Managing Turbulent Hearts

Managing Turbulent Hearts

A Balinese Formula for Living

Unni Wikan

The University of Chicago Press • Chicago and London

The University of Chicago Press, Chicago 60637
The University of Chicago Press, Ltd., London
© 1990 by The University of Chicago
All rights reserved. Published 1990
Printed in the United States of America
99 98   5 4 3

Library of Congress Cataloging-in-Publication Data

Wikan, Unni, 1941–
    Managing turbulent hearts : a Balinese formula for living / Unni
Wikan.
        p.   cm.
    Includes bibliographical references and index.
    ISBN 0-226-89678-1 (cloth). — ISBN 0-226-89680-3 (pbk.)
    1. Balinese (Indonesian people)—Social life and customs.
2. Balinese (Indonesian people)—Social conditions. 3. Philosophy,
Balinese (Indonesian people) I. Title.
DS632.B25W55   1990
306'.09598'6—dc20   90-41019
                                                    CIP

For
Balinese friends
and for
Kim and Suriati

Indeed, I do not forget that my voice is but one voice,
my experience a mere drop in the sea,
my knowledge no greater than the visual field in a microscope,
my mind's eye a mirror that reflects a small corner of the world,
and my ideas—a subjective confession.

CARL JUNG

CONTENTS

ACKNOWLEDGMENTS

The time has come to thank all who helped make this book possible. First and foremost, friends and acquaintances in Bali. Without you, I would have found no point of entry, no way to an understanding, nor would I have enjoyed—as indeed I have—the sheer work of doing this book. Your generosity and friendships have been invaluable and have added new and vital dimensions to my life.

This book is intended as a countergift. I hope you will feel it repays some of my debts and that it may add to Western understandings in a way you can appreciate and accept. I hope my text resonates with you, as you would have it resonate with foreigners. And "if I have spoken wrongly, may I be forgiven."

Some of those who have been most important to me I cannot name, since they figure in the book and I need to protect their identities. You will know how indebted I am. Others may be mentioned.

Drs. I Gusti Putu Antara, I Gusti Ayu Sukesti Antari, Ari Maharani, and Didik provided our first point of contact and our first home in Singaraja. Through the years, they have been a constant source of friendship, generosity, and help. For this, and for introducing us to family and friends in Pengastulan, we express our deepfelt thanks.

Bapak Mohamed Anwar, B.A., Ibu Asiah, and their extensive family of twelve children, foster child, grandmother, and aunt provided our second home and a marvelous working base. Our gratefulness, to Ibu in particular for being an inimitable "foster" mother for our son, Kim, is inexpressible. But everyone in this extraordinary family—Mol, Titi, Ani, and all—deserves individual thanks.

Bapak Abdul Rahman Alawi and Ibu Huriya Abdul Rahman were equally forthcoming and generous in their efforts to help us in every way. For this and for a precious friendship: deepfelt thanks.

I Gusti Putu Mangku Chandi and his wife and family offered us a home at any time and bore our presence at not always convenient hours with the brightest bright face and thoughtful care and concern. For this and for their friendship and generosity: heartfelt thanks.

We are also indebted to Subeidah Husnan with family, Sri Mpu Dwi Tantra, Made Artje, Nyoman Darmi, Sri Darma Yanti, Made Suryati Soegianto, Jero Mangku Sukasana, and Jero Balian Nyoman Lantri with their family, Bapak Drs. Nyoman Suweila, I Ketut Arnatha, Nene Guru and her daughters, Lay, Ping, Ibu Trini Mayun, Sarihati, and Ida Oka.

In addition I wish to thank everyone—also passing acquaintances— who helped us in ways large and small.

Professor Gusti Ngurah Bagus helped us generously in the initial stage and provided valuable points of contact. Without this we might not have known where to start and would surely have made many more mistakes. We express our respectful thanks.

The chief of the Regency of Buleleng, Bupati Drs. I Nyoman Tastera, received us graciously and was surely always in the background underwriting our efforts without making his presence felt. For this we are very grateful.

Except for permission from LIPI—the Indonesian Institute of the Sciences—to conduct the research, none could have been done. Nor would it have been possible without the sponsorship of the University of Udayana in Bali. To both these institutions we acknowledge our indebtedness.

I have left till the end two Balinese friends who have played very special roles in the project which eventuates here. Throughout the research as well as during the writing process I have drawn ceaselessly, and with inestimable benefit, on their knowledge and erudition. Dr. Soegianto Sastrodiwiryo and I Made Bidja Arya Wang Bang Pinatih have been crucial in affecting the shape and contents of this book. I am also grateful to members of their Kawisastra Mandala Foundation.

In Jakarta, Salamah and Abdullah Pope provided me with a home on every occasion and with valuable friendship, for which I am very grateful.

Next I turn to persons and institutions beyond Indonesia. The fieldwork on which this book is based was generously funded by the Norwegian Research Council for Science and the Humanities (NAVF), and the Norwegian Council for Applied Social Science (NORAS). To the latter I am also indebted for financial support toward typing and retyping. A particular thanks to Ellen Vollebæk for seeing this project through at every stage and offering generous practical help and advice.

To the Institute of Comparative Cultural Research I am grateful for funding to enable a last revisit, in 1989.

Acknowledgments

Åsne Tveito typed the manuscript in its several drafts, always with a bright face, and suggested sensitive improvements in the process. But for her, the work of revising would have been so much harder to do.

I am grateful also to Lars Vikör for his help in translating Suriati's poems; to Nancy Frank and Fröydis Haugane, superb librarians, for their efforts to help me in numerous ways; to Paul Weimer and Lis Gerhardt for assisting with the manuscript; to my copyeditor, India Cooper, for a beautiful job; and to David Brent of the University of Chicago Press for all his efforts on my part.

This book has taken me four years to do, and I am indebted to many persons, friends and colleagues, who have sustained me by their faith in it and their encouragement that what I had to say was worth saying, and therefore worth laboring to say so it might be heard. At an early and critical stage, Talal Asad, Mark Hobart, Arthur Kleinman, Gananath Obeyesekere, James Peacock, and Edward Schieffelin offered such inestimable support. Vital in lending me confidence and encouragement were also Charles Leslie, Robert and Sarah LeVine, Byron Good and Mary Jo Del Vecchio Good, Annette Weiner, Joan Kleinman, and members of the Harvard Social Medicine Seminar of spring 1987, in particular Tom Chordas, Janis Jenkins, Paul Farmer, and Don Pollack. Also I wish to thank Paul Rosenblatt, Ronald Simons, Stephen Murray, Anne Krogstad, Henrik Sinding-Larsen, and Solrunn Williksen-Bakker.

Thanks also go to Stanley Tambiah for inviting me to present a short version of my main perspective to the Harvard Anthropology Seminar of spring 1987, and to Naomi Quinn for her invitation to speak to the Society for Cultural Anthropology meetings in spring 1989. The latter offered me the incentive to develop the line of thought which, in a reworked fashion, now constitutes the last chapter of this book.

I should also acknowledge my genuine respect and debt to the person who both stimulated the conception of this study and loomed large through its entire course: Clifford Geertz. Without his knowledge and without my asking, he has profoundly shaped both my thinking and my polemics. .

I wish to acknowledge three journals that published articles derived from my research: *Ethos, American Ethnologist,* and *Culture, Medicine and Psychiatry.* The editors of these journals—Robert Paul, Shirley Lindenbaum, and Byron Good—as well as several anonymous reviewers made important suggestions that critically helped me think through and refine what I wanted to say and why. This book has benefitted much from that. Parts of chapter one have appeared in *Ethos* 15, no. 4 (December 1987): 337–65; and parts of chapter nine in *American*

Ethnologist (1989: 294–310), and are reproduced here with kind permission of the American Anthropological Association.

Gananath Obeyesekere and Buck Schieffelin also commented very constructively on some of these, helping me to shape and sharpen my argument. I acknowledge my indebtedness also for that.

As the manuscript grew, it seemed an imposition to ask people to read and comment on it in whole, and I am inestimably grateful to those who yet did when I asked. Paul Stoller offered valuable suggestions, particularly as regards style and narrative, and though I could follow only some, his advice provided a valuable reference point.

Elizabeth Colson and Laura Nader read the manuscript at shortest notice when at a critical stage I solicited their advice. For their valuable criticism and invaluable encouragement, I am grateful.

Vincent Crapanzano read the manuscript, not once but twice, and has left his indelible stamp on the form and content of this book. To him I owe the crucial idea that I explore and elaborate, as far as I could, the Balinese concept of feeling-thinking, and he also helped me steer clear of numerous pitfalls entailing reification of the "culture" concept. I wish to express my sincere indebtedness and thanks.

To James Peacock and David Napier I owe very special thanks. Each read the manuscript in detail and offered a wealth of critical suggestions regarding content, style, presentation, and analytical structure. This book has benefited enormously from their sensitive reading, and I am deeply indebted to them.

Arthur Kleinman's impact on this book will be evident to anyone familiar with his work. Not only was he a ceaseless source of inspiration and knowledge, but it was to him that I turned whenever my confidence faltered, secure that he would guide me and lend me faith and encouragement. Arthur read parts of the manuscript at several points and at shortest notice, to my inestimable benefit. I hope this book testifies to my deepfelt gratitude and respect.

My husband, Fredrik Barth, has been a lifetime companion, also in work, but in an unequal relationship where it is I who have been the beneficiary. In ways large and small, practical and other, he tried to arrange life so I would have "a room of my own", protected time-space— and this though he deplored the amount of time I spent "there."

I fear it is true that without such inequality I might not have been able to carry this project through. Nor would Bali have become a family project. For this, Fredrik gave up his own desire to continue work in Papua New Guinea, though he exclaimed, "What do you want to do in

Bali! *Everyone* has been to Bali!" I am relieved that in the end he seemed not to regret.

When my own book finishes before his, it is because two minds have been at work on this, though only one voice appears to speak. Let one incident illustrate. When in the end I was searching for a way to open this book (do we all write our introductions last?), and he provided me with a crucial line (page xv, line 1), it was with a sigh: "I had planned to use it myself, but never mind . . . I'll have to think of something else . . ." Nor would he agree to keep it. This book and I owe our greatest debt to him.

Finally, there are Kim and "Suriati." Kim was only seven years old when we went to work in Bali, and though I was immediately made aware that people took to him, I did not quite understand what role he played in opening up homes and hearts before the second visit, when I came alone. "Where is Kim" is what everyone wanted to know, and they seemed more reserved in his absence. So when the opportunity arose, I hurried back to Norway, took Kim out of school, and returned to Bali. Hearts warmed—to judge by expressions—and arms reached out when they saw him. I believe the warmth of our reception with Balinese is in large part due to people's affection for Kim.

To "Suriati," what can I say? But for you, my life and my work would have been so different. I owe a lifelong debt.

INTRODUCTION
Beyond Spectacle and Bright Face

I do not wish to suggest that there is any essential Balinese culture. There are only the myriad statements and actions in which people living on the island of Bali, and calling themselves Balinese, engage.
—MARK HOBART

Any history of the ideas that constitute an ethnological tradition need only presume that mistaken views were likely mistaken for interesting reasons.
—JAMES BOON

"How does one feel empathy for gazelles?" the famous anthropologist Gregory Bateson, who spent two and a half years on Bali studying the Balinese, is reported to have asked. In this he reflected attitudes which have dominated Western interpretations of Bali and cast a romantic and aestheticizing cloak over this South Sea island (Boon 1977).

As artist/anthropologist Jane Belo, who was a contemporary of Gregory Bateson and Margaret Mead and worked closely with them, wrote:

> The babies do not cry, the small boys do not fight, the young girls bear themselves with decorum, the old men dictate with dignity. . . . The child . . . has only to obey the prescriptions of tradition to become an adult happily adjusted to the life which is his. . . . The women accept without rancor the role of an inferior. . . . The system of stratification works smoothly as a rule, and all those individuals who conform to it seem happy. . . . The immutability of all the laws of conduct relieves the individual of any responsibility except that of obeying them. . . . And since they are his habits, he does not even have to think of them ([1935] 1970, 106–9).

My account will be different. The Balinese I came to know during twenty months' fieldwork among them emerged as distinct individuals, struggling, often troubled, lovely to be with and often beautiful to behold, but nonetheless accessible to a degree of understanding as one labors to overcome exoticism and create resonance in oneself to their experienced life situation.

There is indeed much in Balinese life to nourish a distanced, aesthetic admiration. In their collective rituals and their art forms they fashion spectacles of great beauty and complexity. In their social encounters they create a mood of poise and gaiety that dazzles. But for every elaborate offering, there are countless others scraped together from the meager elements at hand. For every splendid ceremony there are numerous inconspicuous ones where people had to make do with what they could ill afford, straining hearts and family relations in the process, and yet the spectacle is so poor that few of us might care to carry its image home in our photographs.

I am struck that even my photographs testify to the extraordinary and splendid. Bali seems to entice everyone into ignoring the commonplace except when it is transformed into dramatic delights, an onlooker's feast.

There is thus a glaring discongruity between people's everyday experience of life on this island and its representation in Western media and works, just as there is between the photos I took and the testimonies my diaries and field notes record.

To grasp how people actually experience their lives, we need to attend more closely than has been customary among anthropologists working in Bali to the ways in which Balinese interpret themselves and each other in their own forms of discourse and in the large and small events of their particular lives: not their terms for gods, institutions, calendars, and rituals so much as the concepts with which they feel and think about, and handle, the tasks and tribulations of their individual existences.

It was here that I became aware of an effort, an experienced ubiquitous endeavor of "making one's face look bright and clear" in a world where there is, as they say, "so much to care about." What Westerners have perceived as an innate aesthetic mood, an ingrained disposition to be graceful and poised, I found instead to reflect a deliberate attitude, a willed response of "not caring," "forgetting" the bad that has come to pass, and "letting bygones be bygones" if one is to thrive, or even to survive.

Why is this observation so important? It provides an alternative key to interpreting and understanding *all* expressions and interactions of Balinese. Realizing it matters profoundly, because it situates people's actions and communications in a different context—a world of effort, struggle, perhaps even covert desperation, not one of tranquility. In such a world, options, acts and statements will take on very different meanings and significance, and attempts at interpretation which ignore this will tend to prove very wide of the mark.

Through my intimate association with Balinese in everyday life I met with the concept which seems to me to be at the root of a Balinese design for living—*ngabe keneh*—what I translate as "managing the heart." It is this that forms the connecting thread throughout the book. In Balinese experience as I came to understand it, all appeals to ancestors and gods will be fruitless unless one engages in a deliberate effort to help oneself by the active deployment of feeling-thought:

"Yesterday, I planted mango stones, for the future, for the children. My husband just watched. I cut down the old branches of the banana trees. He just watched . . . As one sows, one will reap. . . . So I struggle to do always the best. When God sees that, he will reward me . . ."

My book seeks to convey what this implies on an existential level and as a continuing project, never to be set aside. Thus it is indigenous therapy with which I deal, but also much more in that "not so good feelings" are made an *issue* in interpersonal relations: "If people could see our heart, they would laugh and say, 'She does not know how to manage her feelings!'" The sanctions are dire and painfully felt, and "making the face look bright and clear" emerges thus as a moral injunction, a formula for life as well as for living.

As Mark Hobart observes, "Balinese villagers have developed elaborate powers of control by surveillance and discipline, through which people and their doings are subject to regulation. . . . The famed poise of the Balinese is as much a response to surveillance as it is any 'natural grace'" (1985c, 11).

To understand what this "famed poise" means existentially to Balinese, we must know what *it takes* to don the ever-bright face; how the bright face works—when it mirrors, as it should, "a good heart"—for physical and mental health; and how a "happy expression," which reads as synonymous with a "clear, bright face," is even considered to be a social duty with implications for public health: "If someone sits there just brooding, people will say he is thinking about himself only, not the whole of our people."

It was not by design that I came to focus on this. I went to Bali on a project that had an entirely different formulation and dealt with the impact of Islam on Bali-Hindu conceptions of personhood and conduct. Taking as my basis Clifford Geertz's famous study "Person, Time and Conduct in Bali" ([1966] 1973a), I intended to build on this and explore what modifications or changes ensued wherever Islam had replaced Hinduism as a formula for life. Because North Bali has the larger percentage of Muslims, it seemed opportune to do my study there.

When this focus was swiftly set aside, it was because life seemed to will it otherwise. On the second day of fieldwork, I began—still unaware—to be drawn into a life and an experience that challenged my powers of perception and my notions of basic human emotions to such an extent that not only my work, but *I*, was changed in the process. I tell of my experience in chapter 1.

"Another Bali" opened up, one which I would not have anticipated, indeed *could* not have anticipated, on the basis of my previous readings. At issue was not Islam thwarting an essential Hindu base, but the very construction and constitution of that base. Put simply, Balinese, as represented in some celebrated anthropological texts, did not fit with the lives and the fates of the people I perceived. The portrayal of Balinese as all-engrossed in theatrical display and bent on aesthetic pursuit now seemed exoticized beyond recognition.

I realized I would have to begin from beginnings: trying to construct my own understanding of how Balinese experience themselves and others in everyday life and how they represent themselves to themselves and to one another. Nor could I assume that there *is* any essential base. As Mark Hobart has written: "There are only the myriad statements and actions in which people living on the island of Bali, and calling themselves Balinese, engage" (M. Hobart 1986b, 152).

How can it be that the main thrust of my understanding should be so different from that inscribed in the greater part of the anthropological literature? How can I trust my interpretation sufficiently to pit it against those of such authorities as Mead, Bateson, Clifford Geertz, and others? Is it a matter of seeing one fragment only, one particular angle which has happened to loom large in my experience with Balinese and thus come to dominate my interpretation? Or is it a matter of observing Balinese at another time and place, thus that it is actually a different "people" of whom I write?

I think not. First, there are other sources from the 1930s and further back, such as the still highly recognized monograph by Covarrubias ([1937] 1973) which paints a picture much closer to mine; the corpus of traditional materials from Hooykaas (1974, 1978) and Weck ([1937] 1976), mainly from the South, lends further support. Even more compelling, there are evocative Balinese testimonies, such as the traditional poem cycle *Basur* (cf. Zurbuchen 1989) in which a widowed father gives trenchant advice to his two daughters, articulating a social unease and care, a fear of fellow villagers, kinsfolk, and sorcerers, and a stress on gentle demeanors and bright faces that would be most apposite to the concerns I discuss. Indeed, *Basur* is favored by Balinese both in the South and in the North, and we were given a copy by our first host to read long before we were in a position to recognize its relevance.

Finally, a close reading of Bateson's and Mead's own texts indicates that their materials also comprise observations like those I stress. Bateson particularly has some startling insights, as when he sees the individual Balinese as if "forever picking his way, like a tightrope walker" ([1949] 1972a, 120); or when he interprets a Balinese painting as a "symbolic representation of Balinese social organization, in which the smooth relations of etiquette and gaiety metaphorically cover the turbulence of passion" ([1967] 1972b, 150). But such insights were largely left aside, and other and far simpler interpretations were favored, reading essential meanings directly from the surface forms—not least in Bateson's own main text from 1949.

These interpretations by Bateson and Mead which build directly on the overt forms of certain Balinese conventions and conceptions have since been revitalized and elaborated through Clifford Geertz's brilliant and evocative essays ([1966] 1973a, [1972] 1973d, [1974] 1984). These writings may well have been intended by him as both provisional and provocative, occasions to develop general ideas and perspectives on cultural analysis rather than steps in the authoritative construction of an interpretation of Balinese culture. Yet I do not think I am alone among anthropologists in having allowed them to become fused into a coherent, received wisdom about the essential characteristics of Balinese culture, such as I initially brought to my meeting with the field. In my own polemics in the subsequent text, I will thus focus on certain of Geertz's essays and interpretations and treat them as authoritative texts in the corpus of the anthropological literature on Bali, rather than as steps in a particular scholar's pursuit of shifting ideas. Indeed, read my way, they have served profoundly to challenge my own subsequent insights and sharpen my perceptions.

Of course, I fully accept that all views are particular views and that many truths can be told of something as creative and rich as the works and lives of Balinese. But my honest understanding is also that these other accounts of Bali, applied to the lives I have seen and the persons I have known, would have led to invalid understandings and *mis*interpretations of events I have seen, rendering them plausible to an outside reader but less than satisfying for one submerged in the context of those events.

I now believe—and will try to substantiate throughout the book—that the theatrical model in which much recent anthropological discourse casts Balinese is fundamentally misleading. It eliminates the feeling-thinking agent and miscasts people's deeply compelling concerns. Arjun Appadurai has coined the notion "gatekeeping concepts" (1986a) to show how ideas may become metonymic prisons for particular places: they may confine the inhabitants of that place so they seem incarcerated morally and intellectually by their "mode of thought" (1988, 37–40). Gatekeeping concepts

> define the quintessential and dominant questions of interest in the region . . . [so] the over-all nature of the anthropological interpretation of [that] society runs the risk of serious distortion. Here, of course, the central questions concern whether these gatekeeping concepts . . . really reflect something significant about the place in question, or whether they reveal a relatively arbitrary imposition of the whims of anthropological fashion on particular places (1986a, 357–58).

I believe that the theatrical model, enhanced by the attribution of supreme aestheticism, more reflects on Western sensibilities than it reveals anything significant about how Balinese understand themselves and their lives. I also believe it is fundamentally misleading in that it strips Balinese of what they regard as the quintessence of their humanity: the heart—regarded as the motivator of action.

While Balinese may say "the world is the stage of drama" (*dunia adalah panggung sandiwara*), the drama of which *they* speak is one replete with human passion and full of compelling concerns that spill over, causing predicaments, and where things are truly at stake. The actors are full-fledged individuals, and the drama is not for aesthetic delight but is about morality, vested interests, self-esteem, even matters of life and death. I tell the story of a young woman visiting a gracious elderly lady renowned for her religious piety—and the drama veiled by their gracious facades (chaps. 3, 5). It is not an exception but the rule; such or similar dramas are the stuff of so much of their interaction. And Balinese know it!

Or take a man (Hindu) at war with his community over the issue of whether he can or cannot run the electricity at his tourist pension on the occasion of the Balinese New Year, *Nyepi* (a time when everything should be still and dark). In the end members of the community punished him by cutting down the beautiful old trees on his beach; this is high "drama" but tells us little of what was at stake for either of the parties or what actually motivated their actions. Nor does it begin to trace the tragic implications for parties implicated against their will in the conflict and turmoil—in this case, an impoverished man only fortuitously drawn in, who yet lost his capital and critical source of livelihood.

Cares spill over. People may be trapped. The idiom of drama or theatricality captures only one facet of the pattern of life. And when this part is taken for the whole and used to epitomize "*the* culture" we stand truly in danger of imprisoning people in (what we adduce to be) their "mode of thought," besides essentializing culture in a way that is quite unwarranted.

Might it then be that some of my disagreement arises because I have been a different place from anthropologists such as Bateson, Mead, and Clifford Geertz? Is North Bali, where I worked, only superficially similar to the South, from which the overwhelming part of the anthropological literature derives, and in deeper ways quite different?

My fieldwork was carried out during twenty months between January 1984 and March 1989 in and around Singaraja, the capital of Bali's northernmost province, Buleleng. Singaraja is a town of some fifty thousand people, serving a hinterland of approximately one half million. It was the capital of the Dutch colony from 1849 to 1949, and Margaret Mead wrote in 1942 that the Singaraja region was more influenced by Western impulses than South Bali. Today the tables are turned. Since the transfer of the provincial capital to Denpasar in the 1950s and the advent of mass tourism to Bali in the early seventies, North Bali has had considerably less Western influence than the South. Shoestring tourists who come to Lovina, the beach west of Singaraja, generally stay not more than a week, whereas the better-off stay only one day or two, if they include North Bali on their itinerary at all.

Since North Bali is manifestly so much less spectacular than the South, I suspect that the same focus on aesthetics and splendor is reflected in the fact that the lion's share of anthropological fieldwork has been carried out in the South-Central part, comprising only approximately 5 percent of the island's surface and 40 percent of its population.

But Buleleng people contest the idea that they have less spectacular ceremonies than the South. One only has to know where to go to find them; they are not traded off against tourist tickets as in the South. Indeed, when a budding entrepreneur in Singaraja brought a small carload of tourists to a cremation in his local community, this was widely frowned upon, and he did not repeat the experiment. Actually, the South cannot compete with the North, say Northerners, regarding some particularly beautiful customs which are unique to the region: e.g., the *mepeed* held in connection with cremation when all the descendants of the dead, clothed in dazzling garments, parade through the village from the house of the dead to the death temple and back; or the practice on *Kuningan*—a major Balinese yearly ceremony—of women adorned with *real* golden jewelry congregating by the thousands in the death temple (in the South they use only imitation, Northerners say). I have heard astonished tourists remark that the most magnificent offerings they had come across anywhere were carried by women by the roadside in the region around Singaraja on *Kuningan*. Northerners know and are proud of such facts.

I have also heard Northerners say that there are some character differences between Southerners and themselves. Take naming customs and what they reveal: in the South, it is said, people are given just any name, meaningful or not, but in the North names are chosen with care and applied deliberately to shape character. This means it takes something to bear a name. A name compels, it commits: "I said to my son, 'Remember! If you cannot live up to your name, people might laugh!'" The difference in custom indicates to some people in the North that Northerners are braver and stronger.

More important, there are notable differences between North and South in social organization, relevant to the way persons are embedded in society. Relatively few Northerners live in the large, enclosed compounds found in the South, and most households are based on an elementary family unit—though frequently supplemented by other, co-residing relatives. These are traditional, not recent, patterns. Birth rank seems to play a lesser role than in the South: the vast majority of the population is of common (Sudra) birth, and many villages are composed entirely of commoners (Barth 1991). The area is also affected by its focus on an old, established port and urban center (Singaraja), in contrast to the South where life has been rural in its focus and the urban, now swiftly growing, centers are historically recent. Singaraja, moreover, has been open to the traditional cosmopolitanism of the Sulu Sea, with a steady influx of Chinese, Bugis, Javanese, and South Arabians. As a result, non-Hindu communities and congregations are found in higher frequency in the North, including 8 to 10 percent Muslims compared to an island average of 4 percent.

These differences reflect a long cultural history of parallelism, divergence, and convergence; they are not merely the result of the colonial encounter. Whereas early sources of Balinese history from the ninth to the thirteenth centuries give few indications of regional contrast, toward the end of this period Javanese influence increasingly took hold in the South, culminating in the transfer of the Majapahit court from Java to Bali in 1478. The North was not an effective part of this state structure, but continued on with traditional parochialized Balinese culture and local politics until unified by a local ruler, Panci Sakti, in the mid-1600s. The effects of this kingdom were probably neither as deep nor as uniform as those of the Javanese-based state system of the South; and a great variety of local systems, now generally classified as Bali-Aga, have peristed to this day. The differences in both caste organization and in local household and neighborhood patterns can reasonably be explained by these historical contrasts.

Yet the differences should not be exaggerated; and in most situations of interaction between Balinese they are underplayed, whereas common identity, common history, and shared institutions are made salient. Nor is it adequate to speak simply of differences between North and South. It is a ubiquitous feature of complex traditional civilizations that their institutions are locally variable, forms are prolific, and regionalism flourishes on all levels. This fact is often missed and regularly distorted in the usual format of anthropological studies; but I shall not pursue the argument here as it is central to Fredrik Barth's forthcoming book (1991). Suffice it to say that the persons, events, and dilemmas I describe here would be neither startling nor difficult to interpret to Southern Balinese: North and South together compose one people and one civilization.

To what extent can I hope that my data have captured such broad commonalities? With a perspective and method which demand an intimate and comprehensive view of whole persons over time, I cannot rely on large numbers to secure representativeness. May idiosyncrasies of a few of these persons, or misinterpretations on my part regarding the life situation of some of them, or the simple inadequacy of such a small sample, have led me astray?

The methodology I have adopted should protect against such eventualities in two ways. First, my focus has not been on isolated individuals, but on persons-in-interaction: my data come from the relations of each of these focal persons I portray with scores of others, their exchanges with their social environment over a period of time that varies from a few months to five years, intermittently observed. I have shared in their interaction with salient others in the social circles in which they are embedded. I have followed the changing interpretation and appreciation on both sides of such relations and seen something of the course of shifts and changes in the quality of their relationships. My "sample" of unfolding relationships is thus much larger than it might appear if one thinks merely in terms of personal portraits or biographies. Besides this, of course, I have accumulated a broad range of data, as has also my husband, from diverse communities, occasions, and areas, including South Bali.

Second, I have endeavored to use a diversity of differently positioned persons as foci. Within Buleleng, eleven different people can be said to have served as such foci, embracing women and men, young to middle-aged, Hindu and Muslim, and poor to relatively prosperous. Some of these move in overlapping circles, others do not meet at all. The concepts, ideals, fears, and concerns which resonate across such different circles will have a generality and degree of validity sufficient to illuminate the world in which Balinese move.

This then has been my focus: to try and grasp how people actually experience their lives, lives lived according to Balinese ideas, concepts, and conventions. How can we best develop a degree of understanding, a resonance, for the events that happen in Balinese worlds, the meanings they have, and the experiences they induce?

These are the materials I wish to present and the questions I wish to pose; and so my book has become a rather different text from most books in anthropology. I do not enter into an analysis of the main institutions and organization of any community; I do not give an account of customs, or cosmology, or the necessary struggle to make a living. I do not thereby mean to belittle the importance of such facts. As premises and constraints they govern the lives of which I tell, and so their consequences loom large in the very events that I describe: they are there, refracted in the circumstances and scenarios I present. But rather than take apart the events to show the patterns of custom and necessity, I have purposely allowed myself instead to foreground *other* aspects that lead directly to the particular themes that I wish to raise. In part I feel I can allow myself this option because so much has by now been written on Bali from other priorities, and readers can use that literature to critique my account. I also know that Fredrik Barth (1991) will address many of these issues elsewhere, on the basis of our shared pool of field data.

But I also wish at least to have voiced the irreverent question of whether an anthropology of experience really needs to take second place to the description of custom, the interpretation of culture, or the investigation of material patterns. Perhaps a direct approach to the lived significance of other people's concerns should be granted as much primacy as those other approaches.

I arrived for fieldwork in December 1983, having previously visited the island twice as a tourist. We came as a family, my husband, anthropologist Fredrik Barth, our son, Kim, aged seven, and I. My fieldwork took place at first—when I thought I was studying the impact of Islam on indigenous conceptions of person and self—in a Muslim village south of Singaraja, with visits for comparative material to its neighbouring Hindu village and two villages west of Singaraja with mixed Hindu-Muslim population. As I was drawn into the life of the young woman you meet in chapter 1, it became important to have easy access to her circle, and so I settled with my family in Singaraja. We lived in turn with two families, one Hindu, one Muslim, and I worked increasingly in four relatively distinct circles of acquaintances in three town quarters (*banjar/kampong*), one Hindu, one Muslim, and one with mixed Hindu-Muslim population. How I worked, what approach to fieldwork and methodology I followed, is set out in chapter 2. Here let me just note that I tried as much as possible to be a friend and sympathetic listener to people. I never used a tape recorder and rarely took notes on the spot. Thus most of the conversations and observations I relate are rendered from memory.

I made no fewer than seven visits to Bali between 1984 and 1989 and spent a total of twenty months on the island. Revisits were also not planned originally but became the more important with my growing focus on how people cope with life's trials and tribulations through time. Fredrik and I worked in parallel, but not together, and pooled, as we always have, our field notes. After our first and longest joint stay, I next went back alone, a year later, for a stay of two months, but I was made so critically aware of Kim's role in opening up homes and hearts that ever after I tried to bring him along, and on two occasions the whole family went back together.

The linguistic situation in the North demands a note of explanation. It is complex, with two languages, Balinese and Indonesian, in common use and intermixed to the extent that it is not at all uncommon for people to use words of both languages in their speech. Indonesian is the national language and the medium of instruction in schools. It is a Malay language, easy to learn to read and write, and "neutral" in the sense of not being differentiated by words and levels to connote status differences. In Balinese, by contrast, there are at least three different levels, marked by entirely different words, to denote whether one is speaking to a person above, below, or on the same level as oneself in rank. The difficulty of learning the complex vocabulary *and* of knowing when to use the appropriate forms, combined with the danger feared to befall anyone who offends by inappropriate use, is given as the main reason for the increasing use of Indonesian in homes and gatherings. Some parents also say that the particular form of colloquial Balinese spoken in many Singaraja neighborhoods is so coarse that they would rather have their children speak Indonesian, which is inherently polite. Some parents speak Balinese with one child and Indonesian with another thought less clever and more prone to make mistakes in Balinese.

The form of Indonesian spoken and written in North Bali is somewhat different from the national language. A process of Balinization goes on whereby Indonesian words take on Balinese spellings: *sedih* (sad) becomes *sedeh, terkejut* (frightened) *tekejut, jelek* (bad) *jele*, etc. I generally use the Balinese spelling in my text. The glossary at the end may prove helpful.

I have done my utmost not to betray the trust of friends and acquaintances who opened up their hearts to me and revealed secrets which might make people laugh, they fear, if these could be attributed to themselves. I have changed all names and anonymized locales. I have also changed aspects/details of life histories and biographies, but in such a way that the fictitious persons who emerge *might* have been "real." They have the kinds of characters and feeling-thoughts of particular Balinese I know, but without in any way revealing real persons. I hope my deep gratitude and my appreciation and respect for everyone show through. This book is dedicated to Balinese friends.

PART ONE

Experience and Its Interpretation

CHAPTER ONE

Grief, Gaiety, and Laughter

"Be happy, be perfect, be glad in your heart."
(Mantra of *pedanda* when purifying hands before ritual.)

Only one day after my fieldwork began, an acquaintance, a bright and charming young woman, mentioned to me in passing, as we rode the bus down a hill, that a friend of hers in Lombok had suddenly died two days before. He had been sick with diarrhea only one day, and that was it. A telegram from his parents had informed her.

I sympathized with the tragedy of the tale but was not at all clear about the meaning of this to my friend. She related the fragments of the story with such a glittering smile, I could not know whether it was an "event"—something to talk about, though clearly of personal import— or whether perhaps the friend had been special to her. A shy and modest girl, it would clearly be important whether the dead person was a "he" or a "she." But the Balinese do not make such pronominal distinctions, and lump either one under the neuter *dia*. My acquaintance, though highly competent in English, struggled with this same pronominal problem and not infrequently got the two mixed up.

That same evening an illness on the part of my son triggered outspoken fears of black magic on the part of both this friend and others, university-educated people, to whom we had gone to consult for help. They wanted to know whether we had eaten rice in the village where we worked the day before. Well, of course we had. Oh, so the cause of the illness was clear! We *must* know that the village is a center of black magic and take the utmost precautions about where and what we eat. The doctor to whom we went was duly informed of our carelessness. I smiled apologetically at the superstitions of our friends, only to learn later that doctors in Bali themselves generally refer patients to *balians* or *dukuns,* traditional healers and magicians, for a host of illnesses they reckon themselves unable to cure. They also consult these healers themselves.

Our son recovered two days later, and that same evening the girl, let us call her Suriati, brought up the subject of her dead friend again.[1] She had received more telegrams from his parents, imploring her to come to

3

Lombok for a memorial service that was to be held in two days' time. But she had not the money to go. Again my sympathies flowed. Suriati was a poor girl, and the cost of the ticket, twenty-five thousand rupiahs (approximately thirty-five dollars) was clearly beyond her means. Even when she would finish her education and start working, six months hence, her monthly salary would only amount to twice that amount.

I ventured a question about her friend, who, it was by now clear, *was* a boy: had he been special to her? Suriati smiled shyly and confessed: oh, yes, they had hoped to marry, but only her closest family knew. Others must not know for her uncle hoped to marry her to his son and would be angry when, next year as she had thought it would be, she would have to make her refusal clear. Until now she had only said she must finish her education first. (It later appeared she feared black magic in retribution.)

The story so told bespoke a terrible tragedy that had hit Suriati's life. And yet I could not understand. She had been all smiles and "happiness" all through these days, not a tinge of sadness that I could detect in her eyes or facial expressions. She glittered as only happiness glitters in cultures where I had worked before. Now I had read Clifford Geertz's moving rendition of his encounter with a Javanese man who had suddenly lost his wife, impressing upon Geertz the notion that death should be met with "smoothness inside and out" ([1974] 1984: 128). But this was not it. Suriati was not smooth; she shone and sparkled.

A couple of hours later, she approached me shyly. Please, would I excuse her for asking, but could I lend her twenty-five thousand rupiahs so she could go? I was uneasy. Would she really use half a month's salary to go to a brief memorial service—a ritual that, to my knowledge, meant little in terms of Muslim belief?[2] What about her parents, would they let her go? And what about our work? She had promised to assist me for a few days. Suriati assured me that her parents would surely let her go. And she would be gone for only two to three days. I must not fear for our work.

So I agreed, with quite a few misgivings. The story might be true, in which case it went without saying that I must help her. But it seemed too fantastic to be true, given its elements of a prudent young girl invited by the parents she had never seen of a boy now dead and buried with whom she had had a secret love relationship to come speedily to Lombok. I had given her the benefit of the doubt.

Three days passed with no sign of Suriati. In the evening of the fourth I went to her parents' house to inquire about her. They were all smiles and apologies. Suriati would be back in another four days. She had gone to Lombok. I told them she had promised me she would be back the day before. They assured me they would convey the message.

That same evening a letter from Suriati appeared, brought by personal messenger from Denpasar. It contained a thousand apologies and implored me not to be angry. She had not reached Lombok yet. She was in Denpasar, on her way. Her parents had absolutely refused to let her go, but she had cried for two days until they gave in and sent her grandmother to accompany her to Denpasar, where she had hoped to catch a plane. But she did not have the money for the ticket, only an uncle working at the airport who might help her get a cheap seat. But the plane was full, and she was still waiting . . .[3]

I cursed myself for my naivete. To think that her parents would let her go! And what would they think of me for having complicated their lives by lending Suriati the money so she could go? Now there was nothing I could do but wait. And as in the meantime I had learned that a great many, perhaps most, marriages in North Bali are conducted by elopement (*merangkat*), my suspicions grew that Suriati had perhaps gone off to precisely such an affair.

A week later she appeared, apologetic and shy, but otherwise her usual sparkling self. I'll never forget the impression she made on me as she walked the long trail toward our house. She exuded such cheerfulness, carried head and posture so erect, I was in little doubt she must come from a happy encounter.

Sitting down, she implored me not to be angry. The difficulties had been all unforeseen. But her parents *had* refused to let her go, I said. "Oh, yes, they were very afraid . . . from the black magic in Lombok." Really, she herself had been terrified, but her friend had always said, "We must not believe, for if we do not believe, black magic cannot strike us"; and she had prayed incessantly to keep her fears at bay.

Would I like to see the photos of her friend? I nodded, and she laid them out, two thick folders in all, of color photos showing a handsome young man, vivacious in many situations, posing with his motorcyle, joking on picnics with his friends, relaxing on his bed playing his tape recorder, and then—on that same bed—lying as a corpse, white-bedecked but for the face, surrounded by family, flowers, and friends, and then wrapped up and put into the coffin and borne on the way to his last resting place. The last photo showed herself kneeling on his grave.

I was numb, not knowing what to say. Suriati's tragedy was true.

As we sat, regarding the photos, other friends appeared inquiring, with that ubiquitous Balinese curiosity which leaves few matters unexplored, about Suriati's travel in detail. And a curious interaction took

5

place. Eyes shining, teeth exposed in a lively smile, Suriati told of her experience. The audience laughed and joked: how the world is full of men; no use grieving over one; where one stick is broken, another will grow; and, on hearing that the dead friend had two unmarried brothers, well, there was a ready substitute. "Go on, be happy. Let bygones be bygones [*yang lalu biarlah berlalu*]! The world is bigger than a *kelor* leaf [*duniya tak selebar daun kelor*]."[4] And Suriati joined them in their merriment.

The next day when I went to see her again, she was alone. Her mother and grandmother had both gone to seek treatment for *kesambet:* illness from shock or fright (Wikan 1989a). But what had weighed heaviest in bringing these illnesses on, Suriati's friend's death or the danger which she faced from her prolonged stay in Lombok, I could not say at the time. Lombok lurks in the minds of Balinese as the homeland of black magic (no less threatening for being miles away, as many Balinese travel back and forth to see family and friends). And Suriati's family had been hard hit while staying only in Bali. Her grandfather—a practitioner of traditional medicine—had been killed in a spiritual contest by another magician, after he had cured a crazy girl whom the other man had ensorcerized. Suriati's mother had developed "stone pregnancy" (*beling batu*) from black magic as had also an aunt of Suriati's. Another aunt had been trapped by love magic into leading her life in that frightful village where our work centered at that time. Countless illnesses— some of them with deadly import—had been inflicted upon the family as well as on numerous friends and acquaintances by black magic. This only in Bali; think what Lombok may have precipitated.

I knew nothing of this at the time. Black magic is so dangerous to talk about; the air itself may have ears, and the magicians may be enraged by the talking. One avoids talking also to keep one's fears at bay, for fear weakens the person and erodes one's vital resistance. Thus Suriati herself was not told, until she was safe home from Lombok, of the agony her family had lived through in the meantime. Her maternal grandfather, it turned out, had once returned from Lombok with "stone pregnancy," which later caused his death. Her family had not slept a single night while Suriati was in Lombok from fear that she might encounter a similar fate. "Really, I myself did not sleep that whole week," she said, "for my soul [*roh*] being close to theirs, I could feel them tremble." When she returned, safe and sound, they unthinkingly gave their fears away by pointing to her stomach, sighing: "Just wait, it will come." Now, when she reminds them of it, they laugh, a bit embarrassed.

Beling batu—pregnancy with stones—is perhaps the illness most feared from black magic in North Bali, among men and women both. It is believed to have originated with Muslim dukuns—healers/magicians—in Lombok and then to have spread to parts of North Bali and to Banyuwangi in East Java. But its entrenched homeland is still seen as Lombok. Unless powerful countermagic can be found to expel the afflicting spirit—(*roh jahat*)—*beling batu* will kill its victim in a slow and hideous manner: an enlarged stomach is seen as the epitome of ugliness and slovenliness according to North Balinese conceptions of beauty and virtue. Lombok thus looms large in the spectrum of fears with which Balinese battle.

It is a measure of Suriati's grief and of her devotion to her dead friend that she should choose to quiet her fears and face this monstrous place all on her own. So is the fact that her parents should seek to suppress theirs and acquiesce to letting her go. Her mother later told me that when the fateful telegram bearing the news of her friend's death arrived, Suriati had torn it open, glowing with anticipation, because she "knew" it was to bring news of the time and date of his arrival, along with his father, when he would ask for her hand in marriage. She had spoken with him on the phone only two days before, and he had been full of the news that he had now assembled the sarongs, jewelry, and makeup that were to go into her engagement gift (*lamaran*). The marriage, they had planned, would be six months hence.

So her first reaction, as she later conveyed to me herself, had been confusion that the telegram should be signed, not by her friend, but by his father. And when she proceeded to read: "YOUR BROTHER,[5] HAMZA, IS DEAD," she first thought that someone must be playing a trick on her.[6] She rushed to ask her best friend to accompany her to the telephone office, where she phoned her friend's home in Lombok. When the devastating truth was broken to her, tears streamed down her face. Whereupon people leapt at her, laughing, "What's the matter with you, are you crazy [*gila*]!" Such are characterizations that stick in Bali. Suriati gathered herself together, composed her face into an exuberant expression, and smiled left and right to passersby as she walked the long way home.

The day after her return, Suriati and I resumed our joint visits to some villages. She confessed to crying herself to sleep at night, but during the day there was not a sign by which people who did not know her could detect that her life had been shattered. She joked and laughed, and to teasing questions as to whether she had been to Lombok to see her boyfriend, she smiled in the affirmative. When asked whether she was soon going to marry, she smiled modestly, as befits a young girl, but exuding an expression so exuberant as to leave the audience with the distinct impression they were on the right track. Sometimes, when she accompanied me to villages where they grow *rambutan,* a Buleleng fruit delicacy, she would ask if she could buy some, "so I can send it to my friend in Lombok." The notion took hold, among people who did not know her well, that here was a young girl brimming with love for a boy she was soon going to marry.

Our work, however, proved less than fruitful. Suriati, whose usual appearance consummately personifies the Balinese feminine graces of exquisite (*anggun*) and gentle (*lemah-lembut*) demeanor, retracted into a caricature of these same qualities when faced with the dangers of village society:[7] circumspect in all her manner, for fear she might offend, she was at pains to demonstrate friendliness and good grace so excessive it degenerated into a glare. She circumvented all my questions, diluting them to their bare outlines, and reduced answers to skeletons out of fear she might offend someone and become a victim of black magic. Her fears were daily exacerbated by almost everyone we met who learned of our whereabouts. And though she tried hard to convince herself that black magic can only strike us if we believe and make herself not believe, she was quite relieved the day when a *jinn,* a supernatural spirit who had taken possession of her friend's body, entreated her to show the utmost caution and never eat or drink in the place. To avoid offense, she should say that she was fasting. Neither must she tell her birth name to anyone, only her nickname,[8] nor walk barefooted in homes with an earthen floor. The footprints might be used in magic against her. As an attractive young girl, she must be exceedingly careful for she would be a likely target for love magic (*guna-guna*).

With the jinn's authority behind her, Suriati no longer needed to struggle between belief and disbelief. Black magic is not a superstition, but a fact. And Suriati and I gave up our joint visits to the villages. Various ailments I developed over the next few months were proof to her, and everyone else, of the good sense of her decision and the foolhardiness of mine.

Suriati's decision to keep far from village society was indeed sensible by Balinese conceptions. Sadness, as Balinese know, undermines the strength and steadfastness of one's vital life force (*bayu*) to make it "little" or "small" (*cerik*). And a strong life force (*bayu gede*) would be needed to withstand the forces unleashed in village society. Suriati's vital power, on the other hand, was already so low that she was plagued by a series of sicknesses of less than supernatural cause. Headaches, which never used to plague her, had now become her daily companion. Fevers, redness and soreness of the eyes, dizziness, fatigue, and forgetfulness were other ailments with which she struggled over the course of the year to come. Some of these might be attributed to her "sickness from longing or loss"—*sakit rindu*—as generally afflicts Balinese when they have to part with someone beloved, whether by separation or death (p. 200). Others stemmed from her failure to seek treatment for *kesambet*—illness from shock or fright—immediately upon receiving the blow of her friend's death. The shock had been so great, she had forgotten to go. And then it was too late, for the *sambetan* treatment must be taken speedily to be of any use (cf. Wikan 1989a, 37–38). With her life force chronically weakened in consequence, it would be courting disaster for her to visit village society.

In the mornings, when I used to come to her house, she would appear slowly from the back bedroom; her movements were heavy and reluctant, as if she were dragging her body behind her. In her soft-spoken, gentle manner she would complain of the "eye sickness" that had become the center of her attention and speak of how she would go to Denpasar to see an eye specialist as soon as she could assemble the necessary energy and money. Then she would launch into a tale of the headaches, sleepless nights, and overall "confusion" that caused her such pain. Yet afterwards, she would put on her clothes, comb her beautiful long hair, and—as if it were part of that same process of making oneself presentable—put on that sparkling shine and go out into the world.

As a living personification of Balinese values regarding young women, she was indeed praised, but not to her face, for her exquisiteness and charm. On several occasions I heard people esteem her as the epitome of feminine grace:

> Suriati is not only beautiful, her face shaped like the moon,
> but she is also so *polos:* always calm [*tenang*], never high-
> tempered or rash, never asking for much. She is *rimo,* always
> content, accepting whatever you give her, never asking for
> more or voicing complaints. In dress, likewise, she is *polos,*
> always of mute colors, never flashy, and in speech likewise,
> she is *polos,* she does not mix languages . . . To be *polos,* it
> is to be like Suriati.

Considering that *polos* ranks at the apex of the scale of values by which Balinese are judged (cf. p. 70), it was not possible to receive higher praise.

On rare occasions it happened that Suriati's face momentarily lost its shine; her expression would turn "closed" and "quiet" (*nyebeng*), her eyes would gaze emptily into space. Immediately then, by her own report, people would leap at her, laughing, "What is the matter with you, to be always so sad! You make *us* unhappy by that withered face [*mue layu*]! Now stop it! Be happy! Let bygones be bygones!"

She said she felt (secretly) angry (*benci*) with them when they did this, and to quench the bad feeling, she would hurry to drink cold water and wash her hands and face with cold water. Then she would seek out cheerful company "that will make me think of happier things." Thus utilizing time-honored Balinese techniques for dealing with anger, she could make herself "forget" it and "drive it away." It mattered, for anger would further undermine her vital life force.

Little did Suriati know that with her graciousness and calm she appeared to be living proof of the anthropological generalization that the Balinese do not cry at death. A cross-cultural study of grief and mourning in seventy-three cultures found the Balinese to be the worldwide exception to the rule that death calls forth tears (Rosenblatt, Walsh, and Jackson 1976, 15). A source for this might be Margaret Mead's remarks that "tears are disallowed at death" or her statement concerning "those emotions which no adult Balinese displays: grief at parting and death, broken hearts . . ." (1942, 23, 28).

It was three months before I saw Suriati cry. It happened while she was telling her story to an old woman who herself began to cry, perhaps with the resonance born of personal loss (R. Rosaldo, 1984, 187). And when the old woman began to talk of how difficult it is "to find a good heart" and how it is the best who die young, Suriati could no longer restrain herself. Tears streamed down her face.

Afterwards she explained to me why she had struggled so hard to contain her sadness:

> I am afraid to think of it, that I might go mad, so I try to
> be cheerful always that I may forget my sadness. Also I am
> ashamed to cry, except with my closest friends, for if you
> cry, they will laugh. They will say, "Well, he is dead, so why
> do you cry? The world is bigger than a *kelor* leaf!" *Men* do
> not need to smile and laugh if someone they care for dies.
> Like my uncle in Denpasar, people say he is *banci*—homo-
> sexual—because he did not marry. But that is not true. He
> did not marry because he suffers from a broken heart [*patah
> hati*]. His girlfriend died when he was young. But *I* do not

want them to think or say that I have a broken heart, for then they will mock me. They will say, "Oh, you're a widow!" and they will laugh. It is very bad if you are sad and they laugh. That's why we keep our sadness.

CHAPTER TWO

Interpreting Everyday Practice

If one has a short string, one should not try to reach for the sky.
—BALINESE SAYING

Meanings in Context

I have given this story in some detail to render vivid aspects of that world within which Balinese move and qualities required of them, as well as fears that life entails. It is a world of culture, yes, of webs of significance man himself has spun (C. Geertz 1973c, 5). But in my view these webs are not best clarified through elaborate symbolic exposition.

Suriati's successful venture to appear all smiles and happiness in the face of shattering loss cannot be understood merely within a context of politeness and poise—though these are concepts by the use of which Balinese thought truly moves. Nor is the laughter of her friends and foes accounted for by the fact that cheerfulness and happiness figure large in Balinese representations of their moral universe.

It is one thing to delineate cultural notions abstractly, quite another to make sense of the lived predicaments people face, of what is at stake for them in their daily lives.

The anthropologist who goes further to spin out of myriad observations and statements of daily life an elaborate structure of "a cultural system" will fail on three accounts: she will not grasp the lived significance of cultural concepts; she cannot account for, or even make sense of, why people act as they do; she cannot bear witness to the continual contestability of truth and circumstance in people's lives. A view of culture as webs woven into a coherent structure assumes a fictitious harmony of shared interests.

To take this last point first: it has been argued that "few do the actual spinning while the . . . majority are simply caught" (Scholte 1984, 140). This is a powerful warning that issues of meaning and power are generally interwoven. We had an intimation of it in Suriati's plaintive "But *men* do not need to smile and laugh if someone they care for dies." Hers is a poignant reminder that there are real differences of autonomy and power. "Cultures [thus] do not simply constitute webs of significance, systems of meaning that orient humans to one another and their world. They constitute [also] ideologies"; and so it matters to ask who has the power to enforce their views of what is to count and for what (Keesing 1987, 161–62).

Suriati's story, indeed, testifies powerfully to feelings of vulnerability and weakness, for she was triply disadvantaged by Balinese standards: poor, female, and young. And yet this is only part of her story—I believe, of any story. Suriati, like most Balinese I met, refused to be "simply caught" but showed remarkable resilience or even subversion. Mark Hobart's point that we should not mistake deference for deferment is applicable here (1986c, 28). A graceful exterior may mask insubordinate hearts spinning ingenious schemes in forceful counterpoint to persons in power.

Suriati is set on not being branded a "widow" or brokenhearted. She is going to show "them," and she knows that she can. There is a contest going on which involves body-soul and not merely "meaning." In such contests lie the germs of effective social protest, of resistance, and of that sense of personal triumph which may be so crucial.

The imagery of "spinning" versus being "simply caught"—while trenchant in its evocation of *some* salient aspects of social life—invokes a too static view of life and a reified notion of power. The analysis presented here takes the view that cultural meanings are essentially "contested, temporal and emergent" (Clifford 1986, 19). Contention generates a world of essential ambiguity and multivalence—of lived predicaments—different from the simplicities of both cohering significances and imperious power. Indeed, persons in power may also find themselves "trapped" (see chap. 11).

Secondly, we cannot understand Suriati's predicament, or what moved her to act, by appealing to an abstract "culture." Lived predicaments arise in the application of concepts in a particular context in life, not from their abstract contradictions. Beyond that, were we to make sense of Suriati's endeavor by appeal to a Balinese "culture" endorsing "grace," we would come close to reducing her to an automaton: a mere embodiment of "her culture." [1] But her concerns, what was at stake, would be lost, as would also the fact that life presents people with ambiguity and dilemmas. It offers "resistance," becoming at times a "blooming, buzzing confusion" (Kleinman and Kleinman 1989, 12).

As Robert Paul has noted, "We are no longer content to say that people do things simply because that's their culture, or because they've been conditioned by society to do those things"; we have to invoke an acting subject "full of hopes, fears, desires and plans" (1989, 1,4). This means we have to reckon always with actors with multiple, compelling concerns and precious stakes to defend, actors who would be quite helpless without the power of cultural templates to guide and sustain them, and yet the essential fact remains: that for every one of us "life is being lived uniquely and for the first time." As Paul admonishes, we have to take care not to fall back on analyses which counterdict "one's own actual experience of [what] being alive is like" (1989, 4).

Finally, there is the failure to grasp the lived significance of cultural concepts if these are considered in abstract terms. Meanings are necessarily always evoked by actual life and events.[2] Their contextualization is part of their texture and power.[3] What "laughter" or "a clear, bright face" means to actual people depends on many facets of context and circumstance. Thus to know and understand how actual Balinese are moved, gratified, and constrained by the particular significances they recognize, it is necessary to observe people in everyday life and see how cultural meanings are brought by them to bear on their actual, practical concerns.

The anthropological record, in which Bali has found its place as "one of anthropology's most favoured of favorite cases," has presented us with eloquent expositions of Balinese culture portrayed as a web of symbolic structures more or less integrally enmeshed, while being rather silent on this question of how people live or embody their own notions of what they want and why. The assumption seems to be that what the anthropologist distills as culture *is* actually what people enact. Thus Bateson and Mead in their classical account of Balinese character write how they will portray the way in which Balinese "as living persons . . . embody that abstraction which (after we have abstracted it) we technically call culture" (1942, xii).

That, of course, could not be, for that abtraction is an outsider's construct, a fictitious thing, which exists in our minds, not theirs. People do not live and embody culture. That would be too much of a reification. Culture is an abstraction derived from the way people live and communicate. That people abstract from their own lives, and then embody that abstraction, is another thing altogether.[4]

In other words, the anthropologist's construct of culture reflects *our* notions of what guides and propels people's lives, a singular view, based on particular inferences and observations. Mark Hobart puts this cogently: the concepts of "a society" and "a culture" are "in no small part outsiders' constructions of an amalgam of processes, interpreted and disputed in different ways by those involved" (1986a, 8). This car-

14

ries with it the risk of essentializing, as when we seize upon certain elements which we see as integral to "a culture" and then freeze those into a changeless form—an essence—which people are depicted as embodying. This is not to deny that people—every one of us—occasionally do the same. Essentializing—enunciating as definitive what strikes us as salient—is a strategy handy on many occasions.[5] But it is one which glosses over "how knowledge is built up from a plurality of perspectives" (M. Hobart 1985b, 49).

Cultural analysis—the paradigm in which prominent Bali research has been framed[6]—seeks to probe the meanings of key cultural symbols which intertwine with others in a coherent structure that can be read much as we read a text.[7] Such analyses may shed valuable light on the structure of concepts within which people's thoughts move, if generally and abstractly. But three caveats concern me.

First, as noted, meanings do not inhere in "culture," for culture is not a thing. Nor does "it" have any power; only people can have that power. Cultural templates work by deriving their force or power, as well as their meaning, from their ability to mobilize human energy (Paul 1989, 30). Meanings thus are evoked by people bringing cultural templates to bear on their actual life events; and the thicket of connotations which these templates bring to life is inextricably bound up with such everyday events. An account of "culture" detached from this circumstantiality and constrained by canons of systematic and logical representation only runs the risk of being generalized in such a way as to become quite misleading.

An example might be the famous assertion that Balinese composure and grace reflect a stereotyped and depersonalized view of persons (C. Geertz [1966] 1973a, 389–91). It is based on observations of aspects of public interpersonal behavior that, in conjunction with Balinese calendrical systems and naming customs, are seen logically to sustain one another. A cultural system of mutually reinforcing parts is then extrapolated in which grace and composure are depicted as the entailment of a depersonalized view of man.

I question this approach and argue that we should look not for logical connections but for meaningful ones. Meanings should be such as people themselves entertain at some level of consciousness and expression. To understand what the behaviors we term "grace" and "composure" might mean to Balinese, we need to observe actual people, differently positioned, making use of such expressions for particular ends and to make sense of their interpersonal experience. Moreover, we need to attend to the occurrence of such expressions in a variety of settings, formal and informal, and where problems of different interpretation for the actors may also occur. By this methodology, then, we may come to find that what we as observers call "grace" and "composure" have a multiplicity of different meanings for the actors, some of which, far from depersonalizing, even intensify people's preoccupation with the personal and idiosyncratic features of others.

Balinese use the concepts "bright face" (*mue cedang*), and "smooth" (*polos*) or "polite" (*sopan*) demeanor (*semu/penampilan*) to refer to behavioral forms outsiders might characterize as grace and composure. The fact that it is incumbent on all to display such bright faces has the paradoxical effect that the search for signs of the personal and idiosyncratic—the hidden hearts—takes on a peculiar, almost compulsive, character, especially given a world permeated by magic and a society fraught with imputations of sorcery. "Grace" and "composure" may be evocative of social distance and depersonalization to a foreign eye, but the thrust of connotations which *bright faces* and *polite demeanors* carry to Balinese is lost and misrepresented by such exteriorist accounts.

Second, cultural analyses often do not make it clear whether the symbolic interpretations and logical entailments adduced are a product of the analyst's mind or if they truly reveal templates for people's actions. Often we are not provided with the contextual data to judge, and in their absence the assertions of a cultural analysis must hang in rather thin air. The reader is left with few and oblique criteria by which to judge the merits or plausibility of the analysis.

An example might be another famed assertion, that individual Balinese are of "no genuine importance even to themselves. [It is] the masks they wear, . . . and, most important, the spectacle they mount [that] remain and comprise . . . the self" (C. Geertz [1974] 1984, 128). This is a tremendously important statement, for it not only portends to render the value judgments *of* a people but also passes a judgment *on* them. But where is the evidence? Has a single Balinese been portrayed whose self, in own and others' eyes, was limited to her or his public, contrived acts? We need accounts of real persons engrossed in real life situations to enable us to begin to grasp what are people's compelling concerns. People who do not count even to themselves are not likely to suffer as Suriati did.

Thus a third problem with cultural analysis is that it tends to suffer from a one-sided preoccupation with public and ritual events, while the private and less ostentatious domains of human activity are less often in focus. This may reflect a conception that only "public" interaction is fully shaped by cultural processes, whereas people's "private" lives partake of idiosyncratic and personal meanings. It is a viewpoint many now increasingly dispute (e.g. Abu-Lughod 1986). My experience in Bali convinces me that cultural templates penetrate to the innermost of people's souls, so to speak, and mold emotional life and somato-psychic reactions in stereotyped and patterned ways.

This is one reason why personal experience must be attended to. Another is that we cannot understand vital dimensions of public, interpersonal life *except* in relation to private lives and private struggles. To focus on one to the exclusion of the other is to jeopardize our understanding of both. How much of Suriati's trial and self-management would we have understood if we had seen only one facet of her behavior: the sparkling face she presented "in public"? We might even have concluded, as did some Balinese who did not know her well, that she was happily in love.

Balinese are concerned that people carry their hearts (*keneh, hati*) always with them, and that concerns cannot easily be shed: "There is so much to care about" in social life. From their perspective, it is the *effort* (*usaha*) required in bridging, and moving across, thresholds and domains that gives meaning to a host of interpersonal signs, such as a "clear, bright face." This is so whether the effort is thought of as honorable emotion work (Hochschild 1979, 1983), as when Suriati is "keeping her sadness," or commendable cover-up "to make another glad," as when Gede presents her husband with a cheerful face (p. 230), or as feigned good behavior to disguise evil intention or action, as when a neighbor is suspected of black magic.

Salient cultural symbols such as cheerfulness, politeness, laughter, and shame evoke meanings which are only intelligible in a perspective that embraces private matters: the private is part of the *context* from which they derive their significance and force. When interpreting such signs, people make use of information and conjectures pertaining to private life. For their interest, and culturally shared focus, is *the whole person,* not anyone's public persona.

To understand what meanings people attribute to the acts of others, and what is at stake for themselves in everyday life, the total realm in which they move must thus be explored. We should follow people *across domains* to discover what are the meaningful connections *they* perceive and the distinctions that *they* draw. Lives inevitably have some kind of unity—even when compartmentalized into roles and positions

and partitioned by physical structures. It is this wholeness we need to grasp in order to understand what is at stake: and that is not done by relegating existences to either "public" or "private" realms.

Thus cultural models—calendrical systems, conventional customs, sacred symbols, and abstract ideas—lend direction to people's lives in intricate, composite, and impressively orderly ways. But "culture" in this sense is never the only governor. Life is shaped by compromises and dispositions acted out amid multiple practical constraints. To understand the force of cultural templates in people's lives—both their ascribed power to move, and the limits to their role in explanation—I see it as analytically indispenable to give an account of real people and real events. People as they go about their everyday affairs come up against a variety of constraints of which only some are of a normative character. There are biological constraints, spatial, and material ones. And though both space and material assets are perceived through cultural lenses, they pose some problems of their own: Suriati lacked the money to go to Lombok, regardless of the meaning of "money" to Balinese.

Real life is complicated also by the coincidence of events and the multiplicity of concerns that impinge and require simultaneous handling. To gauge the impact of cultural constraints relative to others and to account for the amazing force of the process of symbolizing to endow "bare" facts with thick and meaningful significance, I see no way except to steep oneself in detailed and particular cases. Why is a bride who looks unhappy at her own wedding taken to be a victim of black magic? Or why does the tape recorder that breaks down when one records a speech offer evidence of similar mischief? The answers do not depend on generalized formulas that purport to depict the meanings of either smiles, brides, or magic. It is the conjunction of sets of variables that makes the likely interpretation and thus determines the meanings actors evoke from such events.

The dangers of "misplaced concreteness" against which Clifford Geertz has so eloquently warned seem nowhere more pronounced than in connection with cultural analysis. Actors tend to evaporate, to be supplanted by a corpus of cultural constructs that by their sheer lucidity seem the real thing. The concern with that superstructure, that key-to-all-puzzles concept "culture," would seem to blind otherwise astute observers to nuances and parameters of behavior they would not dream of excluding were it "social organization" they were considering. It is accepted wisdom that actors, differently positioned, pursue different interests and goals, even that they think and value differently. The lessons learned have made little impact on symbolic anthropology.

People Occupy Center Stage

In my account people occupy center stage, while my concern with "culture" is incidental. It enters my story as a major influence in people's lives—something which channels human energy—but not as an object of interest in itself. This is because, along with Jules Henry, "I have to see *that person* before me, and what I cannot see as *that actuality,* what I cannot hear as the sound of *that voice,* has little interest for me" (Henry 1973, xv; italics in original). But beyond that my focus is analytically founded. I argue that the truly significant meanings of symbols, signs, and events are such as propel and constrain people, and thus it is to *their* lives one must look to grasp what is entailed.

I am making so much of these theoretical points because of an important personal experience that profoundly shaped my perspective on Bali and on cultural analysis in general. I came to Bali with the intention of building on previous analyses, particularly those formulated so brilliantly by Clifford Geertz. It came as no little surprise to find that they were a poor aid in helping me understand Balinese. Geertz's portrayal of Balinese as a people lacking in a self behind the mask, as void of individuality and emotionality and interacting "not as egos, subjects, selves," but as remote and detached "contemporaries" (C. Geertz [1966] 1973a, 389–404; [1974] 1984, 128–29) made no sense in terms of the reality I could perceive. There were Suriati and many others who seemed intently conscious of an "I" and a "me," different from others and intrinsically important, whose actions rang with a sense of self-value (*harga diri*), satisfactions, and despairs, and who related to others as well in terms of perceptions of the *personalized* attributes of others, information about which they were avid to collect.

If people did not count even to themselves, who would judge one—and what would it matter if one were judged—a widow or broken-hearted? Why cry, or struggle not to cry, or be preoccupied with matters of health? If the self matters not, why labor to strengthen a precarious spirit as the source of one's vitality and energy? And why the keen, almost compulsive orientation to idiosyncratic and biographical matters if people were really all of a kind—stereotyped contemporaries one never actually "meets" (C. Geertz [1966] 1973a, 365)?

Equally problematic did I find the observation that morality does not count to the Balinese—it is aestheticism which spurs them on. "To please the gods, . . . to please the other, to please the self; but to please as beauty . . . , not as virtue pleases . . ." is, according to Geertz, the Balinese's supreme concern ([1966] 1973a, 400). My observations did

19

not make any sense, if interpreted this way. An ethical code of *sopan-santun*, meaning rules in good order, is constantly invoked to judge behavior, expression, and feeling. As I have written elsewhere, also the Balinese I have come to know "display what, ignoring the squalor and the poverty, one might call refined aestheticism, [but] the intended design of *their* social acts is first and foremost to *please as virtue pleases* with a primary concern to avoid giving offense" (Wikan 1987, 344).

Thus, my personal biography became one of having to recast step by step my initial understanding of Balinese personhood as formulated in major anthropological works. I had to retrace and begin with first beginnings: observations of people in everyday life. This experience has made me profoundly skeptical of the value of cultural analyses that are not anchored in real-life contexts.[8]

The scrutiny of an assemblage of concepts for their logical entailments may lead to the construction of an "ethos" that is wide of the mark of how life in a community is actually lived. If, instead, we anchor our interpretations in *praxis* (Bourdieu 1977), we may hope to better illuminate how an actual range of events, and the specific interpretations imposed upon them by the actors, together create the experience that makes up a socially and culturally mediated "reality." It is by observing the practice of others, noting the interpretive frames into which passing events are placed, attending to the conversations, deliberations, and reminiscences of contextualized episodes in the lives of particular people that we may hope to go *some* way toward participating in the movement of their experience.[9]

Methodological Implications

This theoretical position had methodological implications for how my data were gathered: I tried as much as possible to be with people and share in their concerns and to abandon my own preconceived interests. This meant discarding the project that had brought me to Bali as events were enacted before my eyes that seemed of a distinctly more compelling character to the actors and, therefore, to myself. What is at stake when people laugh in the face of sadness? How can one be heartbroken and yet appear as if one were happily in love? Why would people say "Forget it, this is nothing to be sad about" when a beloved one is dead? And what are the meanings of numerous recurring somatic complaints?

To try to understand, I had to work *from* the occurrence of meaningful elements in actual interaction *toward* an interpretation, not to assume that I knew anything at all from first beginnings. This was not as difficult as it may sound, as I was indeed profoundly troubled by the realization that I could not understand even the expression of basic human emotions. Suriati's cheerfulness was an enigma, as was the laughter of her friends and foes.

To presume these meant that Balinese took a stereotyped and depersonalized view of each other and even of themselves seemed to beg all the questions irrespective of how "logical" such interpretations might be.

I felt the necessity to proceed in a way that would anchor my data and analysis firmly in people's praxis. Thus, I tried to perceive the multiple circumstances of context which seemed to give signs and symbols (such as "a bright face" or "laughter") their often ambiguous and multifaceted meanings. This was not done by searching for "interesting cases" that I could then explore and develop into "extended cases." Every case was potentially interesting if I could only capture the connection between how the world appeared to particular Balinese, what *they* felt was at stake, and how their acts addressed these issues.

Through my involvement and intimacy with particular Balinese, I progressively came to appreciate what their concerns and frames of perception were because I became increasingly familiar with the range of particular matters that were indeed at stake for them. Through continued participation in the unfolding flow of small and big events in their lives I could then, day by day and step by step, build up an increasingly richer context for interpreting the significance of life events to them.

Only then did I feel justified in trying to systematize: first what the particular symbol in the particular occurrence seemed to mean to the particular person(s), then a stepwise generalization from repeated occurrences and similarities to the more general and abstract "meanings" that might enable me at last to make inductive and deductive constructions of "how Balinese are moved."

Take sadness as an example: it was through privileged familiarity with particular Balinese that I began gradually to perceive what is entailed in the experience of being sad (*duke/sedeh*). By comparing the experiences of different persons I could slowly build up an understanding of similarities that held across contexts as well as of situational and positional modifiers. On this basis I could then derive an interpretation of some general dimensions of "sadness" as a cultural concept.

But it was not until I had grasped what Balinese consider *it takes* to "forget" (*ngesapine*) and "manage/guide" (*ngabe*) one's sadness that I began to be in a position where I felt I could understand the lived significance of a Balinese construction of sadness as well as of happiness and "a bright face."

That these should be intimately associated in popular perception was entirely surprising to me and not given by a preoccupation with "grace." I had worked among people in Oman who are as graceful as Balinese, yet evince no concern with the effort, the struggle, the emotional "work" it takes to embody such patterns (Wikan 1982).

The Balinese conception is embedded in *particular* webs of significance that they have spun regarding persons, morality, emotionality, and health. It bespeaks, moreover, a shared, interpersonal perception of others—what we might call the agents of "culture"—as demanding and judgmental beyond what one can at times endure. It is a worldview so different from what I found in Oman, where people are left great leeway in realizing individual natures and where that "nature" is thought likely to assert itself against all restraint (Wikan 1977, 1982). Experientially, then, sadness in Bali is linked with a complex array of concerns pertaining to magic and sorcery, morality, health, social compassion, self-esteem, and social control. As analysts we might separate these into different realms of culture. From the actor's point of view they merge and are all simultaneously needed to render a usable interpretation of the experienced meaning of "sadness." They come together in the body and mind of individuals compelled to grapple with several concerns at once in their efforts to survive and to thrive.

I argue below for a perspective that ties the analysis of experience to the predicaments people face in a world of multiple concerns. Such analysis must utilize different kinds of data: my understanding of Suriati's experience of sorrow grew in bits and spurts over the course of four years and depended on my fitting together a mass of particulars of information that presented themselves piecemeal and haphazardly. They consisted of observations, made in different settings, of Suriati and people who knew her well or not at all; of talks with all of these as well as confidences made by members of her family and acquaintances. Thus, when I understand her to act so she deceived people to think she was happily in love, this is not an imputation on my part but is based on explicit comments made by people concerned. Gestures, mimicry, postures, and other data of a nonverbal sort form part of the material too— and an important part, communication by hint and inflection being essential for Balinese. Last, but not least, somatic complaints and data on illness etiology and diagnosis surface because illness is a recognized means of expressing feelings and interpersonal problems that have no other legitimate outlet.

Not till Suriati married, two years later, a man of whom she said, "His name is like that of my friend who is dead; this makes me hope perhaps his heart is like my friend's too" [10] did I fully recognize the prolonged work of mourning that, as later events were to reveal, did not fully end with marriage (cf. chap. 10).

Positioned Actors and Interpreters

It is in the essence of my field materials that they depict actors differently positioned with respect to rank, gender, age, marital position, life experience, and emotional state, to mention some variables that Balinese deem vital. These predicate one's perspective on oneself and the world, and their juxtaposition in various kaleidoscopic form diversifies a Balinese population as much as any other.

The need of positioning both actors and analysts in anthropological accounts has been forcefully argued by Renato Rosaldo in a seminal article (1984). [11] I draw heavily on the epistemological perspective he formulated there. He argues that all angles of vision are particular ones and thus the sense that people make of their experience, the interpretations they draw, and the actions they embark upon proceed from singular rather than general viewpoints. To analyze meanings and acts without reference to this is to miss the context from which they derive their impetus and force and to distort interpretations.

From this perspective, the anthropologist's lived experience becomes a force to be reckoned with as well as it may foster or hinder certain understandings. Never is its impact negligible, and acting the part of detached observer is no solution. Rosaldo quotes Bourdieu to the effect that to exalt the virtues of distance "simply transmutes into an epistemological choice the anthropologist's objective situation, that of the "impartial spectator," as Husserl puts it, "condemned to see all practice as spectacle" (Bourdieu 1977, 1, quoted in R. Rosaldo 1984, 193).

To apply these insights to Suriati's case: it would be preposterous to try to make sense of her manner of coping with grief in terms of the general meanings that death, grief, and mourning might have for a prototypical Balinese. Suriati is not just anybody, not an abstract persona. She is female, young, and unmarried; she is attractive, well-educated, and upwardly mobile. And the universe of concepts within which Balinese thought and feeling move is, like any such universe, so constituted that people in different positions are implanted with *different* norms and frames for behavior. Balinese men are only required to be polite and composed (*polos*). But a woman must sparkle and shine, be always friendly (*rameh*) and ideally exquisite (*anggun*). Thus a young man whose girlfriend dies may act quiet and grave (*nyebeng*), but a marriageable girl stricken with a similar fate should exhibit unmistakable laughter and cheerfulness.

Thus, though death and bereavement evoke some rather precise cultural meanings that are shared by most Balinese, these are too general and perfunctory to explain the reactions, interpretations, and sanctions that are brought into play in a particular case. Should a girl appear serious and sad, the connotations evoked would be morally very "bad" (*jele*) and of a kind not brought into play with respect to people otherwise positioned. Older people may even overtly show deep sorrow.

We have evidence from Suriati herself that the injunction always to smile weighed upon her and that she felt unfavorably positioned relative to men in this respect. My observations of others similarly struggling to handle sadness with dignity but engrossed in different life situations lead me to conclude that in living with grief, no one is first and foremost a Balinese. This all-encompassing label is not the one brought foremost into play when people search for a way to cope or when they judge the performance of others. Highly positioned, powerful men will even say, "Oh no, people will not laugh if they see you sad!" And they are right. No one would—at them. Also natives may be insensitive to, or ignorant of, the predicaments of social others. In coping with sadness, as with a variety of life experiences, the relevant labels applied are positioned at base. "Balinese" applies equally to all, and in life, all are not equal.

My own perspective on Bali is colored by those of young and middle-aged women. I cannot disengage myself from my associations with Suriati through a crucial period of her life. And even as I have continued to come back to Bali and move in circles other than where we used to go, I recognize the fundamental impact the experiences we shared left on my understanding. Suriati provided my entry into Balinese society. Unprepared, I found myself urged—as if by an inner compulsion—to try to make sense of death, grief, and mourning beside a ubiquitous "misplaced" laughter. It was not by design. It was because she mattered. I cannot escape the effects this had on my analysis.

Most of the people I came to know best are based at the commoner level of society. Most have low or moderate incomes and social rank, which means they are vulnerable and see themselves as such. In the case of interpersonal conflict it is the one more highly positioned who commands the material and social assets that may be used to affect outcomes to one's own advantage.

Thus, my analysis may be skewed in the direction of portraying the fates of people who have the most to lose by being laughed about and "mocked." For people who need all the social goodwill they can muster because they have few other means of influence and help, a good reputation is an invaluable asset.

To expand on my association with Suriati: I met her only twenty-four hours after she had received the news of her friend's death. She came to attach herself to my family and myself, particularly our son Kim, aged seven, who could be showered with affection. My intimacy with her through this crucial epoch of her life meant that, at first, I came to see the world—in a way—*through* her eyes and to be particularly sensitive to the concerns that vexed her. I also became perceptive to the ways the world judged her, from a variety of different angles. Thus a perspective crystallized on the "being-in-the-world" of a particular young woman, who was also attractive, poor, and upwardly mobile.

Retrospectively, I also recognize the extent to which Balinese regarded me as some kind of extension of her. When she moved from Bali a year and one-half later, people suddenly began relating to me as if I were an autonomous person! Previously I had felt as if I did not count *even as* people treated me with palpable friendliness and respect. And I had despaired at my inability to affect the course of an interaction when in Suriati's presence.

Now, I realize how fortunate I had been in this; how people's positioning of me on the edge of their interactions as a companionable but not particularly significant human being sensitized me to the natural flow of events as well as to a mass of nonverbal cues I might otherwise have missed. I sat and listened and looked, for there was not much else for me to do. My questions were brushed aside, and I could not compete with Suriati, or some of the others, in storytelling, expert joking, or hilarious cheerfulness. Nor did I command knowledge of the person gallery required—including masses of particularistic information—to plunge into a portrayal of the vices or good fortunes of others. I felt I was being taken too lightly, and silently I sometimes even resented Suriati's inability to perceive how I must feel.

When she was gone, I realized the goodwill she had built up for me, whether deliberately or not. With her extreme popularity it was only natural that, in her presence, I should be taken as her shadow. And with her politeness, it was only natural that she would disregard me in favor of persons more highly positioned. When she was gone, I seemed to emerge as a person in my own right.

Thus it is that the perception of me, in Bali, links me closely with Suriati, and I have reason to believe that the goodwill I sense toward my family and myself reflects, in part, people's perceptions that we helped her cope with despair. Not that we did anything special. But as new-comers, the arrival of whom could not have been more appropriately timed, we fulfilled a function that Balinese deem essential to helping someone "forget" or "keep/guide" their sadness: to divert attention away and focus it on more pleasurable activities instead. As I continue to come back, I am always aware of the stamp she left on my experience.

In line with the epistemological perspective outlined above, I have chosen a style of presentation that builds on extended case materials with particular attention to individual biographies and life circum-stances.[12] The resultant picture will be a partial one: one person's under-standing of *some* aspects of Balinese life, which I was privileged, thanks to the cordiality and confidences of Balinese friends and ac-quaintances, to share. Yet for all its limitations, I hope to convey the composite nature of everyday life as it is actually experienced by people who are at once absorbed, constrained, and pleasurably gratified by this particular order of things.

The Simultaneous Character of Compelling Life Concerns

Suriati's encounter with tragedy and death conflates different aspects of Balinese life and brings them together in an experiential whole: the role of emotions in psyche and soma; styles of interpersonal conduct, morality, and control; sickness and health; sorcery and magic; and the experienced connections between what we might differentiate as private and public worlds. It thus brings together aspects of life that are apt to be treated as separate domains in a cultural analysis. This is one reason why I chose it as an opening for this book.

Combining concerns that properly belong together in the life of *any* Balinese, whether grief-stricken or happy, Suriati's case seemed an elo-quent point from which to explore the manifold, exacting demands that face Balinese—their sensibilities, bodies, and minds—as they struggle to cope with a world that is, from their own point of view, fearfully complex.

How much easier Suriati's life would have been had she been able to do her work of grieving, *then* concern herself with the threats from black magic, and then subsequently salvage her social position. It was not an option that she had. It is in the essence of life experience that it cannot be compartmentalized into neat and orderly sections to be dealt with sequentially one by one. The Balinese are aware of this and frequently complain that "there is so much to care about" (*liu anu kenehange*) in everyday life. They try to protect themselves in some measure by "not caring" (*sing ngerunguange*), but are aware that this is at best an imperfect solution. The "resistance" that life offers to our actions and relationships[13] cannot be escaped. And despite one's best efforts, one may find oneself trapped.

I consider this an immanent quality of life. Concerns spill over and a multiplicity of cares often cannot be shed but must be handled, several at once, by means of resources that are in their essence limited: energy, vitality, foresight, social goodwill, and material assets. Suriati's experience shows how in Bali even bereavement offers little respite from interpersonal claims and threats. Her concern for her mother with despairs of her own continued to apply. The esteem of peers still needed to be maintained. Money was short and expenses must be considered. Most crucially, black magic does not take vacation, it offers no respite nor does it allow a hiding place, even for the bereaved. Rather, because sadness erodes one's vital resistance, the bereaved are compelled to *intensify* their concern with forces that are ordinarily threatening enough.

Culture versus Lived Experience: What Is at Stake?

"Culture" may be depicted as neat and orderly. Life characteristically is not. "Culture" may be represented as being composed of constituent parts which articulate in a structure of logical and reassuring consistency.[14] But life overflows, messes up things, and strains a person's comprehension and powers of endurance even when the "answers" or "solutions" provided by customs seem simple and clear. It is true that you should not cry in Bali when someone you care for dies. But most people do, even if they manage, like Suriati, to heed other moral injunctions of appearing generally "bright" and "cheerful." "You shall conquer sadness and anger, or you will be sick and your life be in danger" is a cultural proposition of self-evident insight and wisdom. But not the most eloquent exposition of the "fit" and logical consistency of this with other tenets of culture would begin to convey the dilemmas, the trials, and halfway successes that make up the essence of life, from the point of view of the living.

Let an example illustrate: A couple I know labored for over a year in the depths of misery and pain brought on by the deception and injustice they had suffered at the hands of a very close friend. This had left them mired in brokenheartedness and heartsickness (*sakit hati*)—the latter wrought by their own anger. Picture them one day—to everyone's surprise—standing forth at a ceremony given by the man who had caused them such pain, their faces clear and shining, their manners gracious and composed. (They *had* been invited, but no one had thought they would come.) What was at stake?

The wife explained, "We did it to show the world—*and* ourselves—that we are of excellent hearts [*hati mulia*]. But mostly we did it for our own sake. Anger eats away at the heart, destroys the intestines, makes you grow old, ruins your life . . . Better not to care . . ." And she went on to expound on the evils of the bad—*jele*—emotions, reciting insights that are basic premises of Balinese culture.

That sadness and anger are anathema to health and happiness is something Balinese generally know and understand. They have been socialized to an ethos in which this remains a basic premise: the "bad" emotions must be eradicated or they undermine the health of oneself and one's fellow beings.

Such premises and conceptions may be learned also by the anthropologist. They may be be placed in a context of logical fit with other cultural elements to compose a coherent structure. The insights thereby produced may be of undeniable value. But they may also be grossly misleading. They may fail to capture basic ingredients of what sadness or anger means *as a lived experience.*

What It Takes to Enact Moral Commands

By their performance the couple mentioned had won a great personal victory and were praised and admired for it. People who before had shunned them now offered oblique prestations of compassion and respect in the form of gifts and sympathetic smiles and gestures. The couple's feelings of command of their own situation and ability to transcend problems were enhanced. By doing nothing more or less than *putting normative premises into practice* they had earned the respect of themselves and their fellow beings. How could this be? Why was their achievement seen—and experienced—in just such terms?

The answer depends on an appreciation of what Balinese reckon *it takes* to manage emotions that must, by shared convention, be "naturally" composed.

Grace and composure do not come effortlessly to Balinese, nor do they emanate from an innate aesthetic mood set "to please as beauty pleases" (C. Geertz [1966] 1973a, 400). Face (*mue/muka*), expression (*semu/penampilan*), and action (*bikas/tingkah*) are perceived *as* appearances that may require a great deal of emotional work to bring about and sustain. Balinese have a concept—*ngabe keneh*—to connote the effort frequently entailed. Literally, it means to "bring or guide the feeling-thought or heart." Actually it refers to a process of shaping and mustering one's feelings by deliberate, willful effort.

It was because the world perceived the *struggle* that lay behind the couple's resoluteness to appear at the celebration that they esteemed them and granted them respect. It had been hidden from the view of all but intimate others, an ordeal of intense suffering—and yet the world was not taken in. On the basis of the facts of the case that were generally known, people inferred what went on behind bright faces and closed doors. And they reacted accordingly—with compassion (*kelangen/inda*).

It is a moral obligation that weighs on all Balinese to bring or guide the heart or feeling-thought. But this does not reduce the shared awareness of how difficult that may be. People have experience from their own personal lives, and they bring it to bear on their judgment of others, even when those others are remote. "Hearts" hidden from view thus surface nevertheless in that the world takes them for granted and may try to infer what their qualities are. Inner life and public life, "heart" and "face/appearance/action" thus constitute two aspects of the person that cannot be separated but constitute a whole. Any attempt to understand Balinese experience and interpersonal life without consideration of this is bound to lead one astray.

Balinese folk notions of persons and the pressures they face encompass much more varied, and compassionate, understandings than may be inferred from a scrutiny of "public" behavior. A synthetic concept of culture based on "public" symbols and signs has limited heuristic value. It might shed light on Suriati's behavior in public gatherings, but it would not reveal *what it took to enact* that behavior. Balinese would know, for they reckon with the "heart"—concealed from public gaze. Such generally shared folk notions must, even if they are discussed openly mainly in "private," [15] be an integral part of our models of "culture"; and they must be analyzed where they appear: in the immediacy of everyday contexts.

The Experienced Force of Culture as "They"

Suriati's case is enlightening also in that it reveals how Balinese themselves conceive of what we might call their culture as extraordinarily demanding *through* its acting agents: fellow human beings.

People, not culture, act, but people may feel that they in the context of "them" are up against a power of superhuman capacities that forcibly constrains and pressures them. They may also feel that they are at odds with "their culture" in the sense of ideologies and conventions: social or internalized pressures being brought to bear on them *as if* it were an acting agent they confronted. This, then, might be the experiential equivalent of what we call culture.

Balinese acknowledge something of this when they complain how hard it is to have one's heart comply with social rules or injunctions. The menace of "they" always threatens. The laughter (*kedek/tertawa*) that "they" may join in or the slander (*ngumpet*) that "they" may cause to go around are strongly felt sanctions. Reputations are made and unmade in this way. The victim is poorly positioned to counter a challenge to a blemished reputation, once it is made, for there is a strong cultural ban on expressing conflict, quarrel, and self-assertive behavior. Normatively, one should counter assaults on oneself with greater smoothness of expression and speech. Also, labels, once applied, have a tendency to stick. Thus the fear that "they" will laugh sums up the common notion of what is at stake and what is required of oneself to salvage a good reputation. When laughed at, people feel ashamed (*malu/ngidalem*) and often get sick.

"They" are diffuse others, the faceless many. But Balinese also experience their predicament as one of being under pressure from specific others. The concept of *pemaksa* epitomizes this. Literally, *pemaksa* translates as "people exerting pressure or force." It is a problem many struggle with at times, but all the more so if they are in weak social positions. The nature of the force and its peculiar efficacy come across in a phrase young men sometimes use: "We don't resort to love magic [*guna-guna*] any more [to marry a girl]—it has become old-fashioned. We prefer to use *pemaksa*. We sit with the girl and talk with her until her resistance breaks down and she says, 'Do as you like, I don't care' [*sing ngerunguange*]."

Why trapping a girl into marriage by the application of force is experienced as a victory—even though the girl's attitude is "I don't care"—becomes clear once we realize that "not to care" is a highly positive notion. Rather than conveying indifference, it connotes a basic pliability to life's strains and stresses and a willingness to accommodate oneself to the wishes of others. Thus it partakes of notions bound up with the supreme value of *polos* (see p. 70). "Not to care" portrays the person as polite, calm, and sensitive to the situation of others, even while, as we might put it, sacrificing her own best interests.

I shall offer examples throughout of just such a chosen course. Here, my concern is its interrelationship with *pemaksa*. Given a socially sanctioned value of "not to care," *pemaksa* takes on a peculiarly threatening quality, for the possibilities of self-defense are limited. Individuals who are willing to use *pemaksa,* and there are veiled and intricate ways of exerting it so that one may appear gracious and considerate while maneuvering expertly behind the scene, gain an upper hand that is actually fortified from the cultural injunctions, in this case "not caring."

Laughter, slander, *pemaksa,* and "cares" are some notions Balinese apply to express their experience of what we might call culture's grip on individual lives. And "not to care" is a way to protect oneself from inner pressure when outer pressures become overwhelming. "Inner pressure" (*tekanan batin*) is a diffuse but clearly felt somato-psychic sensation that weighs on the heart and mind to unbalance one's life force or spirit. I shall give examples later of persons struggling with this and how they endeavored to cope. But nothing is achieved by assembling such distinct elements or influences into a holistic "culture": the point is to discover what—in actual situations—exerts the power to guide and propel action.

For instance, when in Bali a couple feels obliged to give away a child in fosterage because someone else wants her, what is it that convinces them they have no "choice"?[16] Or when a girl "must" accept a suitor because he persuades her he would get her by magic in any case, what is it that empowers collective representations thus to compel through the agency of others?

I shall try to answer such questions throughout, not by appealing to an all-powerful "culture" but by analyzing actual life situations for what they reveal of powers and constraints. How people cope in the face of such pressures and threats is a recurrent theme. The directing and constraining power of customs may interfere with the realization of personal goals and wishes to varying degrees in different societies. In Bali, I have the impression that cultural injunctions are often experienced as a straitjacket that constricts the innermost recesses of "me" through the actions of "them."[17]

Other Fears: The Threatening Quality of Companions

Besides such diffuse pressures, there is a host of more specific dangers and threats that always appear to be prominent in Balinese awareness. Balinese seem, in a sense, to live perpetually on the verge of disaster, a fact to which their reflections on life, actions, and somatic imagery and ailments all attest.

To live with danger and the attendant fear, and not let it get the better of you—for fear itself is a dangerous state—to tread a balanced course between dangers that loom large so as not to offend and be the butt of evil, this, I would suggest, provides the ubiquitous context which colors most social action in Bali. To recognize and interpret adequately the signs of what is going on between people, and the interpretations *they* are placing on events, this should be kept continuously in mind. A failure to do so is at the root of much of the aestheticizing and other misrepresentation that has distorted our received construction of Balinese culture and society.

Suriati's story also serves to illustrate this. Though needless to say, it is not normal for persons to experience the kind of tragedy that came her way, yet the threat of other calamities abounds and is so forcefully present in everyone's mind as to require careful and comprehensive self-monitoring of behavior, thought, and affect. Socialization consists in teaching the young how to cope, how to steer clear, and how to respond when misfortune nevertheless strikes. Suriati's case thus lays bare parts of an "ethos" that is peculiarly Balinese, but condensed and intensified in her situation of deep and devastating loss. It is an ethos of learning "not to care," of stilling one's thoughts and emotions in preparation for the suffering that life inevitably brings.

Even if we were able to remove from Suriati's life the tragedy of death and loss, we would still be left with a person whose life centered on steering clear of disasters seen as potentially amenable to human control. As an attractive young girl, the fear of love magic would naturally be her greatest preoccupation. At other stages of life, and for persons otherwise positioned, the most pronounced fears would be different. Ordinary and casual sequences of interaction are subject to such precautions. "Have you noticed," asked Suriati one day, "how Mr. S. thinks me childish and immature?" I had. Grudgingly, I had even admitted to myself that he was right, she did act far below her years. She smiled, "Well of course! I *want* him to think me like a child so that he will not take me seriously and be angry with me . . . !"[18] Her eyes widened: "You know, the black magic of that man . . . ?" And an account ensued of the deadly force of the man's power. He was not a professional sorcerer but a neighbor, a teacher, and a family friend. Such are the ones who are most to be feared, for black magic requires the perpetrator to have detailed personal knowledge or personal accessories of one's victim. Everyday social intercourse is profoundly shaped by such fears and protective devices. Patterns of interpersonal interaction are inexplicable except in terms of them.

And yet, life demands that fearfulness be balanced by bold and daring endeavors. Suriati did go to Lombok, though fear was so much her partner that she claims she did not sleep a single night. Her parents did concede to letting her go, though they stood in such terror of Lombok that when her boyfriend was alive, by Suriati's own report, they had failed to accord him proper respect and hospitality. Balinese must constantly venture beyond the line of what they themselves deem safe: to drink coffee served by hosts whose intentions they have every reason to distrust; to remove their shoes and cross the thresholds of many a house with bare feet though they know that the footprints could be used in magic against them.

Precautions and risks must be balanced, and custom provides no simple answer to how one should proceed, only general cautionary advice. In the final instance it is up to the individual to pick her way, even in communities as collectivistic as the Balinese. To portray how patterned responses of feeling, thought, and behavior emerge when such personal choices are implemented within a framework of multifaceted constraints, we need the rather comprehensive and intimate case materials that only close attention to everyday life and ongoing interaction gives.

Ambiguity, Order, and Uncertainty

Cultural analysis is seductive in that it holds the promise of elegance and order. I would go further and argue that some of this order is spurious, an artifact of the analyst's premises and not a finding of our investigations. There lies in the methodology an invitation to speculate and construct connections until all loose ends are tied up. My own methodology errs in the opposite direction, in favoring or accepting disorder unless my findings force me to do otherwise. But I believe that the picture I thereby draw captures elements that are an ubiquitous part of people's experience and ought to appear also in our analyses. Ambiguities, inconsistencies, and confusion plague the lives of people, also in Bali. Through an exposure to persons and the details of their lives, these are made visible and become data. They belong in our analyses, not as imperfections to be eradicated or transformed to paradox on a higher level, but as true aspects of people's humdrum lives.[19]

To take but one example: Suriati's understanding of the laughter directed at her to mean mockery when she was sad is later judged by herself to have been confused (*bingung*), and yet this is how Balinese generally tend to misinterpret when they are sad and confused. A cultural analysis of laughter may succeed in demonstrating its multivalence, including its aspect of mockery. But it misses the way this produces ambiguity and presents people with existential dilemmas when laughter features as part of an actual sequence of interaction. Judging the import of merriment in everyday episodes is indeed a major concern with Balinese and one which taxes their bodies and minds.

Anyone who has lived in Bali and associated intimately with Balinese will know how every day's movements are permeated with their attempts to steer a course by the use of signs, symbols, and hints that *they* perceive as dangerously ambiguous. Uncertainty is a part of life, and essential social information is often subtly muted or hidden.

I will try to show how inconsistencies may be put "to good use"— how they may have disparate meanings on different levels so that a "wrong" interpretation may also lead to rational and constructive response (as I try to show concretely with laughter). But mainly I hope to retrieve the ambiguity and imprecision that adhere to cultural symbols in use: not to ponder their elegance and form, but to convey the practical life implications.

In a previous work I have argued for the need to respect the place and power of silence in people's lives, both for what it says and for what it leaves unasked (Wikan 1982, 13–15). For Bali I would argue for the need to stand back and let uncertainties speak, not to deny that Balinese lives are in so many obvious respects regulated by compelling, even compulsive order. Yet the basic question they ask themselves ever so often is this: "How *can* I know? It is not so easy to tell . . ."

These people who comport themselves conventionally with what appears as effortless ease and grace grapple constantly with questions that concern the hidden hearts—the idiosyncrasies, feelings, and intentions—behind the bright faces of others. The heart, as the seat of emotions, is regarded as the prime mover of action. It is an everyday existential dilemma for Balinese that they cannot know what significant others truly feel and hence what the motivating drive behind their actions might be. Yet they must act in respect of these others with infallible grace and etiquette. And the predicament of living with this groping, grueling uncertainty expresses itself in a variety of somatic complaints of diffuse and multiple etiology. Thus the cultural construction of persons, of emotions, and of health care as well incorporate uncertainty as a basic premise.

Order is not to be denied. It permeates social life, particularly in "public," where deviance from strict norms of conduct will easily earn the perpetrator the stigma of being crazy (*gila*). My point is that we should not mistake this order for Bali. "Heart" and "appearance" are two sides of the coin, and both belong. The heart, seen as a seething cauldron of passions, is a power to be reckoned with, though it works undercover and surreptitiously. Indeed, Balinese see the "acted" or "expressed" order in the form of predictable politeness and cheerfulness as necessitated by the tumults that would threaten were hearts allowed to reign.[20] One may feel forced and restrained by the demands imposed by the agents of an unmerciful culture. But there is no doubt about it: Balinese seem to concur that there is no other alternative. One does not invite tumult and chaos.

Unless this composite and complex nature of social order is also represented in our anthropological accounts, we risk depicting the Balinese as engrossed in their public spectacle, as people without hearts and without compelling personal concerns.

A Consciousness Troubled by Multiple Feeling-Thoughts

"Hearts" is the theme of the next chapters, and I gloss them only perfunctorily here. Yet with my focus on sadness I feel compelled to say a word on "the cultural construction of emotions," a field of strong and rapidly expanding interest in anthropology since the early eighties.[21]

First I should stress that "emotions" are not my focus of interest, any more than "culture" is. It is *people* I seek to understand—namely, the lived experience of particular Balinese. When I employ an analysis of "emotions" it is only as a means to this end. Moreover, the "emotions" I speak of, are not truly emotions in our sense of the word, for Balinese do not recognize feeling (*perasaan*) to be distinct from thought (*pikiran*), but regard both as aspects of one integral process— *keneh*—which is best translated as feeling-thought. Both are rational, both are subjective, and both are *in* the realm of awareness. Balinese have no concept of an unconscious where feelings or memories might be "stored." Consciousness is the essence of feeling-thinking, and experience is being shaped and memories activated by the active engagement of feeling-thought. This emanates from the soul—the *atma*—the person's divine aspect, which also gives the power of vision and of creative development. Consciousness is the sine qua non of the soul, and the senses, intuition, will, desire, and conscience are all part of one concept—*keneh:* feeling-thought integrally bound with the soul.

Balinese laugh when they hear that some Westerners regard feeling as "irrational." "Do you also regard thought as irrational?" they may ask. "Well, if one is not, how can the other be, when they are one and the same?" Balinese with whom I discussed these matters pity people who do not understand the integrated nature of feeling-thought.

I argue that to understand what is entailed in an experience like "being sad" we need to recognize the artificial order imposed when emotions are singled out one by one and analyzed as if they were neat and orderly the way that "culture" is sometimes mistaken to be. Just as life overflows and offers "resistance" to our well-conceived intentions and plans, so in most people's experience emotional life is complex and perplexing, reflecting our daily preoccupation with multiple, compelling concerns. To understand what a particular feeling-thought signifies, we may, at a certain stage, have to consider each as a particular "way of being in the world," a "mythology *in* which we act as well as through which we view the world" (Solomon 1978, 190); yet we should not lose sight of the fact that emotions are rarely experienced in a singular, pure form. They generally occur in a mixture of multiple feeling-thoughts.

People may be restricted in their emotional expressions by cultural conventions prescribing propriety and danger, yet they are not blind to the complex and at times irrepressible feelings that lurk and labor behind. The Balinese say, "So the bereaved look happy when we are there, but we are sure they are sad, and perhaps crying too, when we are gone."

The painful private struggles that may be fought behind cheerful and bright facades are only a fraction as elusive to Balinese as they may appear to us. For they go by signs we cannot perceive and reckon with full-fledged individuals; that is, they go by "their own actual experience of [what] being alive is like" (Paul 1989, 4). I reiterate that so should we. To probe the culturally constituted meanings of expressions such as "cheerfulness" or "bright face," we, too, need to go beyond the chimera of glossy expression to the concerns of which it may be evocative. In one case, as we have seen, a bright face may be to "show the world . . . we are of excellent hearts," in another so as not to be mocked as "a widow." These are exotic concerns which may yet strike a chord. In the words of a balian, speaking of world religions, they are "completely different, exactly the same" (cf. p. 261).

This is to warn against the presumption that emotions are readily comprehensible by virtue of our common humanity.[22] They are and they are not. I hope that Suriati, as represented by me, has evoked the reader's sympathy, that she has emerged with a face and a heart to match. This is necessary for my account to be grasped on an empathetic level as plausible and trustworthy. However, when it comes to understanding how her sadness "felt," and what is at stake in this kind of experience for a Balinese, I ask you to suspend judgment. Even Suriati's moving testimony "it is very bad if you are sad and they laugh," which seems immediately intelligible by virtue of our common humanity, contains complexities that will eventually put both her sadness and the laughter of others in an entirely different light. As I was misled in thinking I understood, so are you.

This is cryptic, but it must remain so for a while. The point I wish to make is that the cultural construction of "emotions" subsumed under feeling-thoughts cannot be treated as a problem of cognitive analysis only. We cannot aim to specify how particular concepts for emotions are constructed and differentiated and then flesh them out for their "content" with an account of the sectors of our common human emotional range that they refer to, the way color concepts can be related to the spectrum. Emotion words bear a complex relationship to each other as in their relations to the lived situations to which they refer.[23] The range of feelings we would partition off as "sadness" can be separated by us from others we distinguish as "fear" or "confusion" because we largely experience them in contexts where they can be separated. If there is a predominant Balinese awareness that sadness makes you vulnerable to illness and sorcery, as I have indicated, then "sadness," "confusion," and "fear" will be experientially linked—not because of a peculiarity of the cognitive taxonomy, but because of their repetitive co-occurrence, the way they are repeatedly mingled in a person's awareness of her "way of being in the world." Again, a holistic perspective on people's practice puts the emphasis on contextualization as the critical source for an understanding. It is here that we must struggle for the subtlest possible grasp of patterns and associations.

A Focus on Lived Situations

Thus, sensitivity to a Balinese concatenation of emotions can provide only one dimension for interpreting everyday experience. We must attend to whole contexts to capture the particulars of people's "lived-in worlds of compelling significance." This need not mean that we see every situation as unique and abdicate our search for generality. Much of my material relates to the pragmatics of people's lives, to that zone between order and chaos Rosaldo has called "nonorder": improvisation, muddling through, and contingent events (1989, 103). Anthropological concepts of norms, roles, and cognitive schema do violence to this important sector of life and fail to retrieve the common key in which it is played. My concept of "compelling concerns," however, allows us to identify salient cultural constructs in the contextualized and particular. People face choices, and choose, that they may conduct their lives with dignity. Their criteria are perspectival and positional, and culturally constructed; they manifest themselves even in responses to unprecedented situations.

What does a man do when his wife suddenly becomes crazy and crawls on the floor like an animal (cf. p. 249)? Or Suriati, when she suddenly finds herself repositioned as a "widow"? They act, even when sick from the shock—and they act in a rather predictable fashion. It is when people fail to do this and shatter expectations of what is sensible and right that they are likely, in Bali, to be labeled mad (*gila*). Suriati ran this risk when, at the telephone office, she cried on realizing the truth of her friend's death. But when she cried in the street, as we left Bali, no such danger was involved. This was a situation which made crying a natural thing to do, according to Balinese.

So people are prepared for the unexpectable and can react in a culturally appropriate fashion. It is a testimony to our versatility and ingenuity that we do, and it attests also to the power of cultural constructs. When social order appears so fixed and action within it so recognizably familiar, this is partly because of the power of "culture." But we err if we reason that therefore all can be explained in terms of cultural constructs. The resultant patterning does not supersede individual variation, nor the fact of personal choice. In each particular situation the person must grapple with discrepant possible courses and interpretations and, having settled for one, is still left with alternatives regarding how to respond. Action reflects these choices: "parts" are multiple and thus cannot dictate responses, even in a society as "conformist" as Bali. If we make our concept of culture all-explanatory, we will in fact destroy its analytical power.

PART TWO

Bridgings, and Cares Carried Across

CHAPTER THREE
Hidden Hearts and Bright Faces

Always when I go out in the street, I make my face look
bright . . . that people will not laugh and say, "She does not
know how to manage her heart" [*sing bise ngabe keneh*].
—BALINESE WOMAN

Public and Private: The Danger of Western Misconstrual

One further conceptualization which emerges from my account of
Suriati's case needs to be explored, since on it hinges much of my
understanding of what is involved in being a Balinese. It relates to Balinese perceptions of self-management and control of the "heart" as the
person in everyday life is required to bridge domains Western social sci-
entists are wont to think of as contrasted and apart: I refer to what are
generally labeled the public and private spheres.

Also, from a Balinese point of view, different settings pose different
constraints in how one must act and appear. But the relevant contrasts
are several, with each constituted in particular Balinese terms. Moreover, to apply an alien distinction without exploring what it might mean
in a Balinese context would be to base our analysis of Bali on assumptions that pertain to other, and principally to Western, social organizational frames.

Western perceptions of the private as a secluded realm in which one
can, to some extent, let one's defenses down is in some respects the
stark opposite of Balinese conceptions of what is at stake in interaction
within small circles of intimates and acquaintances. Likewise, the meaning that "public" conveys also differs in vital respects. What, then, are
the ground rules that pertain to the major arenas in which Balinese
move? And what are the conceptions and constructions on which such
rules are based?

Geertz and Geertz provide an analysis entirely constructed over a pri-
vate/public dichotomy: "A sharp distinction [runs] between the public
and the private domains of social action . . . [an] emphatic boundary
between what goes on in the sitting rooms and kitchens and what goes
on in the streets, fields, and civil arenas" (1975, 158–59). "There is a
warm, intimate, and relaxed atmosphere inside the wall, an atmosphere

41

which contrasts strongly to the restraint, coolness and caution in the road, marketplace, and the village meeting hall" (1975, 75).

"Grace" and Ultimate Concerns

The Bali I know—possibly because the North differs from the South in major features of household and neighborhood organization (Barth 1991)—requires a very different conception. Rather than spell it out in analytical terms, I choose first to provide a glimpse of what is experientially entailed through my description of an encounter between an elderly lady and her young female guest. It was a "private" encounter that took place within the walls and behind the closed door of the hostess's home. I use it as a particular instance of a common type of event I have witnessed or had reported to me innumerable times that epitomizes basic Balinese conceptions of *what is at stake in sitting rooms and kitchens.*

I once went with a friend to a village close to Singaraja where the people are renowned for their civility and good manners. I had repeatedly been told how I need never fear from black magic in the place, which was in stark contrast to some other places where I used to venture. The people of this particular village, Balinese friends assured me, have truly good hearts and good manners.

We visited several homes, including that of the wealthy and high-ranking widow of a former mayor (*perbekel*). She was an elderly lady with the most refined and gentle manner who was also known for her religious piety. My friend, a young woman, was also very graceful (*anggun*), and the atmosphere had that friendly (*rameh*) quality Balinese women, in particular, prize so much. It was cheerful (*girang*) and rang with jokes and laughter. It even turned out that my friend was an old schoolmate of the hostess's daughter, and when she appeared, they shared happy memories and friends in common.

When prayer time came, the hostess asked my friend Issa, a fellow Muslim, if she would like to pray, anticipating that Issa would be too shy to ask. Issa thanked her and withdrew to wash and pray. We stayed on for hours afterwards much enjoying ourselves. It was an encounter that displayed all those elements of graciousness and conviviality for which the Balinese have become justly famous.

Months later Issa happened to mention that when she had been combing her hair after prayer, she had been at pains to collect all the loosened hair straws into her hand bag and bring them home.

"But why?" I exclaimed. "What did you fear?"

"Well, maybe she did not like me . . ."

"Did you see any indication of that?"

"No, but how can I know what she really feels about me? Perhaps I had made her offended [*tersinggung*]? It is not so easy to tell . . ." And when I continued to look astonished she responded, "Oh yes, we can tell. But sometimes not. It is better to be on the safe side . . ."

Indeed, it is. Sanction against showing anger or offense, the injunction to smile despite any displeasurable feelings, leave ego in a limbo as to the true feelings of the other. And this true state of affairs *is* regarded as important. Unlike another society where I have worked, Oman, where the "heart" is perceived as the sanctuary of the person, of no concern to others (Wikan 1982), Balinese are perpetually preoccupied to decipher each other's hidden hearts. So frightful are the consequences that anger or offense may work, it is necessary to be deeply preoccupied. So the "bright face" and composure, while pleasing to humans and gods, also, paradoxically, encapsulate people's fears. For the will to do magic is set in motion by feeling-thoughts that may never be expressed.

This sobering realization, that the true feelings of others are inscrutably hidden behind their bright faces and polite demeanors, presents Balinese with an everyday existential problem. It is one never to be ignored, but to be dealt with scrupulously and perpetually, in the way that scraping for a living must also be. A failure in either or both threatens one's health and one's life in the world.[1]

What Is at Stake in Sitting Rooms and Kitchens?

What might the gracious hostess have done with her visitor's cast-off hair? And why would Issa fear she would *want* to do anything at all? The answer to the first question is: she might have inflicted illness, misfortune, or even death on my unfortunate young friend—this by bringing the hair straws to a balian or a dukun, a magician, with the relevant esoteric knowledge (*ilmu*). Or perhaps she had such knowledge herself? Many ordinary humans do, and it is difficult to know who.

The prevalence of black magic is not doubted by anyone. My data indicate that roughly half of all deaths, in a random sample of the population, are ascribed to black magic or poisoning. This is not conjecture, *but evidenced by the souls of the dead themselves.* Shortly after death, when all Bali-Hindus must contact the soul of the deceased through a special medium (*balian metuunan*) to ask how it fares, the soul is also asked to reveal the cause of its own death. This the soul will do, and the information is important so the bereaved can do an appropriate rite to cleanse the soul in the event of a "bad death" (*salah mati*).[2]

Thus the fear of being put to death by another is not fantasy but based in stark reality, and hair straws, footprints, and photos are among the most prized assets to have if one wants to do another in.[3] The joy of that peculiar satisfaction wipes the heart automatically clean of the anger, jealousy, or envy that ravaged it until then and thus rejuvenates and strengthens the perpetrator's previously sick body and soul. No wonder my friend prized her hair straws and was at pains to collect every single one as she must have bent down to her knees on the floor to check every nook and cranny. Her hair was very long, and it was also very thick.

A Preoccupation with Virtue

Why the gracious hostess would be suspected to *want*, perhaps, to do her visitor harm requires a more elaborate exposition that probes Balinese notions of persons, feeling-thoughts, and morality in depth. This is a connecting theme throughout the book and must stepwise be laid bare. Suffice it here to note that it was not fear that her conduct had been lacking in the requisite grace and etiquette that troubled this courteous young lady. A suggestion that what matters is ". . . to please as beauty, not as virtue pleases . . ." (C. Geertz [1966] 1973a, 400) provides little consolation to a person reared to take a different view of herself and the world. This prescribes in quite minute detail the moral obligations pertaining between fellow human beings and differentiates behavior/action (*bikas*), expression/gesture (*semu*), character (*sifat/abet*), and feeling-thought (*keneh/perasaan*) as emphatically good (*baik/melah*) or bad (*jele/jelek*).

Sopan-santun or *tata krama* is the name given to this ethical code. *Sopan* means literally "polite" whereas *santun* refers to "good rule, good ability." *Tata* means "order," *krama* "rule,"[4] and so *sopan-santun* may be translated as "rules in good order." It is the ethical code of moral precepts and norms to which children are socialized from the earliest age and which regulates all interpersonal conduct. To keep a bright face (*mue cedang*), refrain from arrogance (*sombong*),[5] speak softly and smoothly (*polos*), and be generally friendly (*rameh*) and cheerful (*girang*) are examples of *sopan-santun*. Whoever defaults is said to be *kurang ajar*, that is, "lacking education and knowledge."[6] The sanctions may be dreadful, for a violation of moral behavior causes offense, which may trigger the hidden anger (*benci*)[7] that is the driving force behind black magic and other forms of covert violence. Hence the supreme concern to "please as virtue pleases."

Offense is what my friend feared she might be judged guilty of, and offense is a moral term in Bali. It is linked with clear, concise conception of what is honorable and right between humans; therefore children, who are presumed to be lacking in such knowledge,[8] are also incapable of feeling offended according to Balinese. When adults would react by feeling offended (*tersinggung*), children would feel only embarrassed (*malu*). The difference is significant, for shame generally harms the sufferer only, whereas offense strikes back at the offender.

A failure of friendliness and politeness in interpersonal conduct is also judged an offense. But no measure of this can avail you if your actions are lacking in moral propriety. This is what Issa feared the hostess might judge her guilty of. And it was not unwarranted anxiety on her part. People would agree, if they knew what she knew, that she *had* reason to fear.

Ground Rules

We leave the matter here. It is not important for us now to know what was the nature of her offense, or the moral logic that positioned it so. Suffice it to note that her "offense" concerned acts vis-à-vis a distant relative of the hostess no less than seven years ago! Nor was it a question of premeditated offense on her part, but of being trapped in a situation the relative had forced upon her. Third, it was far from certain that the hostess knew all of this. What is important is that *if* she knew, and knew only the facts torn loose from their proper context, *then* she would probably be angry, still after seven years. This says something of the power ascribed to "hearts" by Balinese.

I have chosen to present Issa's case here to provide an antidote to a preconception we might easily bring to bear on our understanding of Balinese, namely, that their world—like ours—is ordered along a public/private dimension and that their "private" sphere likewise partakes of a warm and relaxed atmosphere. It very often does, of course. Yet, as Issa's case makes indubitably clear, the experiential connotations "private" gatherings occasionally evoke to Balinese are sufficiently different that it is necessary to fully face the dangers of applying a Western scheme to them.

While the domestic realm is often a relaxing kind of place, the fact that it often is not is equally important. We are not served by sweeping generalizations that eradicate such essential differences and portray the

Balinese as relaxing their defenses in the haven of sitting rooms and kitchens. Rather we must *discover* how they think about person and place, and for this, careful observations must be our court of authority.

What then are the ground rules that Balinese perceive "naturally" to apply to different kinds of encounters, occasions, settings, and events? What premises do they act in terms of when they frame their actions and evaluate performance? And what problems of self-management arise as people are required to bridge different settings while pursuing their everyday concerns?

We should explore their recurrent *movements in social space,* the *changes of arena* they must handle, and the attendant *oscillation in interactional mode* for what these embody in terms of rules and regulations that Balinese experience as binding and right and also for what modicum of choice for improvisation and maneuver they allow. A prerequisite of life in society is a measure of freedom as well as constraints, and both must be perceived if we are to capture the actors' existential world. The *enduring concerns* people carry with them from place to place are also likely to show up in the course of such an investigation.

Methodology and Representation

When Geertz and Geertz ascribe an atmosphere of warmth and relaxation to the private sphere as against coolness and restraint in public, what might be their basis? Is the sorcery and witchcraft, which also abounds in South Bali (e.g., Covarrubias [1931] 1973, 320–58; Connor 1986, 68–70; Zurbuchen 1989), experienced as a threat only in public?[9] Or is this the opinion of the authors when they describe caution and restraint as pervading that domain?

We do not know, for the data are not presented to us. And Clifford Geertz might not know, for he explicitly chose to exclude from consideration matters pertaining to magic and sorcery in his most famous study of personhood and conduct in Bali. Labeling witchcraft a "subordinate cultural domain," he suggested it might better be made an object of study in a connection unrelated to Balinese conceptions of personhood with which it did not logically belong ([1966] 1973a, 406).

I consider this methodology untenable. An outsider's conception of logic or typology cannot serve as a measuring stick for what should or should not be included in our analyses. If Balinese, as persons, are concerned with magic and sorcery, and if they believe that fellow beings can do them in, then that speaks tremendously of their ideas of personhood; to exclude such data from consideration is to fabricate a fictitious world, however aesthetically pleasing or logically coherent it may be.

I argue, by contrast, that we should start, methodologically, with people's compelling concerns as they are evinced through their everyday life experiences. The linkages as well as the discontinuities they perceive should be given equal attention to enable us to capture their lifeworld in phenomenological, "lived" terms.

Just as people, in pursuit of compelling concerns, must constantly traverse a variety of kinds of spaces, so our analysis and representation must reckon with their movements and crisscrossings. I have argued before for a perspective that places the person center stage. My search for "ground rules" applies this perspective and follows people *in* social space *as* they move and come up against multiple, at times clearcut, at times vague and ambivalent, pressures and injunctions. The meanings that persons and places carry should show up in the course of such an investigation.

That is one reason why I judged Issa's case a pertinent one to accompany our initial extended focus on a time in Suriati' life. Together the two enable us to begin to spell out the variegated character of interactions pertaining to the domestic realm *and,* by implication, the ground rules that apply and the concerns they are evocative of.

Suriati's case may have seemed to bear out a Western construction of warmth and intimacy in "private" versus restraint and caution in "public," but this was, in part, an artifact of my representation and, in part, a characteristic of that particular time in her life. When I portray her as smoothing her face and posture to go out in the street and report her saying how she would be ashamed to cry "except with my closest friends," a Western reader may naturally infer that such friends together constitute a private, relaxed, and safe place, whereas the "public" consists of "them" conferring restraint and, as Suriati implied, the threat of unmerciful ridicule.

I am going to show that whereas there is some truth to both of these assumptions, when put so schematically they mask rather than clarify. "Private" is much more complex in its experienced connotations, and "public" also appears with another texture and significance. Compelling concerns may indeed make private situations appear the more constraining of the two.

My report on a time in Suriati's life appeared to bear out a Western dichotomy also on account of the particular concerns that at this time vexed and perplexed her. Perceptions of place and person, as Balinese

47

are aware, differ with the "feeling-thought" (*keneh*) one harbors, because this predicates one's outlook on the world and oneself. Sadness or sorrow positions the person particularistically and entails a perspective that is all-enveloping and also "confusing." Hence the experienced contrast between "closest friends" and "them" is thrown into dramatic relief particularly in situations of bereavement and loss.

Any effort to portray somebody else's world must necessarily leave out a great deal, and when this somebody is also of a different culture, efforts at conveying what experiences mean need to provide the reader with a sufficient context for understanding. My initial focus on Suriati could only give fragments of such context. Beyond that, a Western reader may be "naturally" able to empathize with her sorrow, but not at all with her fear of black magic, and thus not so easily able to grasp contrary indications about the meaning of "private" that I also attempted to present through my description of her case.

When I noted her and her family's truly tormenting fear of Lombok and of visiting in village society, did you think it was people in "public" they feared? Not at all, strangers cannot easily harm one, as I am going to show. Their concern was with the kind of danger that is highlighted through Issa's case; and thus this case throws into full relief fears that are the daily lot of Balinese and sensitizes us to watchfulness that cannot be shed but must be intensified particularly in domestic places.

Our task must be to try to discover what are these native models that actors apply in routine daily life as well as on ceremonious occasions. Meticulous orientation to singular instances of putting the frameworks to use is the best approach I can see to unraveling such native constructs. I learn something when I hear a Balinese family reminisce how, when they were going to the death temple with offerings to ask God for leave for the souls of their dead to meet with the living at a balian's a few days hence, they took care to go in the middle of the night. It was to prevent envious souls of other deceased from intruding and obstructing the passage of their own kinsfolk.

In death, as in life, persons (or souls) are ascribed qualities that empower them to wreak havoc with one's own most cherished concerns. An enduring preoccupation for Balinese thus becomes to tread carefully amid dangers while heedful of the constraints that "naturally" apply so valued pursuits are not jeopardized. The qualities ascribed to persons of various kinds and to "souls" and (super)natural spirits are an important part of these constraints, for they inhabit the same social space in which the person moves. A Western dichotomy of public/private is invalid also because it refers only to a world of human persons. But in Bali every kind of social space is also occupied by mystical forces and presences, which participate in encounters and affect the course of interactions.

There are deities, ancestors, demons, witches, ghosts of the dead, and spirits of innumerable kinds—an array of mystical forces that are so much part of people's experience of the natural world that our dichotomy between "natural" and "supernatural" seems inapplicable to them (M. Hobart 1985c, 12; Connor 1982a, 282; also chaps. 5, 11, and 12).

The Virtue of "Making One's Face Look Bright and Clear"

Now let us return to Issa's case to search for the ground rules that apply to encounters in domestic settings. It reveals them in particularly poignant form. First, it bears mention that the hostess behaved admirably correctly by the rules of moral propriety when she presented Issa with a polite and friendly demeanor. She did not evince a trace of that arrogance Balinese deplore, though she was of a status greatly superior to her guest. Exquisite (*anggun*) throughout, she actualized Balinese ideals pertaining to females to the fullest.

Also, she personified moral ideals when she presented Issa with a clear and bright (*cedang*) face. Whatever feelings she may actually have had, she did not stoop to revealing them to her guest. To do so would have been offensive, and offense, as we have learned, is dangerous. The hostess herself might have had reason to fear.

Moreover, to reveal one's heart—that is, one's true feelings—to people beyond the intimate circle of family and friends is also considered shameful (*ngidalem*) and selfish. It is to impose one's own concerns on people who have enough with their own.[10] And it is to run the risk of gossip and ridicule. For reasons of morality and tact, fear of offense and revenge, and fear of shaming oneself people can be counted on to "keep their heart." Provided, that is, that they "have shame" (*tau malu*). And few are those who do not.[11]

Issa, on her part, also did what was commendable and right. She may have been haunted with fear, but she displayed no sign of it that I could detect (and by this time I was quite skilled in detecting such signs). Unlike Suriati, who in a certain mountain village retracted into a caricature of respectful demeanor to please and lessen the danger of magical attack, this young woman acted her part with apparent effortless grace. She also drank the coffee she was served (coffee being much more dangerous than tea, for it conceals traces of poison[12]), though she may have rushed home afterwards to purge herself of the venom she may have feared was placed within.

Thus here are two graceful Balinese, each able to think well of herself and the other in their mutual observance of rigid ground rules. But at the same time they may be seen to be caught in a cultural morass of shared predicament: neither had a way to find out what the other actually felt-thought, and for Issa, at least, it mattered to know. Instead, both kept bright faces that obfuscated disquieting emotional concerns. And it was not to disguise their individuality—on the contrary, their interaction spoke of their mutual, focused interest in the particulars of the other's biography.

The hostess could display her interest more openly on account of her superior social status. Issa was obliged to probe and ferret more secretly. But it was because she was successful in this respect that she hit upon a particularly relevant detail of the hostess's biography that warned her she might be in danger. Provided, that is, that the hostess had similarly been able to trace these significant connections. Issa could fear that she had, but never know for sure.

At stake is not anonymization of the self and the other, but concern with health, morality, and self-value. Concepts like heart (*hati, keneh*), character (*sifat, abet, tabiat*), and attitude (*tingkah*), which feature constantly in everyday discourse, bespeak an ingrained concern with the individual features of others.

Bright Faces: Across Domains

Now if we trace back to Suriati's case, we discover a common concern. She, too, was at pains, and constrained by her social others, to present the world with a bright and happy face. It was to hide her sadness from view, to avoid being shamed by laughter, and also to preserve sanity and health.

Anger or offense, sorrow or fear—the injunction is the same: Be polite (*sopan*) and happy (*gembira*). Laugh and joke. Do not care (*de runguange*), "forget it" (your problem—*ngesapine*) and "manage your heart" (i.e., guide your feeling-thoughts—*ngabe keneh*) behind a clear (*cedang*) and cheerful (*girang*) expression. Be *polos:* of one color, always.

"Public" and "private," exposed street and shielded sitting room, thus enjoin *similar* standards of self-management and performance, at least on *some* occasions. A valued expression of "clear/bright" and "happy" mien applies *across* the boundaries that Westerners draw emphatically; and the "restraint and caution" we position in streets and public places Balinese find to be present also in many private interactions.

This does not mean that Balinese draw no emphatic boundaries between the social spaces in which they move. They do, and we have seen examples of it, such as Suriati being ashamed to cry "except with my closest friends." But it serves to question the *validity* of applying a Western scheme to them and to throw into relief that the bridges and thresholds which Balinese symbolically construct reflect conceptions of what is at stake that are lost by the application of an alien scheme.

The reader may feel that the similarity I point out is spurious, an artifact of the comparison I have drawn in juxtaposing encounters so similar in their emphasis on impersonality and distance as a formal hostess-guest relationship with that of fleeting social movements in the street. I ask you to suspend your judgment. From a Balinese perspective, the connection *is* vital and expressive of compelling life concerns such as what one must do to survive in the world, to protect one's family, and also to prosper. A proper social appearance of polite and friendly demeanor—integral to which is a clear and bright face—is emphatically valued *across* domains. But what is at stake if one fails to comply differs with aspects of the situation, as we shall see.

Making one's face look bright and clear is an abiding concern, *also* in private, *except* among closest family and friends. But even there the injunction weighs. For it is valued in and of itself, not just as a function of relationship and place. One may, without sanction, expose one's heart (*kata hati/tiang keneh*), that is, one's true feelings, to members of an intimate circle of family and friends, but, out of compassion for them as well as for one's own mental calm, it is often not done. One chooses instead to make one's face look bright and clear.

Replied a man when I asked him what his wife had said when he had taken their one-day-old baby away from her and had given it in fosterage to his brother, "I don't know, my wife does not speak much." Suriati's father tends toward a similar attitude. At a time when she felt that the whole family had ganged up against her to make her marry a certain man (p. 203), she said of her father, "My father is *polos* (of one color); he does not show concern one way or the other, but always makes his face look clear." And a woman whose husband suffers prolonged attacks of depression sighs, "I come home from work and am dead beat; but I make my face look bright and smile to him, always with the hope he will get better."

In all other relations, a failure to keep a bright face connotes im-

51

politeness, madness, or an inability to "manage one's heart"—failures that evoke laughter, mocking shame, or, worse, retribution by recourse to magic.

Clear and Bright versus Withered, Cloudy, or Grave

What constitutes a "clear, bright" face (*mue cedang* or *cerah muka*)? Balinese, if you ask them, have difficulties saying. As the normal, natural expression incumbent on all adults to display, it does not lend itself easily to description. "It is an expression (*semu*)," "we can tell," "we can see from the eyes, the eyes cannot lie," and "if the face/expression is not clear/bright, it is like the person is hiding something," was as far as I got when I tried to question. But its *absence* would be noted—with suspicion or compassion—recurrently in everyday interaction when people may refer emphatically to another's face as "not clear" or, more bluntly, *layu* (withered, faded, languished), *muram* (cloudy, gloomy, sorrowful), *seram* (hideous, horrible, frightening) or *nyebeng* (grave, stern).

As the expression "we can see from the eyes" connotes, none of these bad (*jele*) facial expressions are carried by clearly visible facial mimicry, but more by nearly imperceptible signs such as the size and color of the pupil or the color and texture of the face, often in conjunction with aspects of posture and vocal tone. The borderline between clear/bright and withered/cloudy faces is not easily discernible to a foreigner. But it is a signpost Balinese learn to be skilled at reading and by which they orient themselves.[13] The face is taken to be the physical manifestation of hidden forces of major significance—the heart.

For example, a man said to his wife, who had joined us when I had just remarked how his son-in-law's heart was so good, "Unni says Wayan's face is so clear!" I asked why he had substituted "clear face" for my "good heart." He answered, "Myself I believe that the quality of the heart flows to the face, the expression." He was voicing shared, popular understandings.

Balinese are under a moral obligation to manage their hearts, entailing that they should present the world with a "clear, bright" face. *Cedang* (Ind. *cerah*) has connotations of shine, radiance, smoothness. The expression "the air of the face" (*yeh mue*) is often used to convey an image of how the face should be: smooth and clear as water, transparent throughout, and reflective of light and luster. In the Balinese idiom, feelings are thought to "flow" to the face, hence an unruffled, clear, smooth surface should be the outer expression of an inner, good heart, as implied by the man who equated my "good heart" with a "clear face." The facet of brightness that "clear" conveys is also expressed by the term *sinar mue*—the light or ray/radiance of the face. Good feeling-thoughts (*keneh melah*) enlighten the face to cast a hue like that of the sun shining on water.

In practice Balinese are aware that the relationship is not so unequivocal. People produce clear faces when they actually have bad hearts. Indeed, they must. Society does not allow them the freedom of exposing such feelings as they might have; and when dire sanctions meet the one who is not sufficiently skilled in managing the heart, it is only natural that through time people learn techniques of disguise. "The world is the stage of drama" (*dunia adalah panggung sandiwara*), observed a woman who had had more than her share of bitter experience with the attendant burden of having to produce a bright face with some effort.

Clear, bright faces are as much made as naturally created by good feelings simply flowing to the face. And while their "made" component creates some predicaments for Balinese—we saw it with Issa: how was she to know if the hostess was really or only effortfully "clear," and in the latter case, what feelings her brightness concealed—yet the supreme value of a bright face is ideologically sustained. To mask with the purpose of consoling another, or for good social relations, is morally valued and connoted by the special term *pura-pura*. It has none of the bad connotations of pretense for selfish ends, called *munafiq* (see pp. 111).

Contrasted with clear/bright are various expressions that connote socially deplorable demeanor. *Layu* (or *mueg*) is the most common, as it is also used *to* people, not just about them. "*Sapon napi mukane layu?*" (Why is your face so withered?) might be said to someone who is sad to shake her out of her feeling-thought. *Muram* (gloomy, cloudy, sorrowful) also refers to a sad face, but to an appearance of shame, offense, or anger as well. But more commonly, and particularly with men, anger is discerned by a *nyebeng/seram*—grave/stern or frightening—expression. It is a condition much feared by women and children in particular (Wikan 1987, 347). Envy, which is akin to anger, is said to express itself neither in a grave nor gloomy appearance but in a cynical (*sinis*) appearance. Worst of all, jealousy (*cemburu*) might make the face look furious (*galak*).

But again, none of these terms connote clearly demarkable facial expressions. Judgments as to what a face "is" or reveals are as much made as the expression itself. The signs (*ciri-ciri*) and indications (*tampe-tampe*) Balinese go by to probe another's expression are often ambiguous, multivocal, and open to varying interpretations. In an ac-

tual instance, both biographical and situational information and the feelings of the observer affect the interpretation hit upon.

Gender, age, and rank further compound the standards by which expressions are judged, just as such positional modifiers influence the keys
people hold for decoding expressions. What is "grave, stern" to a
woman, need not be at all so to a man, but might be read instead as
acceptably companionable (see chap. 4). Yet the general injunction—to
present the world with a bright face—weighs on all. The *effort* this may
require is on occasion a task of commiserating concern.

One evening a friend and I visited a balian (traditional healer)—he
was a good friend, and we came for purely social reasons. He burst out
in a lament, "I am so tired, I feel as if I have almost no energy, guests
coming morning, midday, night . . . But I always make my face look
clear and receive everyone . . ."

Afterwards, on the way home, my friend commented, "Did you hear
what he said? He also makes his face look bright. Just like me!" In the
morning of that day she had confided to me at length along the lines of
the vignette that opens this chapter: "Always when I go out, I make my
face look bright so that people will not laugh and say, 'She does not
know how to manage her feelings!'" She had said it with satisfaction
and pride. A year before the lament had sounded, "I cannot manage to
make my face look bright and smile when I go out, for I have learned
that a smile is an empty gesture only." Indeed a "bright face" reads also
as a "happy face" (*mue girang*). Brightness and cheerfulness of expression are intimately linked, particularly in women. But it is also possible
to burst with smiles and yet be judged wanting in "brightness," as I had
occasion to find out.

I had let a friend, a foreigner, meet some of my Balinese friends. She
was received with utmost friendliness. But in several houses, the next
time when I came alone, another attitude surfaced. My friend's face was
not clear, said the Balinese, I must take care . . . And when I asked
what they meant, they said her thinking (*pikiran*) and her feeling (*perasaan*) were not of a piece and she acted as if she thought that thinking
alone will do, not realizing one must also have capability . . .[14]

Here, in their judgment, was a person of warring tendencies who let
herself be driven by her thinking whereas all good social behavior requires one "to listen to one's heart." "Thinking is like strategy, tactic,
whereas the heart cannot lie," say Balinese. To me the puzzle was that
this person is as sweet and gentle as any Westerner I know, which is
why I had felt sure she would square well with Balinese. Perhaps, indeed, it was because she resembled them enough in behavioral style that

they felt they could easily read beyond her expression to her heart—and she was found wanting.

Take not this to mean that Balinese read all "cloudy" faces as indicating pretense. They judge every case on its own merits, and when the person is found to be, or known to be, suffering from sadness, a "withered" face may instead elicit compassion.

Anger as well as may be hidden behind a clear and "happy" face: "Did you see how I made my face look bright?" asked a friend, a teacher, when her guests had just left. She had been visited by the relatives of a pupil who had just failed her exams. They tried to persuade her to reverse the decision and let the girl pass. "How could I? It was the decision of the meeting, not just me; and I was angry with them to ask it of me. But I smiled and made my face look bright, for I was afraid . . . they might do something to me . . ."

Thus a concern that we saw in Issa's case, and with Suriati, carries across a wide range of settings and encounters and is explicitly regarded as a protective device. We move on to see what it is about "sitting rooms" that makes it particularly valuable there.

Everyone's Sitting Room Is Feared by Someone

As we have seen in Suriati's case, a home may be a place to let one's defenses down, provided two conditions apply: the right people, and they only, should be there, and one must keep within the rigid bounds set for exposing one's feelings. If these conditions are fulfilled, a sitting room may be a safe haven.

But this space which is protected and private to me is another's threatening and exacting "public": the guest fearing for her life is vulnerable and must exercise as much caution as anybody "on display" in public. *The place is the same,* only the perspective differs according to the position of the person(s) involved. Even Suriati, immersed in tears, will on another occasion be someone's feared and distrusted hostess. Indeed, she knows it and wants it to be that way herself: "Sometimes people here [in Java] say to me, 'You are from Bali, Balinese have the best balians [magicians].' And I let them believe, that they will be properly cautious."

Thus sitting room has multiple connotations: of safety and danger, protected space and exposed arena, intimacy and warmth but *also* of caution and restraint. Which ones will be foremost depends on situational and biographical factors.

Most everyone's sitting room is feared by someone, and it is experienced as precarious even by the self. Why do Balinese keep a *tombal*—a guarding spirit—in their homes? (Suriati even has a lion in the kitchen—her brother, who has "cold blood," has seen it with his own eyes.) It is to avert evil spirits and attacks of black magic.[15] But do not think that these come from the "public"—from the anonymous strangers one accidentally encounters. It is intimates who are feared, close companions with detailed personal knowledge of oneself. "Most dangerous are the neighbors," say Balinese, "for they come all the time." And where do they come? Into one's sitting room and kitchen. Do you then relax, secure in the warmth and safety that inhere to such places? On the contrary, you try to make your face look bright and clear and be as respectful as you can.

That is difficult in the midst of chores and attendant activities. The implication of the saying that those are most dangerous who come at unexpected times is that one may be caught unaware while preoccupied with other concerns and therefore stand in greater danger to offend. Formal visits and public passages are more manageable in that respect. The attention is focused, the expectations drawn, and one goes to the encounter in a set frame of mind that one may anticipate what will ensue. Considering how important spiritual calm and concentrated energy (see chap. 9) are for safety and survival, it is even clearer why those should be more dangerous who surprise one at unexpected times.

Sitting room and kitchen thus have multiple connotations that are shaped and nuanced through the course of everyday life. Some are general, a part of a Balinese cultural heritage of shared assumptions. Others pertain to one's unique biography/experience and the events associated with a place. My understanding is, however, that to any Balinese one's own sitting room is experienced as at once one's safe haven and the place where one is most exposed. It is not, as we may have thought from Issa's case, the hostess relationship alone that confers the power to do sorcery. The hostess herself is exposed depending on who her guests are.

A man described to me how, one evening when he was sitting at home with his cousin, he felt a sudden stroke, as of lightning, hit him in the face. He mobilized all his power and looked the man directly in the eye, making him shudder and recoil. Soon after, the visitor left.

It was his cousin who had been out to kill him. Indeed, this man had two lives on his conscience, as my friend knew for certain. I was given a dramatic account of how the cousin had killed their uncle and the latter's son by black magic not long before. My friend and his kinsfolk had spoken with the souls of two dead men and had verified their own suspi-

cions. But because my friend's spirit (*bayu*) was strong, and he managed to fight back, the cousin was defeated this time.[16]

Another, a woman, fell ill when she had unwrapped the parcel that
her tenant, a friend's daughter, had been given by him. The woman had
seen him deliver it, saying "Take care," whereupon the girl put it in her
closet and locked it. But one day the key had been left in—the girl was
out—and curiosity got the better of the landlady. She found layers of
paper wrapped tightly together and inscribed in strange, Arabic-looking
script. When she found that the last layer was red, a dangerous color,[17]
she quickly threw it in the sea to dispel any evil power. But it was too
late, she fell ill.

Thus a sitting room is, at once, a place to relax; a place to exploit
one's unequal advantage over guests, if one so wishes (they must drink
the beverage you serve and eat your food); or a place to fear for your
own life because intimate information is readily available, which guests
can misuse. Guests may also take advantage of their access to your
house by placing evil materials within it. I have no count of all the incidents of "poison in the pillow" (*cetik candang galeng*) that I have heard
about—the last one concerned a man, an uncle of a close friend of
mine, who was killed in this way by his third and youngest wife.

Also Suriati, now living far away from Bali, continues to have her
private life disturbed by onslaughts of covert violence. Whenever her
husband's youngest cousin comes to visit, Suriati finds herself inexplicably drawn into quarrels with her husband. The pattern is so persistent and compulsive that she has consulted a balian in Bali about the
cause. He confirmed what she suspected and warned her to take great
care: the cousin comes from a place in Western Sumatra renowned all
over Indonesia for its powerful magicians.

Suriati now lives in an apartment that is too expensive for her means.
She was forced out of a previous good and cheap one by the assaults of
black magic from a neighbor, the daughter of her previous landlord.
Even in her new home, the woman continues to pester her. Recently,
Suriati's husband had gone to the old apartment to fetch some things
they had left behind, and when he came back his eyes wore an uncanny
expression. Consumed with fury he launched a vicious attack on Suriati,
accusing her of atrocious vices. She was shocked and collapsed in tears
while the grandmother, who lived with them then, forced the husband
down into a chair and implored him to come to his senses. Soon after he
regained his wits (*kesadaran*) and broke down crying for what he had
done. He explained how at the other house he had met the landlord's
daughter and when she launched an attack on Suriati, he had found him-

self agreeing with all that she said. It shows how important it was for them to move.

One can never protect oneself entirely, however. Sitting in her living room on Friday afternoons, Suriati tends to be suddenly overcome with fatigue and inertia around 6:00 P.M. It strikes her inexplicably and regularly, this feeling of not wanting to go to her boss's home where, at 7:00, she is due to give private lessons to his children. Until that moment she feels fit and fine and it is clearly not "she" who does not want to go, for she is very fond of her boss's family. She suspects black magic from colleagues who are jealous that she is so favored by the boss. Indeed, by the spring of 1989, she had stopped going. She was unable to tell the boss the real reason—for that might enrage her colleagues who might "overhear" (by telepathy) the conversation—and her boss is now angry with her. Yet living with that is easier than with the constant threat of her colleagues' jealousy, for she knows her boss's heart to be good.

Person *and* Place or Person *in* Place

Does it now begin to emerge that place is not the salient variable so much as the constellation of place-and-person combined and that to superimpose a public/private paradigm on Bali is to misrepresent the concerns that compel Balinese and the constraints that *they* must take in earnest?

While the sense of "place" is also important for Balinese in that houses and streets, fields and markets, government offices, hospitals and temples, etc. set different requirements in terms of tasks and demeanors—as when you wear a *sash* (cloth around the waist) to the temple, shoes to a government office, sandals to the market, and walk barefoot at home—yet it would not to do for Balinese to act as if these might be neatly arranged into two contrasting realms, one safe and consoling, the other threatening and exposed. Far more nuanced and particularistic models must be applied if one is to thrive, or even to survive.

This society, which on the face of it appears so peaceful and harmonious, is actually ridden with violence in covert and indirect form.[18] The evidence is unequivocal: massive misfortune, illness and death. But given that it is "hearts" that instigate recourse to black magic, Balinese notions of the critical divide concern *properties that people carry always with them.* The question of how others feel about oneself is more critical than when or where an interaction takes place. It is person *and* place, or person *in* place—of which occasion is one aspect—that foretells whether one may relax one's defenses or be intensely alert.

I find *movement in social space* a good term by which to capture the continuities and bridges that also Balinese deem vital. We shall see, when we turn to what was at stake for Issa with the hostess, that people are presumed to be unable to shed critical concerns even over very long periods of time. It is therefore essential to know what are the movements, relations, and experiences that imprint themselves on people's hearts.

Methodologically, my point is this: our Western public/private dichotomy rings with *particular* connotations like warm versus cool, intimate versus restrained, and safe versus dangerous that we have no reason to expect others to share until they have been actually found to do so. Investigation must be the first step. In the way of the naturalists we must construct, from empirical elements, how people think, and feel, about person and place. It should be done by careful exploration of the notions *they* use to interpret their world and to derive guidance for their lives. Eliciting "texts" or concepts in a vacuum will not do.

As Arthur Kleinman has alerted me, the orientation of contemporary anthropological thinking requires a revitalization of the terminology of experience. And it should come from the lived world and begin with the notions people themselves use to render their lives to themselves and to one another.

Only as a next step may we then search to see if we can find a limited number of such experiential labels which grasp and convey human experience across cultures, and which, by systematic usage, render them comparable through time and space. I suggest some such notions throughout this text: "what is at stake," "multiple, compelling concerns," "cares that cannot be shed," "struggling, coping, striving," "effort," "limited energies," "singular moments," "life world," "bridgings," and "movement in social space." Admittedly crude, and not equally experience-near, they nonetheless attempt to bridge an all too large gap in much of the literature between the fanciful anthropological jargon we use to render people's lives and the quality of those lives as lived.

The Contingent Nature of Intimacy and Warmth

The above representation of endangered and endangering aspects of domestic places is not meant to cancel their comforting and consoling character, but *to question what we think we know.* What are the prerequisites for the warmth and intimacy that also suffuse private life? With whom, when, and how do they obtain? And when does a warm and relaxed encounter cease being one and turn instead into a cautious and cool gathering?[19] It is not place, so much as person and place, which determine this, as we have seen. Equally essential is the question of perspective: who makes the judgment in respect to this? How is the person positioned?

The prerequisites for warmth and intimacy are found, on the one hand, in a cultural conception that singles out closest family members—along with intimate friends—as the only persons to whom one can potentially speak and reveal one's heart. In this respect, all others are bracketed as "them," meaning they might laugh, or take revenge, from offense. Secrets should be kept within the family, for it is both selfish, shameful, and dangerous to reveal them beyond.

An eventual atmosphere of warmth and intimacy in private depends on the constellation of the people present, the quality of their relationships, and the perspective of the person(s) making the judgment, and—under conditions of poverty—economic factors also play a role. One man erased the names of his two dead baby twins from the count of all his children, though it is the custom in Bali to reckon also one's dead children among the total. He could not bear to be reminded of his own failure at the time as responsible household head, though it was economic necessity that caused his problems:

> I was always tense, my mind going off in all directions, and I
> neglected my family. Had I not been so pressured, perhaps
> the children would have lived . . . That morning when the
> first twin died—I found him lying in his bed, suddenly dead,
> at four in the morning, and I woke my wife, but instead of
> staying at home I rushed off to Grogag on my bicycle [forty
> kilometers] to buy the eggs that I could sell at the market.
> When I returned in the evening the other one was also dead.
> They were buried together. I took their death as a warning,
> that I must first look out for my family, second for myself,
> and third only for my duties. Perhaps they saved my life. But
> still, I cannot bear to think of it . . . so I don't count them,
> and I called the next two born with their [birth-order] names,
> as if they had never lived.[20]

In this man's experience his home did not begin to feel like a haven until he himself changed and took up companionship with his wife. I have formed the impression that women are less likely than men to experience their own home as a place to relax. Demands are too many, "cares" are too close, one goes away to "play" (*bermain*), meaning spending time in relaxed encounters with others; or one may even go to work. One woman I know was always tense at home until she opened a stall, where she now spends twelve hours a day. She does not need the money, it is to have a respite, a space of one's own. This may be particularly important for women of whom it is required that they have the gift of "sacrifice" (*pengorbanan*). One teacher said, "I tell my pupils [girls] unless you have this gift [ability], don't marry. You will suffer too much. And I expose my own marital problems to them, that they will learn and know what they must be prepared for." Marriage in Bali is experienced as a fundamentally unequal relationship with women in the weak position; it is only natural then that males and females should experience their sitting rooms and kitchens as *different* kinds of places. For the one it is an arena where one is to be pampered and served and which one can leave at pleasure or return to at will. The other must accommodate, bend, and stretch to make him feel master of the house.

Even a woman very loyal to her husband, occasionally let off a heart-felt complaint:

> Sometimes he comes home late in the evening, not having
> notified me, and I feel like I am angry to be left so much
> alone. But I smile when he comes, and kiss his hand, take his
> handbag and jacket and put them away, and then I serve him
> the food. When he has eaten and rested I suggest carefully
> that it is better not to do like that . . . But sometimes I am so
> angry that I cannot keep myself. I don't wait to receive him, I
> leave the door unlocked, put the food on the table, and go to
> bed. He understands.

But for all, family constellations play a role in affecting the atmosphere of the place. "Look at this one, she has brought luck to the whole family. Ever since she was born, we have prospered, thrived. I hope it is true, it will continue . . ." It was a father who spoke on the good omen of his last-born child.[21] And it was true as he said, I had seen how the family before had been beset with problems. Another, a woman, whose husband was playing around with another woman, struggled with the sensation that she was going mad: "Truly, I want to prostitute myself to shame him. Only the thought of the children and the shame conferred on *them* keeps me from it . . ." A year and one-half later, they were reconciled and had a new child, and the whole family atmosphere was completely changed. A third, complaining about her brother, who set the house on end and unhinged everybody's peace of mind, confided: "It is on account of my grandmother that my brother is so confused. She is ill-tempered and harsh . . . Truly, she is not dear to any one of us . . ." And a fourth: "That's why I want to get married, to get away and get well. These constant soullosses that I suffer, they are from the quarrels and upheavals that ravage our family . . ."

Chapter 11 will give an extended account of the change in family atmosphere and life-style that ensued when a man lost his job and nearly also his mental balance. How a home is experienced, the peace and calm and security, or, alternately, the problems and unhappiness it presents, depends on many factors not grasped by bracketing it as private and leaving it at that, pregnant with the connotations we read into that label.

Abandon "Public/Private"—Center on Person-in-Place

I would like to sum up the position I take in examining the meanings of everyday social space.

I have argued for the abandonment of the public/private dichotomy in the study of Bali and for a general restraint in using the pair as an analytical tool in *any* cross-cultural study. We cannot escape their connotations. They are part and parcel of our Western conceptual baggage. And when we uncritically apply the terms without exploring what, if anything, they signify in a differently constructed world, our analysis rings with probably the wrong connotations.

"Public" comes to connote places like streets, fields, and markets while "private," naturally, connotes the sitting rooms and kitchens. These inevitably carry with them the following connotations in terms of their relationship to one another.

"Private" is to "public" as warm is to cool, as intimate is to restrained, as secluded is to exposed, as safe is to dangerous, as few is to crowd. Homes thus emerge as in their essence warm, intimate, secluded, and safe versus places like streets and markets that are cool, restrained, exposed, and dangerous.

A groundwork is laid that begs the whole analysis, and then to break out and begin to ask "how do actors actually think and feel?" is to jeopardize all we have done. The temptation will be to proceed as if the world we have drawn is the world in which they live. And a graceful and ceremonious appearance in "public" may come to connote stage fright, fear of the self and the other that "must" somehow contrast with a warm and relaxed private face. It is logical that it should.

In the process, people's compelling concerns are misrepresented, for we have misconstrued the world in which they might have been discovered.

CHAPTER FOUR

Movement in Social Space

> Man moves in order to satisfy a need. He aims his movement
> at something of value to him. It is easy to perceive the aim
> of a person's movement if it is directed to some tangible object.
> Yet there also exist intangible values that inspire movement.
> —RUDOLF LABAN

Arrogance among Intimates: What Is at Stake?

Whenever my daughter walks with me to the market, she tugs
and pulls at my skirt constantly from annoyance that we
hardly move. I smile and talk with people all the time, a
friendly word to everyone I know. My daughter does not yet
understand that unless you do, people will say you are arrogant [*sombong*]. They will not like you. It is the most important thing for us Balinese to be liked. So we smile and talk
to everyone, though we may be desperate to get going . . .

. . . I have an uncle, he is different. My uncle likes to go
fishing. And he grew annoyed that every time neighbors used
to see him walking past with his fishing equipment, they
would ask, "*Mau ke mana?*—where are you going?" So he
began answering, "Well, where do you think?" It is terrible
what my uncle did, to be sarcastic [*sigug*] like that. If we do,
the other person will not speak to us again. He will have very
bad feeling against us, he will be angry, and perhaps also
sakit hati [sick in his heart from anger].[1] It will be dangerous
for us.

So the Balinese custom is always to be friendly [*rameh*].
Like myself with my neighbor: whenever I go to work in the
mornings, she asks me, "Where are you going?" She knows,
of course! And I smile and say, "To the office." Every morning of every day . . .

What prompted this reflection on Kede's part was a breach of manners of which I myself had been guilty. One day when I was tired of
having to tell passersby, with a bright smile, for the umpteenth time,
where I was going when I figured they knew full well, I burst out to a
group of young men who particularly annoyed me: "Well, where do you
think?!" Buoyed with my own sense of victory, I arrived at Kede's and
told her what I had done. Her face froze in a flash of panic, and she
tutored me, giving weight to every word.

And with her accelerating description of how "bad feeling" runs its natural course unto "anger-sickness" (for which the remedy is joy through revenge by black magic), Kede imprinted upon me the critical value of always evoking good feeling in the other.

Arrogance among Strangers: What Is at Stake?

The most damning criticism of a Balinese you can make is to say that she or he is *sombong* or *angkak*—arrogant. To brag is to be *sombong*. To walk down the street without greeting acquaintances left and right is to be *sombong*. To wear a "quiet" or "closed" (*nyebeng*) expression, or withdraw into yourself while in the company of people you know, is to be *sombong*. To stand with arms akimbo, or sit with crossed legs, is *sombong*. But the presentation of self required to demonstrate that you are not *sombong*—and it *is* essential to demonstrate that you are not— differs significantly for males and females.[2] Women must sparkle and shine. Men need only wear a companionable expression.

Once with Suriati I was visiting her grandmother, a balian, when in came a young man, a prospective client. On identifying me as a for-eigner, he jubilantly displayed his knowledge of English and came to-tally to dominate the interaction with rather uninhibited self-boasting. I grew annoyed and tried not to show it, even though I could feel how I grew terse and mute. Suriati, on the contrary, beamed and answered smilingly to all of his questions. The moment we had entered into the street, however, her expression changed, and with a vivid display of "bad" feelings she criticized what we had witnessed of self-indulgence.

> "But why were you so friendly to him then?" I asked.
> "Because I was afraid . . ."
> "From black magic?"
> "Oh, no, he does not even know my name [i.e., personal name][3] or who I am. But if I had offended him he might have tried to find out where I live and come to my house and sit in front of my parents and talk of how arrogant I had been. I would have felt so ashamed [*malu*] . . ."

To be accused of arrogance elicits shame whether the accusation is made in a sheltered group or in a more formal gathering. As with a "bright face," the injunction to be "friendly" (*rameh*) or "compan-ionable" (*polos*)—as the sign that one is not *sombong*—carries *across* domains and pertains to a style of being that is valued in and of itself. Though what is *at stake* if one defaults depends on aspects of the situa-tion, as Suriati made abundantly clear.

People who do not know you, even by personal name, lack the prerequisites to do you real harm. And hence the strangers one encounters in the street, and also in some domestic places, are less frightening than acquaintances and friends. Applying Geertz's scheme of "consociates" and "contemporaries" to the Balinese scene—it would be the former, people one actually "meets" (C. Geertz [1966] 1973a, 365) who are truly feared. And in this respect, from a Balinese viewpoint, there is less at stake in what we would call "public" than in "private" places.

"Shame" Pertains across Domains

Shame is not the worst that can befall a Balinese, nor is it limited to "public" encounters. Shame is a feeling that ensues, or should ensue— Balinese believe there are some people who simply do not have the capacity for shame (*tidak tau malu*)—on being found wanting in respect of moral prescriptions. Or on being made to feel like a fool by envious jibes from others. Or on being made to feel embarrassed even when by an act of compassion from another, as ego herself may be aware.

Thus to gloss shame as "stage fright," as does Clifford Geertz for South Bali ([1966] 1973a, 402) would be meaningless for the North Bali scene.[4] Shame, while a judgment conferred by others, pertains also to internalized notions of "good" (*melah*) and "bad" (*jele*) and to a concept of self-value (*harga diri*) that *bridges* distinctions of social space.

Once I was visiting a home where a nine-year-old girl who was mentally handicapped (*cacad*),[5] used to come, and this time she appeared just as we were going to eat. The hostess, who was fond of the girl, invited her to join us. Hiding her face in her arms, the girl let out an embarrassed giggle and slid into the hallway. Another visitor let out an astonished, "She actually knows shame?"[6] "Well, of course!" answered the hostess, proud on the girl's behalf.

Another, a well-endowed man of high political position, was less esteemed in this respect. Notorious for his monetary debts, he was said to greet people he owed money with an inculpable gaze when he ought to have looked shamefaced instead. But the wildest example of shamelessness I heard about concerned a man who was presumed to have killed the mayor in a certain village (by black magic) and yet appeared at the latter's funeral. Nevertheless, he continued to be elected to high political positions.

Among people who struggle to make ends meet, those are considered to be lacking in shame who ask services from them, and fail to pay, or pay poorly, in turn. One poor woman went so far as to ask a well-off family to pay for the clothes she had sewn for them for their daughter's wedding. She received a reaction of surprise (and no money). Were they not neighbors? Would she not help? The norms in terms of which shame is judged vary with social positions.

A girl who had won a fashion contest became sick from shame when the organizers, just before handing out the prizes, decided to disqualify her on the pretext that she was too old to participate. The fault lay clearly with the organizers, who had sent out invitations to pupils of the girl's class; and yet she was beside herself. Friends and family tried to console her, to no avail. She locked herself in a room for several days. An explanation of her extreme reaction was voiced, "She is from Java—the Javanese are much more soft than the Balinese."

Another, a Balinese woman, fortified herself against attempts by a man "to make her down" (*nyajang jelme*) whenever they met at formal political meetings. With a smile and a friendly gesture, he would let the greeting "hi, you woman herb peddler!" resound through the room. She was in fact of higher academic position than him but came originally from a community in which women specialize in peddling herb medicine (*loloh*). She did not react with shame, but with a feeling of anger, and to protect herself against that, resolutely "did not care." Friends of hers agreed that the man made a fool of himself, not of her. It is questionable what *his* friends would think.

Judgments vary as they are made by people of multiple concerns, some of whom have several axes to grind,[7] and most of whom do not carry the fear of shame before them as the ultimate threat. Fear of shame does not constrain people in the way that fear of black magic does, for while it is truly significant, it is of much less import than sorcery. People have ways of alleviating the distress, whereas magic strikes however much a person may try "not to care" (though to avert an attack, it helps to feel strong and brave).

Shame is a matter of judgment, rarely an absolute verdict, and in a sense it truly applies only when it is felt. People may try "not to feel-think"—a self-protective device that is positively endorsed and that Suriati resorted to when envious others tried to jolt her position with me by belittling her intellectual powers: "He laughed while he said it, but it was no joke. And all the others laughed too. Truly, what they speak of you and me, I don't want to know . . ."

Persons may also try to balance the verdicts of one group of people against those of others and against self-satisfaction: one girl was so overcome with joy and pride in her new motorbike that she chose to ride it back and forth to a party instead of walking the long way with her friends. The verdict *"sombong"* sounded harsh and loud among her friends, who did not care to be so friendly with her anymore. Did she care? Or did she receive so much self-satisfaction—and social esteem—from exhibiting her splendid new possession that old friends mattered less? How did the "shame" conferred by them count relative to her own feeling of pride and the recognition conferred by others to whom she also related?

As I have argued elsewhere, "shame" is not an objective judgment, and to understand its experiential significance we have to ascertain the impact of various people's judgments on a person's value in her or his own and others' eyes (Wikan 1984; Pitt-Rivers 1965).

Arrogance is more than contemptible and bad, it is also dangerous in that it is impolite, hence offensive to others. People die at times from having been struck by magic on account of their arrogance (cf. p. 111). And yet, from multiple concerns, or indifference, or ignorance, people choose at times to violate moral ideals. Or they may not consider that they do: the girl with the motorbike may have thought it was stupid to walk when she could ride. The man who yells out, "hi, herb-peddler!" to the academically superior woman may think he is just funny, it is always said with a laugh.

Gender and Moral Judgments

Matters are complicated by the fact that status-modifiers like rank, age, and gender modulate interaction. Let us consider how gender affects the ground rules that pertain to movement in social space.

Ground rule here refers to what Balinese themselves might term behavior (*bikas*) or expression/performance/appearance (*semu/penampilan*). Whereas Geertz asserts that "sexual differentiation is culturally extremely played down. Bali is a rather 'unisex' society, a fact both its customs and its symbolism clearly express" (C. Geertz [1972] 1973d, 417), my own evidence, corroborated by observations also from South Bali, points to extreme gender differentiation both in ritual and symbolic activity and in more mundane life.[8]

Particularly in the realm of body language the difference is marked as females and males are expected to display distinctive patterns of body posture, walking and talking, and facial expressions. To take a trivial example of major significance in everyday life: not only should women eat slowly and soundlessly while moving muscles modestly and keeping their lips closed, whereas men may slurp and expose their gums and emit guttural sounds, but a woman who ate in a less feminine way would be considered offensive and might even provoke danger to herself. A man, on the other hand, who ate like a woman would provoke laughter and be an object of shame.

Elaborate and consistent differences in style and standards characterize males and females[9] and find their schematized expression in symbolic forms such as Balinese dance. Female or male identity should never be set aside, but enacted continuously. Breaches incur sanctions and may also provoke nagging doubts about oneself.

Once I visited a woman who was suffering from the sensation that she had turned mad (*gila*). While I could clearly see that she was upset, and had reason to be upset, to me there was nothing improper about her behavior or appearance. She talked sensibly, acted politely, and dressed impeccably. What were the disturbing signs?

I asked Suriati, who explained, "Oh, yes. She talks persistently and loudly—like a man. She also jumps from one topic to another." Everything in its proper measure in Bali and in accordance with gender-specific norms.

Indeed, fieldwork in Bali has impressed upon me the degree to which institutional segregation may actually obviate or greatly reduce the need for more elaborate codes for the symbolic and social affirmation of gender. Nowhere in sex-segregated Middle Eastern societies have I come across anything resembling the Balinese enactment of difference in body language among the genders (Wikan 1987, 347).

It is important to note that in Bali body language is not like an icing which one adds *onto* one's appearance for aesthetic or pleasing effect. Neither are gestures, mimicry, posture, and tone of voice to be experimented with or chosen at will as part of an effort to find a style that suits oneself to serve as a trapping of self-expression. Body language is dead serious and part and parcel of one's *moral* social performance. And thus norms of social conduct appear deceptively clear when they are not fleshed out with the subtleties of rigorous nonverbal codes by which actual appearance is judged.

It is not fortuitous that in Bali men always speak more loudly than women, always take the lead, always sit with their legs apart, whereas women sit with knees close together and legs slung to the side. Any other appearance would be offensive or ridiculous.[10] It is not a matter of choice. During the early stages of fieldwork I drove Suriati to despair because I used to walk at what to me was a normal pace. She on her part annoyed me because she moved with the speed of a turtle. One day she passed the hint to me that people had begun laughing at her, saying she rushed about as if possessed by a *jinn*. Had we been men, our fast stride would have been entirely proper.

Females should display a soft and gentle demeanor (*lemah-lembut*), to which slow walking and slow talking are integral elements. Women should preferably be *anggun:* exquisite, beautiful, trim, referring to body posture and movement rather than physical endowment. Proper dress is also important. The ethical code of *sopan-santun* incorporates these norms of nonverbal expression.[11]

To rest one's chin in one's hands, as Westerners often do, is both impolite and immoral in social encounters. If done by an adult, it signals laziness. To finger one's face, hold one's hand to the mouth, scratch one's nose or one's hair, switch positions restlessly, and sit with head and posture slightly stooped are also improper and may be offensive to others.[12] But to slurp one's coffee is acceptable, provided it is done by a man. Women say the norms applied to them are much more rigorous and also more detailed and numerous.

The following is an example which exposes criteria people use to judge others whom they meet, though it does not particularly refer to social interaction. Women should abstain from taking afternoon naps. If they do, they might develop an enlarged stomach, a condition called *semug*. And while a big stomach is far from flattering in men, only in women is it considered positively ugly and a sign of laziness. Ideally, the stomach should be level with the waist—a condition called *lang-sing*. Marriageable girls in particular must therefore take great care of their stomachs,[13] so they always sleep from the age of menstruation, approximately ten to twelve years of age, on with tightly swaddled stomachs.[14]

But it is the injunction to always smile in social encounters which women experience as the greatest demand when they find themselves in trying circumstances. I once asked a friend, a middle-aged woman, why women must smile much more than men.

"Because men will have serious business, many problems, so they need not or will not be so friendly [*rameh*]."
"What about women, don't they also have problems?"
"Oh yes, but still we must smile. But . . . young women more than the old. If an old woman smiles too much, people will say she does not behave like a mother. And if a young woman smiles too much, people will say she is crazy . . .
Men, on the contrary, may be serious in the face. They even should, if they have high position, be a little stern [*nye-*

beng], but not so much. But if a woman is serious, you will think maybe she is arrogant and be frightened of her. A woman lawyer, however, will usually be a little stern so as to express her position. But if a woman teacher is stern, the students will be afraid of her, they will not like her, they will not want to study . . .''

On this note we turn back to Suriati's encounter with the young man at her grandmother's house. Faced with his headstrong bout, she did what she had to do to steer clear of being shamed: she smiled, she spoke demurely and slowly with her head slightly bowed and her hands gracefully placed in the lap. Hiding feelings of annoyance was as natural to her as fashioning body posture into a set feminine pattern.

The man, by contrast, indulged himself in a male's right to be self-assertive and dominant, provided he kept within a companionable mode. He smiled, but not too much. He spoke quickly and emphatically, setting the theme and pace of the conversation. His hands asserted points of the conversation, his legs were firmly placed apart in a posture of strength and self-assurance. No need for him to be exuberant and subdued, nor to fear that Suriati might seek him out and sit in front of his parents and speak of how arrogant he had been. It is not the kind of thing graceful girls would do.

Arrogance is judged by appearance/action, but thought to reflect character (*sifat*) as well. As an example of just how bad it is, a story was related to me of a sick old man whose son married when the father was in a critical condition. "How foolish!" remarked a friend, to which the old man retorted, "Not foolish, a foolish person can learn, but a conceited person, never!"

Now it *is* possible to change character by means of ritual (see p. 102), but I never heard it done to erase arrogance. Arrogance might stand a person in good stead, if she or he has power and enacts it with discrimination vis-à-vis inferiors only, as did the boy with Suriati; or the man who calls out "hi, herb-peddler!" to the academically superior woman. His medium position coupled with higher income and male status outweigh hers as a poor female of high academic rank.

The Supreme Value of *Polos*

Balinese men say one cannot understand the meaning of "arrogant" except in relation to *polos* (smooth, companionable). Women differ somewhat in that they contrast "arrogant" not with *polos*, but with friendly (*rameh*). [15] But as they also hold *"polos"* in the highest regard, let us consider first *polos*.

1.   Traditional Hindu healer (balian) who works with texts on astrology.

2.
Traditional Muslim healer (dukun) with an iron rod he uses to take out various illnesses.

3.   Ceremony for the baby at three Balinese months (105 days) when the baby for the first time is allowed to touch the ground. This is when the name is given.

4.   Religious paraphernalia are taken to the beach to be cleansed in the *melasti* cere-
     mony before Balinese New Year (courtesy of Lay, Singaraja).

5.   Cremation tower en route to the cremation grounds.

6.   The *mepeed* ceremony when all descendants of the dead parade in their most splendid garments to please and honor the souls of the dead. It is performed the day before cremation and only in the North.

7. Bidding a dead mother farewell just as her soul is to be released by fire at cremation, thirteen years after death. The mother died when the girl was born, but they had now been reunited for ten days during a major celebration when the souls of the mother and other relatives had been summoned for their final cremation.

8. Baby girl suffering soulloss from the mother's fright. "Bad" emotions in the mother are transmitted to the child through the breast milk and may even cause death.

9. Girls praying on the occasion of Balinese *Galungan*, a recurring festival of the Javanese-Balinese calendar.

10.
Women with offerings on the way to their village temple for its *odalan* ceremony, held every 210 days. Given that there are approximately twenty thousand temples in Bali, most of which have *odalan*, this is a typical scene.

11.
Typical street scene, Singaraja.

12.   Dressing in one's most splendid garments to parade in the *mepeed* ceremony for the souls of the dead. This custom is distinct to Buleleng, the region around Singaraja.

13.   A girl is overcome with emotion after having bid souls of deceased relatives a final farewell on the occasion of their cremation following a ten-day reunion and celebration in the family home. Scene is the same as in plate 7.

14.
Preparing offerings for the banquet of the souls of the dead who honor the family home with their presence before their cremation—an event that may take place thirty, or even fifty, years after death. The same occasion is pictured in plates 5, 6, 7, 12 and 13.

15.
Placing offerings for the earth demons (*buta kala*) so they will not disturb the ceremony. Occasion same as above.

16.
Speaking with the souls of dead family members who possess a balian. The conversations are usually tape-recorded for later replaying, both to soothe emotions and to check what the souls actually said; in this case their advice was sought in a family quarrel.

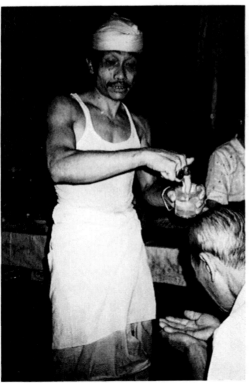

17.
The balian blesses with holy water the relatives who have come to speak with the souls of their dead.

18.
Exhuming the dead the night before they are to
be cremated. On this occasion, five bodies, all
women, were exhumed. They had been dead
from one to thirty years. The whole village,
children and adults, are present.

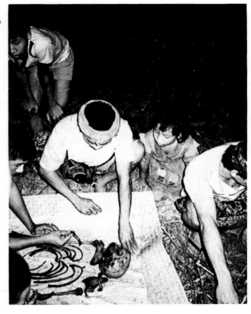

19.
Detail from exhumation above. Some families
do a symbolic exhumation only and excavate
some dust from the burial sites of the dead. It
is believed dangerous to exhume the actual
bodies, for every bone must be found or the
effect would be disastrous.

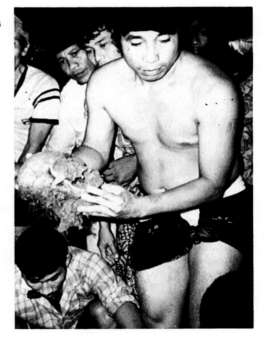

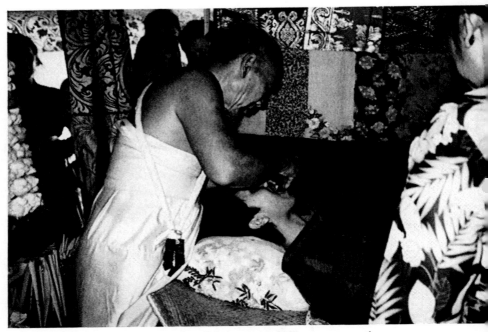

20. The priest Sri Empu Dewi Tantera officiating at a tooth-filing ceremony—the rite of passage for youth—when they are shorn of their animal-like instincts such as greed, anger, arrogance, and sexual laxness so they may cultivate the moral virtues.

21. Same as above.

22.
Kneeling before the parents at a tooth-filing
ceremony—an intensely emotion-laden moment
when this girl, as well as other young girls (and
boys), broke down crying.

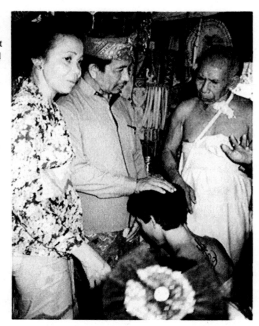

23.
A balian and his wife in their home.

24.   An old priestess in front of the Temple of the Dead (*pura dalem*), Singaraja.

(Photos by Unni Wikan and Frederik Barth.)

Polos refers to performance and action as well as to character and "heart." People may say of another, "(S)he acts *polos,* but truly (s)he is not." But because it is generally difficult to know people's hearts, *polos* is generally judged by appearance or action.

Polos is an exceedingly difficult term to translate with its distinctive Balinese connotations. According to the dictionary, *polos* means "smooth, plain, of one color" (Wojowasito and Wasito W. 1980). In life, as a villager told me, *polos* is a person who is "patient [*sabar*], quiet/still [*pendiam*], and calm [*tenang*]. He knows himself and treats the other person well, even when this other person has talked badly of him or stolen coffee from him" (male-speaking). "She says, 'I do not care or I don't mind, it's all the same [*tak ambil pusing*]. She never mocks or criticizes or ridicules people [*ngumpet* or *demen ngomong*]. She has pity on people [*medalem*]" (female speaking). A *polos* person is of one color, whatever others are and whatever exigencies life brings.

Such is the shared ideal. In practice, one or more aspects may be emphasized according to context or speaker. Women stress the aspects of "never being angry or if angry sometimes, then with good reason and not so much, and the anger quickly passes."[16] I rarely heard this aspect stressed by males, and understandably so. For men should be brave (*berani*), a quality unfitting in women.[17] To flesh the concept out and retrieve more of the nuances of its meaning, let us regard other statements.

> The first meaning of *polos* is no color. Second meaning is only one color, no pattern. A male who is *polos* will be patient, give no opposition, will receive whatever we give and also whatever condition he finds himself in. Sometimes *polos* means "without any interest"; if he gives you something, he will do so without expectation of reciprocity[18] and not be angry if you do not give . . . For women, to be *polos* is to perform like Suriati. To use no makeup, always receive what she is given, voice no protests, to speak softly, not to mix languages. In dress also to use mute colors (male, approximately forty years old, and of good education and poor economic means).

> To be *polos* is to give always what the other asks or needs. I was in Jakarta and I could not find my way, but there if you ask people they will not help, they will point in any direction. In Bali they will accompany you to the house. Balinese people are *polos* (female in her forties, of low social rank).

> *Polos* is a person who lets himself tolerate too much of the behavior of his surroundings. Even if you strike him, he will

71

not hit back. He always gives you what you need. I have a friend, Mr. Ngurah, he does not like *polos*. Whenever I characterize someone as *polos* to him, he immediately retorts "And how much did he give you?" To be *polos* is to let oneself be exploited too much (fifty-year-old male of superior social standing).

My husband likes my father better than my mother, for my father is *polos*. He never inquires about anything. With my mother my husband has to answer to how we are and what is our condition (newly married woman).

To be *polos* means always to say yes, always to follow the other (male).

As these illustrations show, *polos* connotes an obliging, self-effacing, and accommodating attitude. It means "not to care" but to be always considerate of others.[19] Because acting nicely to a person who has offended oneself is also to shame the other into changing her ways, to be *polos* is more than to set a good example; it is to prove oneself superior and to affect courses of action.

A woman was proud of how she had acted *polos* with her sister-in-law when her husband asked her to repay loans of two golden bracelets from the wife and the sister denied ever having seen the bracelets:

I was in the kitchen and heard them arguing, then I could not restrain myself, I went into the living room and just said to her cheerfully, "Never mind the money, you always give me *so* much, *I* am indebted to you!" It is true, I could not care less about the money, but I wanted to shame her, and by being so *polos*, I did. She never came back again.

While it is incumbent on all to be *polos*, some are not, and they are not necessarily sanctioned for it. People expressed admiration for a woman of high social standing of whom it was said, "She is very brave [*orang berani*], never afraid of anything, not at all *polos* whereas her husband is very *polos*."

A person who is brave (*berani*) or hard (*keras*) of character will naturally find it difficult to be *polos*: "You know my son [a fourteen-year-old], he does not like Mr. Bidja for he is not *polos*. He comes here and asks brusquely, 'Where is your father?'" Yet Mr. Bidja was widely esteemed for other aspects of his behavior.

Far from having a stock corpus of terms that apply infallibly to all conduct, Balinese employ a variable assemblage to orient themselves and judge others. As standards the concepts are also weighted differentially in accordance with what is known of the character of the other.[20]

Balinese are always subtly concerned to become acquainted with idiosyncracies so as to better read the signs of affect and attitude.

So long as a person does not appear arrogant, the ideal of *polos* may be dispensed with or not so rigorously applied. One will be esteemed for being *polos,* but there are other sources of esteem, such as wealth, position, education, good looks, bravery. Also the *consequences* that ensue from breaching the norm of nonarrogance will be different depending on context and actors. Finally, criteria by which arrogance is judged vary with positional modifiers, as we have seen.

A man who acts *polos* demonstrates—to other men—that he is not arrogant, what *men* fear most in others. But a woman who sees the same man might think him frightening, unless he is *also* markedly friendly (*rameh*). For women are not brave, as men "must" be. For females the most frightening characteristic—and *they* call it frightening (*seram*)— is a grave and stern expression—*nyebeng*. Hence men cite acts denoting arrogance (such as boasting, bragging, not greeting) as the most negative quality in others, whereas women cite a facial expression indicating anger. Men feel challenged by an arrogant attitude in others, women merely dislike it and withdraw from the conceited person. Thus the behavioral appearance women fear most in themselves, arrogance, is not what they fear most in others (potential anger).[21] Also in order for a woman to prove she is not arrogant she must radiate friendliness in a manner that would be ridiculous—or womanly—for a man.[22]

Generally speaking, a serious expression, a "closed" face, the merest wrinkle in an all-enveloping smiling facade, and a young or middle-aged woman of low or medium position will be labeled *sombong.* When the other is a stranger, she risks being shamed. There are situations where more is at stake, as Kede imprinted upon us in her incisive statement: "He will be angry and perhaps also sick in his heart from anger. It will be dangerous . . ."

Awakenings

Kede had learned her lesson the hard way. A person of exceptional intellectual powers, acknowledged by society at large, and an independent personality, she had used to display a rather "closed" face as she rushed between home, job, meetings, and back home to her seven children again. It would have been all right, had she been of high social position. But she was not. And society criticized her harshly for being arrogant. Then she hit upon hard times and came to cherish the inestimable value of good social relations. "So now, I always make my face look bright and I smile to everyone so that they will like me. I laugh, and I make people laugh, and they are surprised, knowing what I have gone through . . . They cannot see my heart . . .''

Most Balinese do not need awakenings of this kind to stick to the unwritten ground rule of expressed friendliness and nonarrogance. Observing it is as natural as combing one's hair before going out or putting on shoes rather than sandals to go to a government office. One generally wears a bright expression that signals one is not *sombong* in all relations beyond the closest family. This message is also carried by aspects of posture and speech. Allowing for individual differences, it is mainly when sadness and suffering take their toll that the injunction to smile and be bright weighs as a pressure and an exacting demand. And now we are finally in a position to see why my initial portrayal of Balinese society, as diffracted through a time in Suriati's life, seemed to corroborate Geertz and Geertz's generalization of an emphatic boundary across domains.

Feeling-Thought and the Experience of Relations

Nondomestic encounters appear in a certain light to a person torn with internal suffering, just as they do to someone craving to be on display. To a person coping with bereavement or loss in a culture where hearts should be hidden, managed, and kept, all groupings beyond closest family and closest friends are apt to appear exacting or threatening. Provided, that is, that two further premises pertain. Hearts must be defined as difficult to control, and "others" as unmerciful in passing judgments. This is the Balinese case. It is so different from the situation in Oman, where significant others are perceived as mercifully nonjudgmental regarding one's own nature and where that nature is conceived as likely to assert itself despite all effort (Wikan 1977, 1982).

What meaning social encounters come to have is a question of perspective, or positioning, as I have argued before. When life flows smoothly, or one has things to display proudly, large gatherings may be favored arenas offering opportunities for cherished social relations. Or when close relations are ripe with problems—more distant ones may turn into a niche of relatively undemanding and "safe" encounters. When, on the other hand, the heart cries with bitter pain, the enforced gaiety of more impersonal relations may throw into relief an always existent gap between inner feeling and outer expression and make it feel unbearable, unacceptable, and in cases of a "broken heart," even completely unmanageable (see chaps. 8 and 11).

It is a question of perspective, of being-in-the-world in a particular frame of feeling-thought that is changeable, not fixed, and reflective of inner, heartfelt concerns and outer, more objective conditions. A poor peasant of commoner caste views the world differently than a Satria aristocrat, and from a different angle than a sanctified Brahmana priest. But all are human and not immune to the "cares" and tribulations that are our common human lot.

Particularly in Bali, where agents of culture teach people that feeling-thoughts predicate one's view of the world, and one's being within, it goes without saying that perceptions of encounters will change, at times with perceptible behavioral consequences, at other times only in veiled assessments (but these too may have consequences). On no account does it make sense to bracket places as such as cool and constrained versus warm and relaxed. Under no conditions are these the terms actors apply to their existential world.

Crisscrossings and Life-world

Streets and fields do pose some different constraints from sitting rooms and kitchens in the ground rules they prescribe. But we have seen that there is more to bring them together than to set them apart as persons crisscross such spaces constantly and are concerned with a life and a self that are enduring, valuable, and precarious. I use "crisscrossings" in a double sense. On the one hand I refer to the numerous daily exits and entries people make bridging homes, streets, workplace, temple, home of a balian, etc. Just to move from one's own home into a neighbor's usually involves passing through a street. With characteristic Balinese industriousness and engagements in many simultaneous pursuits it is in the nature of things that daily crisscrossings are many.

Second, crisscrossings take place in a more metaphorical sense, as when a sheltered gathering in a secluded sitting room ceases to be intimate in an experiential sense once a person enters who is in some sense feared (this is a recurrent situation in Bali). No longer a protected place to open up one's heart, the setting is redefined, through the actions of protagonists, into a more formal gathering. In an abstract, and interactionally very important sense, people may be said to have crossed a line between domestic and exposed, though they have remained in the same place.

What we may conceive of as a problem of "movement in social space" or as an "oscillation in interactional mode" emerges for actors as a critical social task and an existential concern. Remember Suriati as she prepared for her exit into the street by brightening face and balancing posture and gait. It was a momentous step she was to take, yet one that would *also* have to be taken had visitors entered her home. Indeed, depending on her trust and knowledge of them, she might be even more conscientious about her appearance than when she crossed the threshold into the outer world.

Where the critical boundaries in people's lives go, and what the vital distinctions they make are cannot be decided a priori, but it is a matter for empirical investigation. To render people's compelling concerns, we have to try to grasp their perceptual patterns: how they connect and associate as well as distinguish and separate. Anthropologists have a tendency to partition the world into distinct spheres or fields, a necessary step, in part, that we may begin to grasp a ramifying, bewildering world. There is a danger of simultaneously boxing people in, of forgetting that they move, imperceptibly or with great effort, in pursuit of compelling concerns. It is a *life-world* we partition when we apply Western conceptual schemes without critical examination of what are the notions in which the actors' own significant distinctions are cast.

Judgment, Compromise, and Relative Restraint

Brightness of expression and friendliness/politeness apply ubiquitously to Balinese because such expressions predicate self-esteem, social respect, health, and happiness. These are enduring concerns that Balinese carry with them, yet what it takes to put them into practice as well as the judgment of whether one wants to do so depend on individual circumstances. Balinese also choose at times to be less than gracious: one afternoon a woman selling fruits at a small-town market refused to sell mangoes to a certain customer. He had behaved rashly, and she grew angry, retaliating in kind. In the evening of that day her child fell sick from the customer's black magic.

She should have known, of course, that she ran a risk: a local market in a small town is, by the mere facts of the case, as dangerous a place as any intimate gathering for, unlike markets in bigger towns, here people *do* possess personal knowledge about one another. Yet she let her heart get the better of her and reaped the fruits of what she had sown.

Like Kede, who in her misfortune learned to curb her arrogance, this woman had an "awakening" that reminded her of what reality really is and, therefore, how one ought to behave. It is in the nature of things that people cannot go around behaving optimally all the time; they will fall short, as did these two, whether from bad judgment, indifference, pride,

76

or calculated risks. Multiple concerns, limited energy, exhaustion, confusion, or self-pride may be reasons why one ignores the precautions one "knows" should apply. (Just as fear, self-value, or ultimate concerns may be reasons why one chooses to abide by them.)

Balinese, like any other people, fashion their lives amid multiple constraints and cannot have all that they want. A young woman who traveled alone by overland bus to see her boyfriend was criticized as lacking in self-value (*harga diri*) for this act, even though she was very positively praised for other aspects of her behavior. Another calculated risk in this manner: I had offered to try to talk to a man, a good friend of mine, who had caused a woman's family much pain and had it in his power to ameliorate their conditions. The wife initially welcomed my suggestion, but after a moment's reflection she cautioned against it: "Oh, no! Don't do it! Now we are friends, we sit together and talk together. Perhaps, if you talk to him, he will make you too afraid; you will not dare to come here again . . ." She was alluding to how he had afflicted her through black magic. The most salient sensation had been fear—penetrating fear that almost paralyzed her in normal undertakings. If the man also struck me, she would lose more than she already had: also a trusted friend.

How personal assessments color movements in social space is shown by this case: With a friend I visited an aunt of hers who lived in a remote village. Together the three of us went to pay our respects to the latter's mother-in-law. Ours was a cheerful and vivacious encounter where the talk came to center much on *merangkat*—elopement[23]—as there had just been a notorious one in the village. The mother-in-law spontaneously related how happy she was that none of her four sons had ever done such a thing, but had all married by *maideh*—prior agreement (cf. Barth 1991). She was a Muslim, and Muslims are by ideology more critical of elopement than Hindu Balinese. The daughter-in-law listened with a reverent smile.

Hardly had we entered the street before her expression changed; she did not speak yet, but kept herself until we were safe within her home (to which we leapfrogged, it seemed, not at all observing the norm of slow, gracious walking for women); and here she launched into an attack on her mother-in-law for her blatant dishonesty. "None of her sons having married by *merangkat*! *All* have, including my own husband . . . !" And an account ensued of the mother-in-law's meanness: had it not been for the speaker's father-in-law, of quite another caliber, her children would have starved, since their father, irresponsible bloke, neglected both them and her.

In this case, as with Suriati after her encounter with the arrogant man at her balian grandmother's, the street appears a less constraining place than sitting rooms and kitchens. But it is the sanctity of the home *with the right people* present, and *they only* there, that is truly relaxing. The daughter-in-law passed through a phase of extreme constraint—masked by cheerfulness—in "private," through lessening restraint, bordering on laxness and clearly showing her face in "public," to complete exposure of her heart, orchestrated by a wealth of emotional imagery, in her own home. This is a pattern one commonly encounters. Balinese would seem often to have an urge to give their feelings vent when they come into the street after the extreme constraint of many a domestic encounter. The full emptying of the heart may also take place in the street. Two female friends, in particular, may define a niche of intimacy as they move gracefully along the streets, nodding left and right to passersby, the smile always in readiness to illuminate the face at the appropriate encounters (of which there are usually many) and yet focused intently on speaking their hearts. A home may be so full of people and "cares" that the street appears a haven of freedom and relaxation by comparison.[24]

That freedom is a matter of judgment, or position, and our anthropological assessment should acknowledge the implications of this for our analysis. It may be that my own generalizations partake more of a female perspective than I am aware. Having mainly moved about with women, I think I know something of how they perceive and judge in actual, fluid reality. Men I know only *about*, from what they say and speak. These are vastly different kinds of data, and when I generalize, offering proposals of the kind I have, it is because men give the impression (to me) that the judgments I formulate apply also to them. Yet I have grasped less of their lived realities so I cannot know; and also for this reason I emphasize the situated character of all interpretations.

It seems apt to end with a case which—again—bears out the perspective envisioned via Suriati's case: a "public" demanding and heavily borne and a "private" consoling and all-accepting. Remember, it is a question of perspective or "feeling-thought."

An Accident, a Sullied Blouse, and a Wholly Inconvenient Soulloss

One day Suriati and I collided on her motorcycle with a bicyclist. He escaped unharmed whereas we received small bruises. She, the driver, fell down into the street sullying both knees and one sleeve of her blouse. Gracefully, we smiled at the bicyclist, who was entirely at fault, while we gathered ourselves together and set off toward her house.

There a change of appearance took place, which I shall never forget. Her "face" fell loose, and with a dramatic force I had never expected her to possess, she exploded in a magnificent diatribe against the bicyclist. Truly I know not what she underscored. I could not discern her words at the time as she descended into a colloquial Singaraja low Balinese speaking to her father, who listened spellbound. But her dramatic gestures and high-pitched voice spoke louder than words and stood in glaring contrast to the impeccably soft and graceful young woman who a moment before had crossed the threshold.

The next day she fell sick from "soulloss." But that is another story—for us, structuring reality for a book, where we must take the reader step by step and not mess things up too much by talking of everything at once. Only life observes no such constraints, does not ask "is it in order that this or that happens now or then? Will it make a good story?" Life overflows and messes up things—through a motorcycle accident, a sullied blouse, and a wholly inconvenient "soulloss." And yet life writes the better stories.

CHAPTER FIVE

Could People See . . . All Would Perish from Fright

If we do not believe, black magic cannot strike us.
——COMMON BALINESE SAYING

Cares Carried Across

Life carries "cares" across boundaries, bridges, and thresholds. After her fall in the street, Suriati's blouse would have to be mended, her soul retrieved, and the blow remedied that had been struck to a cherished self-image. Would people who had seen her fumbling laugh? Would they spread the word and mock her? And how was she to manage now for the next few days without her soul, her vital energy (*bayu*)? It would take some three days at least to retrieve it; meanwhile she would be feeling empty (*kosong*), confused (*bingung*), quivering/dizzy (*lengeh*), weak (*lemah*), and suffer piercing headaches (*pusing*). And she would be vulnerable, for without one's soul one is easily prey to evil forces, nor can one exercise sound judgment.[1]

So stricken did Suriati seem to be with this massive assault of bad fortune that when I tried to shake her out of her feeling-thought by showing her my own bad knee with bleeding bruises far worse than hers, she just laughed. And I thought at first, how uncaring! But then I thought, how wise! What better could we do than to laugh in a mocking gesture at the powers that would have us trapped.

Laughing is a therapeutic device that works to shake off suffering, embarrassment, and ill-feeling and seems eminently suitable for a life of "so many cares." And yet the feeling-thought vibrates: how to manage, to cope.

Characteristic for "cares" is that they often cannot be shed nor deposited into boxes to be unlocked only when the time comes to deal with them again. Cares carry across, because hearts cannot be shed. But "hearts" are not often made a focus of inquiry in social analysis. With our Western split-mind vision we tend toward cognitive analysis on the presumption that thinking drives patterned action and feeling is residual. And because thinking is regarded as "rational" and "sensible," we also easily fall into the trap of compartmentalizing "cares" into statuses and roles—ordering elements in everyday life. A lifestring is cut in the process, but we do not see it, for we have eliminated the "heart" through which this string vibrates.

Contrast this with a Balinese perspective and Suriati's existential concerns: they ebbed and flowed in her own heart, and no more than she could shed herself of her heart could she deposit her cares back home or in the street. She was on the move, all the time crisscrossing scenes and encounters, and her concerns moved with her, to some extent. Indeed they should, because Balinese consider feeling to be as rational as thought, so the "heart" must be perennially "listened to." It is the heart, in fact, more than thought, that ensures rational action (see chap. 14).

The nature of the world is such that demands, threats, and dangers abound all around, and the human heart, to avoid becoming a haunted soul,[2] must exercise comprehensive judgment and circumspection in regard to multiple, perennial concerns. We have seen it with Issa in the guest role, with Suriati's husband in the ex-tenant's role, or with Suriati in the position of bereaved. But perhaps the clearest demonstration is provided by just anyone sitting or reclining in her home.

She cannot just close her doors and windows on the world and feel safe and relaxed. She cannot just "shut out" the world by secluding herself in a private space which outsiders cannot penetrate. She may try to play it safe by having protective devices aligning the gate and attached to all openings in the house, as well as offerings for guardian spirits (*tombal*) and amulets on her person, beneath the pillow, etc.[3] If she is left in peace, it is because these objects—which are endowed with mystical power, *sakti*—work and not because physical barriers, however, sturdy, can keep potential destructive forces at bay. Even the back bedroom offers no such refuge, for the person is particularly vulnerable at night.[4]

To live *always* exposed and vulnerable: that is in essence the Balinese predicament, and one that throws into stark relief the difference between being human in their world and in ours. Whatever sanctuary a person is to find, she has to erect it within her own self. By strengthening her vital energy or life force she can hope to repel vicious attacks. By striving "not to care" and rising above animal emotions such as anger, spite, envy, and greed, she makes her spirit "large" and thus stands better armed against evil attacks. Her family, needless to say, must also be meticulous about carrying out their ritual obligations, or ancestors and demons may strike back in anger.

"A weapon under the pillow" is what a balian told me he had placed to save a man who was extremely sick in the hospital and believed to have been struck by black magic. The weapon turned out to be a tiny leaf over which he had read prayers. Balinese make constant use of such weapons—among them a "good heart" entailing a strong vital spirit. But the strain of living with their fears takes its toll and is constantly expressed in everyday life as a most abiding concern.

Relative Dangers

One such concern is their fear of what consequences may ensue if they breach norms of conduct. "I am so afraid"—*saya taku-u-u-t*—is an expression that crops up constantly in everyday talk as people ponder courses of action and decide on options and means. It may be revealing to try to rank different kinds of encounters on a safety-danger axis to give an idea of how their world is ordered along this dimension.

But first a word of warning: fears are also positional in that whom and what one fears depend on variables like gender, age, rank, etc., as well as on matters of biography and situation. A mother with a nursing child will fear "surprise" and exposure to events that may elicit "bad feelings" such as sadness or anger in her, for such feelings may get to her milk and kill the child (Wikan 1989a). Young marriageable persons and their parents, on the other hand, fear "love magic" (*guna-guna*) most; upwardly mobile persons dread being "made down" and becoming objects of shame. High-ranking people fear both laughter and shame less than people of low rank, for few dare challenge them openly. On the other hand, they may be more exposed to black magic, because many are envious of them.

Thus the dangers that loom most gravely vary. But generally speaking, I think, social groupings may be characterized as follows.

Close circles of residential family besides closest friends provide, in the lives of most people, the relatively safe arena of everyday life, though here also, as we have seen, lives may be precarious. Small gatherings of nonintimates, on the other hand, are the most dangerous; larger gatherings of primarily strangers are less dangerous. Big crowds where the person occupies spectator status are safest.

For example, encounters where strangers meet are less dangerous than domestic gatherings. The anonymous others you fleetingly encounter can shame you, but they cannot kill you. "Contemporaries" lack the prerequisites to do that. And if the reader now thinks I am dwelling too much on black magic, I should like to remind you again: many casualties ensue. If you live in a society where many people you know personally have been seriously injured or killed by black magic, you would be a fool not to take your precautions. Indeed, it is for this reason that streets are experienced as relatively safe. Shame, the sanction which threatens one there, is painful and may cause sickness. But there are constraints on people's readiness to shame others because the other might respond with anger that is dangerous to the self. At its most effective, however, shame is experienced as subjectively devastating.

More is at stake in encounters with those who know you better and are more involved in your life. There are many simultaneous strands to the relations; hurt and offense can easily be caused, even inadvertently and unwillingly. And the other person is ideally positioned in terms of sorcery revenge, having both knowledge and access. Magic and other retributive acts also may be worked in intimate relations.[5]

Big ceremonies and crowds, where ego occupies spectator status and the attention is focused on others, are safest. I see the frequency of "startle" responses in such crowds as a measure of the extent to which the person has relaxed her defenses (Wikan 1989a).[6] Also what Mead characterizes as "awayness" (1942, 4) shows up here: the person drifts away in her feeling-thoughts and is unresponsive to the bustle and confusion around. She safely can, there is little to lose; a big impersonal crowd may indeed be the only social occasion in which Balinese women of low rank need not be everpresently bright and smiling. A failure to "manage one's heart" in such settings is of much less consequence than in any other kind of interpersonal gathering.

But this simple scheme does not give a recipe for handling all of life. Assessments of person-in-place crisscross this simple mapping.

A Lion in the Kitchen and Other Beings

Weddings draw big crowds, but weddings are very dangerous. There is magic in the air, directed at bride and/or groom, from envious or jealous people.[7] But magic may be thwarted and deflected and can hit anyone by "wrong address" (*kene tamplikan/salah alamat*).[8] Preparations for weddings are very dangerous: commonly all who engage in helping fall sick, and it is therefore that small children should *never* be brought along. They would be bound to get sick.[9]

Streets, on the other hand, are relatively safe, but it depends on who, and with whom, you are. A girl about to be married ought not to go out at all. Not, as in the Middle East, to prevent men other than the groom from gazing upon her beauty, but to protect life and health. The air will be aswarm with magical assaults from many of her and his rejected suitors, and she cannot expect to go unmolested.

Indeed, perceptions of every place reckon with so many forces un-perceived by us as the earth, air, buildings, and trees abound with spirits and ghosts that, in Isaac B. Singer's words, "could people see all the imps that hover about, they would all perish from fright" (1975, 235). This is an apt rendering of the Balinese perspective. Balinese consider themselves lucky so long as they only sense such spirits but do not see them; [10] but sensing means knowing they are there: they belong as part of one's perception of what a place truly "is."

If you have a lion in the kitchen, you may, like Suriati, feel relatively safe in your own home. Not so if, when building your house, you for-got to get permission from the "earth mother" (*ibu pertiwi*), [11] or un-authorized cut a branch off a tree [12] or filled in the hole which is the living space of some *orang alus,* or accidentally built your Hindu an-cestor temple above the home of a Muslim *jinn* family!

A Balinese, in describing her house, will refer in the same matter-of-fact way to such clearly visible elements as the tree in the front yard as to the (less apparent-to-me) deep sea which surrounds it and protects it from thieves and the lion in the kitchen and *orang alus* in the living room that provide protection and security. Suriati's family is not dis-turbed by the *orang alus* in their living room because they take care to keep their house tidy and clean. Their predecessors, however, were con-stantly troubled because they let small children urinate on the floor and soiled the place, hence the *orang alus* got angry. The balians would then instruct them in how to propitiate the *orang alus* and pay proper care.

My experience with Balinese makes most sense if one considers that they apply a kind of seventh sense (if proprioception [13] is now recog-nized as a universal sixth sense—Sacks 1987, 43) to probe sensory signs for the presence of such mystical forces. Sounds, sights, smells, tastes, and untoward occurrences are omens that portend the presence of such mystical forces when perceived in the right feeling-thought. [14] I was never able to hear the sounds of such creatures as my Balinese friends discerned, nor to be scared witless by some of the sights that terrified them. But I could feel the fright in their hearts and empathize with their predicaments. I had no difficulty in believing in the protective powers that they perceived or the dangers that abounded. Nor was it hard to believe that without the help of their balians (traditional healers cum magicians), Balinese would feel (indeed, be) entirely powerless and vulnerable.

A most important category of otherworldly creatures who constantly make themselves felt are *orang alus*—"refined people." In illness etiology and in the diagnosis of misfortune they feature very often. Because *orang alus* belong in the world with humans, it is of the essence to strike up a peaceful coexistence with them. Their name indicates something of their nature and importance. Ordinary humans are referred to as *orang Bali* (Hindus), *orang Islam* (Muslims), *orang Buddha* (Buddhists), *orang Java* (Javanese), etc. *Orang alus* are of the same basic kind but invisible to us. They look physically like humans, live below the ground or in trees, have families, live in societies, have joys and pains like us. Some are Muslim (*jinn*), some Hindus (*desti*), some bad, some good (just like humans),[15] and they get angry and strike back if you offend them.

Many Balinese fall sick because they happened to step on or inadvertently kick an *orang alus,* not realizing it was there.[16] Then you will become sick in the same spot as where you hit that one. Children often get sick because they urinated on an *orang alus,* as do adults when they visit in villages. Noon and sunset are particularly busy times for *orang alus,* thus it is best for humans to stay in then, not to disturb them. Many people are afflicted because when building or extending their home they accidentally filled in the living space of some *orang alus.* Peaceful coexistence is of the essence.

There is an element of ecological thinking in Balinese conceptions of the (super)natural world, as I was made aware when, in 1986, it was suggested to me by a medical doctor that I research the phenomenon of *belorong.* At the time there was said to be an abundance of them in Singaraja, and many people were plagued. *Belorong* are white magical mice which can sneak through walls and locked doors and steal money and possessions from people while they sleep. They render their owners rich beyond reason.[17] An explanation was spontaneously offered of their sudden abundance. It was the time of *Galungan* and *Kuningan,*[18] great Hindu ceremonies that bring together large throngs of people and cause noise and congestion. Hence the *orang alus* had gone away for they prefer quiet places, and so the *belorong* had been free to invade the vacated niche.

Orang alus and *belorong,* though of different ontological status in that the one is of (super)natural origin, the other—as far as I can understand—"man-made" by magic, compete in the same niche, and the most powerful win and function then also to keep competitors at bay. Another way of putting this would be to say that there should be balance in nature and cosmos.

Against magical creatures such as *belorong* Balinese feel quite powerless. If stricken by one, the person has to enlist the services of a magician to counter the assault. So also when one is afflicted by the bird *kuntilanak*,[19] which sucks the blood of virgins or young women (see 86–87), or by *leak* (witches). The latter are females of inborn evil, with the capacity to transform themselves into any kind of shape: a monkey, or fire, or lightning, and are particularly prone to attacking babies, whom they devour. They are not so common in the North and tend to be subsumed with the general category of black magic as epitomizing all evil.[20] But North Balinese are afraid to go to Sanur, Gianyar, or Karangasem where *leak* are known to be in abundance.

Salient as purveyors of evil in the experience of North Balinese are also *buta kala*. Sometimes represented as the gross aspects of Divinity, these are otherworldly creatures innate to the natural world.[21] They inhere particularly to crossroads and intersections and must be propitiated by Hindus every day and at every minor or major ceremony. Daily offerings are left for them on the ground, particularly at entrances and at the gate. At ceremonies they are given substantial offerings and rituals are performed to keep them happy so that they will not offset the auspicious effects of the ceremony and wreak misfortune. On the night of the Balinese new year—*Nyepi*—the *buta kala* are frightened off with fire brushes, earsplitting noise, and general hackle and cackle.[22]

Kala is often rendered as "demon"; but "some vague idea of abstract, destructive forces might be more apt" (M. Hobart 1985c, 18). They are apparently *not* amenable to human manipulation. *Orang alus*, on the other hand, appear to be sometimes amenable to such manipulation by others and to be accessible to some forms of social interaction. *Kuntilanak* and *belorong* are always assumed to be the instruments of evil human agencies; and *leak* witches are the evil persons themselves in transmogrified form. Finally, there is the whole domain of black magic proper: a terrifying technology of evil purpose.

Black Magic and "We Must not Believe"

There are different kinds of black magic and varying degrees of danger. The genetic word is "science of the left hand" (*pengiwa*)[23] or *ilmu hitam* "black science," but the English word "magic" (pronounced with the stress on the second syllable) is also generally used. Some kinds of magic work at short distance, others over very long distance;[24] some are labeled *"kelas satu"* —"first class"—meaning that the highest, most difficult knowledge (*relajaran berat*) is required to work it; other kinds are within the reach and may be practiced even by ordinary people.

There is magic to create love (generally referred to as *guna-guna,* though *guna-guna* may also connote any other kind of black magic),[25] cause misfortune (bad crops, loss of property etc.), bad appearance (e.g., to make the bride or groom look gloomy or even faint at their own wedding—this is quite common—or to make the food taste foul); there is magic to cause specific sicknesses, such as an ugly swollen face (*sempengot*),[26] a particular form of contagious "hysteria" (*bebainan*),[27] paralysis of a limb (*lumpuh*), paralysis of one-half of the body (*mati setanga* or *angin merah*),[28] "pregnancy with stones" (*beling batu*), and innumerable other afflictions, such as insanity and childlessness. Several of these are deadly, if the magic is not "taken out." There is magic to cause or prevent rain, to facilitate robbery or theft, to make one rich, beautiful, unconquerable, etc. Poison (*cetik* or *pasangan*), though it works differently from black magic, is usually spoken of in the same vein. Both cause illness, misfortune, or death. From the point of view of potential victims it matters little that the means of doing so are different.

Poison works by the application or insertion of evil materials over which spells have been read to an object the victim touches, such as food, drink, or pillow. Magic, on the other hand, is worked by an evil spirit—*roh jahat*—actually entering the body of the victim and taking control of her mind and actions, either by expelling her own "soul" (*atma* or *bayu*) or by rendering it passive.[29] Generally only balians or dukuns (traditional healers cum magicians) command such evil spirits, and persons wishing to work evil need to enlist their services. But Balinese, in my experience, also reckon that there are ordinary people who have acquired bits and pieces of magical knowledge and are able to use it without seeking recourse to a balian. Suriati, in the story above, interpreted her former landlady's black magic as a form of telepathy worked by the power of thought. And to my question as to whether it was then really black magic, she said yes, there is magic (*guna-guna*) that works directly by thought transference.

This short exposition of otherworldly powers far from exhausts their plethora in Balinese perception, but encompasses the ones I have understood to be most salient in everyday experience in the North. From my perspective it is less important to delineate the total realm of (super)-natural creatures and more important to give a sense of how some are evoked in experience in ordinary, everyday life.

Nor do Balinese like to ponder these things. It is important to try "not to believe" in black magic, and I want my representation to carry that flavor. While the sad fact of the world is that black magic abounds in ingenious forms, yet one must try not to feel-think about the matter. Thinking would create fear, and fear undermines the spiritual energy (*bayu*) needed to persevere and to resist actual onslaughts.[30]

So while an outsider might be tempted to try to unravel the "domain of black magic" as a coherent system with its own logic of atrocious practices and counterpractices, this would go against the grain of most of the Balinese sensibilities I have encountered. Therefore, I did not try. What I know of black magic stems from what I have heard in everyday life as people pondered their own or others' plight. My first intimations of it came on the third day of fieldwork when our son Kim was sick, and friends, university-educated people, alerted the doctor that we had eaten yellow rice in a certain village the day before. The terror on their faces told me this was something to take dead seriously.

If so serious, diverse, and pervasive, why should I let an inarticulate sense of its inappropriateness prevent me from systematically exploring and mapping this obviously terribly important "domain of culture"? Because it is a fact of life, all-pervasive like the weather. It is there—not much you can do about it except take certain precautions and adapt to its presence as best you can. The analogue of my own childhood background comes to mind. I grew up in a community in northern Norway, beyond the Arctic Circle, where everybody's life is perpetually affected by a relentless, changeable weather. Two-month-long polar winter nights follow scintillating summers of midnight sun. Storms sweep across mainland and islands, fishermen are lost at sea; blizzards and snowdrifts and sleet and thaw play havoc with life and the best-laid plans. To depict this elemental and manifold force of the weather to shape and wreck human life—should I attempt to describe all its forms, or average temperature fluctuations, or the natives' twelve different terms for snow? Such knowledge may suddenly become essential to be able to act wisely in a crisis in the mountains or at sea, but it does not shape the way one lives in its permanent grip. The impact of arctic weather depends on how it pervades people's awareness as an ever-present potential of unpredictable diversity. All the more so, this should be our main way of trying to grasp the ineffable threat of evil in all its diverse imagery.

Again, we need to remind ourselves that Balinese—some wizards and balians possibly excepted—do not like to ponder these things. One should rather use one's energies in constructive thought to develop the good feeling that may counteract potential onslaughts. Again and again Balinese remind themselves, "If we do not believe, black magic cannot so easily strike us."[31] Saying this they usually look quizzically at one another as if begging confirmation and others join in, "Yes, it is true." Because it is close or even intimate others who can most easily harm oneself—for to work black magic it is a distinct asset to have personal knowledge (such as the birth name) of one's victim, or access to personal accessories such as hair straws, photos, or footprints—caution must perennially be exercised. There is little respite, and no hiding place. As a man said,

> The difference between violence waged with weaponry or with black magic is that in the former case the battle is circumscribed; there is a battle arena, you know you are being attacked, and you can defend yourself. Black magic is so much worse for it strikes at any time and catches you unprepared . . . When Iran and Iraq fight as they do now, it is only because they don't know about black magic. Black magic would be a much more efficient way.

As Real as the Ghosts in the Graveyard

Every kind of natural and social space thus has multiple dimensions overlooked by us if we apply our mechanistic scheme to Balinese. To exclude matters pertaining to magic and sorcery from an examination of Balinese personhood might indeed seem logical to a foreign observer because the kinds of spaces in which we enact a vital part of our identity partake only of social and "natural" characteristics. If we start with Western conceptual distinctions—indeed, even native ones, but decontextualized as semantic schemes—we may end up in a morass where the trails natives actually follow and the signposts they go by remain unperceived by us who do not walk their tracks or struggle with their concerns. The differences that *make* a difference are then not so easily recognized.

To paint a difference clear and sharp and throw into relief Balinese knowledge of how the world is "naturally" constituted, let this tidbit of a long and actually tragic case suffice.

A man, a beloved teacher, decided to make his pupils see for themselves that there are no such things as *jerangkong*—ghosts of the Muslim dead—they are purely a matter of superstition. So he instructed his pupils to camp with him at the edge of a graveyard one night. At 1:00 A.M. they would all go home, for the *jerangkong* are supposed to appear at midnight.

At one o'clock they all went home—the pupils running two and two, even though he had instructed them to walk calmly one by one.

A few days later he was fired and branded as mad. The pupils had all—except one—*seen* the *jerangkong*,[32] and they and their parents had been beyond themselves from fright. Only a madman would have put them through such an ordeal.

The Moral Basis of the Host-Guest Relationship— A Comparative View

As real as are these sensations of the constitution of the natural world, so are Balinese perceptions of the powers that lurk in the heart of someone in the least offended. The powers Balinese reckon with in fellow human beings are not merely presumed or feared. They are felt, perceived, sensed, at times even seen, as palpably clear as were the *jerangkong* on that night in the graveyard.

The generous encounter in which Issa and I participated in such elegant and pleasant surroundings might have been a feast for the spirit and mind had not particular anxiety-provoking indices been present to suggest that reality might "really" be of another kind. As space in Bali explains so much less than in other places I have worked, it may be valuable to draw a comparison with Middle Eastern societies, known for their emphatic boundary between private and public domains, to throw Bali into relief. This will also take us to the core of a problem we left aside earlier: why did Issa fear that she might have offended the gracious lady? What was the nature of her offense?

In the Middle East, as in the West, a boundary between "home" and "street" is emphatically drawn in native conceptualization and with wide-ranging organizational implications. In many Middle Eastern societies, to put it bluntly, it is assumed that the world "out there" is hostile and dangerous and that preservation of critical values such as honor, self-esteem, material and political fortunes depends on hiding from view information that might compromise vital impressions one seeks to foster. Concealment and secrecy are sought through various means; but resort to walls, veils, and physical obstructions usually plays a major role. "Protection" relates not only to critical information about oneself, but to cherished belongings like the women of the house, or "dark secrets" like material poverty or failure (Wikan 1980, 1983). In all these respects precautions are strongly focused on physical dimensions or imagery that actually conceals: garments, shut doors, and high walls.

This is a far cry from Bali. Not because Balinese women are exposed—that is beside the point—but because their perception of what separates relative safety from threat and danger relies on identifying properties that *people carry always about them.* No walls, however sturdy or impenetrable, can keep destructive forces at bay, for black magic penetrates to remote corners and at all times of night and day. Nor do points of "honor" and moral obligations provide assurance in the face of looming danger. Let a comparison of the host(ess)-guest relationship illustrate this point.

In the Middle East, a home is ideologically sacred and protected. When asked how they are, people may answer *mastur ilhal,* "the situation is covered," meaning "we are fine, thank you." Guests who intrude upon this space are under a moral obligation to respect and honor their hosts, meaning they must also not divulge the "secrets of the house" but join in keeping matters hidden, unexposed (Ammar 1954).

The supreme moral obligation remains, however, with the host, who should go to any length and any expense to be generous and protective of the guests. Even if an enemy with whom a man had a blood feud should seek shelter in his home, he would be obliged to receive him cordially, even slaughtering a precious sheep for him. There are no exemptions to these rules of honor, and though life, particularly in poor urban areas, falls far short and there may be breaches of good faith from either party to the interaction, the rule applies and is largely even honored. Generosity is essential for self-respect and social repute.

Compare Bali, where guests are also respectfully received, but where I have never heard the rule promulgated that hosts "should not" poison their guests. It would be meaningless to say, for some do.[33] And the best Balinese can do is remind each other of this abominable fact so that dear ones will be properly cautious. An old man bemoaned a new custom in his village of guests now being served prefilled cups of coffee. It was much better in the old days when all were served from a common kettle and the host had to take the first sip.

Another who has diabetes tells how he always drinks the sugary juice he may be served as a guest. The danger of dying from that is less than from running the risk of offending the host by refusing the drink, thereby implicitly accusing him of sorcery. And this though the host probably knows that he has diabetes.

Offense emerges as an overriding concern, for host and for guest, and in most interpersonal relations.[34] In respect of it there are no alleviating circumstances[35]—only the offended person's heart decides what the outcome may be: "Truly, I was offended, but because my heart is good, he is safe this time," said a man of another who had behaved arrogantly to him by not greeting him. "With another, he might have been in grave danger. . ."

91

But the arrogant man was rich, and the offended one poor; and material status has something to do with the risks one can run. You generally have more self-confidence (which affects your life force) and also can hire a better magician to counter attacks of magic, if you are rich.

In the Middle East guests may also cause harm; but the danger culturally singled out is the inadvertent "evil eye": no one is able to cast the evil eye intentionally. Moreover, strangers may cause the harm as readily as intimates. Balinese, on the other hand, wanted to know if it was really true what they heard, namely, that among Arabs there is an "eye" that could act independently of the person's will?[36] It seemed an incredible thought to them, who reckon only with intentional evil. And we have seen that sorcery cannot easily be practiced against strangers—unless you get them into your home (where they are no longer "strangers"). It is "consociates" who are singled out.

An Overriding Concern with Offense

We may now return to Issa's case and ask why she was so afraid. What was the offense she feared she might be judged guilty of? The answer exposes fundamental trends in Balinese person construction. It reveals the inescapable need of balancing one's life as if one were treading a very high wire. And in regard to morality, it lays bare a requirement of nothing less than perfection, regardless of the human complexities and crossing pressures of real life.

In the course of their conversation the hostess learned where Issa lived, and later she asked her if she knew a relative of hers who lived in a neighboring *kampong* in Singaraja. Issa did. But this meant—the Balinese are experts at tracing distant family connections—that the hostess must also be a distant relative of a boy with whom Issa had been in love seven years earlier. The relationship had broken up when the boy was forced by his father to marry another girl, his cousin. But distressed as he was, he continued to frequent Issa's home. And she, from fear of offending him, could not close her door on him.

His relatives in Singaraja grew angry with her, thinking she encouraged him. But, really, she was innocent. To refuse him entry into the house would be a certain offense. Now his relatives in Singaraja know and are not angry with her anymore. But the hostess, did she know? Was she perhaps still angry? And though Issa did not even know if the hostess had made the connection—they had never before met—it was better to be on the safe side. So, after combing her hair in the bathroom, she carried every loose hair straw home.

But to think that a respected woman, deeply religious, might be so angry seven years after such a trifling event, that she would stoop to using black magic against oneself, bespeaks fear. And it bespeaks a conception of others as boundlessly prone to evil. It bespeaks a notion of anger as easily bred and quieted only with difficulty. It also bespeaks a concern with virtue. To encourge a person engaged to another boy or girl *is* bad (*jele*). The hostess might understandably feel righteous anger.

The "radical aestheticism" of the Balinese, proclaimed to be "the most fundamental and most distinctive quality of their particular brand of sociality" is not, I argue, necessarily artistically motivated. Rather than with social acts, being "first and foremost designed to please, but to please as beauty, not as virtue pleases . . ." (C. Geertz [1966] 1973a, 400), my own data indicate that the main preoccupation is with *virtue*, in a primary concern to avoid giving offense (Wikan 1987, 344).

We now move on to see how such concern with offense compels people to manage their innermost feelings, their hearts, in most social relations. If their design were first and foremost to please as beauty pleases, how content might not Issa have been with her performance at the encounter above? More is at stake. Even the heart must be compelled and shaped to match a model of what feelings should be.

We have seen it with Suriati in her sorrow. We move on now to examine the universe of moral discourse that casts itself as a judge over individual hearts—making them collective concerns of a sort. And we shall consider the *effort* entailed to cooperate in this moral venture.

CHAPTER SIX

Managing the Heart—To Please as Virtue Pleases

*We don't want anybody to know about our heart. If we express
we will make others disappointed, and perhaps angry too.
Balinese do not want to make another unhappy.*
—SURIATI

We bow to each other not simply from the waist, but from the heart.
—ARLIE HOCHSCHILD

"Not so Good Feelings"—An Issue in Interpersonal Relations

Having surveyed ground rules that apply to Balinese movements in
social space and depicted the measure of freedom allowed for personal
expression and maneuver, let us consider the *effort* required of Balinese to manage their social selves. This effort is not of my imagination,
but experienced and expressed by Balinese in numerous locutions and
techniques in daily use geared to helping people "forget," "keep/control/
shape" and "not care" about troubling events. Particularly poignantly
expressed in the concept of "bringing the feeling-thought"—*ngabe
keneh*—this key concept sums up an attitude to life constantly impressed upon others and self to help one to get through trying life or-
deals as well as to cope with minor dashed hopes and losses that make
the person "feel not so good" (*keneh jelek qati*).

A discussion of this belongs here, not just as an exercise in institutionalized means of coping, which is also very important and will be
discussed in detail in later chapters. When "feeling not so good" pertains to a ground plan of movement in social space it is because strict
rules of politeness, friendliness, and composure—as constructed by
Balinese—make an *issue* of these personal "not so good feelings."

They are not allowed expression, but more than that, they are linked
with notions of morality in their feeling aspect and particularly in their
interpersonal form. To evince anything less than a bright and clear face
is an affront to others, or so the person fears. Suriati's story has depicted
this aspect. "Why do you always look so grave, you make *us* unhappy
by that withered face!" said people and laughed when she showed traces
of sadness. Hence "managing the heart," morality, and ground rules for

94

movement in social space belong together and must be considered jointly if we are to understand what it means to be a person—the Balinese way.

I translate the Balinese "bringing the feeling-thought" (*ngabe keneh*) as "managing the heart" for two reasons. First, Balinese regard feeling, thought, will, and desire as inextricably linked, truly one concept. In their native language they do not distinguish among them; all are summed up in the concept *keneh*. And even though Indonesian is making headway into everyday discourse and drawing a contrast Balinese feel from experience to be true between feeling (*perasaan*) and thinking (*pikiran*), yet they are emphatic that the two are linked. Thinking, felt to be located in the forehead, versus feeling, felt to reside in the heart, are two aspects of one process. A balian knowledgeable in the old *lontar* (palm leaf manuscripts)[1] that explicate key concepts of body and soul said that even this experience of feeling and thinking being differentially located is an illusion. Actually feeling-thinking is one process and is anatomically linked with the forehead.

Ordinary Balinese are not likely to dispute that but will add: "Nevertheless, we *feel* our feelings to be located in the heart."[2]

To Think with One's Heart

Feelings and thoughts work on one another, to mutual benefit or detriment. Feeling is experientially prior, in popular perception. My *lontar* instructor disagrees with that and says that thought is ontologically prior (cf. chap. 8) because feeling emanates from thought as an aspect of the soul (*atma*). But people are insistent that it is the other way, judging by their own experience. Apprised of this, the *lontar* expert said that really there was no contradiction between this view and his: "Because without thought there will be no feeling, therefore when you use one, you use the two."

As people see it, life experiences elicit feelings that trigger thoughts such as "when you are angry, you feel it in your heart, and [then] you think you want to act . . ." or "when we walk in the dark we can feel our heart beating from fear, even though we don't think about black magic, and [then] we think we want to run . . ."

Because North Balinese have a conception of themselves as a people "very emotional, we have no defense against feelings . . . ," it is essential to shape feelings into appropriate molds. And the idiom Balinese use to refer to their experience of that which must be molded is "heart" (*keneh/hati*)—a key concept constantly used in everyday discourse to epitomize a person's character, supreme motivating power, and sieve of all experience. It is even used as a synonym with life force, vital energy—*bayu*—indicating that the heart is felt more than anything else to determine the strength and steadfastness of the *bayu*.

Hearts, while invisible, work *in* the world, through their effects on action and expression. They affect all judgment for good or bad, because, say Balinese, "everyone must *think with their feelings.*" Their concept *ngabe* sums up what should be done with this feeling-thinking process from a moral point of view. And we are with the second reason why I translate their "bringing the feeling-thought" as "managing the heart."

The Balinese concept of "bringing"—*ngabe*—has clear connotations of guiding, shaping, composing, controlling: notions perhaps best summed up in the English "managing," particularly when juxtaposed with "heart" (see Hochschild 1983). What the concept of *ngabe keneh* conveys is the need to work on feeling and thought simultaneously to bring them in tune with one's objective circumstances in life—that one may endure and surmount. In distressful life circumstances it may help to seek consolation from God, pray to the souls of the dead for help, appeal to family and friends; but a measure of self-help is absolutely necessary. Indeed, it is not a question of self-help only, but of duties to other than self. *Ngabe keneh* is a question of interpersonal morality.

Managed Hearts—A Matter of External Judgment

Managing the heart refers to a process of shaping inner feeling. Yet the judgment of whether one has succeeded in this lies not primarily with the person but with the world. It depends on *outer expression.* How well has the person managed to hide traces of turmoil, distress, disgust, disappointment, sadness, anger, offense, jealousy or envy— that amalgam of "not so good" or outright "bad" feelings—that are also part of Balinese heartfelt experience?

A person may feel her heart to be "big and strong" (*gede*)—as do Balinese when they feel they have succeeded in guiding their heart. Yet this feeling of smoothly flowing energy, reflecting the life force's immediate receptivity to a surge of good feeling-thoughts, will be quickly arrested unless the world signals agreement with a verdict subjectively felt to be true. A deep disquiet assailed one woman: she believed she had managed to keep her heart, but then people would come up to her in the street and say, "We feel pity with you, may God give you patience." Supreme self-satisfaction, on the other hand, was evinced by another, who jubilantly exclaimed, "I have one principle, always to smile!" She had received ample testimony from people recently that they had no inkling of the turmoil she was living through.

Managing the heart, while it refers to a process of active thinking-feeling to work on inner experience, thus has connotations also of "hiding the heart" (*ngengkebang keneh*), of molding expression onto culturally prescribed patterns. We have seen that making one's face look bright and clear is a necessary but not sufficient part of this. Gracious posture, smooth speech, an overall demeanor expressing politeness and friendliness are also required, as people rely on a host of indications (*ciri-ciri/tampe-tampe*) to ferret out another's heart.[3]

What Is at Stake?

Balinese, when I asked them, gave the following kinds of reasons why the heart should not be expressed: "to make people like oneself," "to make the other person happy," "it is to express friendliness," "it is part of *sopan-santum* [the moral code]," "to show we are not selfish." Invariably this part of the answer would be augmented by another aspect: "we will be shy/ashamed/embarrassed [*malu*] to speak our problem," "it is to keep our secret," "to speak of oneself is to open up the secret."

These explanations have in common that they avoid direct reference to what is truly felt to be at stake: the dangers or sanctions feared to ensue "if people could see one's heart." These come across in spontaneous remarks or as parts of natural conversation when people ponder their own or others' plight—and not in response to an outsider's general questions. Two concerns are then expressed. One is with the laughter (*kedek/tertawa*), mockery (*ejek*), and/or gossip (*ngumpet*) people would likely resort to. It is generally phrased: "If we cannot keep our heart, people will laugh and say, 'She does not know how to manage her feelings [*sing bise ngabe keneh*]!'" The laughter pains, and it erodes self-respect and presumably also social respect.

But there is a more pressing reason why "not so good feelings" should not be expressed. Others might be disappointed (*kecewa*), hurt (*nyakitang keneh*), offended (*tersinggung*), or angry (*benci*) to become thus acquainted with one's heart. Balinese conceptualizations of anger and offense incorporate a view of elicitors so sensitive as to register the minutest breach of grace. No one's heart presumably could stand up to general scrutiny without unleashing a Niagara of bad feelings against oneself. Considering the disaster such bad feelings might work against oneself, it is self-evident why one would take the utmost care to appear cheerful (*girang*), smooth (*polos*), and clear (*cedang*). The gain is well worth the effort.

Managing the Heart so That One Can Smile

One must manage one's heart so that one can smile, say Balinese, men and women both. And while what counts as a smile differs with one's position, and the effort also weighs more on women, who have to be always prepared to smile, yet for everyone to smile is to make another glad (*penggambira*), ideologically speaking. It is a moral duty incumbent on Balinese. A smile is a potent interpersonal gesture that works in two ways: to show respect for and comfort the other, and to assuage the self. It may even *foster* good feeling, as we shall see once we come to consider indigenous theories of the power of expression in nurturing physical and mental health.

Here we need only note that a "smile" is culturally construed as a placating device. As part of the inestimable friendliness that shows one is not *sombong*—headstrong, arrogant, conceited—nor angry nor sad, a smile is something for oneself as well as the other to grasp and hold on to in a world of dire dangers. As with propitiating gods and ancestors with prayers and offerings so that they will be pleased and answer one in kind, so with a smile: it is a prestation of respect and good relations that makes a *moral* claim on another to be well disposed in turn.

Suriati, now living in Jakarta, despairs at having to *unlearn* such an intrinsically good way: "Here if you smile, people will ask 'what do you smile for?' They will be suspicious and think you are masking [*munafiq*], when with us Balinese it is in our character to be like this. Balinese always like to make another person happy and to care about others."

It goes without saying that not any kind of smile will do. The smile should be sincere and honest in its earnest intention to keep good relations. This may be accomplished with difficulty if one bears grudges or hard feelings. Said a man, "If another has disappointed me, and yet I have to congratulate him [with a smile], my feelings will not be so good" (*jele bayune*, literally: my power/life force will be bad). With the intimate relationship Balinese perceive between "heart" and vital energy (pp. 174), one's general well-being also suffers. There is even a danger that this might show through in an expression less than bright and clear, for the feelings of the heart "flow" to the face (cf. p. 52).

One must manage one's heart by an effort so that there will be harmony between inner feeling (*keneh*) and outer expression (*semu*) and action (*bikas*). One can do little to change the world to conform to one's own desires, but a lot to be in the world in such a way that one enhances well-being and ameliorates the chances of disaster. Managing the heart works that way.

Cheerfulness, Self-worth, and Social Esteem

With this stress on smiling, being cheerful, and laughing as ways of assuaging others and making them like one goes a notion that the most potent strategy of hiding one's heart is to resort to joking and humorous storytelling to engulf others in merriment too. At no time in her life was Suriati so deft in joking and animated storytelling as during the twelve months following her friend's death, when she was struggling with the sensation that she might be going mad. This is by her own report. Another, who also set her sights on making people laugh while she was secretly undergoing severe pain, observed, "At the office, every day, I make people laugh [*penggambira*], so everyone is happy when they see me. And if one day I do not come, their faces glow when next they see me. Except for Trini, you should see her; when all the others laugh, she looks down into her desk with a closed face. Probably she is ashamed to think of what her mother has done to me . . . ."

She was alluding to how managing one's heart—or hiding it—is also seen as a victory with respect to the one who caused one such pain. "If only he would forget about his problem and manage his heart, then perhaps he would make Ketut Artje feel ashamed . . . and people would respect him more!" observed another of Wayan Wijaya, who was steeped in sorrow from Ketut's action (chap. 11).

Feeling and Expression as Moral Acts

Success at managing one's heart is indeed a source of self-esteem and social esteem. Both feeling and expression are in Bali collective concerns. Both are encompassed by the moral codex of *sopan-santun* by which persons in all their aspects are judged: as comprising feeling (*keneh/perasaan*), thought (*keneh/pikiran*), character/nature (*sifat/ tabiat*), attitude (*tingkah*), performance/appearance (*semu/penampilan*), and action (*bikas*). None of these escape moral judgment.

While the visible aspects of a person are so clearly distinguished from nonmanifest ones that for any word broadly connoting an emotional aspect Balinese can readily say if it refers to feeling and/or expression, and for some vital emotions (such as anger or happiness) there are different labels to connote whether it is felt or just expressed, yet both are suffused with moral connotations. These come across constantly in everyday discourse as people pass judgment on the feelings and/or expressions of others and self with emphatic verdicts of "good" (*melah/baik*) or "bad" (*jele/jahat*).[4] Or as Balinese say, "It is in our habit to dwell always on the bad. We don't usually say when something is good."[5]

But they do, as in esteeming Suriati for her impeccably *polos* behavior or extolling the good hearts of the couple who appeared at their malefactor's wedding, not to speak of conferring unreserved praise on the girl who received the news of her boyfriend's betrayal with unfailingly good grace. The epitome of good behavior, as we have seen, is the performance which Balinese name *polos*, which expresses a smooth, acquiescing attitude to the vicissitudes life inevitably brings or the "resistance" life offers to one. To be *polos* is to defer one's own wishes and needs to those of the group, the collective.

In extension of this, if you cannot manage your heart, then at least you should hide it and appear before the world as the world likes to see you: a Suriati eminently bright and clear, though she is nearly brokenhearted; a couple pained with distress at a close friend's deceit and yet smiling and cheerful "to show the world and ourselves we are of superior hearts."

Both feeling and expression thus should be chosen, willed, constructed by deliberate mindful action. One owes it to the social collective, one owes it to one's family, and one owes it to oneself. And the reason one owes it is that feelings are dangerous, they are contagious, they are the source of health and welfare, and they may predispose one to death.

"Be happy! Forget it! Let bygones be bygones!" Phrases such as these that resonate through everyday social discourse are more than plain positive advice. They are commands, injunctions, threats, abrasively spoken at times, in their cognizance of the fallibility of the heart.

In their deepest sense individual, hearts are treated *as if* they were social belongings, and one is made to feel one could and should shape one's heart according to morally good precepts. In this sense Balinese culture may be said to have intervened in the innermost recesses of a person's soul: entreating one couple who is utterly sad because their child has been taken in enforced fosterage by the man's brother to "manage their hearts better"; sanctioning another who is visibly distressed with laughter and the verdict "she does not know how to manage her feelings!"

We need not here go into all the reasons for this general disquiet regarding exposure of hidden hearts. Notions about health are critical and will be set out in later chapters. Here we should note its ground-rule aspect. "We have this principle," said a man, "don't you always think about your problem, everyone has it, not just you . . ." Another observed, "If a person sits there brooding, people will say, 'He is thinking about himself only, not the whole of our people.'"

Implied is a conception of feeling as eminently *shapable* by expression and as apt to spread to others when expressed. Entailed is also a notion of individual *responsibility* which may be instructive to ponder before we proceed.

Personal Responsibility

With the notions of *karma pala*—the fruits of one's actions in previous lives—and predestination goes the premise that persons are responsible for their own acts and feelings. At first glance this may sound contradictory, considering that a person's character—*sifat*—which has such impact on her life and deeds—is predestined, the reincarnation of a forefather's or foremother's soul. But as Made Bidja queried, "Would that exonerate the person of responsibility?"

He continued:

> Take my son as an example: He acts short-temperedly at
> times, and in this he is exactly like his grandfather who is
> reincarnated in him. The balian has confirmed the connec-
> tion. But does that relieve my son of responsibility? It is not
> clear that an actual act of misdemeanor can be traced back
> to this reincarnated aspect of his character—and not to his
> own self . . .

A person's character is indeed compounded of several aspects: a part is reincarnated,[6] a part is attributable to the environment, including parents' influence; and a part stems from one's own soul—which in turn may be reincarnated in another when one is dead. This is how an expert learned in the scriptural literature explained it to me. Among ordinary people the opinion is generally voiced that "character reflects the heart," indeed that "the character *is* the heart, they are the same." And while some people nuance this and say it is not wholly so, that "character" refers to a habitual tendency to do things in a certain way (as to be short-tempered, lazy, brave, etc.) whereas "heart" refers to feeling, thought, appreciation, judgment, yet my evidence indicates that in everyday life "heart" and "character" are confounded.

I think this is not fortuitous. Equating character with heart means that character also is regarded as manageable, shapable, amenable to personal control. It means that there is no excuse for bad behavior—except if the person is out of her wits (*kesadaran*) because a victim of black magic or prey to (super)natural spirits.[7] Likewise, when character is clearly incorrigible, as on account of a reincarnated ancestor's bad influence or an unpropitious name, the person's family should have rituals performed to erase and cleanse away the bad impact.[8] Again *responsibility* is at work.

Thus ordinary Balinese come to the expert's conclusion—but by a different route. The premise of personal responsibility they share is unassailable.[9] But whereas the expert accounts for this by a subtle, high-level theory of "character" as ontologically differentiated into three aspects, lay people operate with a simpler theory of a unified concept which they subsume under "heart."

In everyday discourse people are implored to make their heart, their character, and their body the best and thus to take responsibility for their own feelings and actions. It is presumed that they can, if they will. Lack of will connotes also moral failure. Nor is this too much to ask of anyone. Everyone will benefit from observing this golden "ground rule."

Balinese have a conception of themselves as dangerously susceptible to feelings, own and others'. Bateson's image of a "Balinese social organization in which the smooth relations of etiquette and gaiety metaphorically cover the turbulence of passion" ([1967] 1972b, 150) squares well with their self-perception. Constantly reinforced in everyday experience, this explains to them the necessity of extreme friendliness and composure. It accounts for the severity with which the ban on expressing "bad" feelings is enforced, and it ordains the positive value granted to contrived "good" expressions. But contra Bateson I do not believe that the motivating force derives from a concern with macrostructural features, namely, to keep a social collectivity at rest, but rather that it arises from closer-to-home, more parochial interests related to making a living and securing happiness and health (Wikan 1989b).

Person in Place: Incorporating Movement

To link this aspect of self-management with movement in social space, it will serve us to go back to a "ground plan" of groupings and encounters to recapitulate what was seen to be at stake. Perceptions of how critical it is to manage one's heart or simply hide it reflect discriminatory assessments of risks and precautions. It does not matter so much if people who are compassionate to you see your heart. It may cost you dearly if unsympathetic others do. We have seen that it is not given where people of one or the other category are located in social space. Let us extract and elaborate on the main insights.

Cultural notions single out person *and* place, or person *in* place, as the variable to be alert to in most kinds of interpersonal encounter. The critical divide, from an existential viewpoint, centers on properties that persons carry always about them. And hence the Balinese person construction might be said to *incorporate movement,* the going to and fro.

By that I mean to say that Balinese have a fairly precise conception of an immaterial aspect of self that is always present and, hence, of a "double-anchoredness" of persons. The performance you see is but one facet of a self, the one permitted outlet by general consent. But another, as vitally present, lingers behind and responds to everything that goes on. This hidden self [10]—the heart—is a prime mover of action. It is also commonly perceived as the key to a person's character.

What people must do to manage their moves bridging circles of varying restraint, how they must work on feeling and vital spirit (*bayu*) to fashion face, gesture, and posture into stereotyped patterns prescribed for persons of their position in life—this is a perpetual Balinese concern with respect to self and other. Grace and composure do not come "naturally" to Balinese, but hearts, seen as seething cauldrons of passion, must be guided and shaped to allow the socially sanctioned appearance to surface unruffled. It is this socially shared knowledge that beyond every "bright" and "polite" facade there beats a heart of fundamentally different character that enhances popular preoccupation with hearts—in a world that construes them as key movers of action.

This premise entails that assessments of what is at stake for one in a situation depends not so much on *where* an interaction takes place as on *who* the parties to the interaction are. People, needless to say, carry their hearts always with them. But a relevant "who" may be also an immaterial agent. Evil action directed at another may strike oneself through magic by "wrong address." And thus assessments of what is at stake for one in engaging with others in interaction should also include caution about how vulnerable these others might be. Which who(s) might want to strike the who with whom one engages? Life is in essence complicated and experienced as such. And the complaint that "there is so much to care about" bespeaks concern with both material and immaterial agents.

When I speak of Balinese person construction as "incorporating movement," then, it is because of a twofold emphasis I perceive in their attitudes to and reflections on fellow beings. Persons are regarded as being on the move in a physical sense, constantly bridging spaces and groupings. The Balinese standard greeting also testifies to this: "From where are you coming (*dari mana*]?" "To where are you going [*mau ke mana*]?" are their equivalents of a Western "How are you?" or an Arabic "How is the situation?" (*kef ilhal*).

In moving, persons have also to manage their selves by an effort of "emotion work"—to use Hochschild's brilliant phrase (1979, esp. 561–62). Hence "movement" takes place also internally, and a problem in interpersonal relations is the difficulty of ascertaining what the movement is: the bright face, the polished demeanor—from where did they spring? What internal turmoil and suffering or dark motives and vengeful passions may lurk or linger within?

The attention to exterior movement, bridgings, and crisscrossings may be seen to facilitate conjecture and inference regarding people's hidden hearts. What are they up to, who do they see, what takes them hither and thither? Take as an example Issa trying to figure out how much the hostess knew about herself and her long-past relationship with a certain man. It would have stood her in good stead to know something of the hostess's movements at that time and whether she had been in a certain *kampong* (quarter of town) some six to seven years back. In everyday life, knowledge like this is painstakingly collected and hoarded. And the greetings of *"mau ke mana, dari mana?"* which must actually be properly answered, give some indications.

I am struck that there are societies where it would be considered wholly inappropriate and suspect thus to ask people to account for their movements. But in Bali, however annoying it may be to have to tell numerous passersby where one has been or intends to go, it must be done or one is labelled arrogant—*sombong*. The verdict is expressed with a long, drawn-out *o-o-ong*, epitomizing all the disgust Balinese may put into that label.

"Double-anchored Selves"

A second concept I use to facilitate my conceptualization of Balinese person construction is "double-anchoredness." It seeks to capture the unity they perceive between two facets of a person, one outer, one inner, both present, steering interaction while anchored in different pursuits. I refer to the contrast they draw between "heart" and "character," on the one hand, and "attitude," "performance," "appearance," "expression," and "action" on the other.

"Face" (*mue/muka*) is also often juxtaposed with "heart," for "face" is seen to be the surest indicator of another's heart ("we can see from the eyes, the eyes cannot lie"). From ego's viewpoint, likewise, the dilemma experienced in hiding one's heart typically focuses on facial expression. To appropriately mold the face, as in making it look bright and clear, is experienced as the most difficult thing.

The "heart" which figures so prominently in everyday discourse is a metaphor for feeling, character, conscience (*kayun/nurani/kata hati*), and life force, vital energy. All of these are linked in popular perception, and the heart stands as their common denominator. By connecting "heart" with such wide-ranging existential issues, Balinese indeed may be said to have invested the "heart" with key metaphysical power. "It is like we believe that all can be explained in terms of the heart," one hears sometimes said.

Truly the "focal point of a world-view" (Solomon 1978, 181) Balinese hearts are presumed and perceived and are as eminently present in life as are words and deeds. Balinese preoccupation with hearts cannot be exaggerated. Everyday discourse abounds with references to them. The following fragments of a case epitomizes a common concern.

A girl turned down a suitor because he was always grave (*nyebeng*) in the face, though in every other aspect—family background, profession, wealth, and physical appearance—he was everything she could have wished for, as she clearly recognized. His "seriousness," however, represented an intolerable threat. It indicated he might be "given to anger." As family pressure from both his side and her side mounted she strove to overcome her fear, but in vain. "He does not smile, he looks arrogant, what if my children would be like him?" Instead she chose a man not nearly so well off or well educated but reputed to have "a good heart." She had not even met him.

After some months of marriage she sighed, "How difficult it is to know another's heart." She had made a misjudgment, said older women, because she was too young to know the signs by which to read another's heart.

But when I asked why nobody had warned her, they just looked at me aghast. Then a man spoke and said I must understand, it would have been dangerous . . . Nothing more was said. The message was self-evident: She or her spouse or his kin might have been angry and then . . .[11] Indeed, the illness which spurs recourse to black magic also has reference to "heart" and is called "heart-sickness," i.e., "a heart sick from anger."

The two facets of self, heart versus face/performance/action, are present in every situation, conceptually distinct but actually linked. On no occasion was I able to get Balinese to give an answer to a question I tried to frame (in the early stage of fieldwork) eliciting their perception of what heart contrasts most poignantly with, or whether heart was the opposite of anything at all. Mine was clearly a meaningless question as heart belongs *in* every performance, and to single out performance as a thing in itself, or as the obverse of heart, has no meaning. Balinese person construction is holistic, encompassing heart *and* performance, body *and* soul, nature *and* supernature, and to presume any of these to be amenable to pairing on a Western conceptual scale would be a misjudgment—*salah kaprah*, as Balinese would say.

Indeed, it is because performance is *not* seen as a product divested of a heart that people are esteemed for appearing bright and clear when they are known to be, or to have recently been, distressed. Likewise, it is because people of angry hearts—in Bali termed people with a sickness of the heart—carry these with them *in* their performances that grace and goodwill should not be accepted at face value. Indeed, the most dangerous anger (*benci*, or *dendam/dengki*—hatred or grudge) is by definition unexpressed and far more atrocious than anger expressed: *marah* or *gedeg*. [12] Likewise the cheerful (*girang*) countenance which is socially prescribed refers only to appearance and leaves open the question of what the heart truly is. Interpretive problems lie at the heart of Balinese experience. Let us consider further the vital connection in double-anchored selves.

To convey, first, my understanding of how Balinese experience the hidden facet of another's self, perhaps the following metaphor will do: There would seem to be a "hidden eye" in the form of a "heart" always present in any interaction—sieving, sorting, amassing information—for present or potential future use or simply for observing oneself. Compassionate responses stemming from another's seeing through one's hard-won composure *to* one's heart, and evil action fueled by resentment and (concealed) offense, both spring from the same indubitable source: a "heart" equipped with an "eye" to take in vital information and engender heartfelt response, for good or for bad.

But there is also in every interaction present a person, a visible self, whose acts and utterances bespeak real messages and consequences—as do "hearts"—and who is generally not seen as faked. It is important to stress that this more standardized, stereotyped self is socially prescribed, morally enjoined, a vehicle of self-worth and social esteem. It is in essence the social persona with which others deal, since it is the only facet of another's self that they "actually" see. And it goes without saying that this me-in-the-world profoundly engages, gratifies—and occasionally causes despair to—its feeling-thinking agent.

The "shell" must be put on, face smoothed, clothes unruffled, expression, gait, and posture "set" in a proper style. But while with a "hidden eye" one may stand back and observe oneself thus boxed in—as when the heart is ravaged with anger, fear, or despair, or when one is utterly sad—*sedeh*—yet this outer apparent me-in-the-world compels. And persons draw much self-esteem, not to speak of social esteem, from their ability thus to personify cherished ideals that *they* also share concerning the face Balinese ought to present to the world.[13]

The Struggle to Think Well of Oneself

To put a human face on these abstract formulations: Suriati is esteemed for her exquisite and self-effacing social mode. She is praised for appearing always content and composed and for deferring to others' wishes, as should the model young female Balinese. This social persona gratifies her self, and she puts much effort into appearing thus, irrespective of how she feels.

Yet privately she complains, speaking her heart to intimates: "I have this problem, it has been with me always, that I am afraid to make another person unhappy."

Contrasting concerns expressed by two facets of a self, both valuable, both compelling, affecting intercourse. As Balinese have construed collective action, morality, and self, only one of these has general social legitimacy, whereas the other, the heart, belongs, only in relations among intimates. However, even with them there are vital experiences that may be expressed only with difficulty. Anger, envy, jealousy, and offense are so disreputable that I know several Balinese who claim they do not even know how anger feels, having never sensed it in their hearts.

"Double-anchoredness" thus aspires to convey a condition of being-in-the-world that Balinese, as I understand them, perceive as pertaining to other and self. "Heart" and "expression" both belong to and affect what T. S. Eliot termed people's "endless struggle to think well of themselves."[14] In Bali, some ways to achieve this are (1) by morally managing one's heart to dispel bad feelings and let the good ones flow; (2) by hiding one's heart and presenting the world with a bright face; (3) by enhancing oneself at another's expense by deprecatory remarks designed to "make another down"; or (4) by elevating oneself through rejuvenating feelings of joy that spring from success in afflicting another through black magic. In every case, at stake is a composite person's endeavor to make an impact upon the world and reap self-esteem and social esteem.

Predicaments

To understand the predicaments Balinese experience through this double-anchored quality of other and self, we might go off in two directions. We might see the problem from the point of view of an ego engrossed in ordinary, everyday pursuits of the kind that make also Balinese feel at times perturbed and distressed. Or we might take the opposite course of focusing on an other known to disguise her heart and on ego's concern with how the other actually is, perhaps from compassion or perhaps from her fear of what feelings the other's heart contains. Suriati might serve as our model of the first; Issa, who carried her hair straws home, might epitomize the second.

These two perspectives, however, when added one to the other, draw the world too simply. Cast Suriati in Issa's role, and you have the experience—a Balinese dilemma—full blast: a person submerged in a heartfelt experience who must keep smiling and clear for fear of unleashing a Niagara of evil forces upon herself. Suriati's case, as represented by me, did in fact bear out this aspect: Because sadness undermines the vital life force (*bayu*) which is a person's best protection against black magic, it also intensifies her fear and with it the endeavor to appear polite and bright. I depicted Suriati in a certain village as changing almost into a caricature of poise and grace. Consider the severity of her distress and the notoriety of the villagers for black magic, and her attempt to perfect a poise pervaded by fear is also understandable. (Mind you: the judgment of caricature is mine. I have no indication that villagers were anything but pleased and impressed with Suriati's feminine grace.)

We need not go to such extremes to convey an everyday dilemma. Consider a person, any person, engaged in ordinary, multiple pursuits involving of necessity interaction with dozens of others through the day, and the predicament is there—how to steer, move, be with safety in the world, salvaging respect while securing practical ends: making a living, attaining position, nourishing cherished bonds, preserving mental calm.

"I tell myself he is a madman, to keep myself from getting angry," said a woman of a man who had it in his power to decide her possibilities for employment. He had resorted to vicious tactics to make life difficult for her and impress upon her her utter dependency on him in the matter. This was all in secrecy. To her face he behaved as nothing but friendly and polite. But she had found him out,[15] and anger was her natural response.

Yet anger must not be felt, or she would ruin her peace of mind and create havoc in her relationship with him (on whom she continued to be dependent due to his control over resources she needed). So she managed her heart by a technique of casting the man in a "mad" (*gila*) role to show up the absurdity of feeling angry. The result was positive; she felt better and continued to behave towards him as if all was well in their relationship. He repaid her by seeing to it that she had the job she sorely needed.

Or take another example: the girl who deliberately acted immature to make a man whom she feared "think me like a child so that he will not take me seriously and be angry with me." She was proud of herself because her performance had stayed entirely within the bounds of polite demeanor (pertaining to childish girls) so that the man had found no reason to be angry with her. On the contrary, her childishness elicited some sympathy from him. I repeatedly heard him and his wife marvel at her immaturity and express pity with her because she acted thus: the poor girl's home environment was not good, she did not receive proper guidance, etc. Biographical matters explained her, to them, "confused" feeling-thought that engendered "childish" action.

Little did they know that it was highly intelligent feeling-thinking that motivated and shaped her response. She may be seen to have managed her heart rather well through this recourse, alleviating the fear that might have crippled her vital energy and shown through in her relations with the man.[16] He, by information she had, both knew and used black magic.

A third example: Suriati says she has a "problem" on account of her disposition always to want to make others happy. If we trace back to our discussion of the experienced force of culture and the disadvantage to which particularly girls are put, being taught in the face of another's pressure to be pliant and respond, "It's up to you, do as you like"— then Suriati expresses this concern. She is aware that her predicament is aggravated by her particular character, and yet this is how she chooses to be from a combination of fear and pride with herself for excelling to general acclaim.

There is thus a visible self whom the world beholds, in this case, an eminently gracious person. But there is also a hidden self that struggles to find ways of securing valued ends *within* this frame of poise and grace. It makes life complicated at times to manage such discrepant concerns (as we shall see once we come to consider the events that led up to Suriati's marriage). But the "problem," while inherent in Balinese person construction, depends for its experienced force and interpersonal ramifications on matters pertaining to character or "heart." A woman reputed to be brave (*berani*) or proud (*bangga*) might never find herself in the kind of predicament into which Suriati easily gets. People are not likely to try to use *pemaksa* (force) against a *berani/bangga* woman, but they may try more subtle (and perhaps more dangerous) means.

My description of the two girls acting with respect to men whom they feared (but could not withdraw from on account of the men's control over resources the girls needed) was intended to illustrate a common type of encounter where two parties to an interaction are clearly simultaneously "double-anchored." Generally, the polished surface people display is more of an enigma. The experienced nature of their predicament is more often this: "How *can* I know [what (s)he really feels about me]? It is not so easy to tell . . ."[17]

The Intrinsic Value of Good Expression

The distinction Balinese draw between two facets of a self is not like our performance/self, integral to which is a perception of deception since people ought, so we believe, to put their selves into their acts. Beautifully expressed by Santayana: we tend to "urge against cuticles that they are not hearts . . . [and] to be angry with images for not being things, and with words for not being feelings" (quoted in Goffman 1959, vii).

Not so in Bali. The dichotomy they draw is one in which there is general agreement that hearts have by common consensus no place in relations among nonintimates. Impassioned feelings and desires must not interfere with compelling tasks to be done. As a man said, "Society does not need arrogance or unfriendly behaviors. Society needs *gotong-royong*." *Gotong-royong* is the form of communal action which ensures cooperation in numerous tasks Balinese define as collective: irrigation management, agricultural production, temple organization, life cycle ceremonies, and general give-and-take. These might suffer irretrievably were hearts to be exposed.

By a kind of cultural command, then, there is room for a limited range of social personae within the social fabric of Bali. In ordinary, everyday life polite, friendly, and happy demeanors are the elements from which the web of visible social life is spun.[18] Morally based, they receive sanction from gods and ancestors. A man who died from black magic waged by a friend and colleague was characterized by his own cousin as having received his due: he behaved always arrogantly, what could he expect? Implicit is the notion that this was his *karma pala,* fate having acted speedily in this case to inflict holy justice upon a man who had done detriment to another by acting headstrong and conceited.

No concept of hypocrisy or falseness attaches to the morally prescribed demeanors. At an early stage I tried hard to probe whether people did not operate with any such notions, and once a man, having at last seen my point, triumphantly produced a clue. They did have a notion, said he. It is *nyruange* and means "to make an appearance so as to make another's heart happy. It is not for bad thing."

It turned out, they do have a concept of masking, of pretense—*munafiq.* It refers to ill-intended pretense or to a person in whose character it is to be generally masking for selfish ends. Such a person is referred to as *manusia jahat*—a truly bad human being. To put on a good face for the sake of good relations is wholly another thing—*pura-pura.* Once when Made Bidja pointed out to me how a man with whom we had just been together had asked him why his face was not clear ("Truly he was right, I could feel my face was red, for I was angry. But I denied it."), he was quick to point out that this was *pura-pura,* not *munafiq.* He did it with good intent and to express concern for the other.

The general ambience of smiling, in part exuberant, social selves is indeed regarded as facilitating happiness and health. Suriati, now living far away from Bali, said with a sigh, "It is so much easier to be happy in Bali, there are so many smiles . . ." Take not her statement for a way of speaking, superficially pronounced. It is a life-way she attests to, a mode of living seen by its participants as happiness-conducive by way of, among other things, all the smiles. We need to consider Balinese concepts of health to understand why, and other chapters have been set apart for that. I mention her heartfelt utterance here for what it evokes of concern with expression deemed *so good* in itself.

Also she is aware of the turbulence, passions, and evil desires at the base of many a smile. But in general, a person need not relate to the hearts of more than a fraction of the people she meets through the day who are important to her in particular. With the rest, she can draw consolation from their friendliness and their smiles.

All performance is good when it stays within the bounds of moral precepts formulated in the code of *sopan-santun.* And yet individual performance may be judged bad: "She acts *polos,* but truly she is not."

The heart is regarded as not having been managed at all, either because the person lets herself be driven by "not so good feelings" or because she "does not listen to her heart."

Even then moral disapprobation attaches to "heart" and not to "performance." A polite and friendly demeanor is generally good, *even when* it disguises evil intent. It is then the intent that is bad, not the appearance that is inappropriate.

To perform properly is to put oneself into one's act while keeping out a nonappropriate part: the heart's most deepfelt longings, inner turmoil, shameful feelings, antisocial drives. Why sadness is encompassed within the realm of "not so good feelings" we will address later. Here let us just take note of what people said to Suriati: "You make *us* unhappy with that withered face!"

While the moral code of *sopan-santun* formulates precepts that are absolute in an abstract sense, they are applied differentially in practice; rigid codes coexist with a measure of freedom for the person to be and to shape her conduct in harmony with her character (or the character it serves her to act as if she has). The "bright" face and polished demeanor yet permit a myriad of idiosyncratic signs to seep through or be expressed. The surface is porous, permeable, and naturally so, for at the heart is a feeling-thinking person with multiple concerns. Personal judgment, features of character, age, rank, and gender assert themselves to make no two bright faces, no two "happy" demeanors, appear exactly alike.

The Misapplication of the Mask Metaphor

Balinese have instituted an ethos which is intrinsically pleasing and morally good but constraining and disquieting in some of its implications. If people could manage their hearts, all would be well. As a moral guidance the ideal is unassailable. But in practice hearts hide all manner of turmoil and debris, and so when hiding the heart reads as the critical sign that the heart has been managed, problems arise—given that hearts are endowed with potentially atrocious powers.

It is important to note that Balinese do attribute to one another hearts, and not masks and faces (*pace* C. Geertz [1966] 1973a, [1974] 1984). Also, I judge it unfortunate when Keeler assumes his model of Javanese to apply to Balinese: "A person's failure to act suitably in encounter . . . does not reveal a human face behind a social mask" (1983, 162). This mixes the metaphors, for in Bali the face is *on* the person, not something that is masked and hidden. Indeed, as a Balinese doctor said

when apprised of the theatrical imagery in which salient foreign discourse couches Balinese, "If we wear a mask, then it must be on our
hearts, not on our faces." He said it with irony after having dismissed
the imagery as wholly inappropriate.

The difference between faces and hearts, and masks and faces, is essential, and I think detriment has been done to Balinese by reconstruct-
ing them in a language misconstrued: that of theatrical imagery. It
misidentifies their concerns and dislocates them away from the personal
ones of health and family well-being—too humdrum perhaps for a true
interpretive quest—to a preoccupation with aesthetics, performance,
and the pursuit of grace. The latter does indeed obtain, and when a performance is mishandled, it does elicit feelings of embarrassment and
shame. But we must recognize that this shame is in no way the aspect of
the episode which is dreaded most. Unpleasant, disconcerting, it may
unhinge your spirit and put your reputation at stake. But it is anger and
offense that are truly feared.

Granted that the "face" is *on* the person, the "heart" what lies beyond, a person's heart is indeed what Balinese would see in a botched
performance, unless they made it out to be a sign of black magic at
work. Moreover, only when we acknowledge that at the core of a performance is a heart—not a face—a feeling-thinking agent—can we begin to ask questions about motivational force and the meanings of things
to the actors.

Hearts as Forces of This World

Managing the heart to let good feeling-thinking flow, or simply hiding it to cover up the ordinary person's ordinary portion of less than
reputable feelings, is thus a ground rule for movement in social space.
Besides facilitating intracommunal cooperation, managed hearts ensure
a modicum of predictability. People might fall sick from fright should
they come across angry outbursts, sudden uproar, or even an unduly
grave face, glossed by Balinese young women in particular as hideous,
horrible, frightening (Wikan 1987).

But when hearts, invisible, are yet felt it is not only because Balinese
rely on more or less standardized cues to ascertain people's hearts, but
also because invisible yet highly perceptible powers are part and parcel
of the Balinese scheme of things.

We have seen how their world incorporates multiple agencies we cannot perceive. There are place spirits and nature spirits, magical birds,
rats, and dogs, roving souls of people dreaming and scared-away souls

of people suddenly surprised. There are the souls of the dead that play such an important part in the lives of the living, and there are myriad gods emanating from the same source, the supreme being or Divinity, Ida Sang Hyang Widhi Wasa.

These are present, they belong. And persons too are ascribed perceptible powers of potentially tremendous force. Balinese hearts are "things of this world" in a much more immediate sense than symbols in general may be said to be. Not only are they *culturally constructed* and *interpersonally negotiated* through *processes of judgment*—to use key words from anthropological studies of emotion. Balinese hearts are as real as the ground on which one treads or the air that one breathes. They are experienced and sensed in an almost palpable way. And they are treated with as much awe and fear as are (super)natural spirits and ghosts. With the numerous casualties Balinese ascribe to action wreaked by angry hearts, no wonder they tread cautiously to please as virtue pleases.

A Holistic View of the Person

Managed or unmanaged hearts are public "facts"—hence by all measures cultural. But so is the process of fostering the bright face that reads as the sign that the heart has been managed. Nor is this a static product. A bright face is precarious in that it takes an effort to sustain—the strain of which is variously felt depending on one's life experience and situation.

Because this effort is "private," hidden to the world, is it therefore not cultural? Of course it is, in many salient aspects. "Forgetting," "not caring," and "guiding the feeling-thought"—techniques Balinese are taught from the earliest age to employ—bear the stamp of the work of culture (Obeyesekere 1985) as much as the obvious, bright face one presents to the world.

When Suriati, in the privacy of her home, thought about her shock and her grief, she did not invent privatized and particularistic notions there and then. She relied upon a model for shaping feelings, thoughts, and actions that was as much part of her cultural upbringing as any baggage that had been provided her to tackle the world that lay beyond. Cultural templates penetrate to the innermost of people's souls and mold experience and perception of self as much as the outer persona. When Balinese hasten to laugh, when they feel sad, whereas people socialized by other cultural templates may tend to brood and delve deeper into their misery—"culture" is as much at work as in the magnificent ceremonies the Western world has come to associate with Bali.

The implications of this are far reaching. Not only can we not split people up into different realms and analyze each in its constituent elements, but we must assume that people carry a representation *of* themselves *as* they move and that this constitutes part of the cultural construction of self. Moreover, it seems plausible to assume that ego construes alter as *also* carrying such a representation, so that when they meet, each carries a conception of the other as "double-anchored." This then would form part of the cultural construction of the self and the other.

We have seen how Suriati's efforts to meet the world with a bright face did not take the world in, or not completely. People who met her would have an image of a covert aspect of her person. On this basis, those who knew what she had been through—by knowing her friend was dead—might infer some of what was going on behind that cheerful and bright facade. And they could be sympathetic with her, though they did not all express it in a way she could then comprehend.

While Balinese in two influential accounts (Bateson and Mead 1942, 23; C. Geertz [1966] 1973a) have been seen as lacking the quality of empathy, my own data show ample evidence of empathy, but only if it is interpreted in the frame of conceptions which actually governs their experience. Balinese often stress this quality of *kelangen* or *inda*—sympathy or empathy—as fundamental and linked with the "heart": "If you talk sadness, and it does not spread to your neighbor, it means he has no feeling." *Kelangen* depends on a *resonance* of feeling (*ngelah keneh*) between two (or more) persons—and this flows so much precisely because "Balinese are trained to care about others."

Their intense preoccupation with hidden hearts socializes Balinese, as far as I can judge, to acute sensitivity in regard to others. Observed a woman: "People are so kind to me, they come and give me things, even now at *Galungan* [Hindu holiday], and this though I am a Muslim. Why do you think they do it, when I don't tell anyone my heart but always make my face look bright?"

A year before she had complained: "People come to me in the street and say, 'We feel pity with you, may God give you patience!' I am annoyed that they do when I don't complain to anyone or tell them my heart."

People's ability to see through you may constitute a blessing as well as a threat. It is essential to note that Balinese *do* often see through; that they try to do so even if they can't, but may still think they do; and that they attribute feelings, attitudes, and motives to each other on that basis.

We have seen that people are praised or criticized for their ability to manage their hearts. Far from being expected to move about in depersonalized, stereotyped fashion, they are praised when one can infer that the cost of composure is great. Perhaps the clearest example I came across concerned the girl who was given in a public place the news of her boyfriend's betrayal. And yet she did not cry. The story was related to me by several people, and all stressed how "she did not cry until she was home." And she was widely esteemed for acting so *polos* (Wikan 1987, 346).

Did anyone actually see her cry? I know that the several people who told me the story did not. But they *assumed* that she did. It was the natural thing to do, given what she was going through. By coupling emotion with social situation, Balinese perceive ready avenues for deciphering emotion. Feelings are regarded as inscribed in social situations, and so hearts may be probed by assessments of sheer social facts.[19] (p. 162). Perhaps this accounts for the empathy Balinese display even with respect to people they hardly know: it takes a knowledge of situation "only" to infer experience and, with it, the concealed feelings of the heart (cf. chap. 8).

Life is too complicated for the formula always to work, but in many matters it is "given" how people must feel. A presumption that humans are basically the same in their instinctive responses to life events is also at work. Passions, urges, drives assert themselves. And thus vital elements of the self are "exposed," even as people try hard to conceal them. Needless to say, people differ in their ability to guide or hide the heart.

I conclude that the complex world of individual concerns, feelings, passions, and fears of Balinese, though private in the sense of being shielded from the scrutiny of strangers, is also essentially shared and intersubjective, hence *cultural*. Thus it cannot be separated from the "public" surface of behavior—in Bali an edifice of social grace—for it shapes and motivates that behavior. Nor can it be set aside from an analysis of Balinese conceptualization of self and person. Being known by all Balinese to exist and assumed by all to be a highly significant part of personhood, it is necessary to investigate the cultural concepts by which it is structured. This set of concepts forms an elaborate apparatus constantly employed by Balinese to orient themselves and interpret themselves to themselves and to one another. Concepts of heart and feeling-thought lie at its base.

PART THREE

Feeling-Thoughts, Morality, and Health

CHAPTER SEVEN

Feeling-Thoughts and Their Interpretation

Incorporating emotion into ethnography will entail presenting a fuller view of what is at stake for people in everyday life. In reintroducing pain and pleasure in all their complex forms . . . we might further humanize these others for the Western audience.
—LUTZ AND WHITE

Emotional Expression and Feeling

During three months of near daily contact with Suriati, I was at a loss to understand what the death of her friend had meant to her. Or, to be more precise, I intuitively felt I knew a great deal, but the connection between her *emotional expressions* and what I adduced to be her *feelings* was so puzzling as to plague me with a deep sense of confusion.

My inferences about her feelings were based on a variety of observations: the shrouded verbal statements she volunteered; a host of nonverbal signs she gave off in body movement, posture, and tone of voice; the many somatic complaints from which she suffered over the next few months; and the general atmosphere in her home that made one feel a deep concern about her condition.

But above all, there was the sheer fact of her friend's death that made me feel sure she must be deeply sad. She had let me understand that she had loved him dearly and would have married him soon had the tragic event not taken place.

People's reactions were likewise not of a piece, though on the whole they appeared unfeeling and "mocking." Suggestive of other currents were particularly the reactions of some old women. When Suriati told the story to them—and tell it she did often, always making it sound as if it were an acquaintance who was dead—not uncommonly old women would bend down to clutch a corner of their sarongs to wipe their eyes, eyes that from the outside did not seem to water. This reaction, though it did little to clarify things to me, yet evinced that there was more at stake than might appear. The story of the young man's tragic death would seem to carry a meaning—both to those who knew him and to those who did not—that was genuinely masked by my reading of their emotional expressions.

The reasons for my bewilderment are epistemologically and methodologically instructive. I had worked in other cultures before, observed bereavement and loss at close quarters, and been in no doubt about the depth and force of the grief because, I now realize, people expressed their sorrow in ways that were readily understandable to me. They cried. They poured their hearts out. Among the Cairo poor, mothers sometimes become paralyzed with grief over the loss of a child and sit speechless for months on end (Wikan 1988, 452). It seemed an unmistakable sign of deep and devastating loss.

I believe it is, and that my interpretation of their behavior is right, as it is based on a variety of types of data besides the mere observational and on nearly twenty years of contact with the people. But my rationale for thinking I knew was wrong. As Harkness and Kilbride have observed:

> Cultural variation in the expression of affect is one of the most readily observable yet least easily interpretable aspects of human behavior. As a communication system, affective expression is the inverse of linguistic expression: while in language the linguistic symbols are considered arbitrary carriers of meaning, affective expression is perceived as embodying meaning itself. We are not surprised when we cannot understand the speech of a person whose language we do not know, but we assume that an adequate translation would convey a meaningful message to us. Observing the affective behavior of a person from a different culture, however, we "know" what is meant, but are sometimes unable to understand why a person should act in that way (1983, 215).

The last sentence appositely characterizes my own confusion. Though both previous field experience in diverse cultures and everyday life in my own culture had made me aware that positive emotional expressions such as smiles and laughter need not signify happiness or content but may mask—or even *express*—a variety of feeling states, yet I was unprepared for a social order that would associate jokes and laughter with tragic death. To shine and sparkle without a trace of sorrowful expression when someone beloved was dead seemed a contradiction in terms. Suriati remained for a long time unintelligible to me. Yet the problem I had in comprehending her was minor compared to that of trying to make sense of her friends when they said, "Well, he is dead, so why do you cry?" and burst into peals of laughter.

I had no experience, whether from professional or personal life, that enabled me at this stage to incorporate such reactions within the realm of the plausible, natural, or normal. They seemed absurd, plain and simple. Moreover, laughter seemed so grossly inappropriate and objectionable in the situation that I had difficulties handling my own emotional reaction of indignation.

Retrospectively I now realize that I had operated on the assumption that there are *limits* to the meanings that emotional expressions carry across cultures; that affective expression has some invariant biological base that is transculturally universal so that even though laughter *need* not signify a positive response, it *cannot* be the accompaniment of—far less express—deepfelt sorrow or sympathy at death.

It was not an assumption of which I was conscious at the time. Rather it served as a "natural," taken-for-granted notion of how things in their sheer actuality are and was nearly unsuppressible due to an emotional reaction from my side.

Privileged Moments of Insight

Thus I felt a great sense of relief when after three months I saw Suriati cry. At long last she made sense. And when her tearfulness precipitated that spontaneous account of how she struggled to act and be happy from fear of being swept away by grief or made a laughingstock among her peers, this constituted one of those enlightened moments in fieldwork when "vaguely sensed intuitions and observations waiting for their interpretive context suddenly come together and are transformed into clarifying insights and a new basis for understanding" (Wikan 1982, 282). That gripping sense of confusion that had plagued me over the past few months on account of the discrepancy I had perceived between her expressions and feelings now suddenly lifted. And I thought I could see clearly.

Perhaps you can sense some of my feeling of relief? Perhaps also to you, who have been told but the fragments of a long story, things fell into some kind of pattern when you were told Suriati's reasons for hiding her distress.

It is *sensible* to laugh if otherwise people will laugh and mock you as "brokenhearted." Suriati evokes our sympathy because we understand all too well what she means. Her testimony touches strings that appear universal.

Feeling-Thoughts as Predicating Vision

I am going to show you that you have been misled, as I was on that day, that things are considerably more complex than this. Not that

Suriati's statement was not true. It was, but because it was expressed in a state of confusion, as Balinese view it. The positioned character of interpretations, including native interpretations, has received rather little attention from anthropologists.[1] We usually operate with rather monadic descriptions of culture; and when we acknowledge that actors entertain different visions, the variables noted are usually gender, sometimes rank or religion.

In Bali age matters as well, but above all the state of one's feeling-thoughts matters. They are the lens through which perceptions are scanned and filtered and the basis for moral judgment. Robert Solomon's formulation of emotions as being like a mythology *in* which we act and *through* which we see the world (1978, 190) squares well with Balinese conceptions. In their vision of things, whether one is sad and confused or happy and calm makes a world of difference for one's outlook on other and self.

Thus the insight that on this day seemed so clear and sharp when Suriati had told me her heart, culminating in that gripping testimony of why she must hide her sadness, would later have to be recast in the light of contrary events that jeopardized some if its basic elements. *It is true* that fear of laughter keeps the expression of sorrow in check—*from the position of the sad or brokenhearted person.* But it is not true, or not necessarily so, for people with calm hearts and minds. The meanings that cultural symbols such as laughter or sadness evoke differ with one's feeling-thought; and thus to probe for *the* meaning of any cultural symbols seems misleading. Meanings are evoked in praxis, not inherent in symbols (Keesing 1987a, 164; Strathern 1987, 173).

In Balinese conception the sadness of Suriati's mind blurred her vision in a manner that is typical of persons confused and sad, particularly if they are also young and female and of precarious social position. They will then be triply disposed to lean toward a perspective like hers, because such an amalgam of attributes predisposes the person to choose a *particular* interpretation from the options that laughter presents.

A multiplex symbol that may evoke a range of meanings—friendliness, conviviality, ridicule, scorn, shame, shyness, embarrassment, care and compassion—laughter must, like any symbol in everyday use, be *interpreted* by persons in particular life situations. This is why the search for meaning must move very close to the ground: to capture the particular angle of vision—e.g., a confused (*bingung*) state of feeling-thought, or pride and position, or vulnerability—that predicates one's outlook and, with it, the way things in their sheer actuality seem to be.

Crying: Also in Bali a Natural Response to Loss

I am not the only one to have been misled, by Balinese cheerfulness in situations where we expect them to display sorrow, to infer that there is something very special about the way they react to bereavement and loss. When, in a comparative study of seventy-three cultures, they come across as the only people not to cry in (public) mourning, they *are* truly special (Rosenblatt, Walsh, and Jackson 1976, 15).

As Rosenblatt also allows, the enigma they present may be more apparent than real. In my opinion it reflects both their concern to make the face look bright, which baffles outside interpreters, and also their evaluation of smiles and laughter as intrinsically morally good, while they are seen by us as unfitting in connection with death.

But from a Balinese perspective, crying *is* the natural response to tragedy, loss, and despair. Crying, say they, is what everyone will do in the face of such experience. That they speak from experience is also clear: I observed numerous instances of adults crying, in homes, streets, and graveyards, in intimate gatherings and large groupings.

Let Balinese be included with the rest of humanity who do cry when overcome with sorrow. And so the relevant question to ask is rather this: Why do they *also* laugh and strive to convince themselves and others that one had better let bygones be bygones?

Too much is at stake that sadness can be left to run what to Balinese *also* is its otherwise natural course. At issue is a conception that links expression of not-so-good feelings to jeopardized spiritual and mental balance, bodily pain, immorality, ill repute, and even the freedom of the deceased's soul to go back to its source—God. This transposes sadness into a fundamental collective concern that is also suffused with moral and supernatural significance.

Laughter is singled out as the sensible response because expression is perceived to shape and mold feeling. Laughter *makes* happiness, it takes sadness out. This is a premise of life. The relationship is not abstract; it is experientially known and perceived. Just as getting one's feet wet and cold makes one shivering and dizzy; fear makes the blood freeze; anger rushes the blood through the heart and makes one feel hot, ill-tempered, and rash; and sadness gives headache and saps one's vital energy, so the effects of laughter on body-soul are palpable. Laughter helps one forget, makes one feel good, and strengthens the spirit. It also preserves youthfulness of face and body. A connection Western biomedicine is just beginning to acknowledge and use for therapeutic effect (see chap. 8) has been known and practiced by Balinese through ages.

Yet this does not explain why smiling and laughing should be codified as a *moral* injunction. Why are not persons left to their own devices to laugh or to cry as they see fit? Why not grant them the freedom extant among many peoples in the West to drive themselves to despair, if they so wish?

Because in Bali persons are perceived not as islands apart, but as being in touch. They are mutually dependent on one another, for good or for ill. A daughter who was about to marry and move to Sumatra pointed to a key Balinese premise of happiness and health when she phrased concern about her mother thus: "My mother will be left with no one to laugh."

Hers was an overstatement, for the mother belonged to a wide circle of family and friends who would all—for so do Balinese (and particularly women)—smile and laugh at every encounter. But when she was alone and plagued with the problems of the house, who would then cheer her up and help make her heart happy from sadness? To be left with no one to laugh under such circumstances is indeed a predicament.

If my analysis succeeds, then in the end, laughter will emerge as a response as sensible as crying to tragedy, loss, and decay. It is hard for Westerners[2] to escape the conviction that sadness expresses itself naturally in tears or a withered face. The Balinese conception of "natural" links laughter to sadness in a nearly spontaneous response of self-protection and self-value, and also as an expression of compassion and care. It is a question of perspective, in the deep sense of the word. And the Balinese perspective singles out laughter as *the* sound and sensible therapeutic response.

Expression, Process, and Hidden Agendas

The source for the generalization that the Balinese do not cry at death is two anthropologists whose writings have shaped the visions that many Westerners entertain. Margaret Mead characterized the Balinese as extraordinarily lacking in thoughtfulness and as "disallowed" to express sadness or broken hearts (1942, 23, 28). Clifford Geertz represented them as recoiling from emotionality from fear of botching their public performances and as set on the latter to such an extent that the self merges with the role and the act to make them one and inseparable: "Physically men come and go . . . of no importance even to themselves. But the masks they wear, the stage they occupy . . . and, most important, the spectacle they mount remain and comprise not the facade but the substance of things, not least the self" ([1974] 1984, 128–29).

From such perspectives, Balinese noncrying would need no further explanation. People who have no heart beyond the act and are fully engrossed in their performance would not struggle with feelings of sorrow and distress. They would be set on the make-believe (which, Geertz assures us, is not make-believe, but the essence of things) and derive their greatest satisfaction and deepest distress from their role as polished, faceless, and composed enactors. "Stage fright" emerges naturally then as an encompassing fear (C. Geertz [1966] 1973a, 399–404, Keeler 1985, 152–53).

My case materials bespeak other concerns. The Balinese I know do cry, and they are happy, and a graceful and composed performance constitutes but a sector of their experience and one facet of their selves. Their greatest satisfactions and deepest anguish derive from relations with fellow beings who have both faces and hearts; and it is *because* people matter to each other and to themselves that feelings must be channeled into appropriate courses.

Both sanctions against expressing sadness and the affirmation of laughter as a positive response proceed from a view of humans as *in touch;* whose souls (*roh, jiwa-atma*) may reach out and literally connect with one another in sympathy; and who are easily swayed by one another's emotions. To mistake the bright face which Balinese cultivate for this purpose for an absence of feelings and a preoccupation with form is to miss the existential concerns of which it is evocative.

Perhaps Mead and Geertz went wrong because they misapplied a Western ethnotheory of emotions to a Balinese world and assumed that emotional expressions mean—at least fairly closely—what they appear to mean to us. Because Geertz also narrowed the world of Balinese to embrace only "public" behavior, I think he also failed to see that many elements observable within that realm draw on sitting rooms and kitchens (not to speak of back bedrooms, which may be the only place where a person feels she can let her feelings out) for their meanings.

From Mead's perspective, Suriati standing forth with a bright and clear face might be reduced to a prototypical Balinese "disallowed" to cry, while for Geertz she might be a masked player whose self was embodied in the act. Contrast this with a facet of how Suriati saw herself: as someone who must struggle to preserve self-respect and social respect and ensure cherished life concerns; with responsibility for her embattled mother in need of a cheerful home environment; with suitors, threatening sorcery, to be kept at bay; whose mental health and survival were at stake.

We know that she observed and judged herself when with others and in part distanced herself from her performance. It is clear from her exclamation of how angry she was with "them" for chiding her for showing traces of sadness, and also from her comment that men are more favorably positioned in that they need not always smile. We also know that she cried with some and not with others, contra Mead's statement that sorrow is not displayed. We fail to understand the dynamics of what is going on, and we misinterpret the world of Balinese, unless we recognize not only the value of, but also the effort involved in, constructing an appropriate "face" to cover a turbulent "heart."

It is the movement in social space that offers the best entry to the concerns people bring to bear on their self-management and social roles. The meanings of emotional expressions—both in the eyes of the actors and their significant others—depend on a perspective that sees the person whole, not dissected into distinct realms. Take the example of a mother submerged in tears because her child had run away: If you saw her thus you might conclude that Balinese are emotional after all. Conversely, if you saw her when the child had reappeared safe and sound, you might be impressed with her composure and "grace." In either case you would have a view of an end product, whereas *it is the process we must try to grasp:* how are lives composed, and with what views in mind? What are compelling, enduring concerns?

Cultural analyses mislead when extricated "texts" are explored for their general meaning, lending tasteful views of "end products" but no representation of the process that connects the expressions and embodies their logic.[3] That would leave you with a two-faced Suriati alternately cheerful and sad; or a mother first distressed, then calm, but with no grasp of the experience of being sad or that of having a child run away.

Take "cheerfulness" as another example. Cheerful/happy (*girang/gembira*), bright/happy (*cedang*), and friendly (*rameh*)—expressions that to some extent overlap—carry a fan of connotations to Balinese that they apply depending on their perspective and knowledge of the persons concerned. The radiant smile of someone recently bereaved is something else—to those who know—than the equally gleaming perfection of a man, heavily in debt, who greets his (privately sullen) benefactors with a studiously sunny gaze. Both may appear cheerful and composed to us. But ours are "thin" interpretations that grasp but a fraction of the meaning that such expressions convey to people who use symbols to live by, not merely to ponder.

A further reason why Geertz, in my opinion, misrepresents Balinese personhood emerges from these insights. Not only did he assume that the "face" that he could see was all that the Balinese could see, but also

126

that *they did not want to see anything else.* Thus he writes of "that acute sense of embarrassment" that overcomes the Balinese when they become party, always unwillingly it is implied, to another's faulty step or stuttering performance (C. Geertz [1966] 1973a, 385).

I cannot recognize the people I know in these representations. They, on the contrary, seem perpetually preoccupied with deciphering the hidden heart beyond the expression, and with why it is essential—at times a question of life or death—to do so. Their interpretations thus reckon always with a kind of "hidden agenda" within the visible, manifest one. This explains why "cheerfulness" may be variously read as "happiness" or "masking sadness" or "she does not know shame" or "she was so shy she laughed all the time." If, on the other hand, the spectacle comprised their selves, then interpretations that infer different motivations would be meaningless; and the analyst's task would be reduced to exploring the cultural surface of Balinese cheerfulness.

Far from being "embarrassed" at becoming party to others' hidden hearts, Balinese assume that people would be angry, offended, disappointed, or gleeful, or—if their hearts are good—they would be compassionate (*pedalem*). My own observations substantiate this. When confronted with another's mishap or stuttering performance, Balinese manifest a range of reactions ranging from mockery cast as laughter to compassion that is often similarly clad. They make use of subtle signs to convey the difference and to interpret another's response.

I have seen merriness verging on mockery erupt when people suddenly saw shamefacedness dull a person's bright facade. But I have also seen gentle sympathy expressed, as when people who had teased Suriati for being happily in love were apprised of their mistake. When someone succeeds in "making another down," I have seen people turn against the malefactor or join her in gleeful mockery because the attempt succeeded so well. Or they may express pity or dwell on the comic element in the situation.

In no case did I gain the impression that it was a sense of embarrassment with themselves that predicated their responses; rather, people responded in terms of assessments of a situation in which own and other's identities are an issue. It matters "to think well of oneself."

Emergent Insights and Themes

To trace back to that enlightening day when Suriati told me her heart and enabled me to grasp hitherto unintelligible connections between outer composure and inner struggle—it was a day when things fell into

127

a kind of pattern to me that set me on the track of exploring linkages among feeling, expression, morality, and health that have proved fruitful to the present day. With the wisdom of hindsight, let me try to group the emergent insights under a few central themes, though developmentally they crystallized little by little as I continued through the years to struggle to comprehend. Suriati was no longer unintelligible to me, but the world about her continued to be. What was at stake in their divergent expressions of interests and concerns? What identities were at issue?

The following grouping of analytical themes points to the directions in which my attempts to construe an answer moved.

1. *Emotion work.* Emotions are of deepfelt concern with regard to both inner feeling and outer expression. Control of the former relates to conceptions of mental and physical health, of the latter to a notion that expression channels feeling, hence also shapes health. But control of emotional expression is also linked with fears of mockery and shame that implicate feelings of self-respect and self-value (*harga diri*).

2. *Emotional imagery and linkages between affective states.* It appears that emotions are linked in composite ways that reflect deepfelt, culturally constructed notions of self and health. Expressed sadness is met with responses of "Forget it, be happy! Let bygones be bygones!" Anger is seen as the first cause of premature aging, while smiles and cheerfulness are rejuvenating. How are the different emotions conceived, in themselves and in relation to one another? Sadness and cheerfulness, as we have seen, are closely associated, whereas sadness is also linked with "shame." Are there other such syndromes of "linked" emotions, and to what conceptions do they attest?

3. *The cultural construction of fellow beings.* Dichotomized as "closest friends" versus "they" in regard to the expression of sadness, is this a significant contrast that also operates in respect of other emotions? A feeling of shame, as Suriati made clear, would be provoked only if "they," and not if her closest friends, should see her cry. Is the implied contrast here one of person or place? What are the categories of person and place in terms of which Balinese construe their world? What qualities are the different categories of fellow beings ascribed?

4. *The cultural construction of the self.* "I don't want them to think I have a broken heart . . ." said Suriati in a statement that vividly refutes the bold assertion that the Balinese do not count even to themselves (C. Geertz [1974] 1984, 128). She had a clear idea of who and what she wanted to be in the eyes of the world, but also to herself. She was not going to give "them" the chance to think her like a "widow," and she was critical of girls who acted polite and gracious (*polos*) yet seemed to

be lacking in self-respect. What are the standards in terms of which Balinese accord value to the self and to others? What is the place of internalized sanctions versus public control in construing the self or identity?

5. *The signal value of behavior and emotional expressions.* Suriati expressed a clear awareness of the symbolic value of affective language and nonverbal expressions. To appear in public with a "closed" face (*nyebeng*) for a girl is a statement apt to be read either "she is arrogant" or "she is brokenhearted," both of which confer criticism or even shame. Not to marry for a man is an act apt to be read as a public statement that he is a homosexual (*banci*), whereas he may in fact be brokenhearted. What are the major symbols that ego expects alter to go by in construing a judgment of herself? To what extent is there consensus about these signs so that we may speak of cultural models for assigning value to others? How rigid are these codes? Or are persons granted leeway and a measure of grace when their acts are held up for judgment?

The "Endless Struggle to Think Well of Oneself"

Once when I came back to Bali a friend, Ketut Artje, told me something terrible that had happened to his family in the meantime. "It was all in the papers, so everyone knows, yet no one speaks a word to me about it . . . I don't understand," said he, questioning me mutely.

He ought to know. He was a man widely respected, and feared, because of his intelligence, position, and power. To so much as mention the incident to him would be thought offensive and expected to elicit his wrath. It might be very dangerous indeed.

And yet this man, to whom everyone bowed and scraped, was visibly troubled by the apparent inauthenticity of friends and acquaintances. He perceived a gap between what their actions appeared to say and what he himself imagined them to be saying in their "heart of hearts" (*hati kecil*) and perhaps also to one another. Did he "hear" their laughter? Did he "see" their scorn? I do not know. For nothing more was said. But when the chance came not long after, he threw a grandiose party to celebrate an event, and he confided to me afterwards: "I cried, for I was so overcome with all the attention showered on me."

The incident illuminates aspects of Balinese notions of self and other and the complex symbolic valence of nonverbal signs. He was troubled, this man, by a silence that spoke louder than words, and he searched for clues to indicate what was actually being "said," clinging in the end to that rather elusive yardstick of attendance at a party for his consolation.

I offer the case as an example of compelling concerns, of doubts and self-doubt and efforts to reconcile one's notion of who one is with one's fears of who others might take one to be. It thus throws into relief that "endless struggle to think well of oneself" with which, I argue, everyday predicaments connect.

This man was not laughed at to his face, ever. His concerns, on the surface, bore little resemblance to Suriati's. And naturally so, for they were very differently positioned. He is a man, she is female. He is of mature age, she quite young. He is of high social position, she from low origins. He has power, she has none. And whereas he is not trusted but feared, she is widely reputed to have "a good heart."

Nevertheless, in his heart of hearts Ketut Artje grapples with the same kinds of concerns that propel and perplex her. He wants people to think well of him, and he gropes for evidence that they actually do. In this search he is in a sense more unfavorably positioned than she. She has a more or less adequate sense of what people actually feel-think, for they show at times unmercifully little inhibition in making their reactions clear to her. He, a person of high social rank, receives always his due of respect. He meets with nothing but deference and grace.

Does this console him? No. Friendly and polite gestures offer, as we have seen, ambiguous affirmation. For the other is no more perceived to be merged in the spectacle s(he) mounts than one's own self is submerged in the role and the performance one enacts. There is a play going on, as Geertz has so poignantly shown. But there is also a world behind the appearances, and it is primarily there that meanings are constructed: impressions are taken "in," actions are hammered "out," perceptions are filtered, judgments are made. The yardsticks and guidelines by which these actions proceed are culturally constructed, and thus the personal lives of people, whatever their position, share important features: people look to each others' hidden hearts for guidance as to what their expressed behavior signifies.

The position I take in understanding emotion—both feeling and expression—thus delves deep into experiences like this of Ketut Artje where emotions are not singled out and lend themselves to neat classification, but where, on the contrary, ambiguities show up; where people grope and struggle for answers and solutions in the midst of multiple concerns; and where the basic questions they ask themselves are not so much "what does this or that expression mean" but "what does she or he mean, or feel-think (of me, of herself), when (or despite the fact that) s(he) acts like this or that . . . ?"

Difficulties of interpretation may be a concern in every society. In Bali, because the range of expressed feeling-thoughts is strictly limited to a few that are generally endorsed, peculiar interpretive problems arise. It is not only that ego often cannot know what alter actually means, but she is also constrained from raising the point. We saw it in Issa's case. The compulsion of friendliness and politeness inhibits such a course.

This does not mean that people let themselves always be goaded by judgments about what might be the most "graceful" course. To be unperturbed and rise above the situation is easier when one has recourse to *other* means of trapping the world into a favorable response to oneself (as did Ketut Artje). Not so if you are female, poor, and vulnerable.

When Kede Mireh's husband was reputed to be mad, she felt she *had* to know whether people in saying so were right. So she went to ask a not-so-trusted friend whose judgment weighed in the matter. In this she exposed her desperation and vulnerability. She did precisely what Ketut Artje was not willing to do: confront "the said" within people's tacit expressions. She is unusual, and the case was unusual—yet it reveals a common predicament, the difficulty of living with uncertainty. It also reveals the highly personal character of judgments about what is most potently at stake in one's life.

Ketut Artje would not dream of so demeaning himself. He is a man, he is proud, he is also wealthy. He chose another way out of the morass of nagging doubt about what people might actually feel-think: he threw a party. He had this option, she did not. And he chose to regard the overwhelming attendance as proof that people liked him and respected him.

In fact it was not wholly so. I heard much criticism voiced from some people who had attended the party that it had been on too grandiose a scale—epitomizing his quest for power *and* his self-doubt and vulnerability. These were judgments which probably never reached Ketut Artje, yet perhaps he knows nevertheless, for he is both intelligent and sensitive. Or perhaps at this point in his life he could not afford to face such indications—and thus did not see them—though he "must" know they are there?

His own account of how both weather gods and guests had uniquely favored him on this occasion differed in significant respects from descriptions given by others of the sheer facts of the case. Whereas he was impressed that on this day torrential rains and thunder had struck down huge trees all over Buleleng while over his own home the sky was blue and clear—indicating that some guests must have paid a huge sum to a rain-balian to prevent the rain from falling—some guests exclaimed how they had been soaked from head to toe and how the umbrellas of visitors had been stacked to take up a whole room of Ketut's house.

There is nothing strange about the discrepancy of these accounts, from a Balinese point of view. Feeling-thoughts predicate one's vision and steer movement and action.[4] Ketut Artje needed to think well of himself after the blow that a family tragedy had struck to his self-esteem.[5] People hostile to him, on the other hand, would let few occasions for belittling his efforts pass.

Either the rain fell or it did not. (From descriptions of the storm that ravaged Buleleng on that day, I am inclined to believe it did.) My point is simply that interpretations of "facts," both facts of nature and social facts, proceed from particular viewpoints that are anchored in subjective experience. Suriati's interpretations of herself in relation to others were profoundly colored by her feeling-thoughts at different times of her life. I was surprised to find in 1988 that Ketut Artje now tells of the torrential rains that fell over his house on that day. He is now happy and can afford to face such previously disquieting facts.

Because emotions are seen by Balinese as immensely powerful in affecting vision, as ethnographers we also have to reckon with them.

Informants' accounts have in a sense to be checked for "emotion effect." It means that knowledge of their individual circumstances is essential to detect the compelling concerns that modify the interpretations people make.

"Singular Moments"

The three individuals depicted above, Ketut Artje, Suriati, and Kede Mireh, were not chosen for maximum effect or for being aberrant and exceptional. Needless to say, Balinese do not all exhibit such dramatic circumstances at the time of their lives when the anthropologist is there; yet I am struck with how frequently, in most Balinese lives that I know, such "singular moments" occur. For one it is when she is forced to marry a man "so short, she was on the verge of crying all through her wedding"; for another when her deceitful husband returns and starts acting the good man; for a third when she hits upon her daughter's diary and realizes she is just about to run away with a Muslim man; for a fourth when her daughter is sent home from school with a notice that she has not paid school fees for four months—and the mother had given her the money; for a fifth when a beloved daughter is about to move away, leaving the mother with "no one to laugh."

I could run through an almost endless number of such fateful or passing "singular moments" in singular lives. I have the impression that from the point of view of Balinese, life consists of a series of such that mark humdrum existences and give them significance and force, and where linear time and climax (contra Bateson [1949] 1972a, 112–15) are also of the essence. As Balinese construct experience, they seem to spice their lives with a sequence of such dramatic moments that are intensely lived through, somatically sensed, spontaneously narrated, and elaborated in anecdotes. Also, when they speak of others, they seem to "reach out" for such singular moments that are vividly retold in stories full of dramatic effect. They seem to epitomize what the other is, as envisioned by experiences she has gone through or brought upon herself.

Interpretations of the other—and of oneself in relation to her or him—draw on such a store of anecdotes. And fragments of such knowledge become public and circulate in the form of variations on similar themes in overlapping social circles. How can that be when lives are so sheltered, the "heart" opened up to only a few? Partly because of "seepage," indiscretion from the (not always) few. But partly also because the shared preoccupation with hidden hearts creates a milieu in which many are out to accumulate such knowledge; there is a generally high demand for it. Moreover, this focal interest sensitizes Balinese to cues and hints they can use to gain secret information. Such cues may then be used as stepping-stones for further probing interesting cases.[6]

There are other reasons for this interest in "singular moments." First, the criteria of success in sociability applaud the one who is clever at composing and telling stories, both of a humorous and sensational kind. Moreover, because Balinese live in a world where "accidents" do not occur, but minute incidents stand ablaze with moral and (super)natural meaning, they become attuned to reading snippets and signs for what they reveal of momentous significance.

Take the example of a girl who was helping to massage her sick uncle when she suddenly heard him whisper to his wife: "I am not strong [kuat] . . ." The rest was lost, but she imaginatively construes the rest of the sentence herself: "enough to take (i.e., accept) it." What does it mean? Surely, the uncle had asked for *susuk*—a special protection against black magic and harbinger of good luck—to be inserted in him, but he was too weak to "take" the force of the mystical power.[7] The moral? The girl must be terribly careful. The uncle is out to make her marry his son, and so she faces an almost unconquerable contestant.

This is an example of an utterance probed, but I take it the girl drew on a store of cues for her interpretation: biographical knowledge as well as her perceptions of facial expressions and the tone of voice of her uncle and aunt. When next she meets them she is likely to interpret their friendliness in a framework that accords this singular moment essential significance. Indeed, she "must," for it is by being alert to such cues that Balinese feel they can preserve a modicum of control over their health and their fates.

Methodologically the point I want to make is this: emotional expressions always occur with a cluster of *other* signs of significance: nonverbal clues, personal knowledge, "singular moments" are some. People's interpretation of emotional expressions thus draws on a repertoire of "singular moments" that serve to position people with regard to their orientations, and on a "hidden agenda" that serves as a key to what people are beneath (or within) the bright face it is incumbent on all to display.

Methodology: Displace "Emotion" and Place the Person Center Stage

To understand "emotion" it does not work, paradoxically, to focus on the phenomenon, emotion per se. Place the person center stage and see her grounded in a time-space that is peculiarly her own; where she gropes and struggles for value in her own and others' eyes as with such resources as she has at her disposal—energy, foresight, judgmental powers, material and other instrumental means—she attempts to make do and to cope.

Note that interest, both of the actor and her fellow beings, focuses not so much on any one emotional expression, but on a person experiencing and expressing herself while engrossed in multiple concerns. Predominant is the struggle to think well of oneself that we saw exemplified in Suriati's case, in Ketut Artje's endeavor to interpret the unsaid within people's respectful facades, and in the glimpse afforded of the couple who appeared gracefully at their malefactor's wedding.

To understand emotional expression one must thus adopt a perspective that links expression with a particular subject and life situation—what we might call positioning in social time-space. Slight signs under strong control will be read as evidence of strong emotions in a person when one knows that person to be caught up in a situation where strong emotions will be expected. Little wonder people said "may God give you patience" to Gede Mireh when her husband was reputed to be mad. They would know of her turmoil however bright she appeared. We need to apply a Balinese perspective that reckons with "hearts" as the source of feeling, desire, motivation, and will and with actors acting purposively to have an impact on the world. When Kede Mireh made her face look bright it was not only to express herself but to defend herself and accomplish matters of value.

Communicative acts, even in the form of minor displays of emotion, do not merely communicate, they also often serve ends. People express themselves because they have something to say, but also because they wish to make an impact, to affect the course of events and change undesired circumstance. In Bali to laugh when someone is dead is not merely a way of expressing oneself. It is also intended to *change* feeling and perception, *to act upon the world*. Likewise with the effort to control crying; it is not only to convey an image of oneself as someone who can manage one's heart. One also tries to keep oneself—and others—from crying because it is regarded as a way to foster health and happiness and facilitate the way of the deceased's soul to God (see chap. 8).

I am not saying that expression is always for practical ends, but that it may be; and that to get at the nature of experience it is important to investigate not only what people appear to "say" but also what they achieve by their gestures and emotional expressions.

Expressing to Act upon the World

This point may be illustrated if we turn to the case of a mother whose child, a young boy, had run away. She was in a condition of sheer despair, expressed in weeping, huddling in a corner, tearing her hair. Yet the moment she caught sight of her boy, her calm returned. Her voice as she called out to her daughter in the back bedroom betrayed no relief or other emotion. To the boy she merely said, "Have you eaten, slept? Go buy yourself some food; there is none in the house. Then take a bath."

Why did her expression change so dramatically the moment she caught sight of the boy? And how could she manage to effect such a drastic change? It was not that she appeared calm *after* she had managed to calm down. She produced an *instant effect* as one often sees Balinese do, and I presume she did so to act, not merely to express her mood.

It is reasonable to turn to her enduring concerns to understand what this transformation was all about. As the boy's mother, she will have to continue trying to raise this youth, who often made a nuisance of himself. If now he saw what power he had over her—how effective his course had been—how could she keep matters from getting entirely out of hand? Friends had already warned her that the boy's misbehavior was in part because he realized all too well how precious he was to her.

Was this how she thought? I cannot know. I had the impression that she acted spontaneously, the moment she caught sight of him. But it does not follow that the sudden studious calm and absence of signs of turmoil were a spontaneous expression of an inner emotional state. Rather, we must be prepared to look for what may have been at stake for her, and I find it most plausible—and also in accordance with the views I think Balinese would bring to bear on the matter—to ascribe to her a concern with the moment's strategy in her relationship with her adolescent son.

This analysis admittedly is speculative, but let a premise be added which augments its plausibility: emotional expression in Bali is generally pragmatic and often strategic. Balinese are reared to be aware of their hearts and their bodies and of the language they speak. Strategic self-display thus becomes a matter of habit; one is trained to size up a situation quickly and respond by proper emotional appearance. The mother's instant change from desperation to "composure" is more easily comprehended with this premise in mind. She had a lifetime's experience of having on many occasions to produce an instant clear, bright face—in the way that Suriati changed her "withered" face to a bright one as the occasion required.

Emotional expression thus belongs for its analysis within a mode of experienced relationships and life concerns. They are particular concerns, not general ones. Cultural analyses often presume people's activities to be an enactment of culture whether through official or discrepant discourses. In my work I am impressed with people's ingenuity in handling unique life situations—drawing on cultural bits and elements, yes, but fashioning a response that is uniquely theirs. Who but Ketut Artje would have thrown a party? Who but Gede Mireh have gone to a not-so-trusted friend to ask if her husband was mad? And who but Suriati would have answered with perfect grace when a friend sniped at her for less than excellence in mathematics: "And does the rat beget lions for children?"

Thus she positioned both the other and herself, belittling the other's claim to self-pride and underscoring her own achievement. She came from humble origins, had made her way from nothing to learn what she knew by herself. The other came from a privileged position, she had a father who was educated—no wonder as his progeny she excelled.

Lions and rats—evocative images that bespeak a world of compelling concerns when juxtaposed and expressed in the proper context. A party—testimony to economic status and political position, but also to an effort to extract a response of affection and respect when doubts assail and one sees no other way of alleviating them: "I cried, for I was so overcome with all the attention showered on me."

Feeling-Thought as Analytical Category

In trying to make out Suriati's gaiety and the laughter of her acquaintances and friends, I find myself engaged in problems related to the study of a field that has burgeoned in anthropology over the past ten years. I refer to what is generally called the study of "emotion." [8]

Implicit in the preceding has been an argument that the field is somewhat misconceived. On the one hand, I think that a focus on "emotion" encourages attention to phenomena and concepts per se, whereas experience should loom larger. More important, I believe that elevating "emotion" to the analytical level reiterates a contrast Western science draws between feeling and thinking, [9] when the case may actually be, as Balinese are convinced, that they are integrally linked as "feeling-thought." The *significance* of viewing feeling and thought as either linked or distinct is immense. In the next two chapters I deal with some consequences from a therapeutic perspective. Here a more general and analytically fundamental implication should be noted: that of validity.

For the field of cross-cultural psychiatry Kleinman (1986, 1988a), Marsella and White (1982), Simons and Hughes (1985), and others have done much to expose the dangers of applying Western diagnostic labels to experiential matters that may have fundamentally different meanings for people of other cultural backgrounds. I fear that "emotion," as a characteristically Anglo-Saxon label, [10] likewise carries with it connotations that are bound to make us prejudge what we are out to explore: how people actually feel and think about these matters.

Let me be more specific: In our attempts to breach an all-cognitive concept of culture and impress upon the world and ourselves that feelings are also culturally constructed and socially significant, we have been at pains to define "emotion" in a valid way. Major progress was made when Michelle Rosaldo characterized emotion as "*embodied* thoughts, thoughts seeped with the apprehension that 'I am involved'" (1984, 143, italics in original). Catherine Lutz, whose writings have been similarly influential, views as a distinguishing mark of emotion that it refers to "the intensely meaningful as that is culturally defined, socially enacted, and personally articulated." Its value is in "orienting us toward "things that matter rather than things that simply make sense" (1988, 5).

These are major achievements in making "emotion" a legitimate field of study and underscoring both its overall rationality and its culturally constructed character. But I think the time has come now when continued emphasis on "emotion" as a phenomenon in its own right might prove counterproductive. Two issues concern me here. First, I question whether "emotion" as a concept connotes the "intensely meaningful" any more than "thought" does. Rather, I think that this is true of *some* emotions, *some* of the time, but also of thoughtful experience, at times. I believe that the distinction takes as its prototype certain more deep-felt emotions as the sign of authenticity and generalizes those beyond validity. To make "intensely meaningful" a distinguishing mark of "emotion" may be invalid, as I think it is in most people's everyday experience that much emotional life, far from being "intensely meaningful," is rather dour and dull—the way surges of thoughts also are.

Further, is the feeling that "I am involved" any more telling of ordinary, everyday emotion than of ordinary, everyday thought? Does it not emanate from experiences connected with the mind as much as with the heart? Indeed, is the contrast not overdrawn, or perhaps even unwarranted? I think so, and I think that an emphasis on "emotion" is bound to reify a notion we entertain of separate mental processes in which flow different types of experience, when it is only by facing the full consequences of a view that the Anglo-Saxon emotion-thought split might be a myth[11] that theory building will proceed fruitfully (Wikan 1990). From a Balinese point of view, splitting feeling from thought reflects a misguided perception of human experience and an amoral stance (see chap. 14). Because there *is* no difference between feeling and thought—though their embodied sensations may be different—Balinese with whom I discussed the matter advise us to rethink our analytical concept so it will reintegrate what Westerners have split. Indeed, I have grown convinced that feeling-thought or thought-feeling[12] may be the better concept in that it does justice to a *flow of experience* which is neither embedded "in" the heart nor "in" the mind. It flows.

I explore some consequences of this view throughout, but one in particular should be noted here: the Balinese perception that feeling is as rational and as conscious as thought; and that without "listening to one's heart" it is impossible to appreciate (*menghayati*) any situation, to act morally and compassionately. Michelle Rosaldo's point that emotions are *moral acts* in that they involve "a mix of intimate, even physical experience and a more or less conscious . . . judgment concerning self-and-situation" (1983, 139) squares well with Balinese perceptions (although they would be likely to reformulate "more or less conscious," because consciousness is presumed as integral to feeling-thought). So when a person does not "listen to the heart," not lack of consciousness but lack of will is indicated.

Feeling-Thought as Moral Choice

An original presumption of Robert Solomon's, that emotions have a "choice" aspect (1980),[13] is in accordance with Balinese experience and is an essential premise of their ethnotheory of feeling-thoughts, though I think it may be unfounded in general terms. I have worked in one place where people would protest against a suggestion so absurd—that there should be anything volitional about emotions! Poor people in Cairo see feelings as natural and unavoidable responses to set types of behaviors and events. Nothing there for the individual to "choose." The choice remains entirely with the other, who determines one's own response by her acts. (Often it is not even a two-way but a three-way causal chain in which the other is seen as helplessly manipulated by a third person—but that is a complication we need not enter into here.)

In Bali, by contrast, feeling-thoughts are regarded as precisely that: the *choice* and *responsibility* of the person and her closest kin. They are moral acts, truly the structures through which one lives the world (Solomon 1978, 188). Consequently, they cannot be left to a person's own devices, but they must come under the control of the group. As with the air hostesses studied by Arlie Hochschild (1983) who were compelled to manage their hearts for commercial purposes, so with Balinese, but for very different reasons. Culture intervenes, by way of its human agents, to appropriate what we—and the Cairenes—may see as the precincts of the soul: one's heart, one's natural, spontaneous response.

Feelings must be molded and chiseled to comply with societal regulations not only in their outer expressed form, but also in their inner pattern. Balinese part ways with the air hostesses in that control and conscious shaping are seen as a moral good. It is the *only* way to stake out a pleasurable life for oneself and one's social others. Morality and judgment are the essence of emotional life.

Laughter Reconsidered

We will end by returning to Suriati's case and seeing how some of these generalizations apply to emotions as choices and moral acts and to the positioned character of interpretations. We will jump a year in time and meet her as her life had taken an unexpectedly happy turn and she was going to get married. A year of much suffering lay behind (see chap. 11) but need not concern us here. We will look instead at the responses of acquaintances and friends when they were apprised of the happy news.

I was with her as she went about inviting people to her wedding. In the course of the first three days we visited some twenty families. They included both close friends and people who were in the category "them"—people who in some sense were important in her life but with whom she did not otherwise feel close. For most of them, this was the first that they knew of her newfound happiness.

They expressed surprise and happiness on her behalf. In the course of cheerful conversation in which laughter and teasing flowed, they elicited detailed information about the man, who met with the approval of everyone: his reputed good conduct, medium-good position, respectable family background, and looks that were the marvel of everyone earned him much expressed praise. But after a while laughter subsided, joking came to a halt, and what next followed took *me* by surprise. Voices grew soft and sympathetic, eyes filled with compassion and care, and they began to talk of what had happened to her the year before. In detail they went over the story of the young man's death. Also this time there was laughter, but of a different kind. Leavitt's concept of "feeling along with" [14] (1985) springs to my mind. It was as if—no longer remote—they had placed themselves *along with* her, expressing for the first time what they knew she must have gone through. It did not happen in every house where we went, but it did in most, enough to make me sense a pattern.

For Suriati perhaps it was a cathartic experience. For the first time that I knew of she could talk her experience through with people who were in the category "they." And she could do it in a manner "seeped with the apprehension that 'I am involved'" (M. Rosaldo 1984, 143). Previously, when she had talked, she had made the boy seem an acquaintance or even less—the subject of a narrative she had heard.

Afterwards, still filled with surprise at what I understood as a belated declaration of sympathy on people's part, I ventured to remind her of how angry she had been with them before because of their laughter that she had read as scorn (*ejek*).

She leaped to their defense: "Oh no! They laughed to take the sadness out! Maybe they were afraid that I might kill myself because I was so confused, due to my sadness. They laughed to make my heart happy from sadness . . ."

A confused (*bingung*) interpretation is replaced by a fresh and calm (*somboh*) one. A mocking (*mengejek*) response is reinterpreted as a compassionate (*kasian*) one. Laughter, which is inherently multivocal in the view of Balinese, suddenly appears unequivocal: "Oh no! They laughed to take the sadness out . . . !"

Was it her exhilaration on this day of happiness that made her seem so sure? Or had she perhaps experiences from her personal life that corroborated what she now clearly saw? I suddenly remembered the many times I had seen *her* laugh at other people's distress and been disgusted with her as with other Balinese. Mead's interpretation that Balinese were lacking in thoughtfulness had then seemed all too plausible (above, p. 124). Somehow these pieces of observation had remained disconnected in my mind. After all, what *they* did had seemed so much worse: to laugh in connection with death! *Her* laughter had seemed more childish and harmless in its unfeelingness: she laughed at lesser calamities.

A mass of presuppositions that are part of a Western ethnotheory [15] of emotions often unknowingly guide our response. And the confusion under which others labor when at times their feelings get in the way of their vision is also part of an anthropologist's predicament.

We are all positioned in terms of particular life experiences that facilitate and impede certain understandings—not least in the field of "emotion."

CHAPTER EIGHT

Laughter, Sadness, and Death Reconsidered

How can anyone
laugh who knows of
old age, disease, and death?
—THE LORD BUDDHA

That's why, if someone
is sad, we laugh to
make their hearts
happy from sadness.
—BALINESE MAN

The circle is closing, as the last chapter brought us back to where we had begun: with my inability to grasp that laughter may be as meaningful a response as any other to tragedy, loss, and sorrow.

Death in the West calls for a certain kind of "natural" response, to cry.[1] If people cannot express their sorrow, they should be helped to do so. Not necessarily by me, or by you, but by someone. It is a premise of our Western ethnotheory of emotions that people must get their sorrow out, somehow.

As I am writing these lines a friend, an American, has just told me how, after a series of deaths in her family, she went to see a psychiatrist. All she did with him at her appointed hour was cry. No talking, just crying, for an hour twice a week for some months. And he said to her how badly he felt that she must pay him so dearly just to cry. But she did not mind. No one else wanted to see her do it—though she had many friends.[2]

This event took place some years ago. Times are changing, and yet . . .

Our ways of handling death would no doubt seem callous to Balinese. To recoil from the dead body and let strangers handle it; to avoid a bereaved soul because we do not know how to speak or express our compassion; to "forget" the dead once they are buried and let them remain in the soil forever; no daily offerings to them in the houseyard temple; no yearly reunions with them as on Balinese *Galungan* when their souls are invited to the earth to be feted, honored, and pleasurably

142

gratified by their relatives who still walk the earth; no annual wakes in the graveyard where all relatives, old and young, congregate to spend the night with the souls of the dead, again replete with offerings, flowers, and lavishly decorated foods;[3] no searching to placate them in the course of everyday life where health, welfare, and family harmony are seen as dependent on the ancestors' grace and goodwill. And in the end no large-scale celebration to help their souls be released from the cycle of rebirth through cremation in a spectacle as splendid as the descendants can afford, the culminating event after weeks of elaborate ceremony and feasting (see plates 5, 6, 12, 14, and 15).

The latter in fact may be an occasion for intensely evoked emotionality. I have many times seen Balinese burst into profuse, uncontrolled crying. For a brief moment in time they are reunited with the soul of a beloved spouse, parent, or child before the latter will merge into *Moksa* (Nirvana), as they hope, and be released from the cycle of rebirth (see plates 7 and 13).

We have seen that crying is *also* from a Balinese viewpoint a natural, spontaneous response to acute sadness and loss. They are distressed to hear that some foreigners have taken them to be different from what they perceive as the essence of true humanity: that attachment and affection provoke deep and yearning sorrow when the beloved one is gone. Crying, say they, is what everyone must do in the face of such experience.[4]

Why Does Laughter Predominate?

So the question we face is no longer why do the Balinese not cry— for they do—but why do they *also* laugh and strive to convince themselves and one another that "what is dead is dead"?

It is a testimony to their intense emotionality that they do, that sadness cannot be left to run what *also* to Balinese is its otherwise natural course. At stake are the well-being of the self, of the other, and of the soul of the deceased.

Emotions are not to be tampered with or treated lightly, any more than are bodily movement and gestures. Expression works *on* feeling-mind in Bali, and it also works *on* the mindful bodies of others to whom one relates. This is an axiom of all social life and of well-tested indigenous health theories.

Moreover, emotion works *on* the souls of the recently deceased, who continue to care for and be in touch with their beloved who still walk the earth.

143

It is no little responsibility to be saddled with (perceptible) influence on a soul's passage to God. But in Bali it is precisely this onus which weighs on the living, and how they acquit themselves depends in large measure on how they enact/express their feeling-thoughts. It is not, as in many cultures, only a question of performing appropriate rituals that determines whether the soul will be set free to proceed on its way to God. Rituals matter, but not alone. Vital also are *emotional* responses of persons beloved by the soul.

A Balinese ethnotheory of feeling-thoughts is thus sustained by (super)natural sanctions. The microcosm of the self is linked with the macrocosm of society and the (super)natural world through a construction of individual emotional expression as a force to shape health or undermine it, make or break social relations, countervene or provoke assaults of black magic, and facilitate or hamper the soul's way to God.

There might be said to be three parties in this social drama of coping with grief. Their vulnerability to one another and the force and magnitude of dangers that loom explains, I believe, why the drama is successfully enacted again and again. As with Suriati, however much the pressure weighs, one keeps a bright and smiling face—for oneself, for the others, and for the soul of the deceased.

What Is at Stake for the Living at Death?

What is at stake for the living at death—both bereaved and compassionate others—is evoked by this statement of a man, middle-aged, of commoner caste, who has fathered nine children and lost four. According to him, sadness should not be expressed because

> we Balinese are very sensitive [*perasaan*]. We have no defense against feelings. When you are sad, it's like you're being sick in the heart: you feel very weak [*lemah*] and vulnerable, you have no energy or power [*bayu*], you are always confused [*bingung*], you cannot think or plan for your life . . . When we see someone sad, we can become like that too. We will think about their problem, about what the people tell, and feel longing [*kelangen*] with them [that is, remember one's own beloved dead and feel sad]. It will be dangerous. Maybe we will also be sick. So we have this principle:
>
> Don't you always think about your problem.[5] Everyone has it, not just you. You must manage your heart so that you can forget your sadness. Otherwise, if you are sad, it may spread onto another . . .

That's why, when we see another sad, we give advice and laugh to make their hearts happy from sadness [*menghibur hatinya*].

Laughing in an Effort to Do One's Best

To members of many cultures it is not self-evident how laughter may dispel sadness and instead facilitate happiness. Rather, the Balinese response might seem—as it did to Suriati at one time—mocking and unfeeling. I am reminded of an Indian, married to a Burmese from Bangladesh, who told me how for years their marriage had been severely strained whenever they visited her family. Her relatives, and she with them, had seemed to him totally lacking in compassion.

Living in a war zone with many casualties, when his wife met with her relatives after long absences they would speak of the recently dead and burst into peals of laughter. No sadness expressed, but tragedy treated as if it were a gay and joyous event. So it had seemed to him until he heard me lecture about Balinese. And he came running after me in the street, exclaiming how I had helped in their marriage!

That (some) Burmese and (some) Vietnamese (cf. Solomon 1978, 181–82) do as Balinese and laugh instead of cry in situations where *we* expect crying as a natural response does not mean that death and bereavement mean the same to them all. I draw the comparison here only to reduce the uniqueness of the Balinese and, by implication, shake our self-assurance that our way is the natural and right. A large and expanding literature on grief and mourning (e.g., Averill 1968, Danforth and Tsiaras 1982, R. Rosaldo 1984, Rosenblatt 1983, Rosenblatt, Walsh, and Jackson 1976, Schieffelin 1976, Stroebe and Stroebe 1987) attests to great variations cross-culturally in how grief is experienced and bereavement expressed.

The Balinese response attests to *particular* conceptions of life in the world. Theirs is a life-celebrating response that is in part motivated by fear but is also reflective of interpersonal compassion and an ethos that singles the person out as in no small measure the maker of her own fate. This may seem a paradox, given a collectivistic organization and perceptions of predestination (*karma pala*) and (super)natural justice. But in everyday life these concepts are called upon to explain misfortune ex post facto, not to relieve persons of responsibility for "doing their best."

The injunctions to "make one's heart the best" (*melahang ngabe keneh*), "make one's character the best" (*melahang ngabe abet*), and "make one's body the best" (*melahang ngabe ibe*) resound through everyday discourse and implore people to take responsibility for their own attitude (*tingkah*) and appearance/action (*semu/bikas*).

"If we do the best, people will be shy (*malu*) to be jealous (*dengki*) with us," say Balinese, meaning that an inborn tendency to wish ill on people who are better positioned than oneself will be quenched by shame when one meets with the example of goodness and virtue.

To laugh in the face of sorrow is an example of "doing the best" that is crowned with good health, good repute, and a feeling of self-value. To brood and persist in sorrow, on the other hand, is to declare oneself selfish and insensitive to the well-being of others. It is also destructive to good looks—sadness being seen as the first cause of premature aging in this society that puts such value on everlasting youthfulness, particularly in women. "We believe, if the face is bright and clear, we will stay forever young," say Balinese.[6]

They might have said "strong" instead. "Young" here refers to face, soul, and body: one's total embodied self. Laughter makes one forever young. It creates health and happiness and good social relations. This is a premise of life. A further premise is this: that laughter works *on* feeling-mind and body, clearing the heart and with it the face, thus also strengthening the life force—*bayu*.

Health is a function of energy flow—of maintaining a strong life force. It is also dependent on (super)natural sanctions and one's ability to live in harmony with deities, ancestors, demons, and sundry (super)-natural spirits, beside fellow human beings. But in every respect it pays to have good vital power, for it facilitates good judgment. This power—the *bayu*—combats illness and restores health. It has physical and spiritual qualities. And it responds to both feeling and expression.

It responds to expression because expression shapes feeling. This too is a premise of life. But it is more, it is experienced and felt. As sugar is sweet to the tongue, or beauty pleasing to the senses, so does laughter give a light and sweet, fresh and clear sensation to body and mind. Sadness, by contrast, weighs one down, burdens one, and makes one weak. It erodes strength, laughter builds it.

Sadness does more. It spreads. But so does laughter. To see someone sad is to feel-think sadness and thus to be sad. Or it is instinctively to mold one's face into a similar response—as in empathy—and thus re-produce the bad feeling in oneself. One is easily reminded of bad experiences in one's own life and will feel sad also because of that. But if one laughs, one will make others happy as well, for laughter works even on unwilling minds. It changes perception, takes the bitter taste away; and when one wills oneself to happiness by making an effort to laugh, the gain is manifold as the body is swept up in a surge of good energy flow.

Making the Heart Happy from Sadness

The response of Balinese to others' distress builds on such a store of assumptions. Here is the testimony of a twenty-five-year-old man three days after his friend's young wife had suddenly died (from black magic, as they suspected and later had confirmed). I met him after the third night's wake at his friend's house. He looked tired and weak and told me how he had been absent from work for two days because he was so exhausted and troubled by headache.[7] I asked him how they had spent the night during the wake.

> Oh, we sat and talked about what had happened, about her illness and the events surrounding her death, and we laughed and joked a lot to make the family's hearts happy from sadness. We say things like "what is dead is dead" and that they should let bygones be bygones, and because the husband is still young and should remarry soon, we also advise him that "the world is bigger than a *kelor* leaf" and that "where one stick is broken, another will grow . . ."
>
> We say many such things, for we must do all we can to make the family forget their sadness and be happy.[8] As long as we stay, they are happy. Once we go, they will be sad. So we must stay all night every night until the burial and for three nights thereafter. The women are busy preparing food and the materials for the ceremony, while we, the men, gamble to keep ourselves awake, and we give what we gain to the family to help with their expenses.
>
> It is okay to be sad, but not to be crying. A little only when you go to the graveyard. Like when my uncle died—his youngest wife killed him by putting poison in his pillow—I was very sad in my heart, and also sick from shock [*mekesiyab bayune*], for I had seen him well in the morning, and three hours later he was already dead. But I hid my sadness and kept it to myself. I cried only a little when I was alone. It is bad if we express our sadness, for everyone will see and be sad and perhaps crying too. It will be bad for all and very dangerous . . .
>
> So the bereaved look happy when we are there. But I am sure they are sad and perhaps crying too when we are gone.

Of course we know that people are sad even when they do not show it.

Laughing for Catharsis and Health

In voicing these views, Balinese attest to particular conceptions of what is at stake ("it will be very dangerous") and a particular, culturally fashioned theory of health, morality, and social obligation. But they also concur with a steadily growing clinical literature that confirms the effects of emotions and mental state on health.[9] Their experience of feeling as affectable by expression[10] is also borne out by psychological experiments using laughter/humor to induce good feeling (Scheff 1979; Cousins 1976, 1979); by techniques that rely on gestures and posture to train feeling-acting in actors (Bloch, Orthous, and Santibanez-H. 1987);[11] and by explorations into the role of catharsis[12] that stress its somatic-emotional component beside the intellectual one (Nichols and Zax 1977). Laughter may discharge emotion as much as crying does, but it is not common in the West to think that it might discharge suffering conferred by bereavement. The assumption is widely held that tears are the proper discharge for grief (Marris 1974; Nichols and Zax 1977, 95–96).

In fact, laughter is found to be a forceful releaser of pent-up feeling, as it involves the three components inherent to any emotion: neurophysiological, behavioral-expressive, and phenomenological or experiential (Nichols and Zax 1977, 7). It is also found to release aggression and anger, emotions found to be common components of grief worldwide (Rosenblatt, Walsh, and Jackson 1976; Marris 1974, 26; Osterweis, Solomon, and Green 1984, 60, 289).

> Laughter is based on a free release of aggression in a form which is socially acceptable. Freud spent a lifetime looking for a harmless, non-aggressive joke. When he finally thought he had found one it did not stand up to later analytic scrutiny. All jokes are hidden aggressions. They must carry the aggression so well disguised and still so elegantly expressed that it does not interfere with our conscious censorship which does not tolerate open hostility, nor with our conscious . . . (or) unconscious awareness of the hostile trend. . . . The psychic energy which is needed for repression is released in laughter. (Grotjahn 1970, 174)

In Bali, expression of anger/aggression is strongly negatively sanctioned on every occasion. Does this mean that they do not experience such feelings? Clearly not. The prevalence of black magic testifies to their occurrence, and when someone is suspected of having killed a person by black magic, the bereaved express in narratives strongly negative feelings against her/him. Does the laughter they usually engage in on every "tragic" occasion help release such angry feelings? And do Balinese occasionally feel anger even against a beloved deceased? Suriati's poetry which she wrote shortly after her friend's death to express her grief gives evidence also of anger. And when I asked her what that meant, she said she did not know, she just felt like that. Are such feelings then also released by laughter?

Many questions cry out for answers. Because laughter is not assumed to belong with bereavement by researchers in the West, we have masses of studies on the cathartic effects of crying and next to nothing on laughter. It is also questionable what value experiments would have. We would need context-laden assessments of people tuned in to or living by laughter as a formula for health to assess what effects laughter might have as a means of conquering despair. Bali lends itself to such analysis. And let it be remembered: Balinese do cry, sometimes forcefully, prolongedly, other times only "maybe two minutes," as a man said of himself. Laughter comes in as a replacement, a remedy, because there is so much at stake. Perhaps too, in a land of so much laughter, laughter becomes addictive, a bodily need, releasing as it is released, recharging energy in a body that has learned to depend on it?

Crying, by contrast, is less familiar: a spontaneous release that does good in small doses but is frightening if it goes on. It exposes despair, opens up a void that might not heal. But when laughter is resorted to, the mind swells again, the body feels better, one gathers *bayu* (life force). Take as your frame of reference a body-soul swathed since infancy in the bittersweet atmosphere of laughter and clinging to it whenever danger is felt. Try to feel the flow of life that emanates from releasing sorrow by laughing. Feel-think this flow as the essence that keeps you alive on earth. Add the soul of a beloved deceased, whose presence you can feel *trusting* in you to relinquish attachment by letting go.

And laughter becomes sensible, the most rational response. Add fellow beings for whom you care, relying on you not to besmirch them too by your sorrow. What option is there then but to smile and laugh? Perhaps, indeed, this is the better way to handle bereavement?

> There was a lady who wept because she had so many misfortunes. She poured out her misery to Buddha who told her that these miseries would go away if she would obtain a seed from a house that had never known sorrow. The next week Buddha found her singing happily. When the Enlightened One asked if

she found the Seed of Happiness, the old woman replied: "No, Blessed One. I went to every house seeking it and found no house that had not known sorrow. Everywhere I went I saw troubles much worse than my own, and from these I learned that I do not have it bad at all." (Cambodian folktale, quoted in Boehnlein 1987, 765)[13]

The Indonesian sage and scientist Prof. S. Takdir Alisjahbana notes how the Indonesian term for personality, *pribadi* (commonly used also in Bali), derives from *prih* (pain) and *badani* (bodily) and thus "stresses the concepts of pain and effort as being most characteristic of personality. A Buddhist influence can perhaps be discerned in the Indonesian concept of personality." (Alisjahbana, 1966, 16). It is my impression that the Buddhist influence in Balinese culture is pronounced (see also Barth, 1991). And Balinese attempts to cope build on precisely such assumptions as the Cambodian folktale expounds. As the man said, "So we have this principle: don't you always think about your problem. Everyone has it, not just you."

It would indeed be a sorrowful world if the reasons people have to be unhappy should also justify them to expose such unhappiness. The Cambodian legend, I think, would be intuitively understandable to Balinese feeling-minds. When two or more are together and laughter resounds, it is often to the accompaniment of tales recounted of dreadful fates and misfortunes. Laughter punctuates the telling; with exposed gums and wide-open eyes people seem to release muscular tension as laughter explodes in audible bouts similar to the gasps of breath that follow a stressful physical experience. Tragedy and comedy seem interwoven, and comedy is used to bolster the morale needed to face a world of so much tragedy.

> Always we Balinese say, "Lucky you!" If someone has
> broken a leg we say, "Lucky you that you are still alive!" If a
> person has lost her money we say, "Lucky you that you threw
> away your bad luck!" And we laugh to make her heart happy
> from sadness. What more sensible thing could we do?

Bouchet has written of humor as feeding on the grotesque, the absurd, the hopeless, the ugly, the evil, in order to transform it into merriment, zest for life, and constructive response (Bouchet 1986, 131–34). Greenwald notes how laughter may be effective in therapy by making people see the absurdity, the hilarity, the farce of life, and then enjoy it (1975, 119).[14]

Laughter, in these views, emerges as life-celebrating, life-sustaining, food for thought, and the most *sensible* response. Balinese use laughter as a kind of "shock treatment" to shake people out of their despair. When it works so well, it is in part on account of its very ambiguity. With its finely shaded meanings of friendliness, compassion, ridicule, scorn, hostility, humility, shyness, shame—to mention some that are salient in experience—laughter has the power to "shake" distressed souls trying to salvage some self-respect and social respect. I sensed I could detect a kind of fury at times in the determination not to give in and let people laugh at oneself.

"Laughter is man's way of showing his superiority over other men" (Weber 1970, 120). Truly, Balinese feel superior when they manage to laugh in spite of life's cruel fate and have others marvel at their ability to do so. It is also a way of shaming the other who caused one such pain. But above all laughing may work wonders for one's feeling of self-value and command of one's life situation. When one laughs at the "resistance" life offers against oneself, one is not wholly a victim at its mercy.

By an ingenious "work of culture"—to use Obeyesekere's incisive term (1985)—laughter for Balinese works admirable effects on their highly involved body-selves. Because of the way they fashion feeling-expression-body-soul into a coherent *conception* (ibid.), laughter "works" in ways it would not do with us, for its tributaries are other than we have been socialized to sense. We do not seek out situations that would make us glad when we are sad, nor do we like people to laugh and joke in the face of our distress. We do not recognize the sweetness of the taste of laughter as something as soothing as sun to a freezing body; it is not appealing to our senses as a tonic that can "take sadness away" or make one "forget" one's sadness. We tend to be skeptical of such connections, for ours are differently constituted body-selves.

Among Balinese laughter works to enhance bodily well-being by making the blood flow more freely in the veins. It releases pressure, clears the veins and softens tissues and muscles. This flow is felt palpably, emphatically, as a surge of energy, life force, precursor of good feeling-thinking. Laughter changes perception in an immediate, experiential sense. Contra Western views of psychotherapy grounded on the premise that health is best achieved by uncovering layers of suffering and lingering protractedly over them, Balinese views are distinctly the opposite: While "great" problems will require a person to find solutions and not merely to "forget," "forgetting" is always part of the procedure, as is the good feeling-thinking that laughter sustains.

"Forgetting" does not mean what we associate with the term: sup-

151

pressing or repressing. It means simply what it says: not to think of the experience, and thus not to feel it. On the premise that feeling-thinking is one integral process, "forgetting" makes sense. Sadness will dwindle if you stop pondering your distress. For sadness is nothing in and of itself. It is created and recreated by a state of mind and exists in and through this.

Replied a *lontar* expert when I asked how he would explain the "problem" that people sometimes feel sad though they try desperately to think good thoughts: "Then it is because they occasionally lapse into sad thoughts—they do not manage to be constant in their good thinking. If you only think good thoughts, it is impossible to feel sad."

And to my question, "Can sadness not be stored in an unconscious?" he answered, "Oh, no! [laughter] There is no storage room in the body. Even memory is only an aspect of thinking."

Substitute for this premise a Western view of feeling and thinking as separate, and your ability to mold sadness will be considerably reduced. Now sadness exists apart as part of a distinct system of natural urges or affects. Thinking, by contrast is rational, cognitive, and the two are linked by only weak and indirect tributaries. On this premise "forgetting" means steering underground, for feeling and thinking are reified, regarded as "things" and not as processes.

Nichols and Zax observe that it is only because we tend to think of sadness as a thing that can be stored that we can speak of repression or suppression. Actually, there is no such *thing*. What is happening is just that

> part of the natural action sequence [crying] is being avoided. Catharsis, then, [defined by them as "a process that relieves tension and anxiety by expressing emotions" (1)] is part of completing the action sequence. By finishing it, the patient may become clearer about the experience, less tense, and more able to become involved with current events. (1977, 209)

Substitute "crying *and* laughing" for "crying" and Bali may be accommodated within this frame. Perhaps indeed laughing may be as much part of a "natural action sequence" as crying. It depends on what the sequence is intended to accomplish and from whence it sprang. What experience is it a part of, and what meaning does this have to the person(s) concerned?

"Nature," as we know, never appears in natural form in the human body-self. Even allowing for the existence of universal natural reflexes such as crying to relieve pain or laughing to discharge embarrassment

(Scheff, 1979:260), we may still have to take into account a *meaning* component when considering catharsis. When crying is experienced, as among Balinese, as dangerous, its somato-psychic effects are also likely to be other than what Western psychological theories presume. These are issues I think should be explored.[15]

Balinese share an assumption we also preach: that you have to get your sadness "out" somehow. For them, talking and laughing and thinking good thoughts is the way. And in no instance is it advisable to plunge oneself into misery and pain. What the Buddha told the woman, Balinese are wont to remind themselves: "There are problems in every house." If all focused on theirs, the world would be a grim place. We might all sit down and cry, and then who would carry on production, do the work of the gods, and perform the innumerable small tasks needed to keep community life going? Nor would there be any incentive or energy for these tasks, for sadness drains away one's resources.[16] The right to drive oneself to despair—which seems a part of our invaluable freedom in the West—is not compatible with the premises on which Balinese life is grounded.

Bali thus presents a kind of natural testing ground for the hypothesis that laughter is therapeutic under conditions of natural stress. And Balinese have highly involved body-selves to show as evidence for the test. While it may pain one to meet with laughter when one is deeply distressed, the pain relates to fear that one is laughed *at* and not with. And while we should not underestimate the suffering this may cause, laughter experienced as scorn may also have therapeutic effect. Suriati recognized this retrospectively. What would have become of her if the "mocking" had not stirred her to mobilize positive resources within herself?

Laughter works best when it is recognized as compassionate. But even when it veils ridicule it may exact a positive response from the sad person, who will be reminded of one's moral social obligation to be friendly and not *sombong* (arrogant). In this it compels the body-self. As clinical research has shown, it is more difficult to feel sad if one is surrounded with merriment. Moreover, Balinese tend to *seize on* an opportunity to try and be happy.

In a sensitive discussion of an experiment in which he tried to record the frequency of smiles and laughter, Fry observed how his own conscious use of similar expressions to respond to impending mirth steadily inhibited the other's response and froze it midway: "In my anticipating it, it would fail to appear. I had entered a different mood. The intention of recording the smile contributed to the moment in such a manner as to alter its nature and puncture the humor. . . . There were many smiles that died unborn" (Fry 1968, 4–5). But in Bali, if you smile forcedly but with goodwill, the other tends to smile in return. People will also seek out situations in which they will be compelled to smile and laugh—because others do—in an effort to overcome sadness and distress. Take as your premise not a Western "I have a right to happiness" but a Balinese "life is full of sorrows (*susah*)," and laughter may indeed emerge as the way to a happier life.

As the quote from Fry reminds us, laughter in situations where it is unnaturally feigned *means* something different from what it does where it belongs, is expected, should occur, and has intrinsic good value. Suriati, immersed in grief, yet smiled and laughed also to make happy the heart of her mother who had many reasons to be sad. And it did not matter that both of them knew she was making an effort, exercising will. Humans *should* make an effort, and laughing sets off a chain reaction. It compels. Hearts are made happy, as forced good response signals compassion.

But beyond this salient human dimension, laughter works by itself, shaping a feeling-mind socialized from infancy to be malleable to expression.

And we have not yet explored how it works on the souls of the dead.

What Is at Stake for the Souls of the Dead?

Balinese of every religion believe that for a while after death the soul hovers around the house and closely watches the bereaved. Still attached to them and sharing in their concerns, the soul lingers on to see how they fare through this experience of longing and distress. How long it lingers is difficult to say. Muslims believe forty-four days, whereas Hindus and Bali Aga—the original Balinese of animist traditions—are uncommitted in their replies. But all agree that the soul is attached and wants to stay close. Yet it should be freed from the world and set on its course for God. But the more distressed the living are, the more difficult for the soul to depart. A Hindu used the following parable to explain:

> Suppose a mother wants to go to the market, but her child
> cries and clings to her to hold her back. She will be worried
> [*was-was*], wanting to go, but anxious about her child, think-
> ing no, she should not go, but ill at ease, and when she fi-
> nally goes, her mind will not be at rest. So also with the souls
> of the deceased. We must refrain from crying so that they will
> be liberated [from the world] and free to go to heaven. If we
> express our sadness, it will make an obstruction for the soul's

154

going to heaven. We must not cry so that they will meet no
obstacle from our tears.

Tears also must not drop on the body of the deceased as it is being
purified for burial or cremation. This would make the soul unclean and
give it a bad place in heaven. Considering that the body is kept at home
and rituals related to cleansing and purification performed by family
members, here is a strong prohibition on showing distress in situations
where it might be most acutely felt. But as important is concern for the
emotional well-being of the deceased. In Bali as in some other cultures,
e.g., Brazil (Nations and Rebhun 1988) and Bhutan (author's personal
observation), people believe that the soul of the dead will be very unhappy, because encumbered/obstructed, if tears are shed by its beloved
bereaved.

Three years after her friend's death I asked Suriati how she had felt
about his soul at the time. She told me how she felt close to him when in
Lombok, and later also in Bali, after she had brought some of his
clothes back with her. Now I also understand why it was so important
for her to go to Lombok to what at the time I mistook for a brief memorial service, when for her it was a question of being where the beloved
was: present where she could feel in touch. She could commune with
him, she could console him and assure him she would manage, thus setting his soul at peace. And it had to be done in Lombok, for that is
where his soul was. Not till she had brought some of his clothes back
with her to Bali would she also feel close to him there. Balinese of all
religious faiths believe that the souls of both living and recently dead
adhere to their clothes.[17] Touching the clothes of the deceased is a way
to quench illness from longing or loss (*sakit rindu,* cf. p. 200).

I also see now why I never heard people express disapproval of Suriati's decision to travel alone to a foreign land. It was an act that might
otherwise have elicited mocking laughter, but she was doing what she
had to do to put her friend's soul to rest. Burial and proper purification
of his corpse could not alone achieve this. Bonds between living and
dead require nurturing and loosening step by step.

Let this statement, spontaneously given by a man, middle-aged and
of commoner caste, sum up Balinese notions of what is at stake both for
the living and the souls of the deceased.

> At death people will cry, but not so much. Like myself
> when my younger brother died in the earthquake [in 1979],
> and I went to fetch him at the school—I had to dig him out
> with my own hands. My heart was so pressured, I could

hardly keep myself from crying, but I controlled myself until I was back home. Then I cried, but not so much, maybe only for two minutes. If you cry at death, it's like you interfere with God's decision. When someone dies, it is because God calls him, his *karma* is finished. The day of our death is written at birth. His sickness was not haphazard, but because it is the way to death . . . If you cry, the soul will not be so happy because [it is] still in contact with you. You will impede its progress to God. Instead you must be happy and pray to help the soul to go to God. Just like with you, if you are unhappy, you cannot work so well, cannot concentrate, so also with [the souls of] the dead [*leluhur*]. If you are unhappy, they will be unhappy, and it will make it more difficult for them to come close to God.

The body that is dead is okay. You must take care with those who are still living.[18]

The Cultural Construction of Sadness

Implicit in this man's statement is the notion that life requires you to lay problems and sorrows behind if they are of such a nature that they cannot be solved. Let bygones be bygones. What is past is past. You owe it to the living, for to ponder and brood brings you nowhere but to the edge of illness and sometimes beyond.[19] A person needs a steady mind and a good heart to cope with the vicissitudes of life, and this is fostered only if one's life force is steadfast and strong. Sadness undermines the life force. It withers one's energy away, and a person cannot afford to neglect her life force. It is her shield against illness and her asset in the struggle for living.

One therefore owes it to oneself and one's fellow beings to manage one's heart so that one may forget or "lose" one's sadness. Others will help you in this, for it is disquieting to them to see you sad. It places them also at risk.

Thus sadness in Bali is perceived as a problem in need of a solution. Not merely an emotion (*perasaan*) or a state of feeling-thought (*keneh*), it is regarded as a grave threat to health, and the sad person both feels, and is treated, as if she is sick (*sakit*). Likewise, significant others experience the threat of being afflicted by another's sadness: "we may become sick as well." The experience of sadness expresses itself in the following kinds of bodily symptoms.

The person feels confused/disoriented (*bingung*), has headache (*pusing*), and is drained of energy or life force (*bayu*). She feels weak (*lemah/lamas*) and fatigued and has a heavy (*berat*) sensation about the heart. She cannot sleep, loses appetite, and often feels empty (*kosong*) as well. Such an amalgam of symptoms instills fear. Confusion blurs vision, impedes judgment, and makes for forgetfulness and inability to concentrate. A sad person is inclined to be quiet (*diam*) and anxious (*bimbang*) and feel shaky (*goncang*). Bereft of balance, the vital spirit feels as if it is whirling (*jenget*) and might easily fly off.

How gravely these symptoms are felt depends on individual disposition or circumstance. But confusion, headache, fatigue, heaviness, insomnia, and lack of appetite are regarded as intrinsic to the experience of sadness itself. To be sad is thus an affliction of the body-self.

Balinese have no word for grief. They do not think that bereavement engenders feelings basically different from those evoked by other sorrowful experiences. While they do have a concept of a state worse than sad, namely brokenhearted (*patah hati*), this is not culturally associated with bereavement. Indeed, as death is codified, it could hardly be. There are worse experiences in life than to be separated from a beloved through death. Chapter 11 details one such experience.

Brokenheartedness is a condition beyond hope, while for sadness ample hope exists. Brokenheartedness thus meets a criterion seen in the West as intrinsic to the illness of depression: a general feeling of hopelessness (cf. Brown and Harris 1978, 235). Sadness, by this measure, defies diagnosis as depression (though it may still be a depressive mood; see Kleinman and Good [1985] on this distinction). But Balinese sadness is also very different from Western "grief" in that grief is *not* regarded to be an illness, whereas sadness in Bali actually is.

In the West, while there is considerable controversy on the issue,

> the current consensus is that although individuals experiencing grief are distressed, they are not ill or diseased. A number of considerations lead to this conclusion. For one thing, society does not consider them to be sick, nor do bereaved individuals consider themselves ill; they believe they are undergoing a "normal" period of distress. In this sense, bereavement may be compared with pregnancy (Osterweis, Solomon, and Green 1984, 19).

For Balinese, such a comparison would not make sense. While bereavement is as much a normal life event as pregnancy, the feeling-thoughts associated with these experiences are so different that from a health perspective, they bear no comparison.

Sadness is an affliction of the body-soul that threatens a multitude of people, not only the bereaved. It is conceived as likely to "spread" and thus to endanger public health. Pregnancy most definitely does not. I liken Balinese sadness to a contagious disease (*penyakit menular*), and while this admittedly is going further than they would, such comparison throws into relief distinctive aspects of sadness from a Balinese existential viewpoint. Problems of validity and methodology in understanding depressive illnesses cross-culturally have been brilliantly discussed by Kleinman and Good (1985). Sadness or "grief" might warrant a similar analysis.

When "grief" is considered by Western researchers as "normal," not akin to depression, another characteristic is commonly held up: depression entails lowered self-esteem, grief does not (Osterweis, Solomon, and Green 1984, 19–20).[20] But in Bali, sadness does most emphatically. Anyone who is sad will also be "confused" (*bingung*), which entails being disoriented, worried, weak, and dazzled. Alisjahbana gives a similar interpretation:

> If . . . [the] instability of feelings is increased, [the] individual becomes anxious, over-sensitive. His feelings of self-esteem decrease. . . . A person who loses his value orientations in these ways, and thus cannot deploy an effective will, can be said to . . . [be] "demoralized." . . . In the Indonesian language this disorientation which coincides with high tension is termed *bingung,* meaning disoriented, confused (1986, 66 and n. 1).

Sadness in Bali is thus not like depression in that hope exists. It resembles depression in that self-esteem is lowered. It is unlike grief in that it *is* considered to be a sick state. It is "normal" in that everyone will be sad from time to time, yet society takes an emphatic stance against such experience and urges people to get out of it as quickly as they can. Much more than a "mood," sadness is what Obeyesekere calls a "conception" (1985, 135–36) and one that fuses, in a way, a whole vision of life and blends it with bodily experience. For the body-self undergoing this experience, to be sad is to be sick.

Bereavement and Popular Health Care

Underlying this discussion is a perspective I advocate toward the study of bereavement. Bali brought it to the fore. I consider that it may be fruitful to regard culture-specific patterns of bereavement and mourning from the point of view of popular health care: as particular "solutions" to a universal problem which embody basic cultural assumptions of self and health. This is also in line with a stance taken by Kleinman and Good: "Describing how it feels to be grieved or melancholy in another society leads straightforward into analysis of different ways of being a person in radically different worlds" (1985, 3). I take this further and argue that the "crisis" aspect of bereavement is generally pronounced, if to varying extents, and that the way agents of culture deal with such regularly occuring crisis may reflect basic perceptions of health and the measures needed to ensure it.

The "crisis" aspect of bereavement has been noted by several researchers (e.g., Rosenblatt, Walsh, and Jackson 1976; Danforth and Tsiaras 1982; R. Rosaldo 1984). Whereas Osterweis, Solomon, and Green state that "the contemporary Western practice of systematically looking for the health consequences of bereavement is so unusual in cross-cultural perspective (in spite of the fact that most ethnopsychological systems are aware of the more untoward outcomes) that it may be regarded as a result of Westernization" (1984, 205), I am impressed that in cultures where I have worked significant others do anticipate such effects, if not systematically, and try to prevent them (Wikan 1988). Relevant may also be different conceptions of health. However, these authors also note, "with respect to cross-cultural variations in specific health consequences of bereavement, there is so little systematic research . . . that it is only possible to speculate on what contingencies health care providers and prevention experts ought to consider" (Osterweis, Solomon, and Green 1984, 205). In Bali health is seen as endangered in somatically specific ways. In Egypt, which I have compared with Bali (Wikan 1988), people are as concerned with the threat to health, but symptoms are more diffuse and health care measures fundamentally different, mirroring different conceptions of person and health. Even societies that do not fear illness as a consequence of bereavement may yet be concerned with health. What more pregnant testimony could there be than the Ilongot concern to "cast off anger" weighing on one's heart (R. Rosaldo 1984)?

In every culture we know, grieving and mourning do not proceed randomly but are socially hedged about and circumscribed. In their institutionalized forms they reflect "artful" responses to impending "crises" in which health, social welfare, and social relations are at stake. Bereavement thus throws into relief, sometimes in exaggerated form, constraints that apply in everyday life, even though Bali may be extreme in the severity of its social sanctions. This, I believe, reflects that more is seen to be at stake for society at large than is the case in many other cultures. If in the West, sad people were believed to endanger the lives of many others I am sure they would receive more attention and care than is the case under present circumstances.

Sadness in Bali erodes the physical-mental resistance one needs to have a fair chance of surviving in the world. It breaks down what even some Balinese doctors label a person's immune system: the spiritual force or vitality without which one literally dies, as one may quench life-threatening illness by mobilizing this force to the full. Sadness also impairs one's ability to apprehend critical social signs one must go by to avoid offense. When sadness also "spreads" when expressed, the analogy with contagious, life-threatening illnesses is indeed not so far-fetched. The lightness with which Western cultures treat grief (as our nearest equivalent of Balinese sadness) reflects a "light" attitude to the power of the mind to shape health, and a mechanistic worldview with people perceived as separate atoms.

Whereas lingering in despair is just not an option in Bali, with us that kind of freedom may be allowed. Reflected are basically different notions of the constitution of persons and the preconditions for collective life. In the West, to generalize broadly, grief is seen as a personal tragedy, something that engulfs only the individuals most directly involved even when others may be suffering on their behalf. But suffering is regarded as an internal condition. It springs *from* the person and ends *with* the person. The body is the limit, so to speak. Feelings are biological imperatives that happen *to* the person, and to stop them from happening it is necessary to gain control over them or get them out. The hydraulic theory of emotions that William James ([1890] 1950) coined and Freud did much to reinforce is widely embraced.

But in Bali to express sadness is to sadden others and put them also at risk. Feelings, though also here they happen "in" people, are seen to arise *from* social situations and to have social repercussions far beyond the body of the individual. Therefore expression, in particular, must be controlled, but feelings also must be managed, for they sustain the body, life itself. Spirit and body comprise a whole.

The Social Situatedness of Feeling

Balinese have a clear perception of what may, or may not, cause one to be sad (*duke, sedeh*). It is not up to the individual to "choose" how to respond to a particular distressful experience. It is senseless to claim to be sad in a situation that is not recognized as sadness-evoking. I once did and was appropriately corrected and had the "real" feeling pointed out to me. Feelings are not merely contingent on psychological factors (such as "character" or "heart"). The social embeddedness of feeling has been noted also for other non-Western peoples (e.g., Lutz 1985; Myers 1986; but see also chap. 6, note 19).

"To be sad" is thus a symbol which is rigidly codified and circumscribed. And while Balinese recognize that people will differ in the force and intensity of their emotional experience, yet they are emphatic that experiences which elicit sadness do so for all. Feeling and situation/relationship are two aspects of one process.

Does this explain, in part, why they are so deft at detecting sad hearts beyond bright and clear faces? Do they proceed from knowledge of a social event to impute to a person an experience which is culturally perceived to comprise a particular feeling-thought? I think so, at least as regards sadness and their other most salient feeling-thoughts such as anger, envy, jealousy and offense, and happiness.

Entailed is a notion that *humans are the same* in their responses to fateful experiences—and that these are *inevitable* responses. I think they would deny that feelings come in splashes, surges, a conundrum of untamed response. Feelings are particular, as are the situations that evoke them. And the socially shared perception of such close-knit linkages enables Balinese to express empathy with people of bright, clear faces without fear of making fools of themselves. *"Hearts" are "visible,"* as are the efforts of keeping them hidden, *precisely by virtue of knowledge of "sheer" social facts.*[21]

How feeling is grounded in social situation was impressed upon me once when I came distressed to a Balinese friend because another, a foreigner, had deceived me (as I felt) and given herself out to be something she was not, with some dire consequences for myself. Sad, as I truly (thought-felt I) was and was not able to hide, I confided in my Balinese friend, who immediately enlightened/alerted me: "Oh, no, you are not sad! You are angry! The kind of experience you have had—it is very common among us—it does not make one sad, it makes one angry!" And she used the term for hidden anger (*benci*), which is far more dangerous than anger expressed (*marah*).

Sadness is seen as linked with *particular* experiences such as the loss of a beloved by separation or death; or the loss of things of value (possessions, health); or the memory of such loss. It is evoked also when one feels *with* or feels *for* somebody close who is sick or sad or broken-hearted, in which case the whole complex of embodied, physical ailments may be vicariously felt. With more distant persons, one rather feels pity or sympathy (*kelangen*)—a feeling devoid of the sickness connotations of sadness.

Retrospectively, I wonder if the Balinese concise conception of what is, and is not, sadness may not also be linked with their rather precise bodily reference to fateful emotions? With the close integration between body and spirit/life force/heart which they perceive, do they take signals from the body, rather than from the mind, as a clue to what they feel? Of course, body and mind cannot be separated as my formulation might indicate, but we know that cultures differ in their relative stress on one or the other (Kleinman 1986; Wierzbicka 1989).

Balinese seem clearly to use bodily ailments as signs of mindful states. They are ever tuned in to the body and the language it speaks and thus perhaps evolve an experiential focus whereby the body rather than the mind signals to them what they feel. If my interpretation is right, then if I had I been Balinese, I might have taken bodily clues to which I was at the time insensitive as a sign that I was indeed angry and not sad.

Hot flushes characterize anger, say Balinese, and sadness and anger weigh on the heart and create a characteristic nagging sensation: "But they are different. We know which is which. There is no confusing them."

For a Norwegian, encultured to be far less bodily perceptive, there certainly is, and also for people like the Egyptians who comprise anger and sadness under one term, *za'l* (unhappiness/annoyance). It makes little difference; either should be cast off in willful, emphatic response. But for Balinese it is this which should *not* happen. And while sadness is admittable, within bounds, and unavoidable as a spontaneous reaction to certain events, anger has no place even when it might be justified. With such a stigma attached, no wonder Balinese are deft to distinguish sadness from anger.

A clear perception of what elicitors are (or may be) also works to shape emotional response from diffuse reaction to named feeling-thought by the time it reaches consciousness. Whatever my psychobiological response to deception by a friend, as a Balinese I would *feel-think* anger.

How culture shapes emotional response was brought home to me one day when our son, then aged ten, was distressed because his music instructor had been bad-tempered with him. To soften the blow my husband and I suggested that perhaps his teacher had a bad day himself: perhaps *his* boss had been cross with him or his girlfriend had left him or . . . Immediately came the reply: "Then it must have been the former, for he was angry, not sad!" A Norwegian ten-year-old had already learned to associate sadness with losing a lover. Balinese had long since convinced me there was but one natural response to that: anger.

This is when a lover leaves you of her or his own accord or by black magic. But if (s)he was forced to do so by her/his parents, the response might be a broken heart—a state worse than sad.[22] The brokenhearted person has lost hope, a sense of the future, the will to live. (S)he is apt to sit dazed (*bengong*), withdrawn, tuned in on herself. Madness and suicide threaten. Of the cases of brokenheartedness that I came across all were—with one exception—on account of love lost, but not by death.[23] As death is codified it tends to inhibit a brokenhearted response and to help one contain one's sadness better than at other fateful times of despair.

Danforth has observed how the women of rural Greece care for their beloved after death as they did in life: the same pattern enacts itself, a prolongation of a valued relationship (Danforth and Tsiaras 1982, esp. chap. 5).

The analogy cannot be translated fully to Bali, for Balinese souls of the dead go through a complex development to turn eventually into gods with extensive powers—for good or for ill—over the lives of the living. And yet to counter such disaster and express love and care one comforts the dead—as one does the living—by smiles and laughter to make happy their hearts. Intense or prolonged grieving would be a negation of such care. But when a child has run away and is feared to be lost forever, it is as if the bottom has fallen out of one's life. Grief explodes full bore, and there is none of the restraint mothers display when a child is actually dead.

Death seems to offer a kind of consolation certain other life tragedies do not. And I wonder whether for Bali it makes sense to say that people move *between* a commonsensical and a religious perspective on life (C. Geertz [1966] 1973b; Danforth and Tsiaras 1982). Perhaps rather the two merge, so that death appears more acceptable. Gone but present, lost but within reach: so are the souls of the deceased. Lost but living lovers or children, on the other hand, are only gone. *They* are the truly lost ones, and for them only do people cry themselves to despair.

Religious Diversity, Similarity in Coping Response

North Balinese society comprises members of different religions: Hindus, Muslims, Buddhists, and Bali Asli or Aga—the last the original Balinese of animist traditions (see Barth 1991). While they differ

163

greatly in their views on the nature and meaning of death and in their mourning rituals, yet members of these diverse religions share certain fundamental assumptions that induce them to contain their sadness in nearly identical manner.

They are exposed to the same predicaments in everyday living and to a pan-Balinese reality in which, among those who would thrive and survive, pragmatism carries the day. Dangers and threats are experienced as basically the same for all, and though their diverse religions succor and offer meaningful frames of interpretation, it is the *body* which is the most immediate measure of one's viability in this health-oriented culture where minds are embodied and bodies pervaded by feeling-mind.

All need to keep a strong and steadfast life force—*bayu*—for they are exposed not merely to similar trials and tribulations in everyday life, but even to *each other's* demons, ghosts, and black magic, *in addition to* the innumerable (super)natural forces that pertain to their own cosmology. They may even have their own bodies invaded and their souls removed by agents of other religions. And they must be prepared to pray *to* or pray *like* members of another religion to propitiate and get rid of a malignant spirit or human who is wreaking havoc with their life (cf. chap. 12). Experientially, then, the focus is on the *bayu* as the vital essence, source of all energy and power.

The implications of such embodied predicaments are far-reaching for an understanding of cultural complexity in the North. It means that people of different religions are caught up in *one* world which even they recognize as being shared. In the face of such fateful experiences, what does it matter that religions teach different conceptions of the nature of God, life, and death? Is there not an overarching frame of reference which Balinese share and which takes precedence in that it is embodied, while others are only known?

I think so, and I think that this explains why Balinese Hindus, Muslims, Buddhists, and Bali Aga appear so similar in behavioral style and emotional response. On death as in life they tune in to a common pattern: to let bygones be bygones in order to protect their vulnerable souls and also in order not to endanger others: fellow beings to whom sadness might "spread" and the similarly affectable souls of the deceased which live on, only their bodies being dead.

The Soul after Death

Balinese of every religion believe that the hour of death is fated and preordained by God. This does little to deter their fear of black magic.

A belief in God's omniscience coexists with the belief that life is in danger from a host of (super)natural forces, and one must do all one can to avoid them.

On death the soul departs for an existence better than life on earth. To ensure a proper passage Muslims and Bali Aga bury their dead, while Hindus usually bury first to exhume and cremate later. Hindus believe in reincarnation and see death as a necessary stage in the cycle of rebirths that will eventually release the soul from the world to be merged with God. One's fate on earth is determined by the law of *karma pala,* whereby rewards and punishments are meted out in accordance with past actions. Cremation is necessary to enable reincarnation, but most Bali-Hindus are too poor to afford this on the large scale deemed necessary, and so they bury their dead first and exhume and cremate them later when they have accumulated capital enough to pay for that substantial spectacle. Not till the soul is cremated is it considered pure enough, according to Bali-Hindu philosophy, to be worshipped as a holy ancestor (*pitara* or *dewa*) in the family houseyard temple (*sanggah*) (though our data indicate that people in general do not emphasize this criterion but propitiate their dead collectively in the *sanggah*). Cremation may take place immediately upon death, as in well-off families and among priests and high castes, or after many years, generally thirty to fifty, among the less well off. The ceremony accomplishes the final purification of the spirit and liberation of the soul (*atma*).[24]

From a Muslim point of view, death is final, there is no return. A person's actions determine whether she goes to heaven or hell, though living family has some influence in the matter. By giving elaborate feasts in which food is distributed to as many guests as one can afford, one ensures that many people bless the deceased and pray on her behalf. Thus *pahala* is accumulated to compensate for sins the deceased may have committed and propitiate God. In the Muslim community of Pegayaman a ritual called *retipan* is performed in which members of the community take it upon themselves to say prayers in the name of the deceased to make up the full quota of five daily prayers throughout life, should the deceased have been sick or inattentive or otherwise fallen short.

In every religion correct performance of death rituals is of the essence. Among Hindus a first step is to ensure that the soul is actually merged with the corpse before burial or cremation. Because the soul is believed to exit from the body—through the mouth—at the spot where death occurred, it is essential to go there and call the soul back. Thus when a death occurs in the hospital or by accident in the street, a special ceremony is performed by members of the family to invite/entice the

165

soul back and join it to the corpse.[25] Sometimes problems arise because it is not clear where the death occurred, and several attempts may be necessary to retrieve the soul. One may search in the hospital and find none because the deceased expired on the way, for instance. Retrieved the soul must be, or cremation or burial will accomplish nothing but destruction of the body, leaving the soul to roam restless and victimized, inflicting sundry misfortunes upon the living.

At death the body, which consists of the elements of earth, air, water, and fire, decomposes to be merged with its component origins. Old *lontar* (palm-leaf manuscripts deriving from Sanskrit literature) specify where the parts of the body go:

> The physical body (*badan*) turns to earth,
> body hair (*bulu*) to shrubs,
> the skin (*kulit*) to earth,
> the muscles (*daging*) to clay,
> the tendons (*otot*) to branches of vegetation,
> the spinal cord (*sam-sam*) to the axis of the earth,
> the eyes (*mata*) to the sun or the moon,
> the head (*kepala*) to the sky,
> the life force or vital power (*bayu*) to the wind,
> the voice (*soara*) to thunder,
> the liver (*hati*) to fire,
> the heart (*jantung*) to a mountain,
> the pulma (*paru-paru*) to red clouds in the sky,
> the bowels (*usus*) to sunrays,
> the kidneys (*ungsilan*) to stone,
> the spleen (*limpa*) to a shining lake,
> the tissue of the bowels (*dujaringan*) to rain,
> the sour gall (*ampu*) to energy or power,
> the intestines (*ineban*) to the ocean,
> the stomach (*perut*) to crater,
> the hair (of the head) (*rambut*) to dew,
> the sexual organs (*kemalwar*) to the God and Goddess of
>   Love Hyang Semare and Hyang Semari,
> the sperms (*kama*) to their godly origins as Brahma, Visnu,
>   and Siwa,
> the senses (*rasa*) to salt.

Left is the soul (*atma* or *roh*), and where does it go? To God to be reincarnated or, if perfectly pure, merged with the Eternal Soul. In the latter case, release from the cycle of rebirths is attained in the act of salvation (*Moksa*). But for most this is a long and demanding process requiring an endless series of rebirths before the soul is pure enough, according to the law of *karma pala,* to reach *Moksa.*

That reincarnation is to be expected means also that the living should carry out rituals to erase character faults, illnesses, or sins of the deceased so that they will not afflict the person in whom (s)he is reincarnated. A balian told me that many problems arise because the bereaved forget to do this—in which case it is not actually the living person who is suffering but the ancestor who is reborn through her or him. Whatever the logistics, the person will feel afflicted, and the illness's diagnosis will impress upon the living their never-ceasing obligations to placate and respect the dead.

In rare instances persons may be forewarned that this is their last reincarnation, that they are now considered pure enough to reach *Moksa.* It happened to the father of a man I know well. He was an accomplished yogi and teacher of the holy texts (*lontar* and *kakawin*). Two months before he died—God had informed him what the precise moment would be—he began to prepare his family, admonishing them: "Don't you ever be sad! Be always happy!" (*Jangan sedih! Harus gembira!*) "So we never cried or expressed our sadness," said the son, "for it was not allowed. If we had done so, it would have been as if we encouraged the soul to come back and be reincarnated in the cycle of rebirth. It would have constituted an obstacle towards salvation."

But the same precept also applies to people who believe that their deceased may have far to go to reach salvation. Usually it is not for the living to tell. Essentially, one must not hamper the dead in their progress toward God by detaining them through one's tears.

In Coping with Grief No One is Merely a Balinese

Cremation, say Balinese, is a happy (*gembira*) occasion. And yet it is not uncommon to observe among the bereaved expressions of painfully won composure and occasional crying. Intense weeping may also occur. This presents no contradiction to Balinese. An ideology passionately embraced does not foster an automatic response of corresponding feeling and sensation. Attachment is inherent to the human condition, and sadness, say they, is what everyone must feel once it is severed.

But their expressions of sadness may often not be visible to the passing foreigner who is impressed with the "discordant" cheerfulness of the mournful occasion. Balinese facial expressions and bodily posture mislead because the tell-tale signs of sadness (and of anger for that matter) are carried through signifiers that are visible only if one has been

167

trained to see them. The dry-eyed crying of old women has been given as an example. Were it not for that oft-repeated act of lifting a corner of the sarong to wipe their eyes, I might not have "seen" their crying. The muscular movements we expect to precede crying, when the face is distorted and spastic before the tears start flowing, are not, in my experience, apparent among Balinese. Tears erupt suddenly, without warning, in a calm and composed face. And they may disappear as abruptly as they came.

It is not always like this. I have also seen wild, uncontrolled crying more akin to our "normal" tears. In either case the sadness may be as acutely felt; what differs is the self-control and life experience one brings to the situation. Some of the women whose eyes watered when they were told the story of the Lombok boy's death had a personal experience of losing many children: one had borne sixteen and lost all but one before the age of two; another had been much more fortunate—she had lost only seven out of twelve. Did they cry from the resonance born of personal loss, which R. Rosaldo cites as facilitating an empathic response (1984, 187)? Perhaps. But their age also allowed them greater license to express sorrow. Old people are like children, say Balinese, in so many ways, and also in that they are more easily overcome by their feelings.

In grief, as in many kinds of emotional experience, one's position in life channels one's response in accordance with what is deemed proper. Suriati felt the pressure of being a young unmarried woman and observed that men were more favorably placed. It is easy to lose such distinctions from sight when one generalizes about bereavement in other cultures. Yet to the actors, they make a world of difference. In everyday life and the situations that there matter most, no one is just a Balinese: she is a Balinese of a certain status, age, and gender, with a particular character and biography. These affect her reactions to loss, and they affect also the responses of her significant others.

In her struggle to keep her sadness hidden before the world, but also for her own sanity's sake, Suriati was guided by perceptions of what was at stake. It was not that she was a Balinese; that identity was "safe." But she was female and young and ought to marry some day. She ought therefore not to give "them" the chance to label her "brokenhearted" or a "widow." She was sure that they would if they could, for she had ample experience of people trying to "make her down" (*nyajang jelme*). She provoked envy (*iri*) by having climbed to positions that ought to have been barred to her, a female of low social rank. Her particular feminine attractiveness also did little to endear her in the eyes of many.

When now she was assailed by grief, she did not lose her footing. She had to cope to protect an identity of which she was proud and which she had struggled to build. It required her to choose one model of coping among others. It would not occur to her to behave like a man, or an old woman, or a person of securely high rank. She was vulnerable and knew it so well. Nor would she throw all precautions to the winds and say "I don't care." She had precious things to defend.

Whereas Balinese cultural templates endow people with generalized formulas for coping, shreds and fragments of the general models are put to use in a life situation that is experienced as unique and which the world also recognizes as engulfing body and soul. When people say to the bereaved "let bygones be bygones" and give cursory advice that appears saliently void of person-oriented overtones, we should not be misled into thinking that these *express* their attitudes to the bereaved. People are constrained in how to express their empathy, just as the bereaved are in showing they have sadness under control. But there are ways, and they take cognizance of the particular life situation.

A husband and wife were both overcome with sadness. She, after an initial period of despair, bore it bravely with a clear/bright face. He succumbed to depressed ways. She received constant expressions of sympathy in the form of food, gifts, and salutary respect. He was criticized and laughed about scornfully.

Was it because she behaved as a good Balinese, he not? In part, but not alone. She took over the man's role and became the sole provider in a situation of nearly unbearable strain. The world observed and judged her, but not merely as a Balinese. They judged her as a particular woman in a particular life situation. Before she had been not so popular, for she displayed arrogant ways. Now the world changed to a more favorable attitude, even as they criticized her for letting her husband do a tiny bit of housework. They gave her gifts, they smiled encouragingly. She was esteemed and offered responsible political positions.

Two cases are not enough to carry an argument. But they may make a breach in rigid positions. As observers we tend to think that culture prescribes or determines attitudes to life and death. What I try to do is to ask how it looks from the position of engaged participants. From the perspective of people who have an identity to defend, one's status as Balinese is given. *Other* aspects are at stake. And while it is true that "we" Balinese should not express sorrow, that does not mean that the person has license in how *not* to show. She is being watched and judged, *and the terms are positional.* What she risks is not being branded "not like a Balinese," but "like a man" or "like an old woman."

In living with grief, no one is first and foremost a Balinese. She is a person of a certain stature, judged by others who have *particular* stakes to defend. The label "Balinese" applies equally to all, and all are not in fact equal.

Would Anyone Gain from Lingering in Misery and Pain?

To sum up the position I argue: "To make the heart happy from sadness" emerges as a prominent theme and focal value among Balinese. Sadness must be deterred because it is likely to spread and erode the well-being of many. Popular health care measures are initiated to protect life and to counter threats. The misjudgment that follows from "confusion" exacerbates the vulnerability of the sad: the risk of causing offense and eliciting black magic is increased.

Because sadness is life-endangering, to protect people from it is an expression of care:

> When my boyfriend's letters arrive, my mother opens and
> reads them first. I feel pity for him, for he talks about his
> heart and writes words that were not meant for another, only
> for me, and I feel embarrassed. But I know she does it for the
> sake of my own good . . . She does it that she may protect
> me from sadness . . .

Sadness is nevertheless a condition of ample hope. "Forgetting" (*ngesapine*) or "taking it out" (*ngilangang*) is all that is needed. Reflected is the dynamic, creative aspect of Balinese feeling-thinking. Truly, sadness is not a *thing*, but Western popular theory fed by a century of psychoanalytic thinking has misconstrued it as such and reified feeling as if it were a substance locked in some kind of kettle: the body. From this perspective the body might explode if sadness is not taken "out." For Balinese, this danger does not exist, for sadness flows; it cannot be stored, except when thinking *wills* so by pondering and brooding. Banish sad thoughts, and what is there to nourish sadness?

The brokenhearted are those who cannot banish sad thoughts. It is a condition of sadness turned chronic: amplified beyond hope. Faced with such persons Balinese do not laugh. Or they do but in a different way, with gestures clearly signalling compassion. They speak disparagingly of the ones who caused her to be so sick, and extend gestures of pity to the sick one, trying as best they can to help.

But when someone is "just" sad, as on bereavement, community members try to shake her out of a state that may spiral downwards but in which there is still ample hope. Laughter resounds mercilessly, even harshly, in her ears and rebounds at her whenever she succumbs to depressed ways. Not left at peace to be sad, she becomes an object of a kind of shock treatment[26] whereby the humiliation felt at being the object of laughter shakes her out of self-pitying ways and impresses upon her the supreme value of self-protection and care for others.

When she emerges "fresh" (*somboh*) and "clear" (*cedang*) and "calm" *tenang*), she will see how mistaken she was in resenting these efforts to do her good. Laughter read as scorn turns into a therapeutic device in that it shocks and shames the person to come to her senses and "do the best." "Manage your heart better, make your body, your appearance the best" are injunctions that safeguard community life and communal relations. But there is no doubt in the minds of Balinese that the individual is also best served this way. Would anyone gain from lingering in misery and pain?

CHAPTER NINE
Vitality and Health

If a person *feels* sick, who can make him well?
—BALINESE DOCTOR

The life-force may be the least understood force on earth.
—NORMAN COUSINS

Popular Health Care

Kleinman, in his exemplary *Patients and Healers in the Context of Culture* (1980), has criticized anthropologists for an exaggerated interest in the exotic and spectacular aspects of folk medicine at the expense of the more everyday and mundane. Anthropologists have focused excessive attention on shamanistic and ritual healing, whereas popular health care—what people do in their everyday lives to further health and prevent illness—has been neglected and poorly understood.[1] This despite the fact that an estimated 70 to 90 percent of all self-recognized episodes of sickness never enter the domain of either traditional or professional medical personnel but are attended to by laypeople, mainly women, in the home or community network. This predominant interest in ritual healing fosters a misplaced impression that sickness is what preoccupies people when surely *health* is the major concern of everyday life (Kleinman 1980, 51–83).

This chapter seeks to redress some of this imbalance by analyzing aspects of Balinese popular health care in the broadest sense, especially the role Balinese ascribe to feeling-thoughts in relation to body and *bayu.*

We have touched on various aspects of this in the last chapter. Here I take the analysis further by anchoring insights more systematically to a Balinese ethnotheory of feeling-thoughts. The "theory," as I present it, is pieced together from bits and pieces of information gathered in the course of everyday life. It was never laid out to me as a whole, nor did I ever attempt to discuss it with people in this manner. The theory is a construct, my construct, and yet I believe that Balinese would concur with its basic principles as elaborated here. Validity is of the essence, for I try to expound how Balinese *feel-think, act* in respect of, and *use* this theory as a formula for health in everyday life.

Embodied Knowledge

As an example of how the folk theory is invoked in everyday life, we may note again the rationale given by the woman who after a year emerged "fresh" and "clear" (*somboh*), having surmounted pain: "Mostly we did it for our own sake. Anger eats away at the heart, destroys the intestines, makes you grow old, ruins your life . . . Better not to care . . ." (see p. 28).

She formulates in everyday language what is at the philosophical level part of a complex theory of body (*badan*), soul (*atma* or *roh*), spirit/life force (*bayu, jiwa,* or *tenaga*), and feeling-thought (*perasaan, pikiran,* or *keneh*). It is set out in the old palm-leaf manuscripts (*lontar*) of which there are many versions, all comprehended by a small minority of the population, mainly (or perhaps solely) men with the requisite command of old Javanese or old Balinese holy language. Between these versions, each claimed to be authoritative, and the folk knowledge, which also comes in many versions, there are great discrepancies in some respects. For instance, in the case of "soulloss" (*kesambet* or *mekesiyab bayune*), which in the North is a common affliction (Wikan 1989a), people speak of their *bayu*—their vital life force—being lost, and it is this *bayu* that the healer seeks to retrieve. But Made Bidja, who instructed me in the *lontar,* explained that in thus believing people suffer from a misconception—*salah kaprah*. If the *bayu* is lost, a person dies. There is no way one can live, even for a moment, without one's vital life force. What is lost, on the contrary, when one is frightened or suddenly surprised is the soul (*atma* or *roh*), that divine aspect of a person which on death returns to its source, and which also at night takes off frequently, as when we dream. The soul may also be temporarily lost, as when it is captured by evil or angry spirits.[2]

Generally the vital energy or life force (*bayu*) is linked in the body with the soul (*atma*) except on fright, dreaming, or capture by a spirit or in trance—when the *atma* exits, whereas the *bayu* remains.[3] Tenuously linked with the body, the *atma* is lost every so often (e.g., almost every night), whereas the *bayu* cannot be, for it is the essential vitality which sustains the body through life. The *bayu* is the source of life; the *atma* is the source of consciousness, memory, and feeling-thinking. Hence the *bayu* is inalienable except on death when it merges with the wind, whereas the soul departs for God. This is according to expert opinion.

But ordinary Balinese do not think of it this way, for it is not the way they feel. When frightened, or victimized by black magic, they *feel* bereft of energy, *bayu*; they feel weak (*lemah*), tired (*capek*), empty (*kosong*), heavy (*berat*)—and this syndrome of physical feeling tells them the *bayu* has been lost. On its return, they *feel* refilled, refreshed, energetic, and strong, sensations they sum up in the term *somboh*, or *sehat*.

The *bayu* is like a thermometer Balinese constantly check for their viability and what manner of danger they may expose themselves to. When the *bayu* feels low or small (*cerik*), it is foolhardy to do certain things, such as driving a motor bike or visiting persons one truly fears. As did Suriati when she was sad, one must take precautions, be always especially on guard. But when the *bayu* feels big and strong (*gede*), one moves with greater ease, trusts one's own judgment, and dares what others do not. A strong *bayu* makes for an optimistic outlook on life, a weak *bayu* induces pessimism. With a strong *bayu* one has an advantage over others of lesser *bayu*, physically and mentally. The *bayu* protects and refurbishes energy. It also facilitates good judgment.

Feeling, in Balinese experience, is the surest indicator of health, as of many other vital matters. And the *bayu* is an aspect of feeling. So intimately linked are they that Balinese often confound the two and speak of the one when they actually mean the other. *Bayu* substitutes for "heart"—just as "heart" substitutes for *bayu*. Balinese know the difference full well, but in everyday life it *makes* little difference, for the *bayu* is felt to be a reflection of the heart. As a woman said, "Guiding the feeling-thought [*ngabe keneh*] is almost the same as strengthening [*ngedenang*] *bayu*. The real meaning of *bayu* is like energy or power, but we *feel* the *bayu* through the heart."

The soul (*atma*) on the other hand, does not have this embodied quality. It is not felt, perceived, and sensed in the palpable way the *bayu* is. When a person dies, for instance, people can see the *bayu* emanating from the mouth when the dying person takes the last breath.[4] They do not notice the *atma* expiring from the top of the head, the fontanelle, and so they think it is the soul that vanishes through the mouth. Again a misconception, say *lontar* experts, and explicable in terms of the manifest quality of the *bayu*.

It is the folk theory that concerns me here, just as it is praxis and everyday, mundane understandings that have been my preoccupation throughout. I set forth what I understand to be commonly shared perceptions of how feeling-thoughts "work" with regard to the body, vitality, and moral judgment and how one should therefore husband and control them. I detail techniques Balinese use for this purpose and instill in their children from the earliest age. As regards evidence of how well the formula works, I have no clinical tests but statements, spontaneously expressed by people, to indicate what *they* feel are the benefits and costs. Essentially, my stance is to move within the frame of reference they employ, a position I regard as justified, both because health *is*, in Balinese conception, largely a matter of feeling ("If a person *feels* sick, who can make him well?"), and also because, regarding the role of emotions in health, medical tests show contradictory results and the experts argue fiercely.

When, as among Balinese, feelings are regarded not as "free-floating" (Obeyesekere 1985, 135), but as anchored in a *conception* of health and morality which is shared and entrenched, people are further strengthened in their resolve to beat bodily ailments by mustering good feeling and will. What in Western medicine we regard as placebo effects are an integral part of every effort of healing and cure from the viewpoint of Balinese popular health care.

The Concept of Health

Health concerns are salient in nearly all everyday activities and constantly constrain people in their choices of how to act relative to all aspects of the environment: both (super)natural and social. Health and illness feature as ever-present topics of conversation and concern.[5] Health care—in the comprehensive sense of health and happiness—is foremost in people's minds when courses of action are being considered and past encounters evaluated.

This concept of health (*segar*) has a peculiar implication. It refers not merely to bodily well-being or to avoiding what we might associate with bodily/mental affliction. Because body is linked in a *conception* with feeling-thought, vital life force, and balance in the cosmos, to be healthy (*sehat*) is truly a way of being-in-the-world (Solomon 1984, 250). It entails a mind that furthers good action, good expression and proper moral judgment. It bespeaks harmony between oneself and cosmological forces. And it also has ramifications far beyond those we associate with the term because of the way Balinese are constituted as persons: "a nexus of interacting forces" is how Connor lucidly conceives of it (1982a, 263). Distinctions between body and spirit/mind, individual and society, nature and supernature are not applicable to them. A healthy body with a sick mind would be a contradiction in terms. and efforts at staying well by observing mutual obligations, proper hygiene, balanced nutrition, and so on, will be of limited value if not joined by proper feeling-thinking.

Somatization, Responsibility, and Shame

In Bali somatization is prevalent in all segments of the population. That is, problems of a psychological or social order are experienced or expressed through a somatic imagery of physical pain. Or to be more precise,

> individuals experience serious personal and social problems but interpret and articulate them, and indeed come to experience and respond to them, through the medium of the body. Loss, injustice, failure, conflict—all are transformed into discourse about pain. . . . The body mediates the individual's perception, experience and interpretation of problems in social life (Kleinman 1986, 51).[6]

Feelings of confusion, for example, which we have seen to be associated with sadness, are experienced physically as pain (headache), shivering, unsteadiness, and energy loss. Anger, envy, jealousy, fear, and fright likewise have their physical/somatic concomitants, and the connection is "direct; such feelings transpose to the body almost immediately.

Indeed, interpersonal problems will find their way to a person's body and be expressed *through* it, for avenues for dealing with such problems in everyday life are strictly limited. Issues are preferably not brought into the open, and the sick role provides a socially sanctioned refuge, often the only refuge, from the exacting demands of the interpersonal process. To be sick in Bali is not regarded as a failure or shameful, except when a person protractedly does not act as the community feels she or he should act to seek recovery:

> He brings his problem upon himself. When one has an experience like he had, one must not dwell upon the issue and ask why and wherefore. It makes no good. If you have a big problem like his, you must try to forget it or find a solution. If instead of brooding, he looked for a job, people would be shy [*malu*] with him and respect him more. Now, what do they do? They laugh.

Indeed, they did: some from embarrassment, some from scorn, and some from a sense of pity.

Balinese have clear ideas about what efforts to get well should entail. We might speak of a shared model of preventive health and medical help-seeking. People bear responsibility for their health in the sense that they should do what they can do to stay healthy and strong. Ideally this implies husbanding emotional resources. But the notion of keeping control to the extent that one is actually responsible for one's health and is to be blamed when illness befalls is foreign to Balinese thinking. To show foresight and be prepared is the most anyone can aspire to.

Body and health thus provide keys to Balinese ideas of personhood and interpersonal relations. In Kleinman's words, "discourse about pain and disability is a metaphor for discourse and action about the self and the social world" (1986, 51). What in other cultures might be experienced as social, interpersonal, or emotional problems or concerns are in Bali transmuted into bodily symptoms and sicknesses. The body can be likened to a sensitive instrument which they tirelessly scan for "symptoms" of whether they are "in balance" with themselves and their environment.

Because health is embedded in most other activities, to uncover Balinese notions and practice we must analyze aspects of the network of interpersonal relations and major parts of the Balinese worldview—not merely what touches on the medical realm according to Western conventions. Methodologically, this means paying close attention to everyday life so as to discover the multiple meanings people attribute to acts which at first glance may appear to have no relation to health.

Let me plunge into a case story that served me as an eye-opener to exemplify the materials on which I shall focus. Its immediate connection to the theme of health care may not be readily apparent, but that is precisely one of my points.

Laughter and a Mother's Despair

A boy aged fifteen ran away from home after much quarreling with his mother, sister, and grandmother. For days he had behaved obnoxiously, throwing fits of temper, changing his clothes several times a day to make his sister do much laundry, and racing about town on his sister's motorcycle which he had taken, though too young for a license to drive legally. Scolding and other attempts at discipline proved fruitless, and in the end his mother lost her temper and hit him.

Now for a child to run away *ngambul*[7]—offended after a quarrel—is a common enough recourse in North Bali—the only "acceptable" way for children to get back at their parents in this society which so emphatically inculcates proper respect for elders. But the institutionalization of the measure does not detract from its effectiveness. The boy's mother panicked and collapsed in a flood of tears. Twenty hours later, when I came to the house, she sat hunched in a chair by the door, her long hair disheveled, her clothes in disarray, uttering cries so piercing and yearning they sounded primeval.

She sat alone. The grandmother had gone to consult one of the balians specializing in finding lost children. The husband, unable to bear the scene, had extricated himself on the excuse that he had urgent business elsewhere. The daughter soon appeared from the back bedroom, her face also swollen with tears. She had just come back from the telegraph office where she had been to send telegrams to close relations in Denpasar and East Java, urging them to come immediately (oblivious to the 250-kilometer ride this would entail). Before that, she had been all over town, asking near and distant acquaintances if they had seen the boy. Now she and I set out on a second round. When all inquiries were in vain, we finally went to the police, and then to the headmaster of the boy's school. This last we did after much deliberation. Should the boy return safe and sound, he would feel ashamed to have the headmaster know of his unfortunate venture. On the other hand, if . . . The sister's fear won out. We headed for the headmaster's home.

Barely was there time for ceremonious greetings. The otherwise exquisitely polite young woman burst out recounting the tragic tale, replete with dramatic gestures. She had hardly started her tale of woe when the headmaster started laughing. He laughed heartily, infecting the family audience who also joined in the merriment. The girl seemed slightly taken aback. She made new attempts to impress upon the gentleman the graveness of the situation. Her attempts merely provoked more laughter and cheerful talk. We were served some fruit and tea, and then we left.

Identifying the Relevant Context for Health Care

I could not help reflecting again on the callousness toward the suffering of others, of which I seemed, at this early stage of fieldwork, to find much evidence. But that was only because cases are readily misapprehended when not placed in the appropriate context. In the case above, for one thing, vital links with other and subsequent events which might have falsified the first interpretation have been broken. The "story" has been inappropriately sequestered from the flow of events in which it was embedded. For another, the events may be misinterpreted because of failure to recognize the cultural construction of emotion in an affective language that may be difficult to decipher. But most of all, such cases will be misinterpreted unless the implicit purpose and relevance of component acts are identified. What we are seeing here is action saliently guided by Balinese concepts of health care, morality, and compassion. And only when its premises are known can such action be adequately interpreted.

Let me first do something to remedy my first source of misinterpretation: the incident's link with other events. The case of the lost boy had an almost immediate sequel which cast my initial understanding in doubt.

Having bid the headmaster farewell, the boy's sister and I slowly made our way back to the desperate mother. Fifty yards from the house she observed, "The headmaster is with my mother. His car is parked outside." Inside the man was cheering up the distraught woman. Now again he was laughing and joking in ways that might seem unconcerned. But actions besides his rushing to her house bespoke care and sympathy. On the table between them lay fruits he had brought. Soon he stood up to leave. He put a five-thousand-rupiah note in her hand. When an hour later the boy reappeared safe and sound, the headmaster returned. This time he was grave and stern in the face and scolded the boy for the fright and fear he had caused his mother, warning that she had now fallen sick.

In a critique of anthropological studies of grief and mourning, Rosaldo has warned against the danger of confining our reading of people's mourning to institutionalized ritual acts (R. Rosaldo 1984) when the work of grieving persists through time and in everyday contexts as well. A similar warning applies also to popular health care.

It is not reducible to readily visible taboos, personal hygiene, or preventive cosmetics and medicines. Balinese observe a number of such practices that manifest persistent concern with health: they drink daily the sweetened Javanese *jamu* or bitter Balinese *loloh*—traditional herb medicine to counter a variety of plagues; they try to avoid exposure to wind, sun, and cold,[8] seek a properly balanced intake of hot and cold foods, bathe at least twice a day, and take daily medicines "to stay always young" (and strong) (*jamu awet muda*). But any people's concern with health takes a variety of other forms enmeshed in everyday routines that may appear to the observer to be primarily geared to *other* activities. Part of an ongoing process of life, the extent and salience of health care vary dramatically across cultures (Kleinman 1980, 40–41).

That popular health care in Bali is embedded in other activities and only rarely singled out relates to their experience of self as steadily exposed to myriad health-endangering forces; of health as hinging on matters of feeling-thought; and of illness etiology as typically multiplex. Fellow beings, deities, demons, sundry (super)natural spirits, and the souls of the dead can strike a person sick or dead. Hence health is a concern never to be set aside but always to be kept salient.

It should be clear that when I speak of popular health care it is in the broad sense of the term. I am concerned with some of its implications, not with the system as such (Kleinman 1980, 26).[9] I give primacy to a conception of "emotion work," because it presents the ethnography so appropriately; it seems persistently to compel and motivate action; it is explicitly perceived as preventing illness; and it points to the way certain emotions are linked with specific somatic ailments.

The Vital Spirit/Life Force

Health, in Balinese popular conception, depends on an intricate relationship between body (*badan*) and spirit/life force (*bayu*), two mutually sustaining parts of an integral whole. Most decisive is the condition of the life force. As the vital energy that keeps all else moving, it offers the best protection against illness of every kind. This is not to say that the *bayu* can withstand all and every illness. But it is a major asset in a world where innumerable illnesses are caused by black magic.

We have seen that the Balinese live in a world where murder or attempted murder resulting in sickness from sorcery is the order of the day. An assault of black magic depends for its outcome on a contest between the power of the attacker and that of the target victim. Whoever has the stronger is likely to win.[10] But the *bayu* also offers inestimable protection against illness caused by natural factors. Said a Balinese doctor: "The power in all healing is the person himself, his *bayu*. If a person *feels* sick, who can make him well? Medicine is only a means to ease the obstruction, it cannot heal by itself."

Another said: "In recovering from sickness, medicine works only 5 percent; 95 percent depends on the person himself and the state of his *bayu*." Yet others stress the role of the heart as akin to *bayu*.

The *bayu* sustains the body but is not itself a part of it. It represents what is needed to live and grow, and thus all animate things have *bayu*, plants, trees, animals, etc. *Bayu* may be glossed as vital essence, life force, energy or power, and goes also by the names *jiwa, tenaga* or *semangat*. It is perceived as flowing in the blood and refurbishing energy. It is all over the body, flowing in the veins.[11]

But it is also perceived—if in popular "misconception"—to transmute into concentrated form and exit from the body when frightened or suddenly surprised. Bodily sensations such as rapid heartbeat, trembling, and emptiness make this interpretation a sensible one. Embedded in the conception is a metamessage: care for the *bayu,* or it may leave you powerless.

Care is provided in two major ways: by physical and mental nourishment. Food provides physical energy—not any manner of food, but properly balanced and composed. A surfeit of hot foods, such as meat or durian, overenergizes the *bayu* and throws it off balance. Excess of cold foods, such as milk, is less detrimental but may stiffen and make rigid the *bayu.*[12] Both imbalance and rigidity/inflexibility entail lowered resistance and lack of well-being.

Excessive exercise exhausts the *bayu,* but I have not heard that limited exercise should weaken the *bayu.*

But care for the *bayu* is as much or even more a question of spiritual nourishment. Just as plants will weaken and die if they do not receive fertilizer, so with the *bayu,* except nourishment in its case has also an ethereal aspect. To thrive and be well, the person must care for her *bayu* by the power of good feeling-thoughts.

Because of its spiritual quality, the *bayu* belongs medically within the realm of traditional healers. Doctors cannot cope with the *bayu.* Theirs is an expertise limited to the domain of the body, and we shall see that few illnesses have this singular quality (chap. 12). True, if a man vomits, he loses only physical *bayu,* and the doctor may help him by vitamin injections. But for most illnesses Balinese will see balians rather than, or in addition to, medical practitioners (chaps. 12 and 13).

The *bayu,* of such tremendous importance in a world fraught with illness and misfortune, is a sensitive force. It is susceptible to a variety of upheavals from climatic and nutritional causes, but particularly to emotional upsets.

Feeling-thought thus features as a key concept in Balinese popular health care, and managing the heart—*ngabe keneh*—is a moral issue sustained by collective social sanctions to protect the health and welfare of everyone.

Because of the force of expression in shaping health, all should contribute to the maintenance of a cheerful and smooth social ambience.

Balance in Bodily Experience: Calm or Confused

Health, in Hindu-Balinese philosophy, depends on a precarious condition of balance (*keseimbangan*) in body and soul—two aspects of an integral whole. It has three aspects (referred to as *tri hita karana*), indicating the three main cosmological entities that must be related to one another in harmony: God, as the supreme power; the macrocosm about the person, including social relations (*buana agung*); and the person herself as a microcosm with physical needs and feeling-thoughts (*buana alit*) (cf. chap. 12). Disharmony between any of these elements will upset the balance and may cause illness (Muninjaya 1982).

However, these are philosophical concepts, not, by my evidence, part and parcel of people's everyday way of thinking. Balance (*keseimbangan*), while a key concept applied to *some* aspects of a person's relations with the (super)natural and social world, has an impersonal and referential character rather than an experiential one. The body, by contrast, is experienced and sensed. Hence Balinese corrected me when in the early stages of fieldwork I talked and phrased questions as if I believed "balance" was a key to understanding health. Softly one man commented, "What you say is true, but it is not the way we feel-think" (see chap. 14).

Instead, they seem to feel-think in terms of concepts of calm (*tenang, diam*) and confused (*bingung, lengeh, puyung*) as the experienced sensations emanating when one is in balance or imbalance with oneself. Calm and confusion are cultural constructs that link feeling-thought and bodily experience in a distinctive manner. Each connotes simultaneously a state of feeling-thought and a set of physical sensations and links that condition with a view of cause and, in the case of confusion, a state of preparedness for remedial actions. In Robert Solomon's words, to be calm, or confused, connotes a relationship between oneself and one's situation: "It is not merely a feeling, or an inner phenomenon, but an *interpretation*" (Solomon 1984, 48).

In everyday discourse, and on the experiential level, the notions of calm and confused thus supplant balance/imbalance as the reference for a person's assessment of her health and safety.

A feeling of calm entails a state of adjustment to the circumstances in which one finds oneself: an attitude of "not caring," forgetting the bad, letting bygones be bygones, and giving without expectation of return. Relaxed at the center, one avoids disappointment, does not get worked up, combats anger, does not bear grudges, and dispels fear. One feels generally "light and fresh" (*somboh*) and strong (*kuat*).

This is an ideal state to strive for. In most people's lives confusion of various kinds and degrees often mars the desired state. Balinese have a number of terms to differentiate kinds and degrees of confusion, ranging from mild anxiety or worry (as in *bimbang*) through disorientation, being upset (as in *bingung*) to absentminded, dazed (as in *bengong*) to feeling empty (as in *puyung*) to intense shivering and dizziness (as in *lengeh* or *lempuyengan*—also called motion sickness). Most commonly applied is *bingung,* the generic term generally used to connote a "confused" state of being.

The symptomatology of confusion is clear-cut and shared: headache, bodily unease and unsteadiness, and general fatigue. It can be minor or major, depending on the cause. A cause is often extrapolated from symptoms rather than identified beforehand. Headache is always present. Indeed the label for headache (*pusing*) is often used as a synonym for confused (*bingung*). The experiential quality of headache is not so much pain—(indeed "pain" need not be present at all)—but a fearsome feeling of loss of control, unsteadiness, vulnerability. A confused person feels exposed and vulnerable. Not actually sick (*sakit*)—for a confused state is judged so common as to be labeled ubiquitous—one is yet aware that remedies are called for, as one *feels* afflicted, however common that may be.

Increased susceptibility to magical attacks is but one of the expressed concerns. It reflects that one stands in greater danger of causing offense because judgment is blurred, and also that one has less chance of rebuffing an attack. Another liability concerns a host of illnesses from (super)natural causes, of which illness from fright or soulloss may be the most common. The causes of confusion are legion. A survey of differential diagnoses suggested by various people in the case of the boy who ran away exemplifies the scope and range.

1. A spirit medium diagnosed the boy as severely confused due to a critical imbalance in his life. His parents had sent him to a high-ranking school, though he lacked intellectual abilities. The medium advised that the boy be put into a technical school instead.

2. His mother and grandmother (who did not wish to take the boy out of a prestigious school) leaned toward a different interpretation: the boy was severely confused because he harbored a grudge (*dendam benci*) against a neighbor who had unjustly accused him of the theft of a pet bird. What might they do to help him? I asked. Give him back self-confidence ("maybe he thinks we don't believe him") and help him "not to care."

3. His teacher (who was a part-time healer) diagnosed the boy as confused because his home environment was not congenial: his father was too strict and rash. Better if he were moved to a foster home.

4. The boy's sister saw his confusion as a by-product of a spoiled upbringing: "He receives too much attention and gets too high opinion

of himself. I have seen in compositions for his school how he writes, 'My parents love me so much I can do anything I like.' Truly, I envy the children of Ketut Artje. They fear and respect their father."

5. Some neighbors said the boy was confused because he danced break dance. The *bayu* cannot sustain such assaults to stability and calm.

6. A ready explanation of why the boy might be sick was ruled out quickly: his name, which had already been changed once in his childhood because he was always sick, was now checked again and found to be suitable (*cocok*) with his life force.[13] But he had stepped on some *jinn* when he played on the beach, said the balian, and they had disturbed his *bayu*, causing his confusion.

"Confused" in this case was used to connote an affliction of unspecified, multiple etiology and alarming, unpredictable effects. Often "confusion" is an element in illness of another name. Experientially it is a diagnostic criterion. A person feels headache/confusion, perceives herself as weak, and probes for other symptoms that may indicate diagnosis. Often headache/confusion, loss of energy, and dizziness come alone, but the syndrome must be arrested by appropriate remedial action.

A person of weak *bayu* is endangered in the world. Even minor forms of surprise, if startling, may cause illness in various forms. Sudden loud noise as from a quarrel (but not from thunder in the rainy season, for that is expected); frightening sights as from traffic accidents or (super)natural ghosts; frightening sounds as from outbursts of anger (but not from (super)natural spirits, for that is expected); violent motions as from a bus suddenly brought to a halt; to fall down and stumble—these are some common causes of "illness from shock or fright," which is a minor form of, or first stage in, soulloss.

Soulloss implies an intense form of "confusion" connoted by a special word (*lempuyengan*) and sometimes referred to as "motion sickness." The person feels as if she has lost herself, or as if half of her is dead. The spirit feels as if it is flying. She has no energy and is troubled by insomnia. She does not want to eat; the mouth tastes bitter. Fever or alternating hot and cold feelings may be rampant as well. Soulloss is a prime cause of death, particularly in children and old people, and is perhaps the cause most commonly hit upon in the initial diagnosis of illness where the etiology is unknown (see plate 8).

The construction of the *bayu* as eminently vulnerable to emotional upsets has some particularly taxing consequences in the case of mothers with breast-feeding children. The mother is conceived as the greatest danger to the health and life of her own child. Startlement, anger, sorrow, etc., on her part account for roughly 50 percent of all cases of child mortality in some areas where we worked, as these deaths were diagnosed by women themselves (often with the help of folk healers). Because the mother's *bayu* flows in her blood which in turn produces her milk, any untoward emotion will directly affect her milk to make it hot and life-damaging to the child: "That's why it's very hard for us to be a mother. The hardship of a mother cannot be likened to that of any other person" (Wikan 1989a, 27).

A Strong Spirit, a Strong Heart

Balinese are definite that men and women are equally susceptible to afflictions of the body-soul, but the very young and the old are most susceptible. To strengthen and steady the *bayu* is thus of paramount concern. One should also *concentrate* one's energy by calm and unified, not scattered, thinking. "Make your power one" (*satukan jiwa*), say Balinese, or the *bayu* is easily lost. But a steadfast *bayu* will be resilient to surprise, recalcitrant in the face of magic, restitutive against illness. Energy will flow unimpeded, blood will circulate freely.

A Balinese *bayu* has an almost palpable quality. It is experienced and assessed by culturally constructed somatic signs, and the Balinese preoccupation with the state of their *bayu* can hardly be overstressed. As a Western child learns to feel and thus to know that she has a sore throat or a stomachache, so a Balinese child learns to feel she suffers from a weak *bayu*. Neither necessarily entails an illness but more a premonition to be careful lest . . . The forebodings relate in the West to disease, in Bali to viability in a much more basic sense.

Before engaging in important tasks, Balinese will probe their *bayu* to feel if it is strong enough to withstand certain ventures. They may also be concerned to judge others, and their comparable strength, by the actions these others undertake. Whereas in the first phase of fieldwork, when I was with my husband and child, I had no great difficulty in getting Balinese to accompany me to certain villages renowned for their black magic, it proved impossible later: the fact that I had traveled halfway around the world on my own without getting sick meant that my *bayu* must be extremely strong. By extension this meant that it would be dangerous to accompany me to places where I was a likely target of black magic. The magic directed at me would bounce and hit my nearest companion. As magic "by wrong address" is even more dangerous than magic that hits its target, Balinese politely excused themselves when I was set on "risky" courses.

Anger and Black Magic

Certain emotions in Bali are more dangerous than "similar" emotions in other cultures I know because, relegated to secret existence, they are doomed to operate in an unrestrained manner. Anger, envy, jealousy, and offense are morally so deprecable that if circumstances should force a person to admit to the persistence of such feeling-thoughts, she is likely to lay claim to a diagnosis of illness inflicted by black magic. Many Balinese deny ever having been angry; it is not an emotion they have felt in themselves. The balian whose help an angry person seeks will validate this diagnosis and proclaim: "This [the anger] is not you, it is so-and-so."

Anger in oneself is dangerous. It gives a characteristic hot (*panas/ kebus*) feeling because the blood pushes through the body too quickly.[14] It is physically felt as an intemperate sensation in the heart, and it causes sleeplessness. Prolonged anger causes a number of sicknesses such as anger- or heart-sickness (*sakit keneh* or *sakit hati*) and tuberculosis. But more dangerous is anger in another.

The large number of deaths and misfortunes ascribed to black magic is one source of evidence of this. Another reliable source is the body, according to Balinese praxis. When Balinese suspect others of evil, they will examine their own body for illness-manifesting signs. They will also ransack the bed, food, and kitchen for concealed magic materials and be alert to omens in their social environment that portend disaster. Next, they will be alert to signs of illness in family members, due to fear of magic "by wrong address." With illness as a focal concern, the chances are considerable that one may actually feel sick.

So it is necessary to take precautions to protect oneself and one's family members by observing stringent rules of propriety and etiquette. One is not wholly at the mercy of others if one is also diligent in prayer and protects one's soul. Managing the heart is the measure, "forgetting" and "not caring" essential techniques Balinese inculcate in their children from the earliest age.

The Concept and Practice of "Not Caring"

When Suriati felt angry with people because they laughed at her distress, her behavior was eminently sensible by Balinese standards: first she washed face and hands in cold water to diminish the hot feeling, then she sought out cheerful company "that will make me think of happier things." Thus, utilizing time-honored techniques, she managed to deal with her anger and "not to care."

For minor life problems it is best "not to care" but to "forget" the bad that has come to pass and "let bygones be bygones." For major problems a "solution" must be found, and it requires one to "manage one's heart" by willful, constructive response. This is how the difference between these concepts/techniques was explained to me when I asked. In everyday discourse "not caring" and "managing one's heart" seem to be used interchangeably.

"Not to care" (*sing ngerunguange*) is a distinctly Balinese conception [15] that is thought to be fundamental in nurturing bodily health. Expressed in numerous idioms and proverbs, it is an attitude into which children are socialized from the earliest age. A child or adult who sits quietly or with a grave face will be reprimanded: "Do not mind! Forget it!" or "Come on, don't give yourself headache/confusion!" or "Don't be sad, be cheerful!" (*Jangan bersedih, gembiralah*). Less gently, people may say: "Why do you always look sad?" (implicitly "You sadden us!") (*Untuk apa kamu selalu bersedih*). Numerous other expressions are in use to implant the attitude, all bound up with the idea of letting bygones be bygones. One must not care, or one will make oneself unhappy, confused, and given to headaches. One will make others sad, hence vulnerable as well. Concern for all requires that one "does not care."

Yet other expressions used to instill the same attitude are: "You must not be sad!" (*Ede sube sedeh dogenan*); "Don't take headache, do not allow yourself to get confused/distracted/distressed!" (*Jangan deperdulikan* or *jangan ambil pusing*); "Do not mind!" (*Tusing ngerunguange* or *jangan perduli*). *Ede (ampunang) sube kerunguange* has the added reference of "not again" and is often used to a person who has been hurt by the spouse, meaning "It is time you stop caring about him or her!" "Love your spouse/family/friends, but do not care about them" sums up well the meaning of "not caring." *Suka-sukanya* or *acuh-tak-acuh* (I let it be up to him/her, I will not worry myself), a person may say to console herself when struggling to find a way out of unhappiness.

A child who complains about ill treatment from other children will not be encouraged to elaborate on its pain but be enjoined to forget it and not to care. One must learn to elevate oneself above pettiness and misdemeanor—to be high-spirited (*jiwa besar*)—or one is easily hurt or angered and given to sickness. But when persons manage "not to care," the outcome is crowned with personal satisfaction, a sense of physical well-being and social esteem.

"See how much better Kariani manages than Ari," said Suriati to me one day when we had gone from the one to the other. We had found Ari steeped in misery and brooding on her husband's neglect. Her house was messy, the children unkempt. Kariani's house by contrast was spotless, the children nourished and well-clad. "Kariani does not care about her husband," continued Suriati. No implication of failing love was entailed. Loving and "not caring' are not contradictory notions. What she meant was simply that Kariani did not worry and brood.

A poor man in his mid-forties told me a moving story of his effort to better the family's situation by placing a few hens with a peasant to raise chickens for profit. As it turned out, he came to love the chickens so much that he could not bear to think of selling them: every time he would arrive to inspect his fortune, the chickens would rush toward him, jumping on him, thrilled to see him and pecking the peas he fed them from his hand. So he instructed the peasant not to sell. The chickens grew to delightful proportions, but then it began; every time the owner came to see them, some would be gone. The peasant would serve him tragic stories of how one had been taken by a dog, another killed by a truck, his children had been sick and starving so he had to slaughter some to save their lives, etc. Every time new stories of this kind. The owner got so upset that to protect himself he left the chickens there and then, never turning back. It has been a year now, and he has not seen them, though they are his property, worth no small sum (if they are still alive). Precious though they are, more precious was the peace of his soul:

> Never mind the chickens. There must be some three hundred
> of them now if they have thrived and not been killed off. I
> don't care. I told him, they are all yours, just keep them! I
> was afraid of what I might do, and then what about my fam-
> ily! Every time I went there, I would be so upset. Now I am
> keeper of my own peace of mind.

A third example: A woman was suffering gravely because her husband ran about with other women. She neglected her children, and the house was a mess. She went from balian to balian for help, to no avail. But one day she looked fit and fine again, the children were clothed, the house cleaned. She told how she had finally managed "not to care": "*Suka-sukanya*" (it's up to him). She would do her best to fulfill her duties vis-à-vis husband and children; perhaps that would shame him into changing his ways. Her neighbor, happy with this turn of events, spontaneously related how her own mother, years back, had in a similar situation done just that. She did not care, but she served her husband the best of food, treated him with deference and kindness, and kept the house in perfect order. The husband, shamed to see himself by contrast in the mirror she metaphorically held up for him, changed his ways (Wikan 1987, 359).

In this mode of response may be found the basis of Bateson's abstraction of asymmetric schismogenesis as the underpinning of the Balinese "steady state" ([1949] 1972a). A deteriorating performance on the part of one person does not elicit escalating sanctions from the other. On the contrary, the other is sanctioned—and at times even shamed—in a way that does not reflect negatively on the person who causes the shaming, and the shaming cannot truly offend. At the same time the tenor of ceremoniousness and cheerfulness in Balinese social life is left undisturbed. What has not been recognized is that the motivation for this kind of response arises not merely from social ethics but springs from conscious, pervasive welfare concerns.

"Not caring" offers no royal road to happiness but is facilitated through conscious positive response, trying to see the good in the bad. The most moving example that I came across concerned Muslim parents, some of whom had lost up to sixteen children before the age of two, who consoled themselves that it happened because God loved them more than others. On the Day of Judgment, when other parents would boil in the heat of the desert, their own dead children would run forth, each with a pitcher of cold water in its hand, to quench the thirst of their beloved parents. In less vivid images Suriati, as we shall see, set out to convince herself that it was to the good that her boyfriend had died. Even redefining experience to surmount a distressing feeling may provide a way, as when the girl said repeatedly to herself "he is a madman" so she would not be angry with him and thus become sick.

"Not caring" is applicable to present and past worries or pains. It is a moral injunction, a formula for living that also draws on laughter and cheerfulness. Balinese talk of laughter "taking bad feeling out" or "making it go away." What is their evidence?

Their bodies speak. They know from experience that sadness or anger will weigh on the heart and cause inner pressure (*tekanan batin*). But feeling-thoughts, as *processes,* are emminently shapable, and sadness makes one sick *only so long as it is felt.* Thus what counts is to try not to feel, and to think about an experience aggravates the feeling. The idea that one might rid oneself of bad feeling by impelling oneself the deeper into it would seem to Balinese absurd. More rational ways which in their experience actually work are "forgetting" and "guiding one's heart." These are keys to Balinese experience.

In situations where a solution must be found one might have to dwell briefly and temporarily on a bad experience. But for most life experiences "forgetting" will do better, either because one is powerless to change the bygones or because one will always benefit from preserving peace of mind. One will then emerge "fresh" (*somboh*), clear (*cedang*), calm (*tenang*), and strong (*kuat*), and one's self-value (*harga diri*) is enhanced.

Return to Laughter

Making oneself, and others, happy from sadness works because of the intimate relationship Balinese perceive between feeling and expression. More than an abstract model or ethnotheory, theirs is an everyday experience which testifies to the supreme value of good feeling-thinking and good expressions. Physically they feel better, lighter, happier when submerged in laughter than when steeped in pain. Laughter accomplishes the feat of driving sadness away in the way that cold water relieves heat in the body or hot foods neutralize an excess of cold. Anyone who has used laughter to induce good feeling-thinking has experienced the senselessness of "choosing" pain.

Laughing in North Bali is thus a powerful social mechanism that serves the triple social functions of expressing friendliness and conviviality, shame and mockery, sympathy and consolation. An integral element of most social relations, it is generally multivocal and ambiguous. In an actual social instance people might be seen to laugh to (1) protect themselves (from offending another) by acting friendly, (2) create the social gaiety in which everyone, and particularly a sad person, thrives, and (3) ridicule another. In her confused state, Suriati leaned toward the latter interpretation, and this mobilized her fear of being shamed behind a concerted effort to reenter the protective circle of gaiety. Thus the capacity of laughter to drive sadness out may be seen as enhanced by its very ambiguity. It simultaneously provides both encouragement of good emotions and threatened sanction of ridicule if bad emotions are not overcome.

The Problem of Suffering

Not caring, forgetting, and managing one's heart seek to deal with "the problem of suffering" (C. Geertz [1966] 1973b, 104–8). The Balinese solution is not unique. To see the good in the bad is a coping technique well known from other societies as well. What is peculiar to Balinese is their recognition of "the problem of suffering" as a key existential problem, one that entails excessive costs unless anticipated and dealt with in a comprehensive manner. To facilitate this, Balinese have fashioned a solution of a kind: a model of and for life, comprising worldview, feelings, ethics, and pragmatics. By inculcating this vision of the art of living from the earliest age and linking it closely with fears of social sanctions, sorcery, and somatic illness, they have encoded and instituted a distinctive health care praxis. Particularly in its crucial aspect of cultivating "not caring," it represents a natural way of being-in-the-world, a way of responding to life's problems, a state of preparedness for action rather than a belatedly sought remedial solution to particular problems. It thus motivates a pervasive style of being, many aspects of which are strikingly apparent to outside observers, whereas its crucial connection with health concerns is far from transparent to persons who live by other paradigms.

Clifford Geertz has written of a peculiar note, a stylistic nuance that one would not expect to find coexistant with the polished grace and etiquette. He translated this as "playful theatricality," warning that "the playfulness is not lighthearted but almost grave and the theatricality not spontaneous but almost forced" ([1966] 1973a, 401). When its sources are identified in the Balinese complex of emotional imagery relating to body and health, there is no longer anything incongruous about this note, I suggest. Indeed, its association with composure is wholly compatible when recognition is made that from a Balinese point of view "cheerfulness" and "friendliness" constitute indispensable elements of popular health care.

This cheerfulness, which is indeed often forced and dead serious, reads as a conscious, at times nearly frantic, attempt to dispel bad feeling-thoughts that threaten the well-being of one's family and oneself. It is also the indispensable sign to the world that one is indeed free of harmful affects that might threaten and harm others.

In conclusion it may be useful to emphasize some general considerations. My materials emphasize above all the *ongoing* nature of health concerns, their essential embeddedness in daily life and humdrum activities *over time*. It is essential to acknowledge this fact. Sickness may be episodic, but health is a permanent concern—in North Bali nearly an obsession. Sickness is readily apparent, but health and health precautions may be invisible as such to us and easily misidentified as something other than what they are. We must be prepared to pursue the ramifications of health care wherever our data lead us, into any and all realms of life. Otherwise we may be left with a truncated account of health care *and* with wide areas of patterned activity for which we have failed to identify the underlying purpose—tempting us to interpret them, as Geertz does so eloquently for Bali, as empty of mundane purposes and therefore "aesthetic" at base.

PART FOUR

Coping with the Suffering Life Inevitably Brings

CHAPTER TEN

Finding a Way out of Sadness

He who has left
sleeps deeply in his last
resting place. I fashion
his misquito net
from my prayers.
—SURIATI

It was four years after her friend's death, and Suriati and I met again as we had several times through these years. She had been married for nearly three years. Her marriage was not without its problems.

She had not told me before, but I had sensed it. And she, knowing me quite well, probably knew that I could feel her heart. This time, as we talked, she exposed her heart freely to me. And suddenly she made an allusion to some poems she had written during the first year of grief: "Sometimes when I am angry with my husband (because . . .), I place the poems in front of him and say, 'Look here, read this!' "

To my incredulous question, she admitted this was not the literal truth, but what she would have wished to do. Actually, she placed the diary with the poems in a place where he would be sure to find it, in the hope that he would open it and read. She does not know whether he does. She only hopes so.

Sometimes her husband teases her, saying, "He was your first husband, you must forget!" "No," says she, "we must not forget, we should always remember the dead." Is her husband jealous of the dead boy? "Oh, no, not at all! My husband always lets bygones be bygones."

It is easier for some than for others to practice what culture preaches. Suriati's husband is also Balinese, but his character is very different from hers. He is also very different from her friend who died. Their names are the same, which made Suriati hope their characters would be similar. But the relationship turned out to be more complex, and Suriati is left to make the best out of her marriage to a man who is a religious fanatic, of indubitable stature and righteousness, but shallow in his sensivity to people's hearts.

Ideologically committed to letting bygones be bygones, it would not occur to her husband to express jealousy of the dead boy. Perhaps he might not even grasp the force and significance of her poems, should he

195

happen to read them. Perhaps they might strike him as insignificant or immature. But to Suriati they bespeak a world, now passed, of acute suffering and pain. She now wishes them to be read, a testimony to her commitment and loyalty to a man she would have married. They were written during the five first months of grief.[1]

Memories of Dearest Hamza

My love . . .
This life on Earth is laced with deceit
Now you are free of it,
No longer does it make its demands on you
You are free . . . pure . . . cleansed

My love . . .
I am overcome with sorrow
to see the emptiness
                of your bed.
Abandoned we are, I, father, mother, your brother and sister.

My love . . .
Tears sprout
as I lay the blossoms of my sorrow on
        the ground by your resting place.
I cling to the last trace of you
embracing at the very moment we part.
I move without touching the ground
The blossoms of my sorrow fall to the ground
All has turned empty, lonely, still, and dead.

But he who went away
leaves a million thoughts
                a million loves
and a million visions, haunting
a poor body
and stirring in the black night.

He who has left
will never return.

When the pine tree sets new buds
and the jasmine perfumes the air
that is when the kamboja-blossoms fall,
swept down by the melancholy wind.
Clouds . . . rain . . . darkness and loneliness.
The heart struggles
the face grieves.

He who has left
sleeps deeply in his last
resting place. I fashion his mosquito net
from my prayers.
Has he carried away
a piece of my innocent heart?
He who has left and will never return?

I quietly caress the cold night
Tears well forth
The heart cannot restrain them
now that God has called you to his side.

*   *   *

Overcome by sorrow I greet
the people I cherish, I love.
They leave me. Are gone for me.

I submit. I consent.

Every gesture you made in life
speaks to me, is part of me.
With my tears and my prayers
I hold on to
the moment when your shadow was dimmed.

Your train departs
It carries away my pure, white love.
With the black smoke
that rises and mocks me
goes my dark passion.

The whistle has blown
Now only my sobs
and my heartbeat stays on;
and a longing
ever more profound.

I put back in your heart's canoe
the fading picture of my name.
The passing days
swallow up my life
and
my step grows weary.

*   *   *

A moment—a disaster   (written on the first day)
speaks its grief
a maiden who desperately
waits for the love
          of a young man . . . must have her heart shattered.
Her love already stands
before the Almighty
and has succumbed.
Oh Hamza, take me into your world!
The girl with so shattered a heart.

*　　*　　*

The moment
the telegram reached me   (written three weeks after
about Hamza   his death)
    I had to read it.
    I could not believe
    what it said
    —as if the ground under me
    shook.

Oh God. He was truly
my one desire

He was my
most precious possession
Why did he leave me
forever?

*　　*　　*

Farewell, my love   (written after
Wind . . .   four months)
Dry leaves . . .

Rain . . .
Silently
accept January 1984.

After the disruption
of the storm that carried him away
there are no more tears.
I have cried them all
and I should not resist His will
because of love.

Farewell, my love.
Silently.
I have harvested what you planted
Now there are no more blossoms left
to pick.

The days without Hamza are void.
A vase with no
flowers, a sky with no moon.
Hamza was beauty
and refuge.

Suriati says she never showed these poems to anyone. They were her private statement of grief that she would not share with a living soul. I knew she wrote poems at the time, but it never occurred to me to ask to see them. I respected her efforts to appear as she wished even her best friends to see her: as someone committed to coping, carrying head and posture erect even when at times her eyes turned bottomlessly black with sorrow.

She was impressive, and we who cared for her could best help her by sustaining her efforts to endure. My own appropriate role was one of joining others in the effort to surround her with merriment and laughter, to help her "forget," a commitment on everyone's part to the best formula for living: that one had better let bygones be bygones.

The tears she shed, she shed mostly alone, so that not even her mother would see. But she was not alone in this, her most deepfelt experience of grief. She could feel her friend's soul close, touching her, caring and consoling. There is an element of "togetherness" among Balinese in many experiences that Westerners take to be solitary and private. Souls move in their world and touch one another, both among the living and between the living and the dead.

Suriati's friend sustained her, and it was for him and her she wrote the poems. Today they carry another meaning. Still so evocative she is afraid to recite them aloud because they might make her cry, they stand as a testimony to a world long gone to which she feels still committed. Perhaps also she now wishes them to be read—for it was her suggestion that they be published—so her friend will have an impact upon the world. A relationship of secretive character, never consummated before the world, here finds irradicable form and expression.

As on the gravestone that bears his name, his memory is here inscribed, and here it is everlastingly linked to hers.

When in her struggle to find a way out of sadness Suriati turned to writing poetry, it was a technique for which she was culturally prepared.

It is said to be quite common for Balinese to write poems to express their sadness, but I had never seen any, only had people tell me that they have written such. The longings of the heart should remain private, and it was never appropriate for me to ask to see any of these poems.

In her efforts to cope in the first year Suriati also made use of other techniques for which she was culturally prepared. One concerned seeking consolation and comfort from her dead friend's clothes.

> Sometimes I do something strange: I sit on the bed under his large photo on the wall, and I hang his cap on the wall and put his shirt on myself, and then I almost feel he is there in the room with me, and I feel better. Maybe I am mad to act like this, but it does make me feel better. Also, if other men wear his cap in my presence, I almost feel he is alive and with me. When his brother visits, I ask him to wear my friend's cap, and at a celebration a few days ago I asked my cousin's husband to wear his cap. He grew angry, saying he had his own cap, but he finally gave in. It made me feel very good.

Seeking comfort from the clothes of a person one loves to quench feelings of sadness from loss is a time-honored technique.[1] When separated from a beloved, Balinese generally suffer sickness from longing or loss—*sakit rindu*—symptoms of which are intermittent fever, loss of appetite and sleep, and headache/dizziness. A friend who travels much in her work tells how she always brings a piece of her youngest child's clothing along in her handbag. It assuages feelings of sadness and makes her feel close. At night she puts the garment under her pillow, and she also takes care to have a piece of her own clothing under the child's pillow so he will not get sickly. On our return to Bali the family with whom we had stayed the previous year told us how relieved they had been that we had left some of our belongings behind. On the evening of our departure their youngest child had turned very sick with fevers and incessant crying. They diagnosed the cause as longing sickness for our son, Kim, who had always used to play with the child. After some trepidation as to what they could do now that we were gone, someone had the idea of searching through our bags. There was a cap of Kim's, and by placing it on the child's head, he was quickly calmed and cured. He wore it for protection for some time thereafter.

Suriati's friend's family sent her several of the dead boy's clothes, and she often wore his jumpers for protection. It had an effect on her, but also on him. She believed his soul found comfort through her wearing his clothes.

But while she thus strove to stay in touch with his soul, she also searched for ways to *accept* the unchangeable fact that he and she were now living on separate planes of existence. She must shape her life in the world without him and marry some day, thus her concern not to be branded a "widow." She must reduce her own suffering to cope.

Religion teaches her that the day of death is inscribed at birth. Submission to God requires one not to grieve but to accept. But that was not sufficient consolation. In an effort to see the good in the bad that had come to pass, she also set about convincing herself it may have been for the best that her friend died. The abruptness of his death indicated he might have long been suffering from latent tuberculosis. Had he lived, he might have passed the illness on to the children they would have had. If so, she would have suffered even more than she now did.

For her friend, she need not grieve. He is better off now than before. Having led a life devoted to religion, his faults were few and his place in Heaven assured. Death puts the lives of the bereaved at stake—for the dead we need not grieve. It is the bereaved who compel our compassion, not the deceased.

Indeed, Suriati believes that her friend had a forewarning of what would come to pass. Two days before he died, she talked with him at length on the phone, and he closed saying that two days later she would receive a telegram announcing the date he would come with his father to ask for her hand in marriage. But he also added: "If the telegram does not arrive, you will receive a lengthy explanation which perhaps you will not understand . . ." This is all recorded in minute detail in Suriati's diary for December 31, 1983, as I have seen. The next entry reads: "Received telegram at 11:00 A.M. 'Your brother, Hamza, is dead.'"

It took a long time for Suriati to quiet the feeling of sadness that lay as a dark undertone to the shimmering self she presented to the world. She struggled with many somatic ailments, and she knew full well that most of these were caused by her sadness: the constant headaches which had never before plagued her, the feeling of confusion and dizziness, amnesia, fatigue, occasional fevers, and a disconcerting inability to concentrate. Only the eye ailment, the redness and soreness that had troubled her for some months, she did not ascribe to her longing sickness. But this also miraculously disappeared when after some fifteen months she saw light glimmering at the other end of the tunnel. She was in love.

Her new "friend" belonged to a reputable Singaraja family. She had known *of* him for a long time, but when the match was suggested by a family member of his, Suriati could no longer remember what he looked like, for he had left Bali a long time ago. He was reputed, however, to be exceptionally handsome, and this, matched with his and his family's good standing and indubitable religious piety, led her to take a positive stance from the start. When next she received letters from him, with his photos, and then a telephone call, I had the impression she had made up her mind. Not much was said on the phone, as I can vouch, for I was present: "He was so funny, and he laughed all the time, and I also laughed for I was so shy, I did not know what to say . . ." Yet enough had been communicated to strike a chord. A month later they met for a few hours in the company of her parents. And she gave her word that she would marry him.

Her marriage provided a way "out" of sadness, though that is not to say that she did not love this man. I am convinced that she felt that she did. But with characteristic self-reflection she observed:

> I am so happy that this puts an end to my sadness, that I will
> not, like so many girls I have read about in the paper, drink
> mosquito poison. They do it to kill themselves because they
> feel so sad. Recently there was a couple, boy and girl, who
> died in this way in Pulaki temple. People lose their minds
> when they are sad. Truly, when I felt like my life had ended,
> I thought of it too . . .

Now instead she could immerse herself in dreams about happy times to come. Yet all was not bright and romantic. For she had chosen her partner herself—against strong opposition from parents and kin, who wanted her to marry another man, a brother of the boy who was dead. He was handsome, wealthy, and of high position, and she would have wished to accept him to please his parents, for whom she had come to feel deep affection. But she was afraid: "If I marry him, how can I ever forget my dead friend? And his parents, they will also not be able to forget. It will be better for us all if I stay far away."

The man she chose lived far away, and she beamed as she now spilled over with plans for the exciting events to come: engagement, marriage, moving to a new and unknown place "where there will not be so much to care about." At home she felt weighed down by "cares" and suffered greatly from headaches and confusion. There were the men who wanted to marry her, at least three that she knew of at once, each resorting to ingenious devices to try to induce her to comply with his wishes. One used magic, another used "force" (*pemaksa*), and a third used all his influential contacts. She cried because she felt so pressured, and at night she would wake up in terror because she could hear the bird *kuntilanak* flying above with its characteristic *ke-ke-ke* noises. This is a bird sent by someone who suffers pangs of unrequited love to suck the blood from virgins and young brides. Suriati's mother early in her marriage had suffered gravely from its vicious doings.

Then there were the parents of her friend who was dead, who saw in her a semblance of the son they had lost ("my habit—*kebiasaan*—is just like his") and wanted dearly to keep her as a daughter-in-law: "Yes, it is true, they love me, but the son, does he? All the letters come from the father. But it would be the son I was to marry."

Finally there was her mother, the apple of whose eye Suriati was and whom it pained Suriati to distress: "Yesterday I said to my mother, 'If I marry the brother, *you* will be happy, but what about me?' Everyone cares for themselves only, only I care about me."

Everyone had their plans for her, and she felt torn between their irreconcilable wishes:

At last I thought I had made my mother understand that I will not be happy if I marry that brother. But then yesterday my aunt came visiting. And she asked my mother what job does he have, this Hamza [husband-to-be]? My mother replied that he works in a company. "As a sweeper?" asked my aunt. She mocks [*menghina*] him because he does not have formal education beyond elementary school. His parents died when he was young. And she said that in not accepting the brother [of my dead friend] I had traded gold for iron. So now my mother is vacillating again. Sometimes it will be good for us if we talk to others and ask their advice. But sometimes it is bad, it only makes you confused.

She pitied her mother her predicament:

My mother suffers so much, for in the past when my friend used to come and visit, my mother could feel that he was paying me attention, and she did not like it. When his letters came, she would be moody and irritable. My parents were *so* afraid, from the black magic in Lombok. Later my mother understood that my friend's family is not like that, his is a good and religious family. And so she regretted. But there was no time to forgive, and so it is like a *sin* [*dosa*] my mother has committed, and she feels always the pressure. Now she wants to do good to the family by making me marry the brother. But the fact that they are brothers does not make them the same. Truly, it will be better for me if I marry Hamza. His name is like that of my friend who is dead. Makes me hope that perhaps his heart will be like my friend's too . . .

On why she would not marry her dead friend's brother, she also said:

"It would be very dangerous for me . . ."
"What do you mean, it would be dangerous?"
"He suffers from a broken heart, his girlfriend left him. So he will be suspicious of girls, always on his guard. He would make life very hard on me."
"How do you know he suffers from a broken heart?"
"His father wrote me. He asked me to be understanding and patient with his son until he recovers. I was so angry inside. To ask it of me! Everyone thinks of their own happiness only, I alone care about me . . ."

Suriati's choice of partner, though made at a distance, was deliberate, not rushed. She wrote him a letter, stating her conditions that he must accept before she would comply. Among them was that he must not beat her ("It is very common for wives here to be beaten!"); he must follow his own judgment and not that of his sisters; and he must provide good religious guidance and counsel for the children she would have. But as her first condition she asked that he must not be jealous of her dead friend: "Remember, had it not been for his death, I would not have married you."

She told me how she hoped that perhaps one day they would visit his grave together. And for a photo of herself to send her husband-to-be she chose one where she is kneeling by the dead boy's grave. The tombstone, clearly visible, reads:

Hamza Mansur
Born 31-2 1956
Died 2-1 1984

On the evening of the day when she had irrevocably committed herself to her husband-to-be by giving her word of assent to his brother-in-law, the father of the dead boy arrived from Lombok to request her for his eldest son. Respectful till the end, she had not found a way to tell him that she would not ("let him come, it will be more respectful, I don't care" is what she said at a time when she felt everyone was tugging at her to force her to comply with their wishes). She had hoped that her noncommittal letters would carry the message, or that relatives to whom she wrote her heart would convey to the father the truth. They had not.

And yet the parents appeared at her wedding when it took place a few months later. A sense of the quality of her relations with her would-have-been affines is captured in a poem written by Hamza's sister when his family first met Suriati, a week after his death:

Ode to our Sister Suriati

A million colors, whims, surprises,
entered our life with you.
There was laughter, there were smiles, there were
tears, there was disappointment and
a million feelings form the spokes of our wheel
of meetings and partings.
But they only
strengthen our bond
and our kinship ever more
Oh, that it would last . . . through eternity!

Occasional visiting continued to take place between Hamza's parents and Suriati's parents. But for the first year after her marriage Suriati was distressed that when she wrote to them from time to time, she received no reply: "They are disappointed, I think, but truly, if I had married their son, they would have suffered more. And so would I. For we would never have been able to forget."

Suriati's marriage was set for a time that did not please her. Again pressure was felt. Her husband-to-be, so far away, panicked that perhaps before they had reached the safe harbor of marriage, another man might succeed through love magic in capturing her. And so his family exerted much subtle pressure to finalize the precious connection. Suriati tried to withstand what she experienced as force (*pemaksa*) on their part, but after a month her resolve was broken. She had made it clear from the start that she wished to wait about a year for the wedding so she and her husband would have time to get to know each other well and save enough money for a substantial wedding: "It will be the only time when there will be a wedding in my parents' house, so it should be beautiful and memorable." Now plans had to be rearranged, dreams discarded, and ambitions reduced to a dismal fraction. She was sorry but resigned: "Yesterday when I spoke with him on the phone he cried because he is so afraid that someone else might marry me." Her mother bore her disappointment with quiet reserve: "What can she do? Make her husband-to-be so unhappy. He is already almost sick from fear."

Suriati's resolve was broken down so fast in part because the threat of black magic had been exacerbated by the fact that news of her pending marriage had spread far and wide even before she had agreed to marry. (Mischievous tongues said her prospective in-laws had intentionally planted the rumors to frighten her into compliance). It was a dangerous situation, for it meant that competing suitors knew they had precious little time to act. And so she could expect a spate of black magic to be directed at her. The fact that her husband-to-be was unusually good-looking aggravated the threat. It meant that *many* men would be enraged by envy.

For Suriati it was a harrowing experience, and she suffered gravely. She became afraid to go out, and go she must for she had a job to attend regularly. She did not dare to accept hospitality from people she distrusted and often chose to risk offending them, which was also very dangerous. Whenever a letter arrived at her house she smelled it cautiously to sense if it contained suspicious matter; if she thought it did, her mother hoisted up her sarong and passed it between her legs to take away the power of any potential magic.

Suriati's fears were intense but in no way extreme, given that she was extremely attractive and a prime target for black magic. It is quite common for persons about to marry to take such precautions as she did. Every marriage I have heard about has been besieged by magical attacks from persons consumed by jealousy or envy, and for the last weeks before a wedding the bridal couple is particularly precariously placed. Suriati was a likely target for love magic, for she was considered the epitome of feminine attractiveness: "her face shaped like the moon, her hair long and black, and in manner so *polos*, even *rami:* always content with whatever you give her . . ."

Given this predicament, what option did she have except to agree to hasten the marriage? It is one thing to lose one's beloved through death, quite another to be shackled for life with a despised husband one was briefly lured by magic to love. The effect of the love magic wears off very soon; that is precisely one of its characteristics. And Suriati had several acquaintances who had suddenly woken up one day from their enchantment and been horrified to see the true character of the man they had wed. An aunt, a young woman only slightly older than herself, had in particular aggravated Suriati's fears. Such had been her fate:

At seventeen she had been a beautiful young girl whose interests focused on her education: she was diligent, clever, and determined and took no interest in the many men who were attracted to her. One in particular she found despicable. Then one day, a month before her final exams, she suddenly fell head over heels in love with this man whom before she had found ugly and stupid. She neglected her homework, all she could think of was him, and one day on the way to school she let herself be abducted on his motorbike to his village, which lay remote and poverty-ridden in the hills south of Singaraja. The love magic in this case was exceedingly short-lived. Hardly had she arrived before she came to her senses (*sadar*). She cried so hard she did not stop for two days—this by the account she herself gave me—so that on the third day the family brought a balian who gave her a potion that stilled her crying. Since then she has never cried, but she has lived unhappily ever after. "Look at me, what have I become: a village woman of this . . . place!" she says now, her voice quivering with disdain. She lives in a shack of a house with her five children, while her husband is said to have taken a second wife in town.

(Her tragedy hit her family in Singaraja so hard: her father shortly after had a heart attack, and her younger brother enlisted himself as an apprentice to a balian in Sangsit widely renowned for his powers to counteract love magic. The brother now protects other girls; but the sister is beyond salvation. She must make a life for her children.)

Suriati's life experience comprised intimate knowledge of pitiful fates like this, and it served to warn and deter her. Weakened from a year's sorrow from loss, she could not expect to go unscathed should powerful black magic strike. She was diligent in prayers, took many extra antimagical precautions, and did her best to strengthen her *bayu*. Yet she knew she was weak and lived in constant fear of attack.

In particular she feared action from an old man, a prominent member of the community. He, a widower, had tried for months to persuade her to marry him, not by speaking to her directly about it, but by frequenting her home regularly and using all his influential contacts, of which there were many, to try to convince her of her own best interests. Every so often she would be called to the home of one or another accomplice of his, and once recently she had received a message to come urgently to a religious meeting, only to find herself alone with the leader, an old friend. He cried, by her report, as he recounted to her how he had been asked to suggest a match between her and the old man. She cried too, then she went straight to the telephone office to phone the father of her dead friend in Lombok. He calmed her, saying how the old man committed a sin in proposing a marriage to her; but she must not be angry, she must be quiet in heart and mind. Perhaps God put her through the trial to test (*cobaan*) her . . .

He also warned her that she must be careful, never accept food from that man or any of his friends. But Balinese know there is no limit to the ingenuity of people, or the balians they enlist for aid, when someone is set on a course of love magic.

It is against a background such as this that her decision to rush the marriage should be seen. Once the rumors had spread that she was soon to marry, ordinary, commonplace dangers would be exacerbated, and it would be hazardous in the extreme to wait another six months.

So she said to her prospective in-laws (who had never agreed to defer the wedding date!): "It's up to you, do as you like!" And Suriati was wed on a summer's day in July 1985.

When they cleaned up the living room to prepare for the wedding guests, they found it aswarm with butterflies and rodents, but when they sprayed with insecticide, none fell to the ground. It proves how sensible she was not to wait. With more time on their hands, what might not people have accomplished?

Suriati is still childless. It was not what she would have wished, but perhaps it is better this way. What appears as misfortune often conceals superior judgment on the part of God.

> My husband is devoted to his religious training, he has no time for life and social relations. Also in his development, he did not have the experience of harmonious social relations, so he did not learn to care about others. To learn the value of affection and care, you have to receive it yourself. My husband had to work so hard to make his own life, he learned to care only about himself . . .
>
> It will be good for us if he realizes his plan to go abroad to study for some years. No, I will not be sad. Then I can write him the things he will not now listen to when I speak, and he will read and perhaps reflect. Maybe he will change his ways. It gives me hope. Also I can continue my studies then. Now I have no time . . . Sometimes I say [to myself]: it is not just, I train people at the office and even at home I have to teach: to guide my husband to live. If he goes abroad, he will have to make his way in the world among people and perhaps that will teach him to live . . .
>
> I have been fortunate in that I have a model of harmonious relations in many families I know. My mother's foster father, for instance, and his wife, they have a good family and I know it well. From the time I was fifteen, I used to be called there every weekend to help with the housework after my aunt discovered that at home I did nothing. It was good. This way I learned diligence, and I also experienced for myself how a good family life can be. Mr. Bagus, likewise, do you know that despite all the bad things he has done against me, I must admire him for the way he raises his family. His wife and children are so sensitive and good-hearted.
>
> I feel sorry for my husband that he has not had this kind of experience. So I try to teach him. I encourage him to come with me to harmonious families whom I know that he may

experience for himself and learn to value affection and care. I think God is waiting for me to have children until my husband learns. He must change his ways, his character, so that the children will model themselves on a man who is sensitive and cares about others.

CHAPTER ELEVEN

Power, a Fight for Freedom, and Covert Violence

"Don't you see that to fear someone is to grant him power?"
—WAYAN WIJAYA

"In a democracy a procedure like ours would be unheard of, but we go by the rule of force."
—BALINESE MAN

A man and his wife were the good friends of another man and his wife. The junior man, by his wife's report, loved the senior man so much that if she ever spoke a bad word against him, her husband would turn on her in anger. His admiration and respect for his friend were unconditional.

The senior man was a respected member of the community. He held good employment that paid fairly well, and he had in addition other sources of income. His faith and piety were unquestionable, and he had also attained high political position. All of this made him proud (*bangga*)—but in a manner the community could poorly accept.

True, Ketut Artje had reason to be proud, for he was also blessed with a kindhearted, diligent wife and many children, all of whom were impeccably *polos*. But whereas this should have made him feel quietly proud, he had the habit of extolling his person and position. For instance, he liked telling the story of a time when his two young nephews were lost, and yet they did not despair. The six-year-old said to his younger brother: "We need not be afraid, we need only go to the nearest police station and say who our uncle is. Everyone knows our uncle."

Ketut Artje, in other words, was not merely proud, a good and deserved feeling. Some people said he was *megah*—courting fame, splendor, and prestige and bordering on *sombong*—arrogant. Others, like Wayan Wijaya, the junior man, emphasized only his good qualities.

Wayan Wijaya was also well esteemed, but "respect" in his case reflected different notions of the man. He was excessively intelligent—brilliant, by unanimous opinion. But rather than making him proud, Wayan's intelligence and learning inspired him with a deep humility and love for the people. He was said to be good to everyone, kind, and generous, and as proof of this the story was related of how he once, when a pupil had vomited in the class, wiped the dirt up with a cloth with his own hands. He did not reckon himself above anyone—except in matters of intelligence and learning. That was a gift from God to be used for the people, not something to be exploited for personal advantage.

It was only natural that with this vision of life, Wayan's learning had not brought him material riches. He lived with his wife and children in meager circumstances. But for his wife, a woman of pragmatic outlook who was also esteemed for her intelligence and drive, it is hard to envision how the family would have managed. Wayan had chosen to devote himself to a job that paid pitifully little. In his spare time, likewise, he devoted himself to humanitarian activities.

One day Ketut sent a letter to Wayan's wife, Kede Mireh, asking her to come to his house at 4:00 P.M. Expecting her husband to have been similarly invited, Gede went as requested to find the host not with her husband but with another man, a prominent member of the community. She laughed as she saw them to cover up her shyness and unease, for it was clearly to a matter of no little importance she had been summoned. The men also laughed and joked, and cheerful pleasantries were exchanged as coffee was being served. Then the reason for their invitation was disclosed.

Her husband had been fired from his job. It was the decision of a meeting that had been held some time ago, but her husband was not to know until he would receive a letter in a few days' time. She, as wife and mother, ought to be notified first.

Completely taken by surprise, Kede broke down and cried. Pulling herself together by an effort of will she seemed hardly able to muster, she begged them to give him a chance to save his good name and reputation. Please, let it appear the decision had come from himself. She would see to it that he would sign a letter of resignation.

The men declined. It could not be done. This was the decision of the meeting. Kede looked stunned, and then she cried and cried.

The men professed several reasons for the decision. Her husband, as everyone knows, is excessively intelligent, and this unbalances his mind. He follows his own ways and not the ways of the community. In class he is too strict with the pupils and exercises relentless discipline. In gym class he has them march as in a military parade. Recently he had struck a boy who behaved naughtily. Indeed, by his behavior one might think he was mad. This they did not say, but it was clearly implied. And they cited the case of the terror he had struck in pupils' and parents' hearts when he had made the pupils camp near the graveyard one night. True, it was a part of their training as scouts, but sensibility must be exercised. Pupils had been sick from seeing the *jerangkong*—ghosts of the dead—and their parents had also been sick with fright on their behalf.

As she listened to the two men, Kede felt a strange sensation within. It was as if she *almost* believed what they said. A sense of terror gripped her heart. And she, who is ordinarily so brave (*berani*), did not speak against the men. She did not side with her husband and get angry with them for requesting her to put loyalty to them above loyalty to her own husband. Instead she panicked—perhaps it was true what they said. Perhaps they knew things about her husband which she did not. After all, he spent much more time with Ketut than he did with her. A moment's reflection and the conclusion seemed unavoidable to her. Truly if Ketut said so, her husband might be sick or, as he implied, mad.

But please, said she, let him have a warning! If only he had a warning and some rest, surely he would change his ways! There is no ill will in her husband, his heart is so good, but he is tired and his mind unhinged . . . In the end she begged them, please, for the sake of the children, give him a second chance!

The men listened in sympathy but shook their heads. It could not be done. The decision had been made—the unanimous result of a meeting—and it was unalterable. The following words, pronounced by Ketut, have imprinted themselves on Kede's mind: "As unalterable as is the fact that the sun will rise tomorrow morning, so is the decision that your husband must go."

They said they pitied her husband, they pitied her and the children, but God would help them find a way. One's family's welfare cannot count more than the common good. Kede felt numb, she had no more tears.

It was with a firm warning from the men not to speak a word to her husband of what she knew that Kede made her way home that afternoon. In the night she woke and screamed, "*Saya takut, saya takut!*—I am afraid, so afraid!" Her husband woke too and asked what was the matter. "Nothing," said she, "just a bad dream." "Don't be afraid," said he, "I am strong, I can protect us, we have nothing to fear!"

When the letter arrived four days later, he asked her if she had known. She admitted she had. From that day their lives and their relationship changed.

He was devastated with the act of his own, best friend whom he had held in the highest, most affectionate respect. For though the letter of expulsion did not contain Ketut's name, Wayan was sure that he had masterminded the whole:

Ketut is so powerful, everyone is afraid of him. If he had
wanted to prevent this, it would have been an easy task, but
he did not, for he always wants to shine above everyone else.
If someone is a star, Ketut needs to be the moon, if someone
is the moon, he needs to be the sun. He knows I am superior
[in intelligence and learning], so he had to put me down . . .
But to think that for a whole month he made his face look
clear when we went daily to his house; and yet he had been
party to such mischief! I cannot bear to think of it . . . !

And Wayan succumbed to devastating despair. The loss of his job
seemed to matter less to him than the loss of esteem and respectability.
But in the view of his wife, nothing pained him more than the betrayal
of his friend: "He loved Ketut so much, you cannot imagine. So for his
sickness there is no cure. His sickness is this: he suffers from a broken
heart."

Wayan began to behave publicly in strange ways. They were ways
that might be regarded as entirely natural and normal in some other cultures I know, but in Bali they stood out as signs of the madman. He let
his hair grow. He began to stay out for the night at times, sleeping under
the bridge. But as the clearest and most undeniable sign of madness, he
began to give free vent to his feelings of desperation in places outside
the house. He cried on one occasion so it was seen by many people. He
wrote letters of complaint and appeal to people he knew well and not so
well, strewing exclamation marks all over and scribbling handwritten
comments for emphasis in the margins, making the whole look a man's
cry of despair. Which it was.

Not even desperate people should behave like this in Bali. And so
rumors began circulating that he was actually mad. And he knew, and
began to challenge these. Not directly, to people's faces, for he was always polite and friendly to everyone. Moreover, he had a clear perception of who he was and what he did and no difficulty in understanding
that people perceived him as mad. But he became the more committed
to wearing his hair long and standing out as a self-styled revolutionary,
an opponent of the system. Indeed, he was the one against the many, for
even though many people felt sympathy and affection for him and sided
with him against his undoers—yet no one stood up for him in places
where it would have mattered. It is not the way in Bali.

There was too much to risk. Whereas everyone among the poor in
Cairo has allies and defenders who speak up and fight a battle for them
even in high places, Balinese regard it as dangerous to so much as mediate in a contest. One of the two parties is bound to get angry if one tries

to speak directly of a conflict. The safest course is to be quiet and uninvolved.

Wayan's venture was a lonely one: how to convince a community sympathetic to him, but fearing for their lives, of the justness of his cause and move them to act. He was bound to fail, given the elementals of the situation: Ketut's power (due in part to fear among the people that he had knowledge of black magic) versus his own powerlessness and reputation as a man of a purely good heart.

Because of his concern to be always polite with people, he could not talk freely to anyone but had to write—communicate at a distance. Suriati's fear of speaking to her husband of unpleasant things and her belief that if instead she wrote, he might ponder and understand are embedded in a common Balinese conception that writing is more powerful and less offensive than talking.

Wayan sent many letters to people, and they laughed. Reactions were of pity, embarrassment, shame, and scorn. But one reaction was ubiquitous: he should not behave like this. He should contain himself and manage his heart. That would make his undoers feel ashamed, said his supporters. One former pupil of his said she wished he would cut his hair: "I want to tell him, he was my teacher, I don't like people to laugh at my teacher." Wild stories began to circulate relating the things he had done—and people would roar as they narrated these among themselves. Credibility was not the issue, for here was a man who challenged society through his acts, who blatantly refused to conform. So there were no limits to the absurdities of which he might be thought guilty.

"He is the victim of a *sumpah*—a curse.¹ His teacher cast a curse on him when he challenged the system of organization at his college. Pitiful him! What can he do! And yet he should behave himself." The man who spoke expressed a common opinion of the society. Wayan was generally believed to be the victim of a curse, but that did not take responsibility away from himself. Bad fate explains misbehavior. It does not exonerate it. Wayan should prove himself by making an effort to cope as a reasonable man.

At home Wayan became more than difficult to live with. Previously so cheerful and indulgent with the children, he now seemed utterly bereft of his balance. Repeatedly and remorselessly he would turn on his wife, scolding and upbraiding her until she broke down and cried. He seemed ceaseless and tireless in his efforts to drive her into the depths of despair and even to take a secret pleasure in watching her thus: helpless, crushed, and feeble.

The children scurried to get out of their father's way at first when they were stunned to see to what heights his fury could rise. Later they learned to slide smoothly past when they saw that his anger was directed at their mother and not at themselves. But the whole family atmosphere was changed.

Previously the father and mother had seemed happy and well attuned to one another. Now they appeared at complete loggerheads. The children felt pity for their father, and the elder daughter wrote poetry to express her distress: ". . . my eyes water at what they have done to my father, the slander they have caused to him . . ."[2] But it was the mother who received the children's sympathy. A woman, she had to take it all in stride and serve and respect her husband through the skirmishes and accusations.

Accusations were hurled at her numerous times every day. They came to center on one issue: letters of appeal which he had mimeographed and she had failed to post. To her husband the letters—along with her failure to tell him what she knew of his pending expulsion—came to stand as proof of disloyalty and deception so extreme it weighed on him to bring her to her senses.

Both when they were alone together and with very intimate friends he would lash out at her, inspired by fury so intense it seemed as if he was consumed by superhuman righteousness. His eyes glowed with a frightening inner light that seemed to permeate his whole person as if he alone could see reality, the essence of which was completely hidden to his wife. The letters came to symbolize two discrepant worlds; no bridge could be built between them, but the one—his wife's—must be demolished. And he set his mind to this task with singular energy and drive, utilizing his awesome intellectual powers, which were as brilliant as ever.

The wife, worn out by chores and demands and unbearable inner pressure, would make half-hearted attempts to defend herself, then break down and cry. Wayan would go away and let her cry, then come back and start all over again. Two contesting views of reality fought for precedence, and it was only natural that with their different life situations, he would gain the upper hand. He had the whole day to ponder his plight and maneuvers. She had become sole breadwinner for a family of nine. She sold all that she had in the way of material possessions. Still, she had more than she could manage with trying to make ends meet. When her wedding ring was gone, she looked at her hand and whispered barely audibly, "Look, also this gone, and he has not even noticed . . . I cried as I polished it to take it to the pawnshop, for I liked to wear it . . . True, even if I say that I don't care about him, I am still his wife . . ."

As time went by and it became steadily more clear that her husband would not engage himself in serious efforts to find another job, she said to her children: "You must not care about your father but think only about me and be my medicine, my happiness. For if I die, you will be lost too." The children ranged from two to thirteen years of age.

The letters that precipitated such gloom and disaster in their lives were some that Wayan had made Kede type and instructed her to send to various influential people so that they might help him launch a court case against Ketut and his friends. He explained to me what was at stake:

> My case concerns not my position only, but the whole human race. It is about the power of law and justice as against the power of force. Why, if they wanted to fire me, did they hold the meeting in a private home and not at the office? As if the question of my position were a private and not a formal one! Well, of course it was because they were afraid to give me a chance to speak for myself! They knew that if I spoke, people would listen and side with me, for I would expose their selfishness and corruption. Ketut's accomplice, his job is that of accountant, and he earns less than my wife. He has nine children and we have seven. You have seen his house and you have seen mine and you can compare . . . What enables him to live in such luxury? My friend's two brothers like-wise . . . They work in the same kind of position, have the same salary, and yet one is rich and the other is poor. How do you explain it? Corruption is the plight of our society . . .
>
> They wanted to break me because I am not like them. I stay above their pettiness and ingratiation. With them, if someone says, "It is black," they will echo in unison "Oh, yes, it is black!" "No," say I, "It is white," or, "Judge for yourself." It was because I wanted to teach the youth the value of self-reliance and independent judgment that I took them to the graveyard that night. I wanted them to see for themselves that there is no such thing as *jerangkong*. The belief is a superstition. But they must experience and judge for them-selves. Likewise, when I instructed them to make tents of whatever they had at hand—it turned out to be sarongs—well, it was to teach them to be self-reliant and make do in difficult situations. Don't you think I know people called me mad because we made tents from batik? They say we should have bought a proper tent, Western style, and used it. Confor-mity runs in their blood, they cannot think for themselves. So

they misunderstand my education policy, which is to teach
the young to be brave and self-reliant. They take "brave"
[*berani*] to mean *nakal*—obstinate, impudent! Truly, from
their point of view it is!

They are government people, I am a free man. My wife is
also government, she thinks just like them! They don't understand that when at religious festivals I used to force the young
to give exhibitions and dance and sing, it was also to teach
them to be brave and self-reliant. "You must stand on your
feet, be broad-minded and free, you must learn to depend on
yourselves, believe in yourselves" is what I taught them. In
government they cannot understand such an attitude. The
whole system is geared toward bowing to those in power and
reiterating what they say.

Let me give you an example. There was a teacher recently
who was asked by a man how the present system of math
teaching functioned. He answered the truth, that the pupils
were entirely confused. By the use of the current method that
had been imported from Entebbe in Uganda, they did not
learn so much that they could be sent on errands to the market and return with the right amount of change! The teacher
did not realize that the man with whom he spoke was a jour-
nalist, and when his comment was published he was called to
his boss and harshly reprimanded for telling the truth in a
public place. Mathematics from Entebbe! What suits the Af-
ricans does not necessarily suit the Indonesians, and what
suits one Indonesian might be wrong for another! It has been
said about us: "*Rambut sama hitanya, tapi fikiran berbeda*—
the color of our hair is the same, but our thinking is different." Would that persons in power could see that! But they
are narrow-minded and obsequious, so they wanted to break
me, you see!

I want my case to be tried in the courts, but I need support,
for Ketut is a very powerful man. You know how he always
likes to say: "Excuse me [for so saying], but everyone always
grants me my wishes. No one can decline what I ask . . . !"
It is true, everybody stands in fear of him, that is precisely
why he is so powerful. He is an expert at social relations, at
placing people in relationships of debt. He always prides himself on all his friends. Well, I have friends too! The letters . . .

The bare mention of the word provoked a furious gloom in his eyes
that indicated he would go at his wife again. He would set out his plight
in staccato language before an intimate audience. But if she was there,

217

his fury would rise to a crescendo as he delved deep into his marital plight and her deception:

> She *burns* my letters! My own wife sides with my enemies
> to make me down! Would you believe that she never even
> sent the letters that were to help me get the support of people
> and make them understand about my cause! I have been cen-
> sored by my own wife . . . !

And he would tell how she lies to him and says she has sent the letters, but when he searches, he finds some tucked away under the mattress and others under the pillow, and once he came upon her trying to burn a particularly important one in the yard: "It was for her brother in Surabaya, who is in a high position and in a privileged position to help. But she does not want to help me, for she is under the spell of Ketut and his people! Sacrificing her own husband to please them! A coward she is! Obsequious!" And he would explode in a barrage of atrocities that would make listeners bend their heads in shame while his wife collapsed in tears. "That's right! Cry for yourself! You're no longer fit to be called a wife!"

The final verdict pronounced, he would sit back, looking self-satisfied and gauging the impact of his fiery attack. She would be shamefaced at having her marital problems thus exposed and would make halfhearted attempts to defend herself. But whereas he rose to eloquent heights and spoke in a loud and poignant voice, she clipped her words and fumbled: It was not true what he said! She *forgot* to send the letters! She is always loyal, but she cannot manage more than she does with the pressure she is always under. She is completely worn out, so she forgot. That is the truth, he can believe what he will, but she forgot to send the letters.

"Liar! Traitor!" Her husband's words would cut her short as with a voice quivering with contempt he rose to a new pitch of fury. "Forgot, you say! You call burning forgetting? And what about the letters you hid beneath the mattress and pillow, were they forgotten too? Wait a moment . . ." With a nod to the listeners he would speed out and come back looking triumphant with a bunch of letters he would wave in front of his wife: "letters forgotten by my wife under the mattress . . . !" And he would read the names of the intended recipients and tell how this one and that one might have helped him in his cause.

Kede met his charge with the defense that it was *she* who typed the letters, so it is also *her* right to decide what to do with them. Yes, it is true, she did not want to send them, for she is afraid what might happen to the people. Her brother in Surabaya, he has many children. Friends and colleagues likewise, they might get into serious trouble should they be implicated in their own plight. Better for people to be uninvolved and for themselves to let bygones be bygones . . .

Husband: "Let bygones be bygones! What nonsense you speak! You pride yourself on your high education. Now show us you can use it. I will fight for my cause, for my cause concerns not only me, but humankind. How will we ever have justice in this world if we accept the power of force as against the power of law?"

Wife (quietly): "But I'm afraid . . ."

Husband: "Don't you ever speak like that! Don't you see that to fear Ketut is to grant him power? Everyone fears Ketut, that's precisely why he is so powerful. But we must be brave and believe in God and ourselves . . ."

Wife: "He has friends in high positions . . ."

Husband: "He prides himself on all his friends, but we have friends too. They would help me if only they would understand about my cause. But how could they when I was sabotaged by my own wife? I went to Java, to Lombok to talk to people. They were surprised, saying they would have helped me had they only understood. BUT THEY NEVER RECEIVED THE LETTERS! My wife burned my letters! Sacrificing her own husband . . . !"

Wife (crying now): "I don't care! The children are all I am living for! I am so worn it feels as if body and soul are in different places. I work at the office but feel as if the body has been left in the street. When people speak to me, I startle, for I act as if I am present, but truly I am not. I have to manage, to bear it for the sake of the children, but to say that I am deceptive . . . !" And she would collapse in tears again.

Husband: "Yes, you are, because it is your fault that the world did not understand about my cause and come to our rescue. For a long time I believed that I was friendless in this world. But how could my friends help when they did not receive the letters! You have sacrificed your own family! I have told you numerous times that when there are things you don't understand you must ask me to explain. You have to think first of me and my problem, and then everything else will be solved. Like when we go on the motorcycle, if there is an accident, who takes the shot: well first me, then my wife, and then the children. So also with this problem: if my difficulties are solved, then all the family will be well . . ."

I have given fragments of a family tragedy that involved several people but was caused by forces outside the home. Until the day when the letter of expulsion arrived, the family functioned well and had a reputation about town for being particularly harmonious. Wayan, while aberrant in some aspects of his behavior, was very well liked and respected. Indeed, I heard it said by some people who ought to know that the reason he had to go so abruptly was precisely his popularity and brilliance. Had he been given a chance to speak for himself, many people would have sided with him, and the proceedings would have been protracted, shattering the community through moves and countermoves. For the sake of communal peace and social relations, he had to be expelled through undemocratic means.

"In a democracy a procedure like ours would be unheard of, but we go by the rule of force and must always secure loyalty to the system. It was a question of the one against the many, and of the welfare of the community or the one. So it was given how we must act," said one of the men; he was most sympathetic to Wayan's plight but a mastermind behind the meeting. He also described Ketut's plight:

> Ketut did all that he could to avoid having Wayan fired. He respects and loves Wayan so much, his feelings get in the way of his vision. We had to convince him he was going against his own interests and the interests of the community. It was very difficult. He was nearly heartbroken . . .
>
> No, Wayan is not mad, only extreme and deviant, but society does not have concepts to characterize deviance. They call everything mad—*gila*. He is so brilliant, truly imbalanced, and so he follows his own path, not the ways of the community. Society punishes such deviance. It is as if they say: "Who do you think you are to think you will change us, set yourself above everyone else?" And they will never change their minds. In this society "once a deviant, always a deviant." But to say he is mad, no!
>
> Why didn't he explain that when he made tents from sarongs, it was to teach the young to be self-reliant? We thought he was sick to leave the sarongs dangling up there in the air for days. Had it been one day, okay, but a week or two! That's his problem, he never explains himself, just acts, convinced of the wisdom of his cause. Yes, he is brilliant, but he has to live with the people and respect the limits of their comprehension. It is a problem for us that he is so kind, so popular that he easily sways people to think like he does!

To Wayan's wife, the question of whether her husband was actually mad or just sick came to hover as a persistent dark cloud over her life:

I suffer, and so does he, for we are never allowed just to be. My husband is being watched all the time, every detail of his behavior scrutinized from this one point of view: Is he or is he not mad? It is society's supreme interest. Everyone is confused. When they see me too, that's what they think: "There goes the wife of that mad/not-mad man!" It wears me out. So I go from balian to balian, always asking if he is mad or merely sick, and trying to find a cure. Myself, I believe he is just sick from a broken heart. Even should he get his job back, it would not help him in the least, for he loved Ketut beyond measure. For a broken heart there is no cure.

She also said she herself was brokenhearted:

That's why, when I see Ketut in the street, I feel nothing. But my thoughts focus constantly on these times of last year and how we used to go in and out of his home, believing that he was a close friend. Recently, I had an idea. I would write him a letter and ask: "At this time last year, Ketut, how many meetings did you have? Look into your agenda and see!" But I will not, not after a friend of mine, a colleague of Ketut's, told me that when a letter from my husband arrived at their office the other day, Ketut held it up with a sarcastic remark: "Oh, that's from that madman!" I was so sick when I heard it. It proves there is no use. How can we accomplish anything if my husband is dismissed as mad?!

So I will not send that letter. My friend has made me understand that there is no use. And that is also why I don't send my husband's letters. Ketut has friends everywhere in high positions. We are small by comparison. When he has spread the word that my husband is mad, what can we do?

We who knew the couple well could see how she was sick from suffering. In the course of one year she had dwindled to a fraction of her normal, slender self. She had not stooped; on the contrary, it was impressive how she managed to carry head and posture erect. But she seemed to have diminished; probably it was her loss of weight—she was pitifully thin—that detracted from her apparent height. Her face had taken on an air of transparency, her expression was smooth and clear, but smiles that before came easily to her now seemed forced among close friends. And while society continued to esteem her for her bright exterior, she distanced herself from her performance, declaring:

> I cannot smile anymore, for I have learned that appearances are deceptive. When people smile to me, I feel angry with them, and then I think, "Last year, Mr. Artje, you welcomed us smilingly in your house while you conducted your clandestine meetings!" A smile is an empty gesture only. I don't want to join in their deception . . .

But she smiled, and people smiled to her and congratulated her on her endurance and patience. (Brave she was, because she took to working jobs for extra income that would be considered beneath a person of her education—yet were admirable given what she had to do to support her family.) With such sheer persistence, dignity, and self-sacrifice, she might have managed better than she did, were it not for the marital scenes that continually sapped her energy.

People who observed these scenes might think her husband stark mad, for he seemed to thrive from breaking her down. He pranced about, he gained weight, he carried himself as someone out to save the world—and her. Why then would he exploit her, exhaust her, undermine her efforts to cope?

It took some time for me to realize. But one day when we were sitting alone together, he explained to me:

> "She is a victim of black magic, that's why I am angry with her. I want to break the spell of the black magic and save her from the power of Ketut's friend. His father is a balian, the public knows, so the son has knowledge too, I have many proofs of that. When she was called to Ketut's house that day and told that I had been fired, she was instructed not to tell me. And she did precisely as they said. She put loyalty to them over and above loyalty to her own husband! Well, how do you explain that?! Likewise, when I told her I would fight to get my job back, she cautioned against it, saying we should let bygones be bygones! No wonder! So long as he controls her, she will support his cause. So I have to break her, to rescue her from his power. That's why I make her cry. The more she cries, the sooner she will be sane. Do you understand?"
>
> "Yes, but I am afraid that she might break down completely!"
>
> "Oh, no, I see to that! I control my anger and let it out in suitable doses. Then I let her rest, and I go away for a while.

Sometimes I sleep out, stay away, give her time to recuperate so she can collect herself. Then I let my anger out again, until she cries, and so on . . ."

"But she is so exhausted, I fear she might break down, and then what about the children . . . ?"

"Oh, no, she will not, because she prays. And I believe I have white magic that will win over the black magic. I try to make her understand that, by showing they cannot break me. Ketut's friend sees to it that she is busy, sends her on work assignments here and there so that she will forget about my letters and not have time to help me. I show them that I can manage, that they cannot break me. I have no money, and yet my children eat and drink, I eat and drink, I smoke Dunhill . . ."

"What do you mean, you smoke Dunhill?"

"To show them that I am still going strong. That I have power. To make my wife see that my magic is stronger than Mr. Ngurah's . . ."

"Why wouldn't you rather use black magic to counteract the spell of Mr. Ngurah's power?"

"Because I believe in myself. I have self-confidence. I am fighting for a just cause, and I shall win. It is not a question of my position only, but of the whole human race . . ."

It was a few days later, and I thought I might help Kede understand about her husband's maddening behavior, as I was afraid she might truly break down. So I said to her: "Do you realize your husband thinks you are a victim of black magic?" Her eyes widened as she whispered:

"It is true what he says. I was. I know it myself. Really. I never before believed in black magic until I experienced it myself. That day when Ketut called me to his house and told me my husband was sick and would lose his job, I became frozen with fear. I who am always so brave burst out crying! I who had never before been afraid of Ketut, even when everyone was! When he proceeded to list five or six reasons why my husband must be dismissed, I listened, I didn't speak against him! Likewise, when the men warned me I must not tell my husband a word of what I knew, I did as they said! I was completely in fear's power. So I did not tell my husband anything until he forced me, when the letter had arrived. But instead of supporting him, I spoke against him when he was angry with Ketut. I asked him to calm down and let bygones be bygones. When he gave me letters to send to enlist support for his cause, I tore them asunder and burned them. It is incredible but true. Fear held me spellbound. I did not regain my consciousness until about six months ago."

"How did it happen, did you see a balian?"

"Yes, I did. He brought me to my senses. I went from one to the other until I found one that could help. To think that I who had never believed in black magic should come to experience it myself!"

"How did you feel when you were a victim of black magic?"

"Empty of mind, mindless, unable to think; no, not confused—*bingung*—when you are *bingung* you can still think, but when you are under the spell of black magic you have no consciousness, you are ruled by another person's mind. But the strongest sensation was fear, nagging, numbing fear that made me panic at all and everything. It did not subside until the magic was lost. Now I will never be afraid of Mr. Ngurah or anybody else!"

She went on to say how her husband had every reason to distrust her. When he had needed her, she had sabotaged his cause. A year before, when public opinion had been all for him, she had annihilated his efforts to mobilize support. Now it was too late, there was nothing they could do. But her husband does not see it this way and has lost faith in her, so he still thinks she is a victim to black magic.

He is wrong. It is just that I have resigned myself, I have stopped caring. Previously I used to worry myself sick over my husband. My mind centered constantly on him. I thought that if I gave him attention and care he might get well. Now, I have changed my attitude. I will not care, I will live only for my children. Perhaps it is wrong of me to think like that, but when he comes home, I do act like his wife. It is just that if I always think about him, I shall be sick, and without me, where would my children be?

My resolve now is to be quiet and never look back. *Sudahlah*—it's over. Let bygones be bygones. I am praying to God that he has tested us enough. He must help us now, for we have not lost faith. The resignation has given me back my consciousness. I don't nag my husband anymore and ask him when will he begin to work. I don't care. It's up to him— *terserah dia,* let him do as he pleases. But even so, the next moment comes the thought, "BUT WHEN?" Waiting is like a sickness. I must work harder to quiet my mind . . .

She said she also could not refrain from thinking what the people who had done them in would have said if they saw her family's situation now:

> Would that they could experience for themselves how it feels to have one's children go hungry. But they will receive their due, their *karma pala,* I am sure. God is just and will make them pay for their sins. You have heard what tragedy happened in Ketut's family recently? I am sure it was his *karma pala!* Likewise with his accomplice, Mr. Ngurah; just now his son failed in his exams. I think it was his *karma pala*— they are paying for what they did to us.

Kede's efforts to manage her heart and rise above suffering were not without setbacks:

> I was so angry with myself today. I had agreed with my cousin to sell my motorbike to him. I don't need it now. Our debts are driving me mad. All that matters is to clear the debts. So we agreed on a price of three hundred thousand rupiahs. But when he came to fetch the bike, he brought only two hundred seventy thousand rupiahs, saying he had deducted 10 percent because it had some faults. I was so angry, I exploded in hard, loud words. I also got angry with my mother-in-law because she did not support me against him. But I was most angry with my husband. I thought, "If you had been working, this would not have happened. But for you, I would not have had to demean myself." I am angry with others, but it is all on account of him . . .
> The other day my eldest daughter asked me: "Do you hate us, Mama, when with us [children] you are always moody and grim, whereas with the guests you smile and laugh?"

When a year had come full circle from the day Wayan received the letter of dismissal, he seemed to settle into a mood of resignation as a way of life. He stopped torturing himself with the thought of what reality had been a year ago from that day. He spent his days reading and sitting, not doing much. And he no longer tormented his wife to break the spell of black magic. He realized she was cured.

> I myself was under the spell of black magic when I acted like I did. I had no control over my rage. At last I went to see a balian, I who never believed in black magic, and the balian pointed to me and said, "Someone is trying to oust you from your position—*kedudukan.*" I looked at my chair, not under-

standing what he meant. Then I saw that he had spoken metaphorically. Someone was trying to make me ridiculous in the
eyes of the world. It is over now.

Yes, he has heard that Ketut wants to befriend the family and is suffering on account of how they fare.

> We are not ready yet; for the future, we cannot say. He has
> spread the word that he had no influence in the decision of the
> meeting. It is not true. He never lets himself be frightened by
> anyone or anything. He is unshakable, like the foundation of
> a house. He cannot be influenced. He is the leader of opinion
> in the community. Everyone is fearful of him. He has four
> qualities in combination: position, influence, and white and
> black magic. That's why it is useless for us to try to fight
> against him. Our best strategy is to expel the anger from our
> hearts, to make a happier life for ourselves. We believe God
> did this to test our faith and our strength, to teach us we have
> to rely on ourselves. We are the winners, he is the loser.

I do not know that Kede would agree with her husband in this. The
bitterness of the experience was a theme she would revert to, as she had
to make her life in the world, whereas he withdrew and sought consolation in religion. "People say experience is the best teacher, it makes you
wise and mature. They do not know what they speak. Our experience
has been too bitter."

She labored for her children, she grieved for her marital relationship,
and she had to negotiate a new identity vis-à-vis the world: "My husband will never find work because of the rumor that he is mad. You cannot believe how difficult it is for me. I am a Balinese, Balinese have
many friends, and everyone tells me how they pity me that my husband
is mad."

Three years later she said,

> I have one principle now, to work, not to think. We must
> work to bring results, thinking will not do. When God sees
> that, he will help me, but not my husband, for he makes no
> effort to help himself. Yesterday, I planted mango stones, for
> the future, for my children. My husband just watched. I cut
> down the old branches of the banana trees. He just watched.
> Even when he saw that I could not reach the upper branches,
> he did not help, until I asked.
>
> He spends all his time sitting, perhaps reading, does no
> work about the house. My elder daughter is angry when she
> sees me do everything. I just keep quiet, knowing my daugh-

226

ter is right. My husband is no worse than most Indonesian men: they never come to the kitchen, never sweep or wash clothes. That's why Balinese women must work very hard. Modern men are different, like my brother in Denpasar, he cooperates with his wife. But when I tell my husband, he keeps quiet. I have told him he must begin at least to wash his own clothes. But he does not, and I feel sorry for him and do the work. Right or wrong, he is still my husband.

As one sows one will reap. Truly, the law of *karma pala* applies. So I struggle to do always the best. When God sees that, he will reward me. Already I have indications: the typewriter you brought. I do not think about the price but the effort you made. Gifts people give: rice, food, fruits. Sometimes I have so much that I see fruit rot and I must sell rice for we have so much we cannot eat all. The motorbike we sold, I now have a new one—and colleagues love me, former colleagues embrace me when they see me in the street, people offer me loans of money when I need it and even before I have spoken! I have one principle now, always to smile, to make others happy. Sometimes people are surprised and express it, saying: "You're never sad!" They cannot see my heart. I make my face look bright and smile to make all the people like me. I pray to God that they will.

One more year, and a reconciliation had taken place between Wayan and his former best, most trusted friend. Both are happy, and the community is relieved. Many people bestow gifts upon the family. Kede's efforts to "make the best" have brought gain.

One moral of the story is this: The shiny, bright faces hide also such turbulence. The bright face is an expression to the world that one feels committed to the social order, bound by its moral precepts. But the spectacle of a bright face is not a sign that passions have been suppressed. Balinese know what it takes to don bright faces. Perhaps it is precisely because they grant to passions their full power that they collectively concur on keeping them caged in.

Observed a friend when we had visited a woman who was pained with the thought that she might be going mad and had exposed her family problems openly to us: "There are problems like hers in every house. It is just that this woman speaks openly of hers."

There is an element of make-believe in most Balinese interpersonal relations. The clear, bright face assuages and consoles *even when* one knows it to be a surface expression. But the surface also has moral value. So the thirteen-year-old says to her mother: "Do you hate us,

Mama, when with us you are always moody and grim whereas with the guests you always smile and laugh?"

She expresses a dilemma which goes to the core of Balinese interpersonal relations: how to interpret the action, the expression, the finely shaded signs? Personal "needs" are of the essence here, or to put it in idioms more in tune with Balinese: feeling-thoughts get in the way of people's vision.

So Ketut works against the efforts of the meeting to have Wayan fired. Wayan gets angry with his wife for speaking critically of his friend, then upbraids her for not speaking critically enough when he himself feels deceived. He interprets her as being a victim of black magic when she is not so loyal to him as he feels she should be. She on her part agrees that she must have been under black magic when she was no longer as brave as her character "has always been." A daughter in need of a mother's love comes to covet even that smile which is most stereotyped and standard: the one a host(ess) displays to the guests of the house. In the end Wayan was so happy to be reconciled with Ketut that he would not hear a bad word spoken against him!

Far from being stereotypical, Balinese emerge as every one an individual with a character all her/his own and an identity which s(he) cherishes and seeks to protect. Predicaments occur because one *feels* exposed, relations are precious as well as precarious, interpretive frames are conflicting, and power also enters to thwart or impede the attainment of personal goals. Whoever is "unshakable as the foundation of a house," as Wayan said of Ketut, might feel relatively secure. But in Bali I met only one person who might have said this of himself—a yogi of unusual inner strength. Wayan's characterization of Ketut reflects more on Ketut's stature in Wayan's eyes than on Ketut's experiential situation.

True, he was powerful and very proud of that. True, he liked to talk of his ability to steer courses of action ("No one can refuse what I ask") and of people's reliance on resources he controlled. Nonetheless, he was exposed, as are all Balinese, to the sheer unpredictability of life events and had suffered some terrible personal tragedies. He experienced his own powerlessness in many situations. Take the following examples:

He was powerless to prevent political allies from ousting Wayan, whom he held in most affectionate respect. He was powerless to forge a reconciliation with Wayan when after Wayan's expulsion Ketut used to come to his house daily and wait for hours, hoping to talk to him. Wayan refused. Nor did Ketut have any way of letting the community know that he was not the mastermind behind the decision to expel Wayan, but instead had tried his utmost to avoid having Wayan fired.

Ketut was locked in a stalemate of a certain kind of communicative and prestige structure. He had to bow to those in power above him. He had to sacrifice his own personal feelings and interests (a precious friendship) to the "common good." And he had to keep quiet, not raise the issue, or he might offend . . . someone.

The fear of black magic traps people in a net of collective making. This is a Western judgment. From a Balinese point of view, the fear is as real and as justified as is ours of being knocked down and robbed in a dark alley at night. One has to be cautious, to protect oneself. We fear open violence, Balinese covert violence. They are the more exposed, first because of the sheer magnitude of the problem, second because black magic threatens in every place and at all hours.

Take Kede who drank coffee at Ketut's house at 4:00 P.M. one afternoon and "woke up" six months later to find she had been disempowered of her own mind. Take Suriati's husband who at lunchtime meets the landlord's daughter and is ensorcerized to launch a vicious attack on his wife. Take a husband who is killed in the morning by his wife having put poison in his pillow, or Made's cousin who kills his uncle and cousin, or Suriati's grandfather who was killed by "pregnancy with stones." The examples could be multiplied ad infinitum.

Balinese society is extremely violent, as experienced and judged by Balinese. Even if my estimate that around 50 percent of all deaths are attributed to covert violence should prove to be wrong by 50 percent, still one out of every four deaths would be attributed to violence waged by angry hearts. This renders supremely sensible the care they take to avoid offense, but it also explains why people occasionally are forced into extreme positions with no possibility of reconciliation. Not one of Wayan's many friends, some of them in very powerful positions, dared to try to mediate. Driven out into the dark, Wayan was left with massive sympathy and no support. In the West people are afraid to intervene if they see someone being stabbed. The Balinese situation bears some comparison.

When in the end a reconciliation took place between Wayan and Ketut, a severe illness in Wayan's closest family provided the favorable pretext. And I had the impression "everyone" was so relieved. The two men are now the closest friends again. Kede beams, family harmony is restored, and Wayan has, in 1989, been offered a respectable job and is reintegrated in the community.

CHAPTER TWELVE

At the Balian's: Seeking Relief for Life's Strains and Stresses

People believe that the doctor can help, but only the balian can heal. Medicine is a means, not a cure. So my own medical philosophy is: a doctor's first duty is to restore hope.
—BALINESE DOCTOR

When Kede was searching for a way to heal her husband's wounded heart, she first went to a psychiatrist. He instructed her to shower her husband with attention, affection, and care—*kasi senang*—that would restore his shattered self-worth and help him regain hope in the future. But it did not, although "I come home from work, and I smile to him, always smile. I am so tired, and I'm angry with him inside. But I smile. I must be a good actor."

So she set out on a long round of balians until, after three years, she found one who provided relief. The wound was too deep to heal. By then she had spent masses of energy and masses of money, but she did not look back. She was so relieved.

The generic term *balian* is generally translated as "traditional healer," though as Connor alerts us:

> The significance of balians' activities extends beyond this sphere: They are consecrated practitioners who perform many priestly functions, and they are often highly esteemed people (as the honorific title 'Jero' indicates) with some influence in the affairs of Balinese rural communities. There are probably several thousand balians working in Bali today (Connor 1986, 21).

Balians versus Doctors

The realm of balians is different from that of medical doctors, and in North Bali there seems to be a peaceful coexistence, even collaboration, between these different kinds of practitioners of health care.[1] Balians treat illnesses connected with mystical forces that afflict a person's life force or soul. Medical personnel treat the body. But because body and soul are not separate in Balinese cosmology and health thinking, balians also treat the body. It is the medical profession that is left with a kind of residue: ailments of pure physical nature.

Of these there are few. Moreover, when illness occurs, it afflicts persons who *experience* the pain in mental-emotional imagery and *feel* their life force to be affected also by ailments such as broken bones or back pain. As a third qualification, Balinese reckon with multiple causation in many illnesses and misfortunes. Thus, for most kinds of problems and pains, Balinese consult balians *in addition* to doctors.

It is also cheaper to consult a balian. In the North, one pays according to one's means, ideally speaking. Actually, payments of approximately one to two thousand rupiahs (approximately seventy cents) seem standardized, but with variations either way. The balian should refrain from asking for a specific sum and accept whatever his client, referred to as "guest," gives him. It is said that otherwise he will lose his power to heal—his *sakti*. Doctors, on the other hand, demand generally five to ten thousand rupiahs for each consultation, and they prescribe medicines which are very expensive for most to buy.

Considerations of trust, informality, and give-and-take of information further enhance people's preference for balians. With the doctor there is, for most people, a great status difference, and he treats by prescribing a cure, not by explaining things to his patients. The balian, by contrast, elicits symptoms and complaints, and listens to his guests. He also explains to them what has gone wrong and takes time and effort to make sure they will understand. Understanding is of the essence, for healing requires a joint effort on the part of the balian and the family of the afflicted.[2] He receives them in his house, and this is located in an ordinary neighborhood, not set apart in a mercantile or posh area of town. The balian also is often no better off than most of his guests; socially he shares position with them, although an aura of power attaches to him by virtue of his command over mystical forces.

Another important difference between balians and doctors is this: as the relationship between doctor and patient is defined, the patient need not commit herself and harness her spiritual energies to the cure. She presents her body, or a part of it, for examination and treatment and proceeds, if her family has money and believes in the doctor's diagnosis, to buy and take the medicines. At issue is not her trust in the doctor, though some doctors emphasize how their first duty is to induce hope and trust: "If a patient *feels* sick, who can make her well?"

But with respect to the balian, absolute trust is essential. Without it, there is no hope of healing. The sick or troubled person must *believe* in the balian, but more than that, she must be *cocok* with the balian. This means she must be in harmony or agreeable with the balian, in a way that spouses must also be *cocok* or a name must be *cocok* with the person. Without *cocok* there is no hope of recovery or relief.

Fortunately, *cocok* is established ex post facto. It means there is always hope. If relief was not obtained, balian and afflicted were clearly not *cocok*. And the afflicted or the family acting on her behalf must continue their search for someone *cocok*. For Kede, it took three years and visits to more than a score of balians all over Bali. For a medical doctor who was afflicted by a prolonged bout of neurasthenia,[3] it took visits to only two balians (when, after medical colleagues had proved unable to cure him, his wife and mother-in-law engaged him with balians). The first one provided some, but not complete, relief. I asked him why he then switched to another one. "Because I had hope, I might get well."

My question, I now realized, had been framed in terms of my culture-specific assumptions of how best to obtain a cure. Where I come from, sick people tend to stick to the doctor who provides some measure of relief in the hope that continued treatment will ameliorate the condition. In Bali relief should come speedily if not instantaneously, and if it does not, something is amiss in the relationship between healer and guest or doctor and patient. The tendency is to read imperfect relief as a sign that the diagnosis is improper or that balian and afflicted are not properly *cocok*. So the doctor pained with neurasthenia moved on in search of a suitable balian, and experience proved him right.

His realization that his own patients act in terms of similar suppositions with him and do not feel healed except when they have also seen a balian who has soothed their soul makes him remark: "Even when the medicine may have provided relief, the balian is usually given credit for the cure."

The doctor needs, of course, to *see* the patient whom he would cure. That is often not necessary for the balian. "The manipulation of mystical powers," which, as Connor asserts, "is the very foundation of [balians'] therapy" (Connor 1986, 37), implies that a diagnosis may be made and etiology ascertained in the absence of the suffering person. Again, this is a condition conducive to hope. Kede's husband would not hear of her seeing a balian on his behalf, but she did not need his consent. She could go on her own. Even for him to take the medicine, she did not need his consent. Balians are skilled in devising ways in which medicine can be given to unsuspecting persons (in bathwater, soap, coffee, etc.), as this is a problem they daily face: how to help persons who do not see themselves as sick but create havoc with the lives of others.

The balian provides an island of hope and encouragement in a sea of fear and distrust. It is true that balians are also feared, and some intensely so, for they control forces that work evil in the world. But without balians where would Balinese go with their intimate problems and the sicknesses that afflict their souls? That somewhere there is someone who has the answer to any riddle, the formula for any problem, is a basic Balinese premise of life. What matters is to find the particular balian, or one of the many who might each grasp a portion of a many-faceted problem. There is no doubt among Balinese that such balians can be found.

(Though understanding is not enough, as balians are up against mystical forces of awesome powers, and healing is the outcome in many cases of a contest between the mystical power of the balian and that of other agents. However, even this belief harbors hope. To find a balian with power strong enough becomes the focus of one's efforts. Gede in the end *was* successful.)

Different Types of Traditional Healers

Balians are of several kinds, and they cater to different sorts of illnesses and problems. They employ various techniques and come to their calling by different experiences or routes. Their relationships with guests vary in terms of considerations of secrecy and familiarity (Connor 1986, 23–24).

Roughly 50 percent, according to Connor (1986, 33) are literate medical specialists—balian *usada*—whose practice is founded on the possession of classical texts about healing (*usada*) and who acquire their skills by a formalized learning process. Balian *usada* specialize in transcribing and interpreting old palm leaf manuscripts (*lontar*) inscribed in old Javanese or high Balinese that deal with "medicine, magic and mysticism" (Connor 1986: 22–24), or as the balian *usada* with whom I worked explained to me:

> The *lontar* contain *tenung* [predictions, horoscope] for all
> kinds of problems and sicknesses, as well as recipes on how
> to perform black magic. For instance, on how to protect your
> house so that the thief will see it like an ocean and be scared;
> to protect yourself from being burned by fire even when it
> strikes at your house; to capture the thief within the gate; to
> make your daughter not marry except the man of your choice;
> to create harmony, peace between a man's several wives; to
> make the husband want to get close with the wife always; to
> determine the sex of your child; to cure childlessness; to find

lost children. Besides for every conceivable illness, there are also remedies for impotence, for madness, etc.

Balian *usada* dispense advice and medicine after eliciting the symptoms or problems of the afflicted, then consulting the holy texts for diagnosis and therapy. Different systems for producing remedies are in use. But some balian *usada* cannot read the *lontar*. Their claim to efficacy rests on their possession of these manuscripts—thought to have mystical power in themselves—and the holy water they turn into medicine by bringing it into contact with the texts.

All balian *usada* are males. I doubt that in the North there are nearly as many of them as Connor reports from South Bali, but on this point I have only impressions. The balian *usada* with whom I worked had been an apprentice to his father, a yogi, and began his training proper in his late thirties. This was no coincidence, as he explained to me. There are stages in a person's life, and ability to acquire high-level holy knowledge requires remove from worldly pleasures. At fifty, he would withdraw from marital sex to develop the purity of body and spirit needed to attain the heaviest, most dangerous knowledge (*pelajaran berat*).

(To acquire partial knowledge does not work, as to have incomplete knowledge is dangerous. It unbalances the soul and makes for instability in feeling-thinking and acting. This belief, and one which says one should not probe and question too much—"that's like you don't have faith and trust in the ancestors"—work against laypeople acquiring bits and pieces of mystical knowledge and bolster the efforts of the specialists once they have embarked on their track.)

Balian *usada* are highly esteemed members of their communities, although status depends also on personal reputation and biography. The man I was privileged to work with, Made Bidja, had a sensational reputation as brave beyond measure. Once when a man in his neighborhood had gone amok (*ngamok*) and was ranting outside his brother-in-law's house, waving his *kris* (dagger), waiting to kill his brother-in-law before an audience frozen with fear, as a last resort people sent word to Made Bidja. He changed into sarong and said to his weeping wife: "If I die now, mine will be a holy death." Then he went calmly up to the man who was swinging his *kris* and cornered him bluntly: "What are you doing, you crazy man, making yourself a murderer? What of your children, your wife? Well, if you're set on killing somebody, then kill me, here I am!" And he bared his chest and presented himself weaponless to the wild man.

The latter fell to his knees and kissed Made Bidja's feet, his consciousness regained. "So Made Bidja has a large following in Banyuning," closed the man who told me this story.

He was also widely renowned as uncompromising and ruled by his instincts, but that did not detract from his stature though it had made it impossible for him to stick to a secular job and earn a reasonable income. He would not bow to people whom he did not respect, and that meant all whom he considered materialistic, self-serving, or dishonest. His wife had to support him so that he could devote himself to his *lontar*. But all balians, and indeed most ordinary humans, have their peculiarities. And only children, that I heard of, quibbled about Made Bidja's lack of *polos* manners.

Most balians in the North neither possess nor are literate in classical texts. They come to their calling by a process of divine inspiration, apprenticeship with a teacher, and/or inheritance of a practice. The therapeutic techniques they variously use are regarded as efficacious on account of the balian's "mystical power" known as *sakti* or *ilmu*. Balians should use this to relieve suffering by mediating between the realm of mystical forces and their clients' immediate concerns.

Common therapeutic techniques include producing and dispensing holy water, ointments, potions, amulets, and charms, performing massage, and—an essential part—performing rituals on behalf of guests and/or divining what rituals they have to perform to propitiate angry deities, ancestors, or demons. Prescription of foods may also be important.

Expelling black magic is an essential part of every balian's expertise and function. To this end the balian engages in mystical battle with another balian, person, or (super)natural spirit, or he may transfer some of his power to the afflicted person to endow her momentarily with the force to drive out the black magic. This power may even be transmitted through intermediaries when the afflicted one cannot, or will not, come to the balian.

In the North, as in the South (Connor 1986, 25), midwives (balian *manak* or balian *kampong*) and bonesetters (balian *tulang*) are also referred to as balian; this is indicative of the mystical power they are ascribed and lay claim to. In the case of midwives, this power (*sakti*) is said to enable them to change the position of the foetus and assure a moderately painless delivery. Unlike in the South, however, masseurs and masseuses (*tukang urut* or *tukang pijet*) are not commonly designated balian, but rather *tukang*. *Tukang* are craftswomen or men with important functions in curative and preventive medicine, but without the balian's mystical or spiritual power. For this reason, as a woman explained to me, "The *tukang* gives medicine and cures, but she does not say what is the *cause* of an illness. For she is not a balian."

Most *tukang* are indeed females, whereas balians are mainly males. A considerable proportion is, however, females, and no assumption seems to exist that males are more powerful. The most common type of *tukang* in the Singaraja area is, beside masseur/masseuse, the *tukang sambet*. She is a specialist in healing illness from fright or soulloss, commonly called *kesambet*. All *tukang sambet* I met were females.

One type of healer is not easily designated as either balian or *tukang*. This is the medium with a *jinn*—a Muslim (super)natural spirit (*orang alus*). When the medium goes into trance the *jinn* emerges and speaks: he diagnoses illnesses and problems, identifies their causes, prescribes treatment, occasionally performs massage, and produces holy water and ointments as medicines. "Talking therapy" is a vital part of his function. When the *jinn* has left, the medium claims not to remember anything of these conversations.

Both males and females can "have" *jinn*. One woman I know has nine, though commonly only one or two emerge. One is Husnan, an old man of eighty, toothless and limpid, who smokes a lot and loves delicious red Australian apples (not the Balinese sour green ones) and chocolate, preferably of imported brand. The other is Abdullah, a lively, playful little boy of nine, whose greatest delight is ice cream and who loves to ride a bicycle. Because Abdullah is so young, he cannot identify the cause of an illness, but he can heal and give medicine. *Jinn* can see things which we do not, and they have mystical power, *sakti*. Balinese talk of them and act with respect to them as if they were genuine beings.

Because it is the *jinn* who heals, and not the possessed person, a girl was visibly annoyed when another referred to her aunt as a balian: "My aunt is not! She can do nothing! It is Husnan who does it all!" She proceeded to have her mother confirm that it was true, her aunt was not a balian. And she explained to me how much more efficacious is a *jinn* than a balian: "With the *jinn* you can communicate directly, whereas with the balian you have to go through an intermediary to establish contact with the healing power."

At stake was the ambivalent nature of the word *balian*. Because (some) balians work black magic as well as white, the generic term *balian* (as well as its Muslim equivalent, *dukun*) is loaded. "We must not say, 'Balian, balian,'" whispered Suriati to me one day as we were walking in the street talking of such matters. "They might hear and be offended." Another was frightened when in the early stage of fieldwork I committed the blunder of referring to a man simply as dukun, when he might hear. "Had *we* done so, it would have been very dangerous!" The proper appellation is to use the prefix *yeh* (an abbreviation for *Sayyid*) with Muslims, or the honorific title *Jero* with Hindus. Dukuns are also commonly referred to as balians; Balinese may say "Dukun Ali" or "Balian Ali." In fact, dukuns and balians are the same except that a dukun is Muslim, a balian Hindu; dukuns do not go into trance, while balians sometimes (by no means always) do; and dukuns consult Koranic, balians Hindu, writings. Hindus consult Muslim dukuns/balians, just as Muslims consult Hindus.

Balians are presumed to be able to control all manner of (super)natural forces, solve every conceivable problem, and heal or inflict any kind of illness or misfortune. Some have a wide range of expertise. Others are more specialized. Particular balians can stop or cause rain, storms, droughts. Others are experts at locating runaway children. Others again are particularly skilled at finding lost or stolen things and identifying thieves. Yet others can insert magical prowess (*susuk*) into a person, rendering her or him invincible and securing for her or him position, fame, fortune, or bewitchingly good looks.

Some few balians command *belorong*—white magical mice—which can sneak through walls and locked doors and steal money and possessions from people while they sleep. They render their owners rich beyond all reason but demand in return a heavy sacrifice: one should give up what one loves the most. Suriati's father was promised incredible wealth if he would sacrifice his son. And yet *belorong* thrive.

A final type of balian—balian *metuunan*—is of the utmost importance. He can be possessed by the souls of the dead, and it is to him that people go when they want to meet with their dead and have their opinion. For family problems in particular, one's best option may be to consult the ancestors who can apply their wisdom and authority. The dead can also reduce pain from longing and loss, and they can still troubled minds grappling with the question of certitude: *Why* did a beloved one die? The dead are a part of the lives of the living, and one cannot exaggerate the important role that they play (see plates 16 and 17).

Balian *metuunan* attract clients from afar, as there is a certain skepticism about the authenticity of their trances and this is more easily gauged when the medium can have no prior knowledge of the soul for which he is asked to serve as a medium. West of Singaraja lives a balian *metuunan* who attracts people from all over Bali. He is entered by the souls of some ten dead people almost every day.

Multiple Causation, Last Resorts

When a Muslim woman I know was suffering because her husband ran about with another woman, as a last resort she contacted the soul of her deceased father-in-law through a balian *metuunan*. She bared her heart to him and implored him to apply his influence with her husband, which he did. The move was successful, the husband reformed. That she was a Muslim and that Muslims do not "believe" that one can obtain contact with the souls of the dead constituted no great obstacle in this case. As a last resort, one will try anything. And she thanked her father-in-law profusely by performing a great ceremony in his honor—also of a kind Muslims "do not believe" in.

Another, also a Muslim, had great problems with her husband. After having tried a multitude of options—Chinese doctors, Balinese doctors, Muslim dukuns (and I suspect also some Hindu balians)—to little avail, I went with her to a famed Hindu balian. He alerted her to the complexity and triple causation of her problem. First, there was black magic involved. Second, there were the *jinn* in their backyard whom they had disturbed. But third, there was the oath which her husband's ancestors had given long ago to present offerings in "the Muslim holy place" once they became prosperous enough to travel there. But they had not kept their promise and this constituted a great mistake in the eyes of God.

My heart sank as I listened. Knowing she was what she and her community considered with pride a fanatic Muslim, I was distraught to think how she now would have her worst suspicions confirmed. She had warned me before we went that it was probably useless. The balian would treat her as if she were a Hindu and prescribe treatment in accordance with his religion. Therefore she had not gone in earnest, with the offerings needed to request the balian's help and with the right commitment of spirit. She had only accompanied me and chatted informally with the balian. When now he spoke of oaths and offerings in the Muslim holy place (presumably Mecca), he did indeed apply notions pertinent to Hindu religion and meaningless, I thought, to Muslim Balinese.

I was wrong. On our way home her face was luminous and her voice buoyant with hope as she spoke of the perceptiveness of his insights. It was true all what he said. The magic, the *jinn*—her daughter had recently seen the latter in the shape of a beautiful long-haired woman in the backyard—but particularly the oath, which she had failed to recognize till now. She would remedy the fault of the ancestors. She would make a promise to God to take upon herself the burden of carrying it out in practice, once she had money to go to Mecca. She did not say, but I knew, that she did not think of placing offerings there; she interpreted the balian's message metaphorically, not literally. But she would pray and give evidence of her faith and commitment. Understanding between the Muslim and the Hindu had been as good as need be: "You see, it is the law of *karma pala* which asserts itself," she said to me, "but because I am a Muslim I say *taqdir* [fate, destiny], it's all the same."

In terms of religious doctrine they certainly are not, and she should know—she is skilled in religious learning. *Karma pala* is the doctrine of holy retribution founded on the premise of reincarnation: one's present fate is the result of actions in a previous life and God's almighty justice. *Taqdir* or *nasib,* by contrast, implies accepting one's fate as ordained by God according to a rationale humans cannot comprehend. It refers to *this* life only, for there has been no previous one.

And yet *karma pala* and *taqdir* could be accommodated to a common experiential frame. Might not Muslims be punished for the sins of the forefathers, just as Hindus suffer the mistakes of their reincarnated souls? I am not implying that this is how she thought. I think the connection she made was intuitive, not the product of cognitive reasoning. Exposure to common predicaments in everyday life and intimate friendships across religious boundaries create a fund of shared understanding regarding such experiential realities as "fate," "justice," "responsibility," and "oaths"[4] and collapse much of the difference which exists in religious doctrine.

Now the Muslim woman had to go back to the balian in the right spirit. On departure from her home she must invest her trust and faith in him, and he would be able to give medicine for the magic next time. So it happened. She received holy water to pour into her husband's coffee and odorless oil to apply to his soap. A part of the balian's mystical power was also entrusted to her by his grasping her firmly around the wrists while praying to his god to give her power. In the evening she would grasp her husband's wrists and transfer the healing power to him.

The third part of the problem, the *jinn* in the backyard, she could handle herself by asking their forgiveness for the disturbance caused and presenting them with some special foods, including a many-colored chicken.[5]

Two days later she reported her husband to be already better, and when a few months later he fell seriously ill, another cause was diagnosed and help provided by another balian. The adequacy of the above diagnosis and the efficacy of this treatment were not questioned.

A Double Set of Cosmological Forces

Hindu Balinese and Muslim Balinese live together in a world where, in a sense, everything is possible and no options should remain untried when pain afflicts. *Jinn* and *memedi* are analogous powers, two names for the same kind, as are Muslim death magic, *sihir,* and Balinese *pasangan.* People believe in both and all. Balinese witches (*leak*) are all Hindu but afflict Muslims too. Muslim ghosts of the dead (*jerangkong*) scare the wits out of Hindu Balinese. Not to speak of the dreaded illnesses from Lombok, neighboring island in the east, which are said to have spread through Muslim dukuns but afflict everyone. Agents of illness and misfortune thus abound in this multicultural universe. The acculturation and syncretism of society render North Balinese vulnerable to a larger population of demons, ghosts, and spirits than would have afflicted them had they lived in a religiously homogeneous society. Perhaps it also entails a greater availability of remedial options. It is hard to gauge the balance.

It is beyond doubt that Hindus and Muslims acknowledge each others' (super)natural powers and treat them with proper awe. Illustrative is the following case: the family of a Hindu mayor of a Singaraja *kampong* propitiate daily and present offerings and food to a whole family of Muslim *jinn* who live on the lower level of their houseyard temple (*sanggah*); their Hindu deities live on the two upper levels. The *jinn* have resided there since they obtained permission from the mayor's grandfather two generations ago. When occasionally a family member steps on or bumps into one of these *jinn,* she or he falls sick, and to get well has to pray like the *jinn,* that is, like a Muslim. At the five daily Muslim prayer times, when *jinn* flutter about to the bathroom for their ritual ablutions before prayer, the Hindu family of humans hardly move about their house, so as not to disturb the *jinn.* So also on Fridays, a particularly busy day for the *jinn.*

A reverse case: A Muslim boy was chronically sick until a balian diagnosed the cause as anger on the part of his Hindu ancestors (of three generations ago) because he had not performed the tooth-filing ceremony! Probably the diagnosis was done by a Hindu balian, but it made sense to the afflicted; they performed the requisite ceremony, and because the treatment was effective, the diagnosis was proved right.

Hindus and Muslims use balians of either religion, even when the preference may be to consult first one of one's own kind. Because people can be afflicted by deeds done by balians of the other religion, one's best option may indeed be to contact one of them. He might know best the riddles and rules of repelling the black magic. But essentially one tries one's luck where significant others, and particularly the old women in the neighborhood, who are especially experienced in such matters, advise one to go. A visit to any balian quickly shows middle-aged or elderly women to be in the great majority among visitors, as they often take it upon themselves to go on others' behalf.

No concept of accident attaches to Balinese sickness, as we have seen. Everything is caused.[6] And though illness is recognized as stemming also from dietary imbalance or harsh climatic exposure, the ultimate agents of causation are (super)natural beings who "are not under direct human control but may be approached through ritual specialists and offerings" (Connor 1986, 30). Thus when a boy broke his leg in a traffic accident and after three operations the fracture would still not heal, his mother came to a balian asking "why *my* son?" and "why is every operation unsuccessful?" She was informed it was on account of the boy's *karma pala*. An ancestor who was reincarnated in him had committed a serious ritual mistake. The boy actually improved when the mistake was remedied.

The Concept of *Sakti*

What enabled the balian to diagnose the (or this) cause? It was his *kesaktian*, a condition of being spiritually powerful/full of *sakti*.[7] *Sakti* equips balians with the personal power to intervene on behalf of guests with a variety of mystical forces.

> More humble practitioners are cautious in acknowledging that they have such power. They may deny that they are balians, although they work as healers. Many people are reluctant to use the term balian in describing others because *sakti* can be used for good or evil ends; it is a morally neutral force. Thus it is not necessarily a compliment to describe someone as *sakti* (Connor 1986, 27).

Once I was with a balian who was treating a relative who had come to her from Java. He was suffering from weakness and frailness of the limbs so strong that when he came he could not walk; now, after two treatments, he was better but still weak. She diagnosed the cause as anger on the part of the gods because he did not acknowledge his own *sakti.* He had worked as a healer since people spontaneously started coming to him for help, and word had spread of his healing powers. But he did not acknowledge himself as a balian, and so guests did not bring him offerings. For this the gods were angry, for they were denied nourishment from inhaling the smell of incense and flowers. So in turn his energy diminished, as did the sources of his mystical power.

The cure consisted in asking forgiveness of the gods and performing retributive rituals. The balian was able, through massage, to transfer strength to the man by leading it through her right forefinger to his forehead. Holy water was also essential. Later the man would return to Java and acknowledge his status as balian (or dukun, as they are called in Java).

Sakti, as mystical power, has two aspects. It is a quality immanent in the natural world, as an aspect of certain places, objects, substances, or persons. But it is also "supernatural" in the transcendent sense, as a force at the command of deities, ancestors, and demons. It is morally neutral and may work good or evil.[8]

Sakti occurs in the natural world at certain kinds of places such as wild woods and particular trees, springs, or streams referred to as *angker* or *tenger.* To trespass on these without uttering the proper apologetic formulas (in high Balinese) causes illness. Children particularly often fall victim to this. *Sakti* is also an essential quality of many kinds of objects such as *lontar, kris* daggers, Koranic script, offerings, batik sarongs, old Chinese coins, some stones, etc. Many people are afflicted because they have picked up some stones or pebbles that caught their eye and placed them carelessly, not realizing that these were *sakti.* *Sakti* pertains also to substances such as the brass of the gamelan, the powder used to decorate the bride or purify the body at death, the *lalang* leaves used to thatch roofs and also to purify the bereaved after death (and for many medical purposes as well), and the *jangu* leaves used to decorate the ceiling at weddings. If the *jangu* leaves were not fresh, the guests will fall ill, as Balinese commonly experience.

The powder (*boreh*) of the bride is used to *cure* illness, (after a wedding, when many of the guests are usually sick, they flock to the bride to obtain some powder to cure illness from magic by wrong address); the brass dust of the gamelan (*rajun*) is used to *inflict* poisonous illness. Thus *sakti* may be activated for good or bad ends, and it abounds in the world of the Balinese where the fates of humans and (super)naturals are intertwined. The "supernatural" pervades the "natural" world, not least in the form of *sakti.*

Sakti, as the mystical force or spiritual power which balians possess, is a quality of which ordinary humans too have ample experience. They sense it, they perceive it, they fall sick from it or are miraculously and blessedly cured by it. *Sakti* is thus very different from a Christian congregation's perception of their priest's charisma. *Sakti* is not an abstract quality, for it is *also* tangible and close. It is not otherworldly, for it is also a prominent facet of *this* world. Like the miracles that convince believers in famous Christian curative centers of divine powers, or the evil that stands as proof of the devil's doings, *sakti* evokes both good and bad powers in manifest form. But it does more; it is itself a manifestation of these powers, combining them in one concept, one force. The separation of good and evil, inherent to Western cosmology, is foreign to Balinese thinking. Mystical power may be used for both ends. As a quality suffusing every aspect of the world, *sakti* is both *of* and *for* this world. It both shapes people's experience and is itself shaped by it. And it is morally neutral.

For a person to refer to himself or herself as *balian* is to lay claim to public recognition as someone who is *sakti* (Connor 1986, 27). Connor notes, and we have also seen, that some may be reluctant to do so, preferring to practice as healers without calling themselves balian. That is because *sakti* is multivalent in its connotations and can be employed for morally evil purposes as well as good. This may go part of the way to explain why, in their reference to this mystical power, I find that even recognized balians do not use the word *sakti*, but subsume it under *bayu*—the vital energy or life force which is also ordinary people's ordinary reference for their state of being in the world: their embodied, felt power of resistance. And just as ordinary people speak of the need to have a good heart and be calm to foster strength, so balians stress the necessity of cultivating power (*bayu*) by good feeling-thinking.

But I think the reasons for this speech usage may be even more profound and reflect experiential realities with methodological and epistemological consequences for an understanding of indigenous healers and cosmologies.

Much anthropological insight into ritual and cosmology is the outcome of efforts to probe the minds of particularly knowledgeable individuals with the ability to explain things to an outsider.[9] In negotiated encounters between the interrogator and the interrogated deep knowledge is tapped—and produced—and pinpointed onto patterns of sometimes formidable symbolic dimensions. Such encounters are removed from the context of everyday affairs, and it is unavoidable that many of the interviewee's experiential connections with this are broken in this concerted effort to probe words and meanings.

I speak from experience. Toward the end of a fieldwork that had been oriented toward the everyday and mundane, I engaged in just such an effort in collaboration with two brilliant men with exceptional explanatory powers. One was a (Hindu) balian *usada,* the other a Muslim medical doctor who was an apprentice to him. A world opened up to me of deep knowledge and understanding of a kind I had never come across in ordinary, everyday life. But *because* I had this background I was a skeptical apprentice. When they told me things that did not fit with what I perceived to be ordinary people's understanding, I would counter them, saying, "but people say," "but people think . . ." And thus a world of "misconceptions" (*salah kaprah*) was laid bare, a world of partial, at times "wrong," understandings. Yet these were wholly appropriate signposts and guidelines from the points of view of people I knew! Were they then to be relegated to secondary standing or denied validity?

This was not the perspective of the men who instructed me. While they were at times surprised to hear of the *extent* of people's "misconceptions," they had little problem understanding why these occurred. Moreover, they could explain to me the rationale behind people's views, being themselves part of a world in which family and friends acted in terms of just such conceptions. The literally *embodied, physically felt,* reference people use to interpret the world around them was also an experiential frame for these two men. But I suspect that had I begun at the other end—with the experts—and then moved on to the world of everyday affairs, I might not have learned about these discrepancies, for I would have read other meanings, other cosmologies, into people's action. And by being something of an "expert" myself, or having this as my orientation, I might have subtly induced people to play "my" game and engaged them in rather farfetched, because remote, understandings.

As it was, I was not keen to play the experts' game, because I felt committed to those who had first taught me. And I was fortunate in having as collaborators men who were humble enough to come part of my way in laboriously explaining to me the sources of everyday (mis)understandings, as they saw them. Thus I came to understand better why people think they lose their vital life force (*bayu*) in soulloss, when it is actually their ethereal aspect, the *atma* (soul) that they lose. But how would I have understood the *experiential* meaning of *bayu* if I had not for a long time "believed" and taken in earnest what people said, that they actually lost their *bayu?* A contrary (and, by the scriptures, truer) understanding, that it is the *atma* they lose, gives an entirely different perspective on things and has epistemological implications.

If you think without your heart, you will have no moral guidance, say

Balinese. Nor can you appreciate any situation or gain knowledge. If we apply this to the fieldwork situation, it entails that one must apply feeling *and* thought. The *bayu* has a palpable, embodied quality for people and balians alike that neither *atma* nor even *sakti* possesses; hence *bayu* emerges as a daily tapped resource of understanding for them, uniquely experience-near. But it is also of the essence for the anthropologist to tap the sources within oneself which enable one to share in some of people's experience. "Feeling along with" is the term John Leavitt coins for this perspective (1985, 10). I find it a felicitious term which evokes precisely the betwixt and between position of the anthropologist, straddling worlds and trying to bridge between them. Nor is this so different from what we all do in our ordinary, everyday encounters when we struggle to understand other minds, other hearts, aware of their ultimate elusiveness.

"Feeling along with" evokes separation yet closeness, unattachment *and* compassion. It invokes embodied understanding and attests to the nature of knowledge that is filtered or refracted through the body as a *privileged* means of creating resonance between another and oneself. Also for ourselves, the body functions as a crucial source of knowledge about the world and its essential features (Lakoff and Johnson 1980).

So balians, while they may *know* that they have *sakti, feel* it through the *bayu*, often as an electrical charge, a surge of vital energy. *Sakti* is real, just as is the *atma;* but compared with the *bayu*, both become ephemeral and transcendent. Also of importance to understanding why balians use such a humdrum term for such a mystical quality is that most come to their vocation midway in life. They have a background of ordinary living and have for a lifetime already oriented themselves with reference to *bayu*. Moreover, because *bayu* is itself spiritual and has an ephemeral as well as a physical quality, it may indeed emerge as the experience-near reference for *sakti* in a world where even the *atma*, the person's godly aspect, is relegated to second place, experientially subsumed into *bayu*.

Powers of Darkness, Powers of Light

The balian should use his *sakti* on behalf of the community to mediate between "this-worldly" and "other-worldly" powers. Or, to be more correct, he should allow himself to be used by it (McCauley 1984, 170). Refusal to follow the god's calling may cause illness to the person or members of her family, and is often a way for the gods to alert people to their *sakti* and force them to use it as a community resource.

The world of everyday, manifest affairs is referred to as the realm of light (*lemah*). The realm of darkness (*peteng*), by contrast, is comprised by mystical forces beyond the capability of ordinary understanding. It encompasses, among other things, white and black magic and their physical manifestations in such creatures as the bird *kuntilanak*, white mice (*belorong*), witches (*leak*), demons (*buta kala*), ghosts (*jerangkong*), and *orang alus* (such as *jinn, desti, memedi*), the souls of the dead, both unpurified (*leluhur, arwah*) and purified (*dewa*), and the gods (*bhatara*), such as Siwa, Brahma, and Visnu. We have seen that the realms of light and darkness are not actually separate, as mystical forces impinge constantly on ordinary, everyday affairs and are very much a part of people's experience of the natural world.

Balians should deploy their spiritual powers to relieve the fear, suffering, and pain of community members by mediating between the realm of mystical forces and their clients' immediate concerns. Occasionally, to this end, some will go on evil errands. The rain that falls when least expected and maximally inopportune, as well as many other misfortunes, illnesses, and deaths, testify that such evil work is being done. I never met any balian who admitted to working black magic—all emphasized how they work white magic only—but what is white and what is black may be a question of perspective. A famous dukun was proud of his skill at working love magic (*guna-guna*): "Of course, it is good to create love!" said he, with a broad, toothless grin. Others would emphatically disagree.

Balians should manipulate mystical forces for the benefit of the afflicted, and those who do not are said to think only of the here and now and to be unconcerned with their *karma pala*.

Balance versus Detrimental Anger

We have seen that in everyday popular health care the notions of "guiding one's feeling-thought/managing one's heart" and "not caring" are crucial. The balian operates in terms of another formula, but one that is compatible with this. He as well urges clients to keep good hearts, for in so doing they bolster their vital energy (*bayu*), making an effective resistance against attacks and onslaughts.[10] The balian will tell people to concentrate their power (*satukan jiwa*) and to strengthen their spirit (*besarkan jiwa*), appealing to broad, popular notions. In tune with this, his first concern is always to instigate hope. I have seen persons arrive very ill at a balian's and be told with a bright smile how easily their illness will be cured, provided they do what they need to do to help

246

themselves. That the illness is dangerous is never communicated to the sick person or her family, who need all the hope they can muster to bolster their efforts.[11]

The assumption of balian and populace alike seems to be that if a person harnesses her spiritual energies, and her family also properly fulfills their ritual[12] obligations, they perform vital preventive functions. If they also fulfill social obligations, such as treating others with proper deference and respect, they have done what they can to protect health and welfare.

The balian takes over where these efforts have failed and illness or misfortune indicates that something is amiss in the world: the balance which should obtain between good and bad powers is upset, either because of ritual omissions or mistakes which provoked the wrath of deities, ancestors, or demons; or predestination, whereby the living are paying for the sins of the dead; or evil action grounded in sorcery. The balian's function is to restore the balance on which health and happiness depend.

This aspect of balance is fundamental in Balinese cosmology and receives its elaboration in the *lontar* texts. Between the "small world" (*buana alit*), as the person, and the "great world" (*buana agung*), as the whole of existence or cosmos, balance should obtain. The "small world" refers to the "human body" as an anatomical structure which is also a vessel for the manifestations of (super)natural forces. Each element of the body also corresponds to features of the natural universe, as we have seen in the *lontar*'s prescriptions of where the parts of the body go upon death, e.g., the eyes to the moon, the head to the mountains (p. 166). The two structures are further defined by a constant flow of energy between them, and both are suffused with mystical power. In their healing ceremonies, balians

> attempt to influence the condition of their patients by deploying spiritually powerful elements of the "big world," such as medicines, offerings and mantra syllables. People with great spiritual power may also effect changes in the natural universe by the correct manipulation of mystical forces within their own bodies. . . . Knowledge of the correct way to manipulate natural objects allows control over their corresponding cosmic elements and thus creates and defines the person of power (*wong sakti*). (Connor 1986, 28)

She also notes how the principles of correspondences are known by ritual specialists only. "For ordinary folk, uninitiated into the mysteries of cosmic correspondences, offerings (*banten*) are the means by which they can influence the supernatural determination of their fate" (1986, 28).

My own fieldwork indicates that the ordinary person's conception of correspondence seems to be summed up in the notion *seimbang*—balanced—as the condition of harmony which should obtain between a person and all aspects of the universe. A world in balance is one where good and bad powers hold each other neutralized, or the good dominate the bad. "Balance" applies also to personal situation and experience. Excessive happiness may be dangerous: "We believe it will be followed by something bad so there will be balance." So is photography of an uneven number of persons: it is believed one person will become sick or even die. Names must be in balance with a person's vital spirit (*bayu*), and name change because a name turned out to be too light or too heavy is common. Physical or mental handicap is also assumed to highlight critical imbalance, in this case between a person's parents and their social environment. It is taken as evidence that they have mocked or ridiculed someone with a similar defect, and thus a handicapped person is referred to as *cacad*, from the word for scoff or mock (*nyacad*). When the balance which should obtain between a person and all aspects of the universe is obviously upset, the balian is called upon to restore it.

However, while "balance" may be said to be an underlying assumption and a condition for health and order in the universe, it is rarely invoked in everyday discourse. People feel-think along other dimensions, and when things go wrong, *anger* is assumed: anger of the gods, the ancestors, demons, fellow beings, or what have you. It is *feeling-thoughts* which are presumed to move the universe, just as it is feeling-thoughts which are presumed to determine the actions of people.

Let us look at one case which highlights how the anger of the gods worked dramatic changes in a couple's lives.

CHAPTER THIRTEEN

The Power to Heal

I am so tired. Sometimes I wish I had another life. But I surrender. The god
has chosen me.
—JERO MANGKU

Becoming a Balian: A Case

Some fifteen years ago there lived in Singaraja a couple who was famous all over town. She was a beauty so striking it is reputed that
President Soekarno himself wanted to marry her. She was a famed Balinese dancer and led an exciting life traveling about the world.

He was only marginally less famous. He was said to be handsome
beyond description and champion of all kinds of sports. He belonged to
a high-ranking, affluent family and led a free and independent life.
When the two married, people could not think of a more glamorous
couple.

For ten years they stayed happily married. Then, by the husband's
own description, his wife turned suddenly mad. She spoke wildly and
obscenely; she could not walk but crept on her knees (but very quickly!);
her eyes were hollow and staring; she would sit with her face resting in
her palms and stare out into space, *bengong* (dazed). She never slept,
and sometimes she would take a knife, threatening to kill herself.

For three months she was sick. Her husband and kin went all over
Bali in search of a balian who could heal her, but in vain. Then suddenly
one day, the husband's mother was possessed by a god from the Pulaki
temple. He was very angry, and the medium stood with her arms planted
at her sides (a provocative gesture) as the god accused her son of not
having listened to him. That was why his wife had become mad. He
must now become a priest (*pemangku*) and consecrate his life to religion, let his hair grow long, and give a specified set of offerings in
Pulaki. Then his wife would recover.

Jero Mangku told me:

> I did not believe, and I was angry, because I did not want
> to give up my freedom. I very much enjoyed the life I was
> leading, traveling around and seeing places. I loved doing ex-

249

ercise and wearing my hair short, like the other young men.
I did *not* want to become a priest!

But the god threatened him and said this was his choice: either to have his freedom or to make his wife well.

I cried for I was so tormented, and finally I said to the god,
"Okay, so I will go! But on one condition, that you make my
wife well immediately! I am not willing to wait a week or a
month, it must be done now or never!" The god laughed as I
said this. But I wanted to test him, for I did not believe!

He wasted no time to carry out his resolution but went the next day to Pulaki with the offerings as prescribed. Still he did not believe; he just did what he had been told, and in a recalcitrant spirit. When he returned home, he found his wife in the kitchen, cooking the food. "I believed! Never will I be brave again to resist the god. I cannot risk my wife going mad."

So he clothed himself in the white garment of a priest, let hair and beard grow, and relinquished his previous work and freedom of movement.

All I did was sit, I just sat in my house for three months, and
I was so unhappy to give up the life I had known. Then guests
began to come, at first some great dukuns [Muslim balians]
and three *pedandas* [Brahamana priests]. And I was so ill at
ease, I did not know anything, how to perform, what to do, I
had no experience, I was stupid (*bodoh*)! So I just sat with
my arms crossed, like a sulking child, and said to them, "Do
it yourself! You have experience, I know nothing!" For these
were old *pedandas*.

They entered his sacred room which his mother and his wife had prepared for him, according to the god's instructions. There they proceeded to pray and make devotions, while he just watched:

I had not the faintest idea what to do with the offerings, with
holy water, etc. Then suddenly I began to feel my body growing big and my face filling out, and I lost my consciousness.
When I began to speak it was in holy language at first, I did
not know what I myself was saying, but the *pedandas*, of
course, understood, and then I spoke in Balinese. For over an
hour I was possessed by the god until they were satisfied and
had been helped. They had been instructed by their own gods
to seek me out. Then they went away, and others began to

come, until now, you see . . . [he pointed to his porch where
he had guests from early morning till late at night]. The gods
have chosen me that I shall devote my life to helping others.
And I do not dare to resist from fear of the consequences for
my wife. And now I believe. Still I often do not understand
why the god tells me to do this or that, but I believe.

Two gods have chosen Jero Mangku. One is from the sacred temple
of Pulaki, the other from Bali's holiest mountain of Gunung Agung.
Both are very old, and when either enters his body Jero Mangku speaks
like an old man, slowly and with difficulty; he walks very slowly, and
even when he tries to move faster, his legs will not move. He feels old
and knows that he looks old. As the sign that the god is coming his jaw
begins to move uncontrollably, as do his eyelids and the muscles about
his eyes, and then this spreads to the nose and the mouth. But he does
not remember any of the words afterwards.[1]

He owes all his knowledge to the gods, nothing to humans, and thus
considers himself superior to balians who have learned by studying. He
knows all about the different properties of different flowers and holy
waters. In Pulaki, for instance, there are five sources of holy water, and
every one has a specific usage. Sometimes he has tested other balians
and found that they do not know the difference but think that holy water
is of undifferentiated kind. He makes many kinds[2] of medicines and
ointments: the gods give him the recipes. He does not understand, just
proceeds as instructed, doing everything with the help of his wife, without whom he could not manage anything. New recipes he tries out first
on himself, then on his wife, and only after that on his guests.

Word of Jero Mangku's healing powers had indeed spread far afield.
He had practiced for six years now and received guests from as far
away as Denpasar and Karangasem, and occasionally even from Java or
Madura. He never rested but received guests every day unless he had to
lead some ceremony at a family temple. In an ordinary day some ten to
fifteen guests would come, making him often moan how exhausted he
was at the god's ceaseless deployment of him in the service of the
people. He spoke with longing of his past, of his freedom of movement
and his short hair, and had an insatiable curiosity about the ways of the
world and a memory like glue for political and geographical affairs portrayed on television. How did it look now in Denpasar, he asked me. He
had heard that tourists went naked about Kuta and that there were tall
buildings, fast cars.

The porch of his home had been his window on the world for the past six years. He would tell me how every now and then he would decide to take a day's vacation and go away in the family car. But when he went outside at sunrise, early enough so that guests would not have had time to arrive, there on the porch some would be, waiting. And he would turn back, heedful of the god's message: to be ever in the service of the people.

A Weapon Under the Pillow

Here is an idea of the range and kinds of problems he treats and the diagnoses and treatments he gives.

1. One early afternoon two frantically tense young men came with their high-strung mothers. One was Balinese, the other Chinese, and they seemed on the verge of violence, so tense were they. The women's voices were shrill as they spoke.

The boys were chicken traders in the market and had long been friends. Today, the Chinese had asked the Balinese to keep for him two hundred and fifty thousand rupiahs in his pocket. But two hundred thousand rupiahs had disappeared. The Chinese boy and his mother looked ferociously at the Balinese boy.

Jero Mangku's god emerged and spoke in a furious voice. He berated the Chinese boy for his gambling proclivities. No need to look for the money. He is never going to find it. It has been taken by the god in punishment for his sins. But if he reforms and begins to lead a decent life, the god will pay him back manyfold. If he buys a chicken for ten thousand rupiahs, he will sell it for twenty thousand, people will give him money; he will gain more than ever before.

Rituals to be carried out at a Chinese temple were also prescribed, and the boy was given holy water to drink. The boys and their mothers shone with relief as they left Jero Mangku's home. They appeared convinced of the validity of the diagnosis and treatment.

2. A mother, her face swathed with pain, came on behalf of her twenty-five-year-old son, who had been seriously wounded in a traffic accident. Both his legs and one arm were broken, and after three operations the fractures would still not heal. Now he was lying in the hospital, frantic with pain, imploring God to let him die. The doctors had given up and advised her to see Jero Mangku.

The god revealed that the soul reincarnated in her son had committed a serious ritual mistake in his former life which her son was paying for according to the law of *karma pala*. That is why he in particular was caught in the traffic accident. The family would have to remedy the ancestor's mistake, but not till the son's fracture had healed. Jero Mangku requires people only to make a *promise* of performing elaborate ceremonies, not to enact them until healing is secured. The young man was also given efficacious oil and ointments to make him well.

The mother came back a week later and a week later again. The tension was gone now; she smiled as she told how her son was so much better and might soon be able to walk. When I returned a year later, she reported that her son limps but can walk. She has brought Jero Mangku many new guests.

3. A woman came from the hospital where she had been for a week because she could not urinate. The doctors had stuck a long probe into her, to no avail, and now they had advised her to see Jero Mangku. He diagnosed that she was suffering an illness of the kidneys because the ancestor who is reincarnated in her was poisoned by a rejected lover. This happened approximately forty-five years ago, but the poison had been slow to take effect. The treatment included no ceremony, but a particular herbal medicine, for there had been no ritual mistake. This illness also was regarded as "so easy to cure." Because the woman lived in a remote area of Bali, I was not able to follow up the case.

4. Two old women came on behalf of one's son, who was sick, his body and face alternately swelling and retracting. Diagnosis: The boy had been eating out of a plate with his siblings, and this made the gods angry. In the boy's body are reincarnated several souls, so he is very holy and should eat alone. Moreover, the god was angry because the family altar had collapsed and not been repaired. Indeed, so angry was he that he even refused to allow Jero Mangku to give medicine that day but required the women first to go home and make a promise by the family altar to remedy it, then come back in two days for the medicine. Before they left, Jero Mangku called to his wife to return the money they had brought him with the offerings, for the god had revealed that his guests were so poor that the money had been borrowed.

5. A mother and grandmother came with a young child who for ten days had been suffering bad sores behind his ears. They had seen many doctors, to no avail. Diagnosis: It was not the child but the ancestor reincarnated in the child who had the illness. The family had made a mistake in not performing the ceremony of *meseh lawang* after this ancestor died. The purpose of this ceremony is to ensure that illnesses or defects of the dead person will not afflict the person in whom (s)he may be reincarnated. The ceremony should have taken place before the corpse was taken to the cemetery.

Jero Mangku is convinced that many people forget to perform this ceremony.

> So they come to me and ask, 'Why, when the parents are healthy, is the son blind?' Or, 'Why is my child born with a defect?' Well, it's so easy to explain. If a man falls down from a tree and breaks his limbs and dies, well of course the person in whom he is reincarnated will suffer fractures, unless *meseh lawang* is performed. But people don't understand. Why has everyone in my family many debts, is always sad, has always bad luck? they ask. Often it is because of failure to perform *meseh lawang*, but it may also be because the ancestors are angry for other reasons.

The treatment in this case included herbal medicines mixed with Jero Mangku's special black oil and ointments. The family also had to promise to make the required ceremony after the boy was healthy. Ten days later he was reported to be well.

6. A man lay ill in a hospital in Denpasar, diagnosed as suffering nervous exhaustion. Jero Mangku was contacted when the man showed no sign of improvement but lost both the power of speech and movement. His wife was frantic and sure he was dying.

In his holy room (*kamar suci*) in Singaraja Jero Mangku consulted his gods, who revealed that the man was sick from two causes. First, he sold antiques that were then transported out of the country, and as these are *sakti* objects, the gods were very angry. Second, he was a victim of black magic from his stepmother and her children, who were envious of his wealth, and because many people had ganged up against him, he was very seriously afflicted. Jero Mangku ordered that he go off the doctor's medicines and be taken home, for the medicines were antithetical to his body and upset the souls reincarnated in him; he must also change his diet, go off meat and hot foods and eat only vegetables and fruits. Holy water to drink was sent to him in Denpasar.

The sick man loved meat and was furious with this prescription. He refused to eat, became mute, and lay as if he was nearly dead. His family did not dare to remove him from the hospital, so Jero Mangku finally went there (I went along) and, seeing the man's serious condition, advised that he remain in hospital for intravenous feeding. But he performed exorcising rituals and applied holy water to the man.

Afterwards, he told the weeping wife that she had nothing to fear. True, the magic was very strong, but he had put a weapon under the man's pillow to vanquish it. "A weapon?" I asked. "Yes, a small leaf; it will protect him and repel the black magic."

He also explained why the man was so weak: the god, to protect him, had taken away one of the two souls reincarnated in him so it would not be harmed by the black magic; when the magic had gone, he would put it back. Naturally, bereft of half of his usual spiritual equipment, the man was very weak. Not to worry.

As days passed and the doctors in the hospital fed the man milk, Jero Mangku's worry increased. Milk was antithetical to the sick man, for a priest, a *pemangku,* was reincarnated in him, and cow's milk is forbidden to a priest. He said that so far the gods had protected the sick man, but with this offense it was questionable how long they would continue to do so.

A few days later, the man died.

The Person Vulnerable and Exposed

The above cases illustrate a formula to which ordinary people commonly testify when they say "health and happiness depend on the ancestors' goodwill." They show how "anger"[3] rather than "balance" is a diagnostic criterion and exemplify the intimate connection perceived between a person and macrocosmological forces. The explanatory framework balians deploy also points to the peculiar ephemeral nature of Balinese person construction. As Connor has put it so well:

> The Balinese view of personality . . . defies the distinction many other cultures draw between the self and macrocosmos, between mind and body, and between the natural and supernatural realm. . . .
>
> If we look at the practices of the therapists in Bali, coupled with the elements of personality as articulated in classical medico-religious texts, as well as by informants, it appears that the Balinese "person" is not an isolated, indivisible unit but is rather a nexus of interacting forces, macrocosmic and microcosmic, natural and supernatural, always in delicate balance. . . .
>
> [This] portrayal of personality is, of course, overwhelmingly cognitive and . . . emphasizes the exotic at the expense of the more mundane cultural interpretation of human behavior. . . .
>
> [However,] the subjective experience of self, coupled with the Balinese belief in the manifold representations of the supernatural which pervade their lives, is analytically crucial to any explanation of why these people not only suffer from unbalanced psyches but also recover from such disturbances (1982a, 263–64).

Mind in Psyche and Soma

"Unbalanced psyches" is, of course, a Western way of describing things. For Balinese, as we have seen, psychic stress and disturbance translate usually into physically experienced complaints. That is, a process of somatization takes place which Kleinman defines "for the purposes of simplifying and unifying a complex, contested term . . . as the normative expression of personal and social distress in an idiom of bodily complaints and medical help-seeking" (Kleinman 1986, 2). The body is the medium through which Balinese experience and express personal complaints. The diagnostic framework applied by balians often defuses guilt and antisocial feelings by positing the causative agents beyond the person—on the other hand, it also sows seeds of suspicion and dissension by diagnosing sorcery. Illness yet might be said both to function as a safety valve and to offer respite, in many cases, from the pressures of everyday living. Connor asks the important question of whether Western psychodynamic theories can have heuristic value or offer any real therapeutic effects when applied in a culture which denies their basic conceptual foundation (1982a, 264).

At issue is the illness experience which contrasts with the disease as "the way the illness experience is reinterpreted by practitioners in terms of their theoretical models and through clinical work. . . . Illness connotes "the way individuals and the members of their social network perceive symptoms, categorize and label those symptoms, experience them, and articulate that illness experience through idioms of distress and pathways of help-seeking" (Kleinman 1986, 225).

The "illness" and the "disease" may differ dramàtically, as Balinese often find when they consult their doctors. Commonly I was told that doctors could cure about 10 percent of illnesses, balians some 90 percent. Salient distinctions Balinese draw are between sicknesses that affect the life-force/soul (*bayu*) and those that involve only the body.

With respect to most afflictions balians and their clientele share understandings of many of the cosmological principles in which diagnosis and treatment are grounded. Indeed, they must, for balians act *for*, but not to the exclusion of, the afflicted. Every effort at healing involves a joint effort on the part of balian and family of the afflicted. The balian is concerned with their commitment and trust and their ability to carry out requisite rituals. The involvement of a person's relatives in the therapy process and the release of pent-up emotions in uncontrolled outbursts may indeed make a substantial contribution to the resolution of a sufferer's problems, particularly when they are of mental-emotional nature (see Connor 1982b, 790).

I also presume placebo effects to be triggered by the absolute condition of placing full trust in the balian and committing oneself in spirit and heart, that is, mobilizing all one's energy resources. As the concerned family commit themselves, they may be counted on to "do the best" to enact care and compassion, in the way that Kede always smiled and heeded the psychiatrist's command of bestowing affection on her husband.

It works best when the sick person is aware of the balian's efforts on her behalf, but perhaps it works also at times when she does not know (cf. Hahn and Kleinman, 1983, 17).

Scheper-Hughes and Lock argue that placebo effects and what they, after Hahn and Kleinman, term nocebo effects, as the opposite—that is, strong and pathogenic emotions—are integral to "all sickness and healing, for they are concepts that refer in an incomplete and oblique way to the interactions between mind and body" (1987, 30). Typical nocebo effects might be the anxiety and fears in which sorcery beliefs are embedded (Hahn and Kleinman 1983) and that at times induce death from magical fright (Cannon, 1942), also in Bali. A common illness that implicates nocebo effects in etiology and placebo effects in healing is "pregnancy with stones." Jero Mangku is particularly renowned for, and proud of, his ability to cure this illness.

Pregnancy with Stones

Pregnancy with stones—*beling batu*—is the magical illness most frantically feared in the North. Other illnesses, such as the "black wind" (*angin hitam*) which paralyzes half the body (and is therefore also referred to as "half is dead": *mati setanga*) or the famed *bebainan* in which small creatures, *babai,* have been inserted in the victim's body and cause hysterical fits and uncontrolled speech (Suryani 1984), are feared very much. But they do not compare with pregnancy with stones, which gives a most hideous appearance and spells ultimate death if not cured. Suriati's grandfather died from this, and everyone seems to have family or acquaintances who have suffered this abominable affliction though, fortunately, many were cured.

Pregnancy with stones connotes that the stomach is swollen and stone-hard to the touch. It may be filled with stones, with the husks of coconuts (*sambuk bangrok*), or with fish or other creatures. This is revealed when in successful healing the revolting substances are expelled coated in sickly smelling emulsions. It is distinguished from stomach tumor (*abeh*) which produces an enlarged but soft stomach and must be cured by medical personnel. Only balians with superior mystical power can heal pregnancy with stones.

It afflicts both males and females, generally those beyond puberty. Jero Mangku says that teenage girls are the most frequent victims, for their hearts (read *bayu*, life force) are weaker. A Balinese doctor also told me this, but I did not hear it from ordinary people, who expressed a belief that both sexes are equally exposed.

Beling batu originates from Lombok, which is another way of saying that it is held to be Islamic in origin. But some Hindu balians have been trained by Lombokese dukuns, or by their (Muslim) apprentices in Bali, to cause it. Banyuwangi in East Java is also presumed to have become by diffusion a main locus for *beling batu*.

I had the occasion to meet several guests suffering this illness at Jero Mangku's. Some had come a long way, from Denpasar, Kintamani, or Karangasem. They looked pale and exhausted, were withdrawn, and shied away from onlookers (for instance, reclusing in his living room rather than on the exposed porch where guests usually sit and chat while awaiting their turn). I had the impression they felt ashamed of their affliction. And understandably so. An enlarged stomach is the epitome of ugliness and immorality to Balinese. It evokes images of laziness, self-indulgence, and inability to control one's animal instincts. In women in particular it is awful. Ideals of female beauty dictate that the stomach should be even with the waist and lower bosom, whereas breasts and buttocks should protrude in a form called *pingul*. To cultivate this desired form girls sleep tightly bound in a cocoon of yards of elastic wound around the stomach from the age of menses, around ten, and women do so for forty days after giving birth. Females also should not sleep in the middle of the day, for it predisposes one to a large stomach and a condition of laziness.

If, as Hahn and Kleinman assert, the mindful body responds to its biopsychosocial environment in terms of cultural expectations and beliefs that facilitate or impede nocebo and placebo effects, then pregnancy with stones might be seen as peculiarly Balinese: a culturally constructed expression of particular fears and despairs. It embodies basic Balinese conceptions of beauty, morality, and interpersonal evil. The physical embodiments of fears work, to quote Hahn and Kleinman, to retard "integrated biopsychical processes, [they are] demoralizing, reducing immunological competence and physiological activation" (1983, 19). Conversely, contact with a balian might activate hope and, with it, the person's internal therapeutic system. "We know that 'hope' is associated with heightened activation of the autonomic nervous system . . . , personal animation, and social connectedness. It is believed that this biopsychosocial integration corresponds with an associated multitude of physiological processes that represent, as it were, the person's internal therapeutic system" (1983, 18–19).

Both balians and ordinary people emphasize the importance of hope, of vital energy as the power of resistance, and of fears as debilitating. A doctor even told me how *bayu* flows in the white blood cells, hence *is* the person's immune system. But Balinese do not regard pregnancy with stones as psychosomatic in the sense of being psychologically induced. Black magic is a fact, an objective attribute of the world. Activating hope, keeping an optimistic outlook on life, works to strengthen the spirit and deter attacks of black magic. Fears debilitate, but they do not "produce" attacks. The principles of causation are other.

Pregnancy with stones is caused by the insertion of alien elements into the victim's body. One man claimed to know that filling a jug with water containing pieces of paper with special magical script and shaking the jug wildly while keeping the spout closed was a way to cause stone pregnancy. Most people have no idea how to cause it, and they would not even think about these matters, which belong to a realm of mystical knowledge—*kelas satu*—of the highest, most dangerous order.

Contrary to popular belief, Jero Mangku finds that pregnancy with stones originates not in the stomach but in the head. The gods have revealed to him that it is the soul (*atma*) that is afflicted (aspects of which are thinking-feeling and visualization). This is connected with the spinal cord, which is continuous with the brain (*kondalini*). The illness starts in the brain. From there it moves via the blood to the eyes and on to the stomach. All of this takes time and indicates a progressively deteriorating condition.

When stone-pregnant persons come to him, they usually feel desperate. He treats by massage with his sacred oil and ointments, beginning with the arms and the legs and proceeding to the face, the neck, the chest, and then the stomach with downward movements. The god has taught him how to massage. If the genitalia must be massaged, he calls on the sick person's mother to do so. When the illness goes out, either through the genitalia or the mouth, the smell is sickly and the emulsion contains hairs, nails, sand, coconut husk, fish, or other magical elements. Refuse also gushes forth from the mouth, and the sick person may sit a whole day vomiting, meanwhile moaning and groaning. When the magic is out, the stomach turns soft and normal again.

But the fight with the attacking spirit(s) may be prolonged and necessitate exhausting battles. While the balian massages, the spirit fights back and yells and screams, threatening death and everlasting punishment. Sometimes Jero Mangku is deathly tired after a successful treatment. Prolonged negotiations may also be part of the battle, and the spirit, if he is Muslim, may put as a final condition for retreat that the (Hindu) balian pray like himself. This seems a small concession, and so Jeru Mangku often agrees. He may also have to accompany the spirit to the door in a final gesture of respect and good grace.

Afterwards, the family of the sick person will have to conduct a major, expensive ceremony (costing approximately three hundred thousand rupiahs or two hundred dollars) to purify and cleanse the sick person and thank the deities for their support and further secure their goodwill. Realignment of a person's four spiritual siblings (*kanda mpat*)[4] who protect against illness and had been displaced by the magical spirit is also secured, though the *kanda mpat* are so dangerous to think about that I did not find reference to them among either ordinary people or ordinary balians, but only among balian *usada*.

Magic by Wrong Address

By their power to heal balians also *attract* evil forces, who are furious because they are challenged and try to strike back when least expected. They also strike at members of the balian's family in deviation of the target, and for this reason balians often do not wish family members to follow their profession and may refuse to bequest their *sakti* to them. One balian I know had lost thirty of his thirty-four children (from four wives) in early childhood. Both he and his community leaned toward the interpretation of magic by wrong address. This balian was very famous and strong, and he would describe to me how at night when he is just about to fall asleep, he will have a sensation of wind coming from all sides and whirling up around him or of a multitude of fluttering butterflies in the air about his head, or see a mass of intertwined snakes writhing and squirming around him. All of this indicates that he is under attack from another wizard and that he must mobilize all his strength to withstand the onslaught.

Jero Mangku also has evidence that some are after him, and sometimes he challenges them, "Just come, try if you will!" Disturbing signs are sounds in the ears, a terrible smell as of a burning corpse, and the noise of little cackling chicken running about the house (but when they search, none can be found); he also sometimes hears a little girl weeping. All portend magic trying to strike.

To counter the attack it is important to be calm (*tenang*) and have a good heart, says Jero Mangku, reiterating popular judgments. Only once has a child of his been sick from black magic, and he believes that because all family ceremonies are complete, black magic cannot win over him or his family.

So the balian urges people to manage their hearts and strengthen their life force, as well as to honor deities and gods, heed dangerous spirits, apply countermagical formulas or substances to their persons, gates, doors, and windows, and be cautious in all interpersonal encounters. He reinforces popular notions and acts in terms of a cosmology sufficiently broad and a language of interpretation sufficiently vague to make sense to people of any religion. A Hindu balian, after lecturing my husband on the differences among Hinduism, Islam, and Buddhism, concluded with a bright smile, "You see, they are completely different. Exactly the same!"

The world indeed has several facets, and what matters is to be pragmatic, flexible, versatile, not fastidious in religion.

The Self in Relation to Multiple Causation

In medical care this pragmatism implies a willingness to try several alternatives, simultaneously or consecutively. The exposure of the person to myriad influences and forces all through the day and everywhere explains in part why illness etiology is initially open to so many diverse interpretations that are not seen as contradictory. To exemplify: A girl, two years old, was sick for two weeks with crying, sleeplessness, occasional fevers, and lack of appetite. The initial diagnosis by the child's mother and grandmother was that she was suffering from *sawan nganten*—an illness from magic by wrong address which particularly strikes children when they accompany their mothers to a wedding (Wikan 1989a, 35). To cure it, "the powder of the bride" was applied— a *sakti* substance efficacious against *sawan*—but it proved useless. So the family reasoned she might have fallen off a chair, and they took her to a masseuse to bring her veins back in order. Again, no use. Symptoms worsened; the child cried more, and even began to resist being held by her grandmother, whom before she adored. So she was taken to a Chinese doctor who provided some medicines, but when after a day no improvement was noticed, she was brought to a Catholic hospital. Here the diagnosis was "pending typhoid," which alarmed the family, and when after two days the girl was not better from the medicines she was taking, neighbors recommended a particular dukun. He diagnosed a severe attack of black magic and gave her holy water to expel the magic and a particularly efficacious amulet to wear. Still no improvement, and then the father suddenly remembered that a few days before he had played with the child under a big tree on the beach. Perhaps they had disturbed an *orang alus*. Flowers were brought and placed under the tree with apologies to the *orang alus* for any disturbance caused. Then the girl was said to have become much better and was pronounced cured. To mark her recovery, the family gave a huge *slametan* to thank God and have many guests pray on her behalf. The next day her symptoms returned; the family panicked and were relieved when shortly after measles broke out. She was taken to a Balinese doctor and got well after a while.

There is no way to determine that measles alone were responsible for her condition, or that "the powder of the bride," the massage, and the amulet were not partially effective in its cure. That causation is typically complex seems reasonable given a nexus of body-spirit-mind bound up with a universe of cosmological forces. Even in terms of Muslim praxis the premise of multiple causation makes sense. Concepts of holy justice, magic, *orang alus,* and interpersonal evil commit Balinese across religious diversity to a common praxis of health care.

A Case of Extortion

The case of the little girl reveals another aspect of balian-guest relations: the powerlessness of clients vis-à-vis a balian who misuses his power. It was the only instance I came across of economic extortion, though I was told that very successful balians never last long because they would become arrogant and set high prices, leading to punishment by the gods and loss of *sakti*. In this case the balian demanded the equivalent of a bus driver's monthly wage (twenty thousand rupiahs) from the impoverished father, who became sick from the shock; to protect his family, he did not tell them why he was ill. But they found out and were beyond themselves with anger and despair. I was there when the news broke; the women began crying hysterically and threatening to counter the balian (he had taken the father aside and asked for the money in secrecy from him, because, said the women, only men would agree to such an outrageous request: they consider it beneath themselves to bargain). But hardly had they voiced the threat before they withdrew in panic: really, wasn't the girl better? Come to think of it, she cried less than before, was calmer. At stake seemed to be fear of what the balian might do if they offended him.

I offered to help. I spoke Arabic and so might converse with him in a language of whose knowledge he was proud. Perhaps I could explain their predicament to him without offense. At first the women seemed to welcome the thought. Yes, truly, that could be. All he had done was to write a piece of Koranic script in an amulet. Isn't the Koran everyone's property, and not for him to make a fortune from? But they had no sooner pronounced this than fear again rose and they panicked. It was then that the father came to remember about the *orang alus* under the tree on the beach, and it was then that they decided to give a huge *slametan*, thinking they had seen significant improvement in the girl.

Theirs was a truly painful experience: to be trapped into paying a month's wage for an amulet that did not even work (or had not worked yet). Neighbors who heard about the experience were shocked, and the balian lost a few of his former "guests."

Always to Maintain Hope

I have presented this case for what it is: unique in my experience. Power may be misused in any relationship, and stories abound of evil and self-serving balians. But as a category balians are esteemed, and many are held in affectionate respect. When clients are poor, balians may give help for nothing except flower offerings worth a nominal sum.

Balians serve their communities as well as individuals by procuring and sustaining hope in the face of life's strains and stresses. They heal a variety of illnesses and are also ever accessible as a receptacle for suffering of a kind Balinese cannot easily share with others. With them feelings may be given free vent, fears voiced, and interpersonal problems exposed. The bright face which the afflicted wears all along the way to the balian's porch here eventually may be shed. And the heart is exposed, posture and facial expression cry out, as, in a privileged relation, Balinese are (relatively) freed from the fear of causing offense. The balian is there to listen and help, and so he does: numerous guests come away buoyed and relieved every day.

Perhaps indeed the effort of appearing bright before the world would be too much at times if people did not have access to such persons of authority and wisdom in whom to confide and to whom to express their sorrows, with the attendant expectation that they will be helped. The knowledge that one has recourse to relief, somewhere, somehow, may lessen the strain of maintaining an impeccable appearance. Teamed up with a suitable balian, a person can overcome most everyday tensions and problems.

Let this testimony by Jero Mangku sum up how one balian looks upon his life and his work:

> I am so tired. Sometimes I wish I had another life. But I surrender. The god has chosen me. I only wish I had not more than three or four guests a day; truly one would be enough. A doctor does not spend more than ten or fifteen minutes on a patient, but I may spend an hour or an hour and a half, and the massage is very hard work. Often my body is aching. I am so tired, I feel as if I have almost no *bayu*. And yet I always make my face look bright. I receive everyone the same, whether poor or rich, ugly or handsome, it makes no difference with me. I do the god's work.

PART FIVE

Culture and Translation

CHAPTER FOURTEEN

Going Beyond the Words:
A Plea for Resonance

If we do not use our feelings, we will be captured by the illusion.
—MADE BIDJA

The view I am offering says that there is such a thing as moral
progress . . . in the direction of greater human solidarity, . . . thought of as
the ability to see more and more traditional differences (of
religion, . . . customs, and the like) as unimportant when compared with
similarities with respect to pain and humiliation.
—RICHARD RORTY

Underlying this attempt to depict the lived experience of Balinese has
been a certain orientation to methodology and epistemology. I advocate
the need to ground oneself—heart and mind—in relationships to people
one seeks to understand: to be subjective in the sense of deploying oneself and one's own, always limited and partial, sources of insight—
a particular vantage point. Indeed, we might as well acknowledge that
one's vantage point is necessarily always particular, whether we deal
with "large" or "small" issues. Which issue is which is also a matter of
perspective.

Practitioners of social science, we are easily tempted to forget this.
There lies in the conception of our discipline an invitation or even compulsion to overgeneralize and stereotype. Suriati becomes one of "the
Balinese." Wayan Wijaya, Ketut Artje, and Gede Mireh are easily
blended into "a people," "a culture."

I have tried to resist. And when I have failed, as no doubt I have, I
hope that the reader on closing this book yet will have been brought sufficiently into touch with particular Balinese that this is what will remain
with you for the future: the memory, a distinct feeling-thought, of how
different they are; how human in that they have each their own characters; and how vulnerable, like you and me, to the unpredictable, at times
cruel, nature of life itself. Also for Balinese, life is what happens while
they are making other plans.

If my book has accomplished this, then I will have repaid some of my debts to Balinese friends who steadily impressed upon me that my task was to create resonance (*ngelah keneh*) between you and them. I must bring the reader, or the audience, in touch with the stories I tell, said they. Otherwise there would be no empathy, no compassion (*kelangen*). Nor would there be understanding, for understanding presupposes this quality of resonance.

Balinese have a suspicion that Westerners do not see it this way, that we believe we can think only with our minds and yet arrive at genuine insight. In this we are captives of illusion (*hayacan*), say they, for feeling is the more essential for comprehension: "Without feeling it is impossible to appreciate (*menghayati*) any situation or problem."

Made Bidja said to me:

> Take as an example Muslims in Bali who have no concept of *karma pala* [that one's acts, good or bad, will affect one's future life and condition of reincarnation]. And yet they understand what it's all about. How do they come to appreciate? By the power of resonance. They use their feelings, and so they understand its basic idea as just returns, heaven and hell. But Westerners have no resonance with the idea of *karma pala* because they use their thoughts only, and so ideas and understandings do not spring alive . . .

I was reminded, as he spoke, of my Muslim friend who had accompanied me to a Hindu balian and on being advised to cure her misfortune by "presenting offerings in the Muslim holy place" immediately understood what he meant. I had thought his words would reek to her (who prided herself on being a fanatic Muslim) of idolatry and ancestor worship. But she went to the core of the meaning of things, for she saw beyond the words. It was I who was at a disadvantage, for I saw as far as the words only, and so I could not grasp their true significance.

Made Bidja continued (we were on the point of how ideas and readings do not spring alive):

> Take my friend Dr. Soegianto, who now writes the story of Panci Sakti [Balinese hero and reputed founder of the Buleleng dynasty c. A.D. 1660–1680]. How do you think he can? Well, because of his earlier readings about Hannibal and Alexander the Great! He used his feelings then to understand about their lives, and so there was resonance between him and them. Now he uses this appreciation to understand [i.e., interpret] the texts about Panci Sakti and to communicate an understanding to others.

Resonance thus demands something of both author and reader: a joint effort at feeling-thought; a willingness on the part of both to engage with another world, life, or idea: to *use* one's own life experience, on the example of the Muslim "fanatic" faced with the Hindu balian, to try to grasp the meanings that reside neither in words, "facts," nor text but are evoked in the meeting of an experiencing subject with the text; in the next instance, then, to share such understandings with others.

It is the essence of this view of things that knowledge is for being shared. To seek knowledge in itself, for oneself, bespeaks less than honorable motives.

Hannibal, Alexander the Great, and Panci Sakti had something in common, as my Balinese friend saw it. Separated by some two thousand years in time and by great distances in space, yet they were men and warriors, heroes; they had friends and enemies, lovers, parents; they fought for things that were dear to them—and in this they had some commonality of experience.

So it is with Muslims and Hindus, or with Balinese and us. We can use this commonality of experience to try and understand one another. Indeed, we must, for we have nothing else. Made Bidja's advice was that I make this the very foundation of my study.

I have tried, and I was fortunate in having as guides along the way persons who painstakingly took me by the hand and exercised much patience, intelligence, and good-natured (I like to think) laughter in trying to make me understand. Theirs was a difficult task, for there was much for me to unlearn before I could grasp what mattered to them and how it mattered. Sometimes, when I struggled so hard to comprehend that deep furrows showed on my forehead, friends would interrupt me gently: "Stop thinking! You're going about this the wrong way. You'll never understand what we mean if you use only your thinking!"

And when I, puzzled and slightly hurt, asked whether they could not conceive that some kind of knowledge were best attained by the power of thought (alone), some laughed as heartily as if this were the funniest thing they had ever heard: "Oh, no! Feeling is the more essential for comprehension!"

Read that sentence again. It does not mean what it appears to say, for there is no such thing among Balinese as what we term "feeling." What their injunction calls forth is the notion that there should be balance between feeling and thought but that, *on balance,* feeling is the more essential. Preferably there should be more of neither one nor the other but harmonious integration between two aspects of an integral process that people try occasionally to split.

Said a man, "If we use our feelings only, we'll all sit down and cry, for there is too much suffering in this world. But if we use our thoughts only, then we will be selfish and greedy."

The group of men who were present nodded their heads in emphatic response: "Exactly! If feeling is not tempered with thought, we will all be sad and sick. But if thought supplants feeling, there will be no resonance, no sensitivity . . ."

Knowledge and experience, in this formulation, are two aspects of the same. It does not work to proceed to search for knowledge otherwise than one proceeds to live in the world. Learning is for life, just as life is for learning. Here then is a vision of the world that integrates what we have split. And on writing these words I am reminded again of the balian who, lecturing my husband on the differences among Hinduism, Islam, and Buddhism, concluded with a bright smile: "You see, they are completely different! Exactly the same!"

Might he have said, "Humans are the same; religions deal with the same kinds of problems; God is the same; the rest is irrelevant"?

I have tried to ask some Balinese friends if this stress on feeling as essential for understanding would not lead to mere subjectivism. "Oh, no!" was the answer, and always to trills of laughter. All knowledge is subjective *and* objective, neither one nor the other, for the concepts are misapplied. But because feeling is as rational as thought, this gives no grounds for pessimism or unease. Deeper insights will be reached if we use our feeling-thoughts. Again and again the advice to me would be, shed your presumptions of what feeling "is."

It was not that I started with a blank slate in my efforts to understand Balinese. I was, on the one hand, privileged in having worked and lived in several cultures, thus having some experience in the ways of the world that I could bring to bear on my understanding of Balinese (the way Dr. Soegianto used his familiarity with Alexander and Hannibal to understand about Panci Sakti). On the other hand, I was, as I came to realize, profoundly handicapped by being captive to ways of understanding, including a view of how best to *obtain* understanding, that had served me in good stead other places where I had lived yet were now judged to be "illusory." Like Suriati, who in Jakarta has to unlearn a lifetime's ingrained belief in the supreme good value of smiling and being "happy" because she finds that by this manner of response she forfeits what she needs—in Jakarta—to live successfully, so I too had to discard valued parts of myself.

In the end I felt the richer for it; but in the beginning, and for a very long time, it was hard. Not only did I have to learn to smile always so my muscles ached (for my muscles were not trained in this way of being); not only did I have to reenter a world long gone where (as a child) I had taken in full earnest the presence of supernatural beings (Balinese now made me question *who* were captives of superstitions: "we" who know about such things, or those of you who [think you] live in a mechanistic world). But the most difficult, I had to rid myself of basic constraints which arise from Western epistemology—i.e., conceptions of how best to attain knowledge—in which I had been reared since my school days.

It was hard because the Balinese contrary vision was not spelled out to me early the way, say, the "fact" of black magic was when I stumbled across it and, aware that I had stumbled, started searching for the obstructions that impeded my progress. Their vision of the way to knowledge did not challenge my powers of perception the way my encounter with Suriati, laughing with grief, did. For the longest time I simply did not understand that here was anything to understand. Balinese and I talked past each other. And one reason we did was their use of the words *perasaan* and *pikiran* which translate readily as "feeling" and "thought." How was I to understand that they meant the one *and* the other? That they are, as Balinese say, "the same"?

They say *perasaan*, and they mean feeling-thought. I say *perasaan*, and I mean only feeling, of course. And we do not know that we are talking past one another, for the words appear to be readily translatable from one language into an other. In a nutshell it is this problem of translation which anthropologists must confront and solve in the most sensitive way possible, and that even requires that we are prepared to let our very epistemology be subtly undermined by the perspective of "the other."

In bringing this book to a close, I will try to take you with me part of the way I had to travel to begin, as I say, to understand. It may seem paradoxical that I do so now. Ought there not rather to be a conclusion, a summing up? I think not. In my view, this is what life is all about: a groping for understanding, followed by the feeling that one has reached that and gone beyond, only again to plunge deeper into an awareness that the profoundest answers conceal genuine riddles. "You must love the questions themselves," Rilke said (quoted in Maslow 1966, 14).

For me, nearing the end of my mental journey into Bali brings with it the realization that it is now I begin. It was from here I should have ventured. And so I close by a detour: reflections on sheer beginnings that to me came as belated afterthoughts. I trace some singular moments in my own progress toward understanding that now appear with the luminous clarity of hindsight, pointing ahead to new discoveries. Were I to begin, this is where I now would begin.

I use deliberately an evocative mode in keeping with friends' advice that what matters is to achieve resonance.

One day in Bali I was sitting with a couple trying to make out—once again—how notions of balance and harmony (*pantas/keseimbangan*) translate into personal experience. From the literature it seemed clear that such notions were crucial in Bali-Hindu cosmology and person constitution. But how, I wondered, did they compel action? What did they actually mean for people whose lives they presumably governed?

As with my friends I explored linkages I thought I could detect between bodily imbalance, emotional imbalance, and moral and ritual transgressions, logically all cohered, yet my friends seemed bewildered by my questions. In the end the man cut me short and gracefully said, "You know, it's right what you say, but it is not the way we think."

And he went on to expound how Balinese think, substituting for the notion of "balance" I had used more experience-near concepts of pragmatic consequence in everyday life and relegating my kind of usage to the discourse of literary and textual specialists.

To me his warning was timely. As I saw it, he did not merely juxtapose two kinds of discourses, two ways of knowing, one expert, one folk. More was at stake.

By setting "truth" against "the way we think," in a superb gesture—using the simplest kind of words—he had challenged the relationship I conventionally perceived between them and made "truth" seem the indubitable loser. With perfect grace, granting me a measure of truth, he yet held out before me the prospects of superior insight, would I go for experiential knowledge rather than abstract truth. It was not that the latter did not matter, but that the former mattered more, given what I was out to gain: an understanding of "ordinary" Balinese like himself.

Concretely, the words he invoked to impress upon me "how we think" were "calm," "confused," "angry," and "happy"—as the experience-near referents for the more abstract "balance" and "imbalance." Like the abstractions, they can refer to cosmos as well as to person and social relations, in accordance with the merging of macrocosm and microcosm which is a tenet of Balinese philosophy and feeling-thought. Thus a "calm" feeling in oneself indicates a world—one's world—in balance. Other tangible evidence—say, rain showers on a clear, sunny day during the dry season when one is staging a major celebration—indicates imbalance.

It was such a day in May 1986, and I was standing in the graveyard with the man in charge of his family's cremation: a splendid ritual of exhuming and etherealizing after thirty years of burial. We had reached the climax: after twenty days of preparatory rites and celebrations the cremation towers and caskets were now to be set ablaze. At that very moment, the sky opened up in torrential rains. The man looked at me and said: "I don't know what *you* think, but I . . . !"

A world—his world, in imbalance indeed! Except this would not be "the way we think." Rather, the salient concepts would be those of anger, envy, and jealousy: unresolved social relations/conflicts motivating sorcery and spitefulness.

The anthropologist's way out, to take care of both "expert" and "ordinary" forms of representations, is suggested by Quinn and Holland (1987). Realizing that researchers have tended to privilege "experts" above the "folk," it is suggested that "folk" and "expert" models be redefined as "cultural models," equally pertinent and valid. This is a major step forward, yet it raises problems. In my view such models *are* not equal, and framing the issue thus sidesteps the problem of how to identify valid knowledge, relevant knowledge from different existential viewpoints. Nor does a view of cultural knowledge as distributive and situated resolve what is at stake—for it is a question not of fitting pieces into a jigsaw puzzle but of grasping *lived-in worlds of compelling significance.*

That "balance" is a key cosmic principle may be good to ponder for some, but singularly inept to live by, and thus rather irrelevant compared to models that "work" (Obeyesekere 1985), that guide and compel experience and have, as D'Andrade puts it, "directing force" (1984). In Bali what works with directing force are models anchored in bodily experience, and this, as we have seen, has implications for attitudes to expert knowledge.

Thus "balance"—like *atma* (soul) and to some extent even *karma pala* are intellectually powerful glosses *on* the world, yet experientially rather bland and remote. Take the example of a man at war with his community over the issue of what restrictions apply on Balinese New Year—*Nyepi*—"silent day." By tradition no light may be lit. But he defines his tourist hostel as beyond bounds and runs the electricity. The community is enraged and interprets his bad action as the result of his *karma pala*. His father had been a spy for the Dutch. But what good does it do to know (or attribute) a cause ex post facto? The man should listen to his heart and come to his senses, and also propitiate the gods to still their anger—that is the essence.

On the remoteness of "balance," take a girl dissolved in tears at her own wedding because "her husband is so old and short," and so they are not suitable (*cocok*): "Whenever they go out together, she will feel not so good, for they look odd together." Imbalance (*tidak seimbang*) indeed—but what can she do? Manage her heart, of course! And the women of the family can take note of the imbalance to recognize her father's ulterior motives and to safeguard another daughter's interests by helping her stage an elopement. Human motivations and will, i.e., feeling-thoughts, are the salient and explanatory variables. "Imbalance" is a means to reflect on it in general, an index for the result, and a contingent one at that.

Is there not "imbalance" when a man marries two wives? I asked Suriati. She answered, "It depends if he is rich or poor. If he is wealthy, perhaps there will not be imbalance . . ." [1] Far from modeling the world for forethought, action, and repair, "balance" comes in *after* the experience/event and does not determine it. The driving forces in a Balinese universe are feeling-thoughts; so "balance," "soul," and the whole panoply of similar concepts are indubitably right and true, yet relatively secondary and remote compared to embodied concepts such as vitality, energy, calm, confusion, happiness, or sadness.

It was such a challenge my friend Nyoman Artje posed to me when he questioned my preoccupation with "balance." It concerned the ontological status of experience versus interpretation and the production of knowledge: How do we come to know what we think we know? What is to count as truth, and for what purpose?

It was a challenge that was to be brought home to me time and again in fieldwork, for instance when after a year an expert told me that knowledge I had gained that Balinese lose their vital life force when they are frightened or suddenly surprised was a misconception. Whoever loses it will be actually dead! Yet here were all those Balinese I knew who had lost their *bayu* and were most undeniably alive. Where then was truth? What was I to believe?

I carried my confusion to a friend and shared with her my sense of problem. She thought for a moment, also perplexed, then she shrugged her shoulders and said, "Well, I suppose it's right what the balian *usada* says, but it is not the way we feel!" And she went on to expound so graphically the sensations of emptiness, trembling, confusion, and fear that ensue when one loses one's *bayu* that anyone who thought otherwise was made to seem slightly—bewildered.

I don't suppose my friend thought any more about this. It was I as the anthropologist who was left with the problem of how to reconcile these different views, or even account for the fact that people could be so naive. Next, what troubled me was the realization that *I* could be so gullible. Clearly I had not done my homework, read the literature well, or I would not have been misled in the first place into thinking that people lost their "souls"!

In the end what came to trouble me more was the insight which might have been lost had I *not* been so naive! Had I gone to the experts first, or been more familiar with philosophical doctrine, would I have been able to take in earnest the notion that people lose their *bayu?* Instead of accepting the relevance of their claims and letting it resonate with myself, would I not have shrugged it off as a "misconception," less than true?

To revert to the scene where my friend alerted me to "how we think": In throwing differences between the two models of balance and of feeling-thought into such stark relief, he might seem to be adopting a contrary, though politely formulated, epistemology from that of the balian who enunciated the stark differences between world religions only to conclude triumphantly with a declaration of their sameness. But that would be just going by his words, and not beyond. Also he conveys trenchant testimony to "sameness" in the sense that the world has different facets and thus presents many truths—but with one being primary in the sense of being experienced, sensed, and acted on. What is his measure? The game of life in which relevance is of the essence, and so, needless to say, there *are* winners and losers.

His warning, as I saw it, was that I should get my priorities clear, or I would be bound to lose by messing up truths of different orders and relevance. I must focus where I needed to focus for the task at hand. "Balance" was relevant, but not for me, not now, in that it did not compel experience.

Do not think these insights came to me there and then. It has taken me much and laborious hindsight to distill and put into words what at the time was vague and diffuse. His basic message I got—"it is not the way we think"—for it seemed embedded in his words; I did not need to go beyond. When I began to understand that I had misconstrued even this—that he had never in fact said what I had made him out to say— then I truly lost my footing and, staggering to gain firmer ground, embarked at last on the trail that eventually leads here.

What did he say? He used the word *mekeneh*—"feel," "think," "feel-think," or "think-feel." These are different, not the same, for people like myself who have been reared to think of "think" and "feel" as opposites. For Balinese it might make little difference how one glossed *mekeneh,* for they are trained to distill sameness from such labels—depending on context, of course. But for me, out to bridge worlds and compel resonance among peoples it makes a world of difference—as Nyoman Artje warned me—that I get my priorities right.

What is the relevant translation of *mekeneh* given that I want to create resonance?

When I finally realized the insidious distortion of which I had been guilty by rendering *mekeneh* into English as either "think" or "feel" (depending on how I felt!), it came to me as part of an existential insight: in going for the easier solution, I had been dissecting a process of knowing, splitting it off from its ontological base—as if lived experience could be reduced to a way of thinking, or even as if the latter reigned supreme.

And I had impeded resonance. However awkward "feel-think" might sound in English, a strange concept may yet compel understanding by slowly becoming familiar, losing its strangeness, appearing at last "natural." *Then* we may, if we wish, revert to "think" and "feel," for they will never again be what they once were but will be realigned as one *and* the other. We will have gone beyond the words.

The point is important, for Balinese insist that knowledge must be felt-thought or else one will be bereft of moral guidance and unable to think rationally. Balinese have a proverb which says, "If you have a short string, you should not try to reach for the sky." They use it to refer to precisely the sort of people who split feeling off from thought, letting the latter be their driving ambition when to climb high in any venture, including the pursuit of knowledge, one has to exercise feeling-thought.

I was in Bali constantly made aware that my string was too short and that there was no way of extending it by going by the power of thought. A radical re-feel-thinking would be necessary that would entail diminished striving, increased alertness, more of what Maslow has called "keep[ing one's] brain out of the way . . . [in order] to be . . . receptive, passive, patient and waiting, rather than eager, quick and impatient" (1966, 10–11).

Let me contrast a prevalent Western epistemology with a Balinese approach by drawing on Lakoff and Kövecses (1987). After uncovering a series of notions that seem embedded in the way American English talks about anger, the authors proceed in a perceptive concluding section to pose a number of important questions: How much of the model they have uncovered do people actually use in comprehending anger?

Do they base their actions on this model? Do they have awareness of it? How much of it do they consciously believe? And finally and "most intriguingly: does the model have any effect on what people *feel?*" (1987, 220–21, italics in original).

The Balinese vision of knowledge I espouse here would render superfluous such questions, for it is experientially anchored. What in the one vision may appear as crucial afterthoughts, reflections on one's own beginnings, in the other would *be* true beginnings, framing the process of research. A cognitive model would be flawed in its very conception for segregating one part of a more encompassing process which can be split and then reaggregated only at the price of misconception. This process shapes all experience. It should also shape models of experience, i.e., research designs and methodology. Crucial is the power of resonance which is required for knowledge as for life.

Balinese models of anger derive from a pool of felt-thought experience—different *and* the same for people differently positioned. So do their models of black magic, social inequality, or the jurisdiction of the gods. Indeed, my friend who brushed aside my use of "balance" as misapplied, if right and true, proceeded to set out precisely those "basic level concepts" (Lakoff and Kövecses 1987, 218) that were sensible/relevant because felt-thought. They were used, they were conscious, they were believed—and they were *embodied.*

Much anthropological writing on cultural knowledge assumes the models by which people act on and interpret their world to be largely outside awareness, tacit, and unexamined (e.g., Quinn and Holland 1987). Among Balinese the opposite has struck me. While undoubtedly also here "culture" may be said to be "what one sees *with,* but rarely what one *sees*" (to borrow an incisive expression from Quinn and Holland 1987, 14, italics in original), in Bali I am impressed with how explicit, how aware, how able people are to ponder even such models as "grant a seeming necessity to how they live their lives" (11).

Perhaps if feeling-thinking is *the* crucial process of gaining knowledge about oneself and the world, then awareness is increased because embodied? Perhaps it is our Western thought-splitting tendency to shut feeling off as all too irrational, no partner for thought, that accounts, in part, for the degree to which we lead shallow lives, unaware of basic presuppositions?

Balinese contest that knowledge can be out-of-awareness. And they do not contest it cooly, unperturbed. They laugh heartily at such an absurd notion. "Unconscious? Absolutely not! Impossible!" Consciousness (*kesadaran*) is the essence of the soul (*atma*) from which derive all powers of comprehension. The person is in essence conscious (*sadar*) and aware, if not steered by other powers.

Awareness is also enhanced by the palpable bodily repercussions of so much feeling-thought. As I have argued before, Balinese seem to rely on their bodies for clues to what they feel-think, or indeed, to "what is" and "what it means." The body is emphasized as a medium of the most relevant insight regarding true facts of the world. So also experts, when disagreeing, will point to embodied evidence to back up their claims. On one occasion I heard a group of men, several of whom are learned in holy texts, argue over what happens to a person's soul—the *atma*—when she or he is victimized by black magic. Does it exit from the body or stay vanquished within? They reasoned completely within a frame of bodily experience, not adducing any evidence from texts to support their contesting claims. Reflected are shared attitudes about what constitutes prime evidence, based in a common epistemological frame: there is no point in arguing by mere thought. "Can anyone think but with their heart?" ask Balinese.

They know some people can, in a self-inflicted action that severs their powers of comprehension and ability to live ethically. What the "think" in the above statement is meant to convey is proper, sound, indeed rational thinking: "Thinking is like strategy, tactic; the heart cannot lie." In the Balinese vision of things "feeling" is not antithetical to rationality, but *insufficient* feeling is. It marks the selfish, the greedy, and those who have lacked proper guidance. It may therefore also be inflicted as a punishment from the gods. The man who is at war with his community over the issue of what restrictions apply on Balinese New Year is said to be so truly bad (*manusia jahat*) because he does not listen to his heart. It is his *karma pala*—punishment for sins of his father. But that does not exonerate the son, who should make every effort to temper thought with feeling.

Just how essential feeling is for life and learning becomes clear once we consider the requirements of attaining the highest degree of knowledge, that compiled in the holy texts. The apprentice must still his thoughts completely. Now resonance requires nothing less.

It is a puzzle to Balinese that Western epistemology should be premised on a self-defeating base: that the sky can be reached with an amputated string. One man, himself an expert, phrased it thus to me: "Westerners do not understand about the basics of gaining knowledge because they do not have the concept of the soul—*atma*—and so they don't understand about their own feelings. They mistake their feelings for thoughts. The result is that they create disturbance, for when they think without their feelings, they will misapprehend and also cause offense." Ethics, experience, and knowledge are interwoven in this view of science. Validity and relevance are also of the essence.

Let not the word "soul" in the above distract attention from basics. That would be like letting oneself be diverted by words to think how "different they are"! And so the man's message would be lost. On the injunction of resonance, go beyond—in the manner of the Muslim woman who could overcome the potential barrier of an infidel, Hindu gloss to get at the balian's real message to herself. This is the meaning of resonance: to deexoticize and strip away the layers of exotica which impede understanding; to make familiar, to acknowledge our common humanity.

"Take Muslims in Bali who have no concept of *karma pala,* and yet they understand," said the Hindu. "They say *karma pala,* we say *taqdir,* it's all the same," said the Muslim. And the anthropologist jumps at such seemingly absurd statements, until she sees the relevance of going beyond words to the core of the meaning of things, shared human experience.

Balinese regard that Westerners may be inept at such resonance because we "mistake [our] feelings for thoughts [and so] . . . [we] create disturbance . . ."

What was the experiential evidence of the man who spoke? Tourists who throng into religious ceremonies such as cremation (*ngaben*) dressed as if they were on the beach? Or who mistake a beach for a beach when it has in fact been transformed into a place of homage for the gods—as on Balinese *melasti*—as is plain for all (who think with their hearts) to see? Or did he have in mind persons like myself who are out to understand Bali and get entangled in illusions because we, like the tourists, get stuck on the thought level?

I do not know, but his words bespoke benign advice from a sage in his community of Balinese, questioning both our moral practice and our epistemological stance. A humanistic science must be built on a foundation of cross-culturally valid insight, and so I suggest that the prevalent Western epistemology is fundamentally culture-bound. It may need re-feel-thinking to allow for different constructions of reality and with them greater awareness among people of insight relevant to their lives than we concede, or even are capable of, who seem committed to what Balinese might term an "art of the absurd": to think but with our thoughts.

Such a re-feel-thinking, by its very nature, cannot be limited to a purely intellectual enlightenment and an act of will. It must be reflected in the concepts we privilege—and embodied in our method and our praxis. What brought me to this realization was obviously within the paradigm of anthropology's shared emphasis on participant observation, reflexivity, and "letting their voice be heard"; but it goes somewhat further in specifying a way of being and a praxis and in favoring ways of conceptualizing which are in harmony with this praxis.

First, let it be reflected in our basic orientation to the unknown which we wish to explore and know: we should try to approach it without fears of its complexity. In this, I have benefited from a certain delight with the breakdown of logical neatness and order and the victory of "non-order," rather than disorder (R. Rosaldo 1989), over schemata. This also makes it attractive to celebrate the particular, seeking to know it not by assigning it to categories but by embedding it in meaningful contexts—thereby only enriching its particularity.

I opened this chapter with a call to ground ourselves, heart and mind, in relationships to people we wish to understand. This proved a felicitous starting point among people who emphasize feeling-thought, for it is in our cultivation of close human relationships that we in the West come closest to observing and integrating the cross-connections between what we usually try to differentiate and assign to "thinking" and "feeling." In building up a context to understand the particular persons I encountered, I spent much effort in simply attending to them and listening to them. Context, then, did not entail a systematics (in which case it would necessarily have been *my* systematics) of observation, but an immersion in the relationship through participation in those parts of the flow of their lives into which they were willing to incorporate me. Such participation certainly does not preclude questioning and struggling to understand, as I did with Suriati, Kede Mireh, Jero Mangku, and many others, but it does entail casting this struggle in concepts that prepartition and prejudge reality minimally and encourage openness, alertness, and—as the concept slowly emerged for me—resonance.

Note the concepts on which most of my analysis has been built. Starting by trying to orient myself by learning *what was at stake* for particular persons in particular situations, I was led to acknowledge and attend to their *multiple, simultaneous concerns* that they carry with them *as they move, bridging* scenes and encounters if we are to grasp these concerns, and how they, people in various positions, *feel-think* and act. I have stressed the need for a discovery procedure that seeks out knowledge *they deem relevant* to their lived experience as the basis on which to build understandings.

From a concern that an anthropology of experience requires a revitalization and redesign of our conventional concepts (cf. p. 59). I have further sought to elevate some key experiential concepts among Balinese to key *analytical status*. That is, I have taken some notions which they use continuously and which strike me as having potential general relevance and applied them technically, not metaphorically: "multiple, simultaneous concerns," "cares which cannot be shed," "effort," "what it takes," "bridging," "movement in social space," "connecting links," "hearts which carry across," and "what is at stake"—these all derive from an experienced, oft-evoked realization among Balinese that there is "so much to care about" in life and that bright faces shield all manners of hearts which should be "managed"—but never can be shed—indeed, *must* not be shed, or one would be left with "only thoughts."

Furthermore, I have chosen *not* to break in—where I was aware of it and thus could avoid it—and order this multiplicity of concerns with categories of my own: classifying and grouping them, "operationalizing" my interest in Balinese priorities by asking people to rank order them, etc. Instead, I followed them *as* they moved. Again, this meant recognizing a separability, and a degree of distinctness, between scenes and encounters—a plausible sociological perspective. But my next step was not to group such scenes and encounters in classes—such as public and private—so as to impose (my) order on them: they were separated so as to observe the bridging, to discover what was at stake, to uncover the connecting links and the symbolic thresholds people construct. It is in this sense that I have used them analytically and technically, not just evocatively.

Because Balinese stress the continuing links in people's lives, I have also been at pains to try to capture the webs they forge in their lives which go to make, as Kleinman says, "of each life a seamless whole" (1988b, 39), but without assuming deep, embracing coherence in this whole. It was their steadily expressed emphasis on bridging aspects and "so many cares" which also compelled me to try to connect—as I hope I have—and it was their stress on resonance which stirred me to try to find evocative words which would also be analytically compelling.

I read this plea for resonance as basically in tune with a growing call in anthropology for deexotization (e.g., Appadurai 1986a, Keesing 1987a, Clifford 1988, McHugh 1989). "Resonance" evokes shared human experience, what people across "cultures" and through time have in common. Unlike the concept of "culture," which tends to underscore differentness and extol the exotic, "resonance" bridges—from a lived realization that this is the only practicable way. It does not deny difference (Hinduism, Buddhism, and Islam *are,* as the balian said, completely different) but renders difference relatively insignificant in the face of that which counts more: shared human experience.

I read the plea for resonance as a plea that we *reempower thought,* better to understand and better to live. And then the day may come when people like Made Bidja will say, "Tourists have no concept of *melasti* [ceremony on the beach], and yet they understand its basic idea as homage to the gods . . ."

The essence of my methodology is thus centered on the existential concerns of particular Balinese, the core choices in life which cannot be escaped. I argue that we need to try to grasp those connecting links which they forge in their lives and to attend closely to the analytical concepts which *they* use to shape their action on the world and their moral sensibilities in it.

Crucial among them is their conception of feeling-thinking. Putting it to use I have sought to articulate what their acts and concerns evoked in *my* feeling-mind and to escape the traps of illusion in which Balinese warn one will be captured if one uses only thought. I have tried to respect and to apply their notion that feeling is the more essential for comprehension in that it spawns intuition, evaluation, and moral judgment. From a Balinese perspective a Western epistemology based on intellectual reasoning and objective thought appears an act of hubris. It cannot prove adequate, I agree, to an anthropology that aspires to know the women and the men of this world.

This may have been the insight A. L. Kroeber was groping toward when as early as 1949 he made his unheeded plea for a unified conception of affect-idea system (Kroeber 1949, 1369). But we should not need to appeal to an anthropological authority to legitimate the concept. Let us show enough humility toward other traditions of knowledge that we are open to the insights they teach.

There has been much emphasis lately on "letting their voice be heard" in our writings—but in a patronizing way this has almost always been limited to their accounts of *themselves* and their particular worlds. I submit that we should also be willing to learn *general* lessons from their insights and analyses of the human condition. It is in this spirit that I propose to employ a Bali-inspired model of "feeling-thinking" or "thinking-feeling"—written with a dash and not a slash—to replace the previously so successful, but Western culture-bound, notion of "emotion."

In Bali in March 1989 I sat with a group of men discussing a paper I was to give at a conference in the United States and testing my exposition on them. They listened intently and laughed heartily when I explained that "emotion" had gained acceptance in anthropology recently after years of neglect during which it was deemed irrational and subjective. "Do Westerners also regard thinking as irrational?!"

Made Bidja then spoke: "Westerners do not understand about feeling . . . and so they think that they think with their thoughts when actually they use their feelings . . . If we do not use our feelings, there will be no resonance with life . . ." He paused for a moment, then went on: "I have one piece of advice for you. When you go to Washington, tell Suriati's story, and then when you finish, ask the audience, 'What did you think when you heard this?'" Made's face brightened into a wide smile. "Then tell them, 'That which you thought, it was not your thinking, it was your feeling.' They will understand."

NOTES

Chapter One

1. That she had not done so before was probably due to consideration for us as well as concern for her own best interests. The Balinese consider it selfish to approach people outside the close family with concerns of one's own, the more so when the other is in a state of worry. She might also have counted on me to be more receptive to her when I was happy again because my son was well.

2. Her dead friend was a Muslim: my inference about what the ritual might mean was based on fifteen years of familiarity with Muslims, including having lived and worked for five years in the Middle East.

3. She had originally told me she would travel by bus and boat and would bring her brother along (as it would be inappropriate for a young woman like her to travel overland alone by bus). What accounted for her change of plans I cannot say. It may have been her delayed departure due to her parents' initial refusal to let her go; or it may have been her brother's and her parents' fear of black magic which entailed that her brother would not accompany her.

4. The *kelor* leaf is about the size of a little fingernail.

5. "Brother" is the common metonym for a lover or boyfriend.

6. Balinese do consider that people occasionally resort to such devices to harm others: they may intentionally startle or frighten others to cause illness from fright or soulloss (cf. Wikan 1989a).

7. Then her face would become "flat" and expressionless/immobile: her jaw was stiff; her mouth pulled lengthwise; when she spoke, her lips moved hardly at all and her voice was barely audible. Such extreme expression of respect/fear alternated with excessive smiling and laughing in a mode of feminine grace and friendliness.

8. To work black magic it is a distinct asset to have knowledge of the person's real name. North Balinese generally have nicknames and keep their real names a secret to strangers and people whom they fear.

Chapter Two

1. A compelling analysis alerting us to the pitfalls of reducing people to products of "their culture" is Edward Said's *Covering Islam* (1981). He shows how assigning people to the category "Islam" or "Muslim," and then explain-

ing their actions with reference to those, is a way of denigrating and making less-than-human persons who can be counted on to act on the basis of motives just as complex as our own. That "they" may invoke the category "Islam" to explain their own actions is to be seen as a strategic maneuver and does not change this fact.

2. I recognize the multivalence of the word "meaning," which seems to mean just about all and everything. Mark Hobart characterizes it as "a weak notion" (1985b, 40), "a very Casanova . . . in its appetite for association" (Black 1968, 163, quoted in Hobart 1985b, 41). He criticizes Geertz's use of both it and of "symbol": A symbol, according to Geertz, is "anything that denotes, describes, represents, exemplifies, labels, indicates, evokes, depicts, expresses—anything that somehow signifies" (1980, 135). Hobart concludes: "It is hard to see how almost anything does not, on some reading, fulfill at least one of Geertz's verbs. . . . This rather deprives meaning of any meaning" (1985b, 40).

I do not regard, however, that it is necessary for my analysis here that I enter into a discussion of the meaning of "meaning." I refer the interested reader to Mark Hobart 1985b and 1986a. To me, as to Robert Paul, "the heart of the issue" is that "meaning is something which can only be fully grasped in terms of the purposes, intentions, desires, and fears that are put into play in sociocultural action—in short, by the examination of the question 'what do people want?'" (1989, 3–4).

3. "Context" is a concept as problematic as "meaning." Again, it is worth quoting Mark Hobart: "Appeal to context involves a kind of confidence trick—for everyone invokes it, but no one knows quite what it is." Etymologically, the word refers to "connexion, order, construction, something woven together . . . [but] incomplete and hinting at something else as its locus: activities, ideas, speech, texts, or whatever. In some sense almost anything can serve as a context for something else. . . . For context is just an analytical convenience, designed for a particular purpose . . . but there is a danger of it being seen as somehow substantive" (1985b, 34).

Context, then, is negotiable: "Differences in roles, interests, power and perspective make the potential context different for those involved. . . . Stressing 'context,' rather than 'text,' is a way to emphasize a plurality of perspectives" (1985b, 44–49).

However, "contextualizing also raises the delicate issue of whose formulation of relation and whose criteria of relevance are at stake? . . . The ability to assert and have one's assertions accepted as legitimate knowledge, are important aspects of power" (M. Hobart, 1986a, 8).

4. I am indebted to Vincent Crapanzano (personal communication) for alerting me to this and for having urged me to rethink my use of the concept "culture" as applied in previous drafts. In response to that I fully rewrote the introductory part of this chapter. Any faults remain, of course, my own.

5. On essentializing, see also Appadurai 1986a, 1988; M. Hobart 1985b, 1986b; and Keesing 1989a, 1989b. Keesing notes "the crowning irony that our

own conceptual diseases should [now] be deployed against us," namely by the essentialist concept with its exclusivist focus having entered common parlance, political rhetoric, and power games (1989b, 5–8).

6. I am thinking in particular of Clifford Geertz's works, [1966] 1973a, 1973c, and [1974] 1984.

7. For a critique of the text metaphor, see Keesing 1987a and M. Hobart 1985b. "Culture is not a text, nor a set of rules, nor even a discourse. Culture is complex and cannot be captured in any single metaphor. But because it is easier to handle there is a widespread tendency to focus upon text and its sense rather than the range of social contexts in which text is used. . . . The focus on text tends to de-centre context, and encourage the search for something essential rather than a plurality of perspectives" (M. Hobart, 1985b, 44).

8. For trenchant critiques of C. Geertz's interpretive program as shown in practice, see Austin 1979, Shankman 1984, Keesing 1987a, and Nader 1988. Crapanzano (1986) provides a lucid analysis of the literary techniques used to convey an impression of the ethnographer's presence while decontextualizing ethnographic data. Roseberry (1982) likewise critiques the Balinese cockfight as a text which is separated from its social context, to make unclear who is speaking to whom about what. Connor expresses concern about "the ethnographic standards such a subjectivist approach fosters. Geertz sometimes ignores basic (and admittedly rather prosaic) rules for the presentation of ethnographic evidence. . . . To those of us with a more pedestrian concern with such issues, thick description sometimes appears to come out of thin air" (1984, 271). For a critique of Geertz's "Person, Time, and Conduct in Bali" and a forceful exposition of the need to attend to context and actors' diversely positioned interests if we are to ferret out the meaning of words, rules, and things, see Mark Hobart 1986b. Hobart (1986d, 15) notes, in respect of Geertz's study *Negara: The Theater State in Nineteenth-Century Bali* (1980), that it "blissfully ignored the categories Balinese actually use [see C. Geertz 1980, 135], or even the possibility that they might not conform to his!"

9. A fine example of such contextualized interpretation is Newman (1988), methodologically specially useful because we have some of the participants' sense to judge and critique the ethnography her analysis produces.

10. Names are believed to shape character and are often carefully chosen to that end.

11. See also Bruner and Plattner 1984 and Hallowell 1955.

12. For a cogent exposition of life story narrative, see Peacock 1984: "The narration is, after all, what the native places before us; he himself organizes his experience into a form with its own integrity and force. Unforgivable is a psychological, sociological, or any other kind of reductionism that ignores this form to go straight for some allegedly deeper structure, which of course also reflects the abstracted categories of that frame of reference selected for emphasis. This is not to say one should end with the narrative form, but one should start with it" (97).

While not using a life story method here, in the sense that I ever sat down with people and tried to elicit their biographies, yet I sought to handle such materials as I obtained with the humility and caution Peacock impresses upon us.

13. I am indebted to Arthur Kleinman for this formulation.

14. See R. Rosaldo 1989 for a critique of the classicist notion of culture with its built-in assumption of hegemonic order, coherence, and homogeneity. His book was not yet in print when my manuscript was completed. See also Appadurai 1986b and Keesing 1987a, 1989b.

15. But such intense emotional aspects of persons are also publicly vividly represented in theater and performance, e.g., in the *wayang* (see A. Hobart 1987 and Zurbuchen 1987). They are moreover displayed in trance.

16. In one case I am thinking of, a man's elder brother (who had children of his own) took by force his brother's three-year-old daughter on the pretext that she was a reincarnation of their grandfather; moreover, because he was wealthy and the father poor, the girl would be better off with him. The parents were heartbroken and tried repeatedly to get their daughter back. But when the elder brother added as the ultimate threat that if they took her, the two "would not be brothers any more," the case was settled. The parents acquiesced though they continued for years to mourn the loss of their daughter.

17. James Peacock (personal communication) reports having a tape of a Malay in a mental hospital in Surabaya "who actually does see 'culture' as representing 'them.'"

Note also M. Hobart again (1985c, 11): "The famed poise of the Balinese is as much a response to surveillance as it is any 'natural' grace (at night it becomes another story, which is when most theft, violence, arson and philandering goes on)."

18. Arlie Hochschild interestingly notes that a similar strategy is practiced by air hostesses to contain their anger vis-à-vis obnoxious passengers: they deliberately think of them as "children" (1983, 8).

19. Fundamentally, Goodman's dictum applies: "Coherence is a characteristic of description, not of the world. . . . What we must face is the fact that even the truest description comes nowhere near faithfully reproducing the way the world is. . . . [No true description] tells us *the* way the world is, but each of them tells us *a* way the world is" (1972, 29, 31, quoted in M. Hobart 1986d, 10).

20. Compare Colson (1974, 37): "It should . . . be no surprise to us if some people live in what appears to be a Rousseauian paradise because they take a Hobbesian view of their situation: they walk softly because they believe it necessary not to offend others whom they regard as dangerous."

21. Cf. Abu-Lughod 1986; Lutz 1988; Lutz and White 1986; Myers 1986; M. Rosaldo 1983, 1984; R. Rosaldo 1984; Schieffelin 1976, 1985; Solomon 1978, 1980, 1983, 1984; Shweder 1985.

22. Shweder details six different questions that must be addressed in asking whether people are alike or different in their emotional functioning, and then concludes: "Undoubtedly, there are universals and cultural specifics with regard to each of these aspects of emotional functioning. It is ludicrous to imagine that

the emotional functioning of people in different cultures is basically the same. It is just as ludicrous to imagine that each culture's emotional life is entirely unique" (1985, 193).

23. Crapanzano, in an important article (1989), urges that the *glossing* of emotion be considered independently of either emotional *expression* or emotional *experience*. The glossing of emotion can have a pragmatic function—to "call the context"—but this is often masked by Western notions of the self and our psychology of emotion. Studies of emotion that conflate its expression and its gloss entail giving dominance to verbal expressions over other modes of expression, thus overlooking the possibility of disjunction between the different registers in which emotions are expressed. More important, taking people's "words for" emotion as a method to lay out their "psychology" of emotion is to confound the pragmatic features of an utterance with context-independent aspects, and thereby to reinforce a particular Western philosophy of the locus of emotion as in some way being *in* the individual (1989, 79–82).

Crapanzano's perspective links up with the theory of language and expression formulated by Donald Davidson and elaborated by Richard Rorty in his latest book (1989); this underscores the need to look at language and locution in all their forms as ways *to act upon the world* rather than as media of representation and expression. The anthropological study of "emotion," I am convinced, has suffered gravely from its disregard for the pragmatic functions or purposes of emotion and its overemphasis on meaning or interpretation. See also chap. 7.

Chapter Three

1. Elizabeth Colson makes a strikingly similar observation in her complex and sensitive discussion of the balancing of fear with grace among Tonga. She observed a woman who filled a visitor's basket to overflowing with grain, "in the best tradition of Tonga hospitality and . . . with every indication of gracious generosity." Colson at the time took it to be an expression of kinship obligations within a system of generalized reciprocal exchange. Later she heard the woman warn a man who suspected sorcery in his granary how he might have caused envy or offense: "You saw me give grain to that woman who came the other day. How could I refuse when she asked me for grain? Perhaps she would do nothing, but I could not tell. The only thing to do is give" (1974, 47–49).

Colson observes: "I once took for granted the surface amiability of present Tonga community life but seventeen years of following the members of certain Gwembe Tonga villages have given me a better grasp of their involvement with each other. I now look around a neighborhood gathering and wonder at the tough-minded determination that keeps hostilities from surfacing and disturbing the business of living" (1974, 48).

2. Muslims also, while they do not (read: should not) believe that one can obtain contact with the souls of the dead, nor that death could be "caused" by anyone but God (the time of one's death is written at birth), still subscribe to a

view of "bad deaths" caused by black magic, poisoning, or witchcraft. The evidence to them is sudden unexpected death, "strange" symptoms, or the testimony of a balian (healer cum magician) whom they consult.

3. Covarrubias ([1931] 1973, 351) notes the use of "clothes, locks of hair, nail-cuttings, saliva, and even the soil taken from a footprint . . . to gain control of the physical and mental condition of the person."

4. Mark Hobart translates *krama* as "progress, succession and manner" as well as "customary behaviour, conduct, order, the rules according to which something happens" (1986c, 10).

5. I use generally the adjectival or adverbial form of norms applying to people or conduct, even when in English the sentence may call for the noun. This is because the adjectival/adverbial form is generally used among the Balinese.

6. Duff-Cooper (1984), after Wojowasito and Wasito W. (1980), translates this also as "impolite and rude."

7. Balinese are emphatic that unexpressed anger—*benci*—is far more dangerous than anger expressed—*marah* or *gedeg*. The latter is of short duration, *benci* remains. *Benci* is akin to envious (*iri*), jealous (*cemburu*), hateful (*dengki*), and *dendam* (bearing a grudge). See also note 12 to chap. 6.

8. Children below the age of seven are regarded as lacking the power of reasoning. From age fifteen they are regarded as adults (*beligh*). Cf. M. Hobart: "Children are excused breaches on the grounds that they do not understand and cannot be responsible for their intentions—the same holds of idiots and Europeans" (1983, 13).

9. Hildred Geertz, on the basis of her study of Balinese drawings collected by Bateson and Mead in the 1930s, observes: "The collection as a whole reveals that a concern with . . . sorcery was pervasive and intense, an important source for graphic images for the young painters" (1989, 46).

10. To give an example of how strictly these norms apply, and, I believe, particularly among men: One man found his friend with a less than "clear, bright face" when he came to visit him one morning. Not a word was spoken to indicate that anything was wrong. But afterwards the visitor went to a relative of the host to inquire. It turned out that thieves had broken into his friend's photocopying shop the night before and had stolen expensive (uninsured) equipment! As good friends as they were, yet the host kept the secret so as not to appear selfish and impolite, as he himself explained to me when I later asked him about his motives.

11. Such people are called "thick-faced" (*mue tebal* or *tebal muka*).

12. It is advised that one look into the cup as into a mirror. If one can see one's own reflection, then the drink is safe.

13. I am struck that Balinese are extremely sensitive to, and attribute major importance to, changes of skin color and texture, the size and shape of the pupil, and the speed and tone of a voice which I could hardly perceive. The dreaded hidden anger (*benci*), for instance, is said to reveal itself in a heightened, slightly reddish skin color and in faster-paced speaking with a slightly

louder voice. When cases were pointed out to me that involved people I myself had seen, I often had to admit that I had not noticed such signs.

Given that recent research in the field of nonverbal communication has shown that only 10 percent of human communication is comprised by words, while nonverbal behavior makes up all the rest (Moore and Yamamoto 1988, 1), it is also likely that I missed innummerable other clues. On the power of the eye and the pupil to convey emotion, see Napier 1986, 280.

14. Cf. Bateson: "For the attainment of grace, the reasons of the heart must be integrated with the reasons of reason" ([1967] 1972b, 129). Balinese may advise one another, "Don't make your heart/will/spirit too large (*de gedenang keneh* or *tidak besarkan jiwa*)"; that is, don't unbalance emotion and reason, or don't will more than your capability allows.

15. *Tombal* may be in the form of a magical substance the inhabitants of a place have obtained from a magician and placed in their house or buried in the ground (e.g., in the houseyard, rice field, orchard, shop, etc.). It may also be an actual (super)natural spirit who belongs to the place or has been invoked to protect the people and their belongings. Such a house protector is called *penungang karang*. The problem with an actual spirit is that once it is there, it may not be willing to move, which may create a problem when the *tombal* has developed a special liking for food which the present occupants do not know. In such a case the *tombal* easily gets angry and harms the family.

Demonic figures—*aling-aling*—which frighten intruders also line the courtyards of Hindu houses. Muslims place pieces of paper with Koranic script above all entrances to the house, every door and window. Finally, all place red onions (*bawang*) and chilis around the house—in the courtyard, under the pillow, etc.—for protection.

16. A man explained to me that it is actually the soul (*atma* or *roh*)—the source of thinking and concentration—which fights, and not the spirit or life force (*bayu*), for the life force cannot think. When the life force is yet perceived to be of such crucial importance, it is because it empowers and energizes the force of the mental resistance.

17. Red is the color of challenge, arrogance, bravery, and danger. Balinese may be upset if they receive a note or postcard written in red ink from unsuspecting tourists. It carries the connotation that the sender might be angry.

18. Balinese sorcerers and witches are rarely openly accused. The confrontations take place on a mystical level, or justice is left up to the gods to apply. Stories sometimes circulate in the North of sorcerers in the South—particularly in Gianyar—who have been openly challenged and punished. I never heard of a case from the North, despite consensual reports of the most atrocious deeds being practiced by particular balians. For instance, there was much concern at a time in 1986 about a particular balian who was said to create havoc with marriages. He would get into the bed between husband and wife and seduce the wife. She in turn would be so pleased that she turned against her own husband. But no one would dare to challenge the balian.

19. Zurbuchen notes: "At the very least, perpetual feuding and estrange-

ment . . . are an uneasy counterpart to the cooperation and mutual dependency of the family, *banjar*, temple congregation and village group" (1989, 264).

20. Balinese prefix names with labels connoting "the first" (*Putu* or *Loh* [fem.]/*Wayang* or *Gede* [masc.]), "the second" (*Made* or *Kede* [fem. and masc.]), "the third" (*Komang* [fem.]/*Nyoman* [masc.]), and "the fourth" (*Ketut* or *Chatut* [fem. and masc.]). The fifth child is referred to as the first again, and the formula repeats itself. To "erase" the twins, who had been born as numbers three and four, the father called the nextborn "the third" (*Komang*) instead of "the first" (*Putu*).

Changing name order may also be done to cheat or confuse evil spirits out to kill children. For example, the grandparents of the man above lost three children in succession. To protect the nextborn as well as the remaining children they changed their birth order names so they became the fourth, third, second, first, second, third, first, third.

21. This was a child who insisted on being reborn; that is, the soul of the ancestor to be reincarnated in her did. Signs of pregnancy in the mother, who was using reliable contraceptives and was desperate not to have any more children, did not show until she was five months pregnant. Her doctor, a Muslim (Muslims do not "believe" in reincarnation), confirmed that the case was truly extraordinary.

Chapter Four

1. Literally *sakit hati* means heart-sickness, but it refers to anger-sickness, and only that. I have heard a youth who was very sad describe herself as *sakit hati*, only to be corrected by her parents. *Sakit hati* has very bad connotations. Characterized by a burning hot sensation in the chest and a lack of appetite and sleep, it is perceived as the driving force behind black magic. Synonyms are *sakit keneh* and *iri hati*—the latter literally "envy-sickness."

2. The very popular poem *Geguritan Basur*, which in Mary Zurbuchen's superb translation (1989) only came to my attention after this book went to press, gives a vivid exposition of the dangers of arrogance. In this poem, which is commonly performed/recited on special occasions and also invoked in everyday life, a widowed father counsels his two young, lovely daughters how to comport themselves not to offend or attract envy. Their mother had died from sorcery (poison) venged by a neighbor, and the father is concerned to instill in his daughters the virtues of good behavior. On arrogance he has this to say: *"Be careful about how you sit / If low, the fall will then be soft / But if your seat is much too high / Should then you fall, you will break your neck . . . / Don't lie or make rash promises* [Don't behave in an arrogant manner, don't talk to excess, don't chatter, children] / *And let your laugh be moderate* [As for your laughter, let it be moderate, children, and bear a humble manner] *Use [your books] to enlighten yourselves / . . Yet don't be proud / because you have learning and power / It's dangerous to boast and brag / . . . So don't you ever*

idly boast / If you should lie or talk too much / And waste your words in idle speech / Then people will in anger hear / Disgusted kin become your foes" (Zurbuchen 1989, 245–55).

3. Cf. note 8, chap. 1. While people disagree on the absolute necessity of knowing a person's personal name in order to do black magic against her or him, all agree that such knowledge is a great advantage. In its absence, a photo, hair straws, or nail cuttings might substitute; these would also be difficult for a stranger to obtain. Knowledge of the intended victim's mother's birth name is as good as having the name of the actual victim. Hence this also should not be disclosed.

4. I would also question the validity of glossing "shame" (*lek*) as "stage fright" for South Bali. A problem with Geertz's use of this metaphor, as I see it, is that his actors are portrayed as on the scene, but as if emerging out of nowhere and having no existence in their own right. How could such faceless persons have "stage fright" or any other fears and ambivalences of identity?

5. The term for handicapped—*cacad*—is derived from the verb *nyacad:* to scoff or mock. Entailed is the notion that handicap/abnormality reflects retribution (*karma pala*) by the gods because the parents of the person mocked or scoffed at another with similar defects. It is particularly dangerous if they do so while the mother is pregnant. Because handicapped persons are made so by God, it is considered particularly meritorious to be kind and compassionate to them. God will reward one many times over.

6. On Balinese attitudes to eating and the observation that they consider it shameful, like defecation, see Bateson and Mead 1942 and Duff-Cooper 1985.

7. For an excellent analysis of an extended case that shows how composite judgments are made by a multiplicity of actors exercising varying personal interests and invoking value hierarchies of different orders to suit themselves, see M. Hobart 1986b, 138–39. This article is a forceful critique of the view that values can be objectively ranked, or that symbols have meaning in themselves.

8. My own observations come from a village in Mengwi and in Sanur where I spent time to obtain some comparative materials.

Writing from South Bali (Klungkung), Suryani observes how "sons are much more valued than daughters. Sons are the focus of the family hopes and ambition, the potential source of support for their parents and sisters, and the potential helpers of the parents in the performance of their customary and religious rituals and obligations. In contrast, daughters are regarded as potentially useless, for upon marriage they enter their husbands' families and thus are lost to their own" (1984, 100). She also has vivid descriptions of the strain under which in-marrying wives are put. M. Hobart (1986c, 6) notes how women are in many contexts not, or only partly, "considered agents. . . . They are not able to act, or else are not responsible for their actions."

9. As regards body ideals, however, these converge: the physical appearance most admired for both sexes is that they should be tall and slim and have black straight hair, pure skin, and long, straight fingers. The face should be moon-

shaped (*lonjang*), that is, the temple area should be convex (not concave, as in Westerners). To foster this desired shape, the baby's head is placed to rest in a towel shaped as a circle with a hole in the middle—a form called *sounan*.

10. These patterns show up even after death. When the soul of a dead person possesses a human medium, a male person's soul characteristically speaks loudly and stridently (*keras*), while the soul of a dead woman (who may be impersonating a man) always speaks softly, gently, with a low voice and slight mouth movements.

11. Many of the themes I set out here are salient and evocatively rendered in the poem *Geguritan Basur* (cf. note 2). The widower's daughters are introduced thus: "*Of graceful form, slender and tall / Their sweet smiles were so enchanting / They were just like Nilotama / Each gesture captivated minds / So respectful toward their father / Many did praise / Patient, polite and generous, too / With family all affectionate / Incapable of meanness, greed / Their father loved them very much / His wisdom guided all their thoughts*" (Zurbuchen 1989, 225–27).

12. Interestingly, when a Balinese acquaintance of mine realized that a girl who looked normal and also often acted properly was indeed abnormal (*cacad*), the signs he noted were that she held her chin in her hand a short while, and sat with legs nearly but not entirely slung together.

13. The *Geguritan Basur* contains a beautiful passage in which the father counsels his daughters thus: (the part in italics is the original wording, the part in roman type is the modern translation): "*And don't be greedy when you eat / Who'll notice if your shit is large / But many notice how you look / Yet if your sarong's torn, with holes /* (From extravagant eating your sarong ends up in rags and tatters, dear children) / *With the stitching trailing down / then I'd be troubled and ashamed / Full-grown people / Must learn how to conduct themselves*" (Zurbuchen 1989, 242–43).

I find many interesting parallels between Balinese ideals of female beauty, slimness, and morality and those prevalent in the Victorian age and even up to our day in modern Western society. These have been brilliantly exposed by Joan Jacobs Brumberg in her prize-winning book (1988). In Bali, "how one [eats] [speaks] to basic issues of character." A thin body—as epitomized by a flat stomach—is an expression of "sublimity of mind and purity of soul"; it implies "asexuality and restraint" and is also an expression of "intelligence, sensitivity and morality" (178, 185, 187).

14. Pregnant women must do so for three months after birth, ostensibly "so they will not be tired." The critical importance attached to a flat stomach is also seen by the fact that women daily drink a particular herb medicine—*jamu langsing*—to nourish the (ideal) condition of a waist-level stomach (*langsing*). Buttocks, by contrast, should protrude.

A main reason why women welcome Western clothing is that they experience relief with its fit, both physically and psychologically: it allows better breathing, and it conceals the features of the body.

15. Reflected is the following kind of gender contrast, as explained by one

woman: "*Rameh* is an expression of gladness, especially among women. It is expressed in [telling] many stories. Women, if only two of them are together—there will be *rameh*. Men will only smile." *Rameh*, from my personal experience, connotes laughing, joking, vivid storytelling involving lots of gestures, and gossip.

16. Thus women also give *engal-galak* (quickly taken to anger) as the obverse of *polos*.

17. A woman confided: "My relatives think I am too brave and not sufficiently modest/shy (*malu*). I speak English, I have built a house, I am a business woman. If only they knew how often I feel *malu* (shy/timid), but I struggle to overcome it. Can it be wrong to be brave when one must?" Her husband had left her, and she had to be the sole provider for four children.

Berani has connotations of being challenging, unruly, even obstinate (cf. p. 217). It is fitting in men, on occasion and within limits, but not at all in females—from a male point of view.

18. In regard to gift-giving this ideal of *polos* entails that the link between giver and gift is underplayed. No card or name should accompany a gift: it would mean that one expected a return. This creates some problems for recipients, who are concerned that the giver may be offended if she does not receive a proper countergift, so one struggles to remember givers by the shape and wrappings of their gifts, which is difficult at ceremonious occasions when gifts are many. Givers, likewise, may try to facilitate identification by always using the same kind of wrapping. However, gifts must never be opened in the presence of the giver. These rules are unwritten conventions (*kebiasaan*) testifying to the basic notion that "it is bad to hope." A man who did identify his gifts was characterized as "of another manner" (*paling lain*).

19. Once when I resented the prospect of having to get up at four o'clock in the morning to get a ride to a ceremony with a friend, after discovering that another friend leaving at seven would reach there in time, I looked for a way to get out of my first appointment. Another friend, who heard me deliberate on how best to do it without causing offense, exclaimed, "Why don't you just be *polos* and accommodate yourself? That's what we would do!" I did.

20. For a fine exposition of a similar argument, see Howe (1984). M. Hobart (1985a, 125) notes how Balinese commonly recognize "the agent with his, or her, tastes, perceptions, emotions and interests. Rather than typify some 'essential' person . . . , the Balinese I know tended to stress the differences between people, even among family and friends. If we assume homogeneity, the Balinese come close to assuming diversity."

21. I take this to mean that women regard anger as so deplorable they do not even conceive that they might frighten others by an angry expression. The worst appearance of which they can think themselves guilty is probably arrogance.

22. Suriati complained, "Sometimes I am the only girl in my class, and the boys like laughter, and so sometimes they touch me on the arm, and when I get angry they say I am *sombong* [arrogant]!"

23. On elopement, see Covarrubias [1931] 1973, Boon 1977, and Barth 1991,

who discusses this in relation to other forms of marriage.

24. For a comparative perspective from India, see Appadurai 1985.

Chapter Five

1. To retrieve her soul, she would have to go to a healer who would summon it back through a particular ritual. This is normally easy to do, but sometimes the soul is retrieved with difficulty, or it is found and lost again. For an exposition of what "illness from fright/soulloss" (for which a wide range of terms is used in various parts of North Bali, namely *kesambet, mekesiyab bayune, turutan, kecapathan, betus*) entails of etiology, subjective experience, and treatment alternatives, see Wikan 1989a. It is popularly regarded as a common cause of death in children.

2. Balinese, indeed, tend to conflate the concepts of heart (*keneh, hati*), life force/spirit (*bayu, jiwa*), and soul (*atma, roh*) in everyday discourse. Experientially they are intimately linked. See chap. 9.

3. Such protective devices may be red onions and chilis which are placed around the house. Women may put pieces of red onion beneath their waistbands (*stagen*) and safety pins on their sarongs, both regarded as countermagical devices. Cf. also note 15, chap. 3.

4. Black magic and witches both strike particularly (but not only) after midnight. Cf. Belo ([1935] 1970, 101): "The Balinese are universally afraid of the dark, and fear of *leyak*, living male and female sorcerers in supernatural form, is intensified between the hours of midnight and dawn. . . . His [the Balinese person's] court is his haven. The encircling clay walls, the high ceremonial entrance gate, and the magic strip of wall immediately within this gate (to block the path of evil spirits) give him a feeling of security. . . . But he prefers not to sleep alone."

5. 15. Cf. Zurbuchen: "Fears of the bad results of a relative's jealousy or disaffection play a powerful role in the management of kin-group and hamlet relations; the Balinese fear that a supernatural force will be enacted by even the closest associates—hence the saying, *musuh tekén gigi* 'the enemy is as close as your teeth'" (1989, 263–64).

6. On hypersensitivity to sudden fright or startle see also H. Geertz (1968) on Javanese *latah*, and the volume by R. C. Simons and C. E. Hughes on the culture-bound syndromes (1985), especially R. C. Simons (1985). In North Bali such a syndrome is known as *gigian* (pronounced with *g* as in good); it occurs most commonly in women, particularly above the age of forty, in group context, e.g., when they are making preparations for a ceremony or watching one. Then if someone pokes (*jail*) one of them, suddenly throws a stone, or makes a sharp sound, the syndrome may be triggered. It is characterized by trancelike movements, waving arms, and a stream of talk (*omong*) with pornographic reference combined with a tendency to always repeat what another person says. To stop an incidence, it is necessary that the monotonous rhythm of some sound nearby, e.g., from the gamelan or pounding tools, come to a halt. A Balinese medical

doctor explained the syndrome thus: "It may be obsessive behavior which serves the function among women, who in Bali work very hard, to break the monotonous situation and give release, but the release may be hysteric."

7. There is said to be evidence of such evil action at work at all weddings, e.g., the bride or groom makes a bad appearance, looking unhappy or tired; the bride may even cry; the food may be rotten or the rice unboiled; pouring rain may prevent the guests from coming; etc.

8. If magic is directed at a person strong at heart, that is, with a strong vital life force (*bayu*), it may be deflected and hit someone close by who is weaker. Or, if magical materials have been placed below the ground, or venging spirits (*roh jahat*) are operating in the air, persons other than the intended victim are also easily afflicted. This too is spoken of as a form of "wrong address" (perhaps because the perpetrator's evil action is seen as directed against a particular person, even when to get at him, he had to harm a whole group).

9. Because envy and jealousy are particularly operative at life cycle ceremonies, women who help in preparation commonly fall sick "by wrong address." The condition is referred to as *poyok, lelah,* or *capek* and connotes sudden, unnatural fatigue. It is healed only by obtaining some of the ceremonial rice used for the occasion or the powder used for anointing the child, bride, or corpse. Children in particular are exposed because they are weaker; the illness is called *sawan nganten* or *sawan bangke* (literally: ensuing from wedding or death) with symptoms of listlessness and loss of appetite. If left untreated it may result in death (see Wikan 1989a, 26).

10. Mark Hobart (1983, 39) observes how Balinese consider the senses to be ranked hierarchically. Sight is universally held as the most important and reliable, hearing as the least. The illustration Hobart was often given was of the difference between seeing a cow walking in the road wearing a cowbell, as against merely hearing a cowbell. The source of latter might be a cow or a small boy playing. Cf. also Wikan 1989a, on the diverse emotional and subjective implications of seeing versus merely sensing an upsetting event. Hearing engenders fear, so it is of far less consequence for health than seeing, which causes fright. Only the latter leads to soulloss, though fear may also be debilitating.

11. A special ritual, *ngulap ngambe,* has to be performed before building. Illness or misfortune results if people "forget," as they sometimes do.

12. Cf. M. Hobart who, in a beautiful essay on the agency of plants, observes: "Finally, perhaps, we should also consider how we speak of the natural world in Bali. By calling plants and animals 'natural' we circumscribe sharply their capacity to act as agents, most certainly as agents apart from instinctual drives" (1986c, 31).

13. Proprioception refers to "that continuous but unconscious sensory flow from the movable parts of our body (muscles, tendons, joints) by which their position and tone and motion are continually monitored and adjusted but in a way which is hidden from us because it is automatic and unconscious." First "discovered" by Sherrington in the 1890s, this sixth sense is indispensable "for our sense of ourselves; for it is only by courtesy of proprioception, so to speak,

that we feel our bodies as proper to us, as our 'property,' as our own" (Sacks 1987, 43).

14. Balinese operate with a distinction between *sekala* and *niskala,* i.e., between what is visible, embodied, and what is invisible and unmanifest. But this distinction, as Mark Hobart points out, is not equivalent to the dichotomy between either present and absent, or true and false. The relevant context within which Balinese interpret and act "is likely to include *niskala,* however unverifiable its effects" (1985a, 112, 125).

15. One renowned Muslim dukun said, however, that all *orang alus* are worse than humans.

16. They may not realize what they have done, but on their falling sick, the healer may suggest/diagnose this as the cause and ask the family to remember. Then they may recall, for instance, that they closed a rat's hole, which the healer now identifies as the home of an *orang alus.*

17. But at a terrible price. The fortune-seeker must go to Agung Kawi in Java, said to be the home of *belorong* (also called *bikolpoteh*) and give an oath that he is prepared to sacrifice whatever the evil spirit (*roh jahat*) who will embody the rat asks for. It may even be his own child.

18. *Galungan* and *Kuningan* represent the major ceremonies of the Balinese calendar. On *Galungan,* which occurs once in the lunar year, every 210 days, the ancestors come to the earth to be feted and entertained; they return to heaven on *Kuningan,* ten days later. The period between *Galungan* and *Kuningan* is marked by joyful celebrations and a wealth of beautiful offerings and decorations.

19. *Kuntilanak* can take the shape of either a bird or a beautiful woman. When men approach her, she suddenly turns and reveals her back as a hollow. The female form may actually be the evil spirit of a woman who died in childbirth. The bird, which is the more common form, has a characteristic *"ke-ke-ke"* sound and may be clearly heard at midnight. It is sent/summoned (*suruhan*) by a boy in love with a young girl or pregnant woman to make her sick; the diagnostic symptom is bleeding from the vagina. When the balian is successful in healing the patient, the *kuntilanak* will sometimes say who sent it (but the information is never revealed to the sick person's family). The affliction may be contagious. If a mother touches a *kuntilanak*-stricken girl, she will also fall sick. I was told that the afflicted will cry a lot and want to sleep. The mother of a close friend of mine was severely struck immediately upon marrying. To me, it seemed not coincidental that she intensely resented her husband at the time (as she told me herself). But neither she nor anyone else hinted at the connection I made.

20. Northerners speak of witchcraft and black magic as if they were the same thing, but black magic is by far the more common reference. Probably this is because either stands for them as proof of evil human action, against which similar precautions must be taken. *That* is what is truly significant. What form the evil takes is of quite secondary importance. Hence, while speaking of black

magic, they may suddenly interject reference to *leak* (witchcraft), only to continue to speak of black magic, and so forth. Indeed, it seems that they regard the *leak*'s ability to change into the shape of an animal as one of many techniques employed by sorcerers.

Precautions against black magic and witchcraft are similar: placing red onions and chilis around the house and also on one's body if one feels particularly exposed, as do pregnant women; throwing salt with all one's might while holding one's breath when one senses an attack, as by a sudden flash of light or gust of wind or the sight of a snake. In any actual instance it is, of course, usually impossible to say if it was a witch or a sorcerer who caused the attack—their evil actions are similar, nor does it matter. I did, however, hear about a special way to repel (*penolak*) witches: by nudity. A friend told me how, when he was a child, his grandmother would now and then suddenly unwrap her sarong. This meant she had seen a witch. I was also told that witches cannot penetrate bamboo houses.

Interestingly, while witchcraft (*leak*) is an indigenous Bali-Hindu category, and the homeland of witches is traditional Hindu areas, Northerners believe that Muslims can also transform themselves into *leak*.

21. See Howe 1984 for a detailed description of various forms of *buta-kala*. Regarding their ability to inflict evil, however, Goris observes how "a *leyak* is a much more gruesome being than a demon" (1960, 51).

22. *Nyepi* connotes "silent day." Following the noisy ceremonies and parades of the night before, on *Nyepi* all traffic stops, and people may not move in the streets. It is forbidden to light fires or cook. The island comes to a halt. Muslims and Buddhists also observe these regulations; only some Balinese hotel owners do not.

23. *Pengiwa* is derived from *kiwa* (left). Hence it means literally, according to Goris, "sinister actions, that is to say black magic." He continues "It is practised primarily by the dreaded *leyak* or werewolf" (1960, 51).

On black magic, see also Hooykaas 1973. Black magic is presumed always to stem from, and to be more prevalent and dangerous in, the eastern direction.

24. *Pasangan* and *rajja* are forms of short-distance magic, the materials for which must be placed within the house of one's intended victim. *Pasangan* is the Hindu category, *rajja* the Muslim, but they work similarly and afflict persons of either religion. I was told that *rajja* is evidenced by a red stripe across the foot and was shown a terrible case of a woman who had the flesh eaten away from her foot up to a distinct red line. *Rajja* and *pasangan* may also be placed in the village bath, a stream or pool where the villagers go to wash.

Sihir is the common word for death magic and long-distance magic, but *bangrok*—said to stem from Lombok—is also frequently used. The latter manifests itself most commonly, I was told, as "pregnancy with stones."

25. Actually, *guna* means use or advantage, and so *guna-guna* literally refers to any form of magic that is used to gain something of value: a lover, a material object, position, or the like. But because love magic often is what un-

married persons, their parents, and married people as well fear the most, they tend to use the word *guna-guna* to designate love magic, whereas other forms are referred to by other specific names.

26. I developed this illness myself shortly after my arrival. My face swelled and retracted in odd undulations, giving me an appearance so ghastly that I tried to hide from people. I was found out and taken to a healer who treated me with red onion (efficacious to lose the effect of [*pemunah*] black magic) and with holy water. Immediately, my face returned to normal. A medical doctor told me that the symptoms of *sempengot* are identical to those of the medical diagnosis Bell's palsy. The vital difference is that Bell's palsy takes a minimum of fourteen days to cure, whereas *sempengot* may be healed immediately, as in my case.

At the time of my illness, no Balinese so much as hinted to me that it might be caused by magic, probably so as not to disquiet my spirit and thus weaken my resistance. They also made me believe I had only been given herbal medicine for it. But, as I found out much later, word about the incident had spread all over town, and a common interpretation was that someone was trying to "test" (*cobaan*) me to see if I was immune to magic—as Balinese tend to believe foreigners to be. Retrospectively, I believe that the incident had the effect on the Balinese of making me seem more like them. Later, when people described how they themselves had been afflicted, they would sometimes add: "Well, you know it [how it feels] yourself. Remember the time . . ."

Sempengot is worked through actual contact with magical materials and may be motivated by two different kinds of concerns: it may be a form of love magic; or it may be to frighten thieves, as by placing *sempengot* materials in an orchard. If it works, the thief is brought to shame because his face swells up the next day. *Sempengot* thus is for trees what *tombal* protection is for the house.

27. On *bebainan*, see the excellent article by Suryani (1984). It expresses itself in hysterical spasms, crying, wild screaming and shouting, and sometimes also in the emission of sounds like those made by ducks and geese. It afflicts mainly, but not only, teenage girls and is very contagious. An attack lasts generally one to two hours. Two teachers reported independently that "there is not a week when it does not happen to someone or other in my class." Most crucially, through the victim speaks the voice of someone in love with her or him, for *bebai* (the process of making sick, the materials used—contra *bebainan*, the sickness) is a form of love magic (*guna-guna*). An enraged suitor who has sent an evil spirit into the body of the victim entrances her or him by disturbing the soul (*tergangu roh*) and monitoring her/his actions. People are emphatic that it is the actual suitor who speaks through the victim and not an "unconscious self." Balinese in fact deny that there is anything like an unconscious.

To halt an attack, the victim must be grasped firmly by the wrists (which may be difficult due to the force of the convulsions), and those trying to help should stand by the head, not the feet, of the victim and not look directly at her. Otherwise, it may very easily spread to them. A teacher told me how afraid she is to help at all when she feels her heart (i.e., life force) to be weak (*cerik*). "But if I have to, I do."

On the force of the contagion, I was told of a case recently in an identified village where a whole class of forty pupils—boys and girls—was afflicted.

Information as noted above came to me from many different sources, and I believe there is general agreement about such "facts." I also observed two cases myself. A Hindu medical doctor further told me the following: "*Bebai* is transferred through telepathy and gives hysteria. We believe the thinking of everybody is electromagnetic." *Bebai* takes two forms, he went on. More commonly, it is a form of love magic (*guna-guna*). Alternatively, it may be motivated by evil alone. For that the most efficient way is to obtain a foetus one to four months old, put it in a plastic bag, and bury it in the ground in the enemy's yard, preferably between Monday and Tuesday (he said for the Muslims the best time would be different). But a balian who is very *sakti* (has high mystical knowledge) may be able to work the same effect by intense concentration only.

Medical people may think *bebainan* is a form of epilepsy, but that is wrong, the doctor continued. It is a form of hysteria. The difference: a person may get epilepsy attacks in any place, but hysteria occurs only in safe places (e.g., on the floor). Arm movements are different: in epilepsy the arms are stiff, in hysteria they go in all directions. Also, in epilepsy there is foam around the mouth, in hysteria not. He also said *bebainan* erupted with a stream of sounds like *ke-ke-ke* (cf. *kuntilanak* sounds, note 19).

The doctor had oberved a fascinating case with his own eyes. A patient, a young girl, came into the hospital, very weak; she needed blood transfusions every week or she could not move. Then suddenly one morning she had a hysterical attack followed by a flow of sounds (*aura*). To test her, he grabbed her by the hand, which was now extremely strong, though she had not received blood transfusions for a week (cf. Suryani [1984, 102] on the extraordinary strength of sufferers). Her father asked for permission to bring a healer/magician, as it seemed the girl might be suffering from two diseases and not just one. The balian prayed and went into trance, whereupon it was revealed that no fewer than (the souls of) three persons lived in her stomach. They, in fact, were innocent. They had been planted there by an enemy "who needs you to die as soon as possible." A battle ensued between (the mystical power of) the evildoer and the healer. Eventually the former said, "I want to surrender, please don't kill me!" The souls of the three men in the girl's stomach became desperate. The balian begged them to go home. They said they could not, for they did not know the way; "It is not our doing that we are here!" So the balian showed them the way. The girl drank holy water mixed with flowers—"whereupon both diseases disappeared."

Another doctor described *bebainan* as a specific design (*pola*) of Balinese culture serving as a release mechanism for inner pressure.

28. *Angin hitam* (black wind) and *angin merah* (red wind) both cause dreaded illnesses. From the "black wind"—which usually comes as a gush from the seaward direction and may be so strong the victim is thrown to the ground—the body becomes crooked and bent (*bengkok*), and the face may turn black. By the "red wind" half of the body is made "dead," paralyzed (*lumpuh*), and the

eyes become bloodshot and protrude. Both may be deadly and are caused by the stroke of an evil spirit called *digetug hanto*.

In efforts to cure *bengkok*, the face may be smeared with pigeon's blood; for the *lumpuh* red onion is smeared into the eyes so the illness comes out with the tears and the evil force goes "into" the onion. Often there is no cure.

29. The *roh jahat* does not work on its own behalf but for a magician who sends it to possess the victim and wreak evil on her. The *roh jahat* is of the category *orang alus* and may be either Hindu (*desti*) or Muslim (*jinn*). Experts disagree on whether the victim's own consciousness/soul (*atma* or *roh*) is expelled from the body or remains conquered within. I do not know what ordinary people think. Cf. note 3, chap. 9.

30. Suryani (1984, 105–6) notes how only those who are mentally weak will succumb to attacks of sorcery. She adds: "Certain categories of people in Bali, especially young women, are generally regarded as 'mentally weak.'"

31. A woman told how once when she was a teenager she extracted a piece of hair one and a half meters long from her breast. "But because I did not think (then) that it was black magic, I did not get sick."

32. *Jerangkong* appear in the form of an animal (e.g., a rabbit, a hen, or a bird) wearing the white shroud in which the person was buried, sometimes with a piece of cotton across the face. They emit evil smells, and they jump rather than walk. Only adults can become *jerangkong*, for only those who are sinners become such. The earth will not receive them, and so they are forced to be ghosts for forty days. It is believed that to see a *jerangkong* is to fall immediately sick.

33. Mark Hobart (1985c, 21) observes: "The Balinese did take the view that lying, treachery to friends, political intrigue and so on were so common that there would be no room in hell!"

34. I was told a sad tale—it began by a woman suddenly starting to cry as she was showing me the photo of a little girl, and concerned a young man, the girl's father. He was working as an assistant on a pickup truck (*bemo*) when he unintentionally came to offend a passenger by being reluctant to overload his *bemo* with some building materials. The owner of the timber grew angry, as transporting the load in two turns meant he would have to pay double price. The assistant and *bemo* driver both grew afraid and decided to run the risk of a fine above that of retributive offense. But after the assistant had unloaded the freight, he suddenly felt convulsively sick and his tongue started to grow. It continued to grow until it took the shape of a snake and paralyzed his mouth so he could not speak. In a few days he was dead. The fact that magic struck him immediately meant also that it was no ordinary human he had offended. It must have been a *tukang sihir:* a death magic specialist who had no need to waste time seeking a magician's help.

35. My interpretation is contrary to Bateson ([1949] 1972a, 119): "The offense is felt to be against the order and natural structure of the universe rather than against the actual person offended. The offender, even in such serious matter as incest (for which he may be excluded from the society) is not blamed for anything worse than stupidity and clumsiness. Rather he is 'an unfortunate

person' (*anak latjoer*), and misfortune may come to any of us 'when it is our turn.'"

36. There live some fifty families of Arab (Yemeni) descent in a certain area of Singaraja. It is from them some people have heard about "the evil eye."

Chapter Six

1. *Lontar* are traditional texts inscribed in Old Javanese or Old Balinese on palm leaves that have been dried, treated, and bound. A famous collection of *lontar* is in the Kedong Kertya Museum in Singaraja. On *lontar,* see also M. Hobart 1986c, 21.

2. Said a man, "Scientifically, you feel with your brain, but Balinese say: with your heart!"

3. Mark Hobart notes how in Bali "more stress is placed on behaviour than is allowed in most accounts of Balinese culture in that intention is regarded as unknowable, action not" (1983, 34), and thus one will be judged by one's actions, for which intention is inferred ex post facto. Hence the need to show extreme caution about action (1986c, 6). He also asserts that "Balinese have intended action and motivation as the private sphere of individuals and beyond the proper business of others to inquire into" (1985c, 19). Barth suggests that "to inquire into" should be rephrased as "adjudicate into" (personal communication). In my experience Balinese are constantly and tirelessly inquiring into the motivations of others even when they know these cannot be known, only inferred. All aspects of the person come up for inquiry, and all are encompassed by the moral code, even when, as I agree with Hobart, action takes center stage. A man explained the absolute necessity of good action thus: "We cannot know what it is in another's heart, but at least this is the action . . ." This is in keeping with Hobart's "one is responsible for one's normal acts because one did them, but not because one intended them" (1985c, 19).

4. *Jele* (Indonesian *jelek*) refers to feeling, thought, character, or action, whereas *jahat,* which is stronger, refers to a permanent character defect that results in bad action at all times.

5. Cf. M. Hobart (1986d, 9), who notes how Balinese evince concern less with explaining the normal than the idiosyncratic or unexpected.

6. Balinese, both ordinary people and balians, tell me that several souls (*atma*) may even be reincarnated in one person, indeed, that this is not at all unusual.

7. An example: An old village priest (*pemangku*) made advances towards his own daughter-in-law, once she was a widow. The family was appalled and regarded the action as so inexplicable that it must be due to evil spirits. But as the widow's son-in-law, who told me the story, added: "Had he been a young man, probably society would have made a different judgment." In other words, actions do not speak in and of themselves, but to people who make contextual judgments.

8. The ritual is called *metubah* and entails putting a special offering (*tubah*),

which must consist of seafood and not meat, by a river or stream or under the eaves of the house. It may be used preventatively or therapeutically. Parents who are informed (three months after birth) that a particular ancestor is reincarnated in their child may dislike some of this person's known characteristics and have *metubah* performed to "erase" such traits, e.g., bad temper, laziness, womanizing. Or the ritual may be performed in adult age. The brother-in-law of a friend was notorious for his gambling proclivities. After *metubah* he is said to be completely changed, industrious and responsible. *Metubah* may or may not be accompanied by name change.

9. Mark Hobart has a slightly different interpretation: He notes how Balinese "resort to extra-human agencies to account for abnormal and violent behaviour," indeed that "violence and absolution from responsibility or even intention, seem to go hand in hand" (1985c, 17–19). But he also notes, using the example of *amok*, how priests waive personal responsibility by seeing the person as a victim of evil forces, whereas villagers "were more sceptical about claims that responsibility for actions were [*sic*] waived" (1985c, 18–19).

10. Mark Hobart (1986a, 4) notes how the Balinese word *atma*, which is usually translated as "soul," derives from the Sanskritic word *atman*, which is better rendered "self" than "soul." The relevance of this for my present discussion relates to the fact that "the heart" (*keneh*)—as a metaphor for (and abode of) feeling—is perceived by Balinese to be an aspect of or emanate from the *atma*, that is, from "the self" rather than "the soul," if we accept the above translation.

11. I have heard Balinese express regret that their society lacks mechanisms for warning people (outside the immediate family) against bad courses they are taking. The responsibility and danger of saying anything to them would be too great.

12. I was told that *gedeg/marah* is also easy to erase; it is a function of the moment. *Benci*, by contrast stays. *Benci* relates to notions such as *nyakitang keneh* (hurt, offended, angry), *puik* (not on speaking terms), *sakit keneh* and *sakit hati/iri hati* (anger-sickness).

13. This visible social persona, separated from its inner anchoring, seems to have served as the empirical source of all features with which Bateson, Mead, and Clifford Geertz constructed their representation of the Balinese person. Without that whole other side of their double-anchoredness, and therefore also without attentiveness to their largely small and discrete behaviors aimed at eliciting information on the hearts of others, these materials could indeed lead one to see only that outer grace and formality which Geertz—in that sense rightly!—characterizes as being devoid of a self.

14. *The Cocktail Party:* "Half of the harm that is done in this world / Is due to people who want to feel important / They don't mean to do harm—but the harm does not interest them / Or they don't see it, or they justify it / Because they are absorbed in the endless struggle / To think well of themselves."

To manage one's heart is said to be a way to build self-confidence and counteract feelings of inferiority (*minder*). See Wikan 1987, 361.

15. Balinese distinguish degrees of uncertainty of knowing: words for knowing are set apart from words for believing. To know something (*uning/nawang*) is to have evidence that it is so, which is different from "making something out in the half-light" or "guessing" (*meturah-turahan*). Likewise, believing comes in degrees, with *ngega/ngugu* to imply a conviction backed by evidence and *pracaya* as a kind of commitment where evidence is weak (M. Hobart 1983, 38–39). In this case, the woman used the word *nawang;* she actually had evidence that the man used vicious tactics.

16. "There is an interesting connexion between deferment and deference. One should not assume that outer behaviour entails inner submissiveness." Cf. M. Hobart 1986c, 28.

17. A way to alleviate one's fear when one suspects bad feelings in another's heart, yet intends not to follow the course that would make the other glad, is "to give understanding" to the other. This offers that modicum of confidence one needs to persist in one's way. Before a couple marries, it is generally necessary for both "to give understanding" to jealous competitors to lessen the danger of magical attacks. Thus Suriati, before she married, put as a condition to her husband-to-be that he "should give understanding" to his former girlfriend, who otherwise might feel angry and do evil. Reflected again is a perception of hearts as eminently manageable provided there is will.

18. Ceremonies permit a wider range, e.g., trance.

19. Indeed, I believe there is nothing unique about this; this is what we all do in our daily lives; this *is* what empathy amounts to. I am reminded of an interview with a Norwegian poet, Kolbjörn Falkeid, who reflects on his grief and people's reactions after the death of his daughter: " 'How are you?' people ask. It can serve as a gentle way of approaching, a light brush across the cheek, words that wish to remove bandages with caution so that the wound does not begin to bleed again. And I could have answered with long explanations, I could have told of all the tears in the fabric of life. I could have told everything. But I answer, 'Fine, thank you!' *Each in their own way knows it so well. And it is good to have the trivialities of everyday life to conceal things behind.*" (Rie Bistrup in *Aftenposten* 11 [April 1990], Barth's translation and my emphasis). See also note 8, chap. 8.

Chapter Seven

1. There are notable exceptions, e.g., R. Rosaldo 1984, 1989, Bailey 1979, Newman 1988, to mention a few.

2. Several readers have warned me that in using Western grief reactions as a foil against which to characterize Balinese patterns, I end up simplifying the former too much—and thereby perhaps blurring my characterization of the latter. Sociological descriptions, literary accounts, and our own personal experience all testify to the emphasis in many Western subcultures and circles on both self-control and graceful demeanor in the face of sorrow, and the mingling of sociability and laughter with grief on occasions such as funerals. In some Euro-

pean folk cultures, this latter aspect is proverbial in the context of the wake.

But such forms clash strongly with middle-class ideas of decorum and visible sorrow as the proper signs of attachment and respect for the deceased. In many parts of the West we further envisage a tension between the appropriate, genuine personal emotions and public propriety, the uses of sociability as a reaction to the fatigue of grieving, and the place of laughter as a sign and a promise that the grieving person will in due course be able to overcome her grief. Other voices emphasize the health-restoring role of the permitted expression of desperate feelings of loss.

To evoke what I am reporting from Bali, however, I need to draw a picture of control and gaiety of an entirely different order: the obtrusive circus-like tone in many postmortuary processions and gatherings; the rejection of signs of grief as inappropriate to the proper honoring of the deceased; the fear of the debilitating effects of crying on the mourners and their associates.

3. For similar concerns expressed regarding the analysis of "body movement," see Moore and Yamamoto (1988, ix): "Like a wave that furls and curls and rolls and crashes, then suddenly is no more, how does one pin human movement down? Just as every wave is different, moreover, every body movement is different. There is no one way of folding arms, for example. If words are used simply to describe a person as having the position of 'arms folded' the reader is denied an understanding of the movement that got the individual into the position. For the movement to be described we have to know the process by which the person folded his or her arms. If this is not given, it is like taking a photograph, of a wave, freezing in time the furling and curling motion of the sea, and allowing us only to infer the character of the motion."

4. Cf. also M. Hobart (1985a, 123): "The agent's thoughts or feelings are seen as an active part of knowledge, speculation and speech."

5. For though he tried to explain it away as black magic, and thus cast himself as an innocent victim, he had no way of inducing others to share this judgment with him. The case simply could not be aired, even by him, because of moral notions that would render such talk selfish. In a way, he was caught in the trap of "grace."

6. My interpretation differs from Bateson's: "The formal techniques of social influence—oratory and the like—are almost totally lacking in Balinese culture. To demand the continued attention of an individual or exert emotional influence upon a group are alike distasteful and virtually impossible; because in such circumstances the attention of the victim rapidly wanders. Even such continued speech as would, in most cultures, be used for the telling of stories does not occur in Bali. The narrator will, typically, pause after a sentence or two, and wait for some member of the audience to ask him a concrete question about some detail of the plot. He will then answer the question and resume his narration. This procedure apparently breaks the cumulative tension by irrelevant interaction" ([1949] 1972a, 114).

7. *Susuk* is a form of magic from Java worked by the insertion into a person's

body of gold leaves over which spells have been read. It is expensive to obtain and ensures good fortune, position, or looks. Girls with bewitchingly good looks are likely to be suspected of having used *susuk,* as is any person of unusual good luck. Visible signs of *susuk* are said to be moles or warts.

8. I have benefited from a number of works, in particular Leavitt 1985, Lutz 1985 and 1988, M. Rosaldo 1983 and 1984, R. Rosaldo 1984, Schieffelin 1985, Shweder 1985, and Solomon 1978, 1982, and 1985.

9. Scheper-Hughes and Lock (1987) suggest that "emotion" transcends this distinction by fusing cognitive and feeling elements. I am more sceptical that it actually works that way, because our concept so clearly evokes the feeling aspect in particular.

10. Wierzbicka (1989) in a brilliant article lays bare the fundamental Anglo-Saxon groundedness of concepts such as "mind," which is used in social science literature as if it were a "Western" or even a universally valid concept. "Emotion" to me, as a Norwegian speaker, appears to suffer from a similar kind of problem. While "feeling" and "thought" can be translated as *fölelse* and *tanke,* "emotion" cannot be translated—except in the loan-word *emosjon,* which is purely academic. Wierzbicka traces the implications of such groundedness for ethnopsychology and cross-cultural translation.

11. Warnings by Colson and Nader are apposite here: "Be careful not to attribute to all Westerners what may be true only for some (intellectual) Westerners, as with the separation of heart and mind" (personal communication). Cf. also Wierzbicka's article (1989) on Anglo-Saxon contra German, French, and Russian notions of the constitution of the person.

12. Both Catherine Lutz and Fitz John Porter Poole make use of labels that join feeling and thought in their analyses of Ifaluk and Bimin-Kuskusmin, respectively, namely "thought/emotion" (Lutz 1988, 92) and "thinking/feeling" (Poole 1987, 4). I go further than both in suggesting that "feeling-thought" or "feeling-thinking" *substitute* for our anthropological key concept "emotion." I prefer it written with a hyphen rather than a slash because the slash seems to me to reflect or reinforce the divide.

13. It seems to be an aspect he reformulated after coming up against criticism; compare Solomon 1980 and [1976] 1983.

14. The concept of "feeling along with," as coined by Leavitt, is more akin to sympathy than empathy. It is "not a feeling *inside* what someone else is feeling, but a feeling *along with,* a realignment of one's own affects [on] a model of what others feel." Thus "it is very different from spontaneous empathic communion" (1985, 10–11). Leavitt uses the term as an analytical device to expose and help solve methodological problems in the study and rendering of "emotion." I find his article an outstanding piece of work which has aided my own understanding significantly.

15. I take the concept "ethnotheory" from Lutz 1985.

Chapter Eight

1. The comparison with "the West" is roughly drawn but builds on generalized evaluations such as Stroebe and Stroebe's excellent book *Bereavement and Health* (1987): "In the West . . . [those] close to the deceased person tend to be overcome with grief and shed tears, sob, or even cry out loud. This is permissible behavior and evokes sympathy rather than censure from others" (35). "Sadness and despair are so much part of normal grief that, at least in Western cultures, it is considered pathological if a person who has recently lost his or her spouse does not show signs of depression" (21).

2. Cf. Nichols and Zax (1977, 99): "The reality of death is denied or at least not dealt with openly in the majority of American families." Osterweis, Solomon, and Green note, "The mourning process in America today is supposed to be brief and private" (1984, 200).

3. Relatives congregate in the graveyard around 3:00 or 4:00 A.M. on the day of *Kuningan,* which marks the return of the soul of the dead to heaven after their ten-day visit on earth, starting on the first day of *Galungan.* All families bring baskets with prize foods, beautifully arranged; and each family sits on their grave site eating, drinking, and chatting until the sun rises and the souls of the ancestors depart. On *Galungan,* see note 15, chap. 5, and Goris 1960, 124–26.

4. I have to generalize broadly here, but it is worth keeping the following observation in mind: "Just as each type of relationship has special meaning, so too does each type of death carry with it a special kind of pain for those who are left behind" (Osterweis, Solomon, and Green 1984, 4).

5. Literally: Don't make the feeling-thinking bigger (*de gedenang keneh*).

6. A teacher told me: "I always say to my students: 'to be pretty, don't you go to the beauty parlor, but make your heart the best.' " To preserve youthfulness is a prominent concern of both sexes, but perhaps particularly of women, who fear that if they are not attractive the husband might take another wife. Herbal medicine to keep one young (*jamu awet muda*) is daily taken. Thus also the value of the husband being older than the wife: "Indonesian women age much faster than the men. Look at my parents: my father was eleven years older than my mother, and now they are [look] the same age!"

7. I understood his headache and overall anxiety to have been also caused by the fact that a close friend's wife, mother of small children like his own, had been killed by black magic.

8. Contrast Stroebe and Stroebe on condolences: "However difficult it may be to find the right expression in condoling the bereaved, platitudes must be avoided. Quite consistently these elicit resentment and annoyance where they are meant to help." As examples of such "unhelpful statements that were meant to be condoling" they give, among others, "life is for the living," "at least you're young and can remarry," "time heals everything," "one can't live with the dead" (1987, 243). I suggest that how such sayings "work," and what they mean, depend on many factors—chief among them "culture." See also note 19, chap. 6.

9. For example, Cousins 1976, 1979; Frank 1975a, 1975b; Lynch 1977; Moody 1978; Osterweis, Solomon, and Green 1984; Stroebe and Stroebe 1987; Zajoric 1985. Osterweis, Solomon, and Green note: "The findings from hundreds of studies have generally supported the proposition that life stressors of all types place individuals at greater risk for a variety of physical illnesses and mental disorders" (1984, 9).

10. The most famous theory of the interconnectedness of emotional experience and physical health with bodily expression is of course the James-Lange proprioceptive-feedback theory (James [1890] 1950, Lange [1885] 1922). "James not only assumed that facial feedback was one of the sources of bodily information which patterned our emotional experience, but he also suggested that one could block feelings by enacting expressive patterns which were in conflict with the emotions one was experiencing at the moment: 'If we wish to conquer undesirable emotional tendencies in ourselves we must assiduously, and in the first instance coldbloodedly, go through the outward movements of those contrary dispositions which we prefer to cultivate. The reward of peristency will infallibly come, in the fading out of the sullenness or depression, and the advent of real cheerfulness and kindliness in their stead'" [1950, 463]. Since facial and other outward expressions are frequently affected by social norms, the assumption that voluntary control of facial expressions can shape the emotional experience suggests one mechanism by which cultural norms can influence emotional experience" (Stroebe and Stroebe 1987, 29).

This hypothesis of facial feedback has been strongly supported by Laird (1984) on the basis of his experiments. Also Rosenblatt (1983, 148) notes: "Although one may feel very intensely the discrepancy between one's external expression of cheer or equanimity and one's internal feeling of grief, working at putting on a cheerful front may actually reduce the feelings of grief." Hochschild's theory of emotion work (1979, 1983) is also most apposite here.

11. For an evocative fictionalized account of how artists are trained to emulate emotion by working on expression, see Davies 1987, 114–18.

12. I use catharsis in the broad sense as "a process that relieves tension and anxiety by expressing emotions" (Nichols and Zax 1977, 1).

13. This same tale is referred to in Obeyesekere 1985, 144–45: "She soon came to the realization that her own personal grief was simply a part of a larger universal problem of suffering. In this recognition of the nature of life lay her redemption."

14. Cf. Nietzsche: "Man suffers so deeply that he had to invent laughter. The unhappiest and most melancholy animal is, as fitting, the most cheerful" (from *The Will to Power*, quoted in Siegel 1987, 46).

15. Rosenblatt has done so in a beautiful book (1983) where he compares twentieth-century grief theories to nineteenth-century diarists' expressions of grief and mourning. Among the fifty-six diarists, he found that "none expressed a desire for catharsis of grief, to vent reined-in emotion." And several sought deliberately to control their grief (100). He proceeds to ask why that should be. The answer is too complex to render here, but Rosenblatt observes: "From the

perspective of the diaries, the ego defenses involved in the emotional control of grief are not necessarily maladaptive. . . . Such turning away [from grief] seems to be normal (in the sense of being common), to be rarely associated with pathology, and be typically a sign of coping" (1983, 148).

Osterweis, Solomon, and Green note: "It is a commonly assumed, particularly by clinicians, that the absence of grieving phenomena following bereavement represents some form of personality pathology and will have later adverse consequences. But the empirical research in support of this assumption has not been undertaken. . . . A fundamental research problem has to do with the definition of outcomes. There is no argument on the criteria of adequate recovery" (1984, 18, 41).

16. Cf. Rosenblatt (1983, 153): "Freud wrote about the energy absorbed by grief work, and it may be that people back away from grief work in order to save some energy for other tasks or to save themselves from exhaustion. The fact that several diarists said . . . that they had to deal with their young children or their work could be taken to mean that emotional control allows energy expenditure for other tasks. People may also back away temporarily from grief work for the same reasons they might back away from other combat—to get fresh perspective, to restore energy, or to heal wounds that are being rasped too painfully in the struggle. . . . It seems that only the person who is isolated from others and lacks responsibilities or necessary chores can afford to allocate all energy to grieving."

17. In several heterodox Bali Aga variants of mortuary ritual, the deceased's clothing, rather than the corpse, is the focus of ritual and cremation; and the link between the departing soul and the leftover clothes is explicitly acknowledged in a number of widely disseminated folk practices (see Barth 1991).

18. Cf. Wellenkamp (1988, 490) for similar notions among the Toraja: "Don't think of [the dead person] [if you do], later, many things will be neglected. Your heart should only consider the living."

19. Cf. Belo ([1935] 1970, 89): "There is an undercurrent of superstition in the Balinese mind that to 'give up' will cause sickness and increased vulnerability to the dangers of illness. . . . That is why people who have undergone a trying ordeal are not spared and pampered but urged to get up and go on as if nothing had happened to them."

20. This criterion, however, is not unproblematic, as Stroebe and Stroebe (1987, 24) note. But they also argue that though "depressive symptoms represent a 'final common path' (Akiskal and McKinney, 1973) "between grief and depression, ... [they] form two distinctive and distinguishable syndromes" (25).

21. Only after this went to press did I come across similar analysis by Kleinman and Kleinman (1989), building on a theory of emotions launched by Taiwanese scholar H. K. Hwang: "If a person understands other persons' emotional responses to various circumstances in life, and if he emphatically can respond to their actions, then he is said to 'know *ren gin.*' Emotions need not be

expressed openly. A sensitive person 'knows the tone' (*zhih yin*). Thus emotions mean a contextualized response, a response one feels or senses in experiencing the concrete particularity of lived situations. The person who knows *ren gin* reads his and others' responses to the situation through all the senses: sight, smell, sound, and other sensations, including an inner resonance" (23).

22. I take this to mean that anger against parents should not be felt.

23. Cf. Cousins (1976, 1462): "The will to live is not a theoretical abstraction but a physiological reality with therapeutical consequences." On brokenheartedness in Western cultures, see Stroebe and Stroebe 1987, 1–4 and 163–65.

24. Balinese cremation is a theme too large to enter into here, I refer the reader to Connor 1986, C. Geertz 1980, M. Hobart 1978, Ramseyer 1977, and Weck 1976.

25. The ritual is called *ngulapine*. If the place is very far away, or unknown, a priest will be asked to call the soul from afar.

26. Interestingly, a Balinese doctor and a balian *usada* with whom I discussed Western psychotherapy interpreted it as a kind of shock treatment: to delve into misery could have no other purpose, as they saw it.

Chapter Nine

1. Kleinman differentiates three sectors of the health care system: the professional, the folk, and the popular. The professional sector is made up of the medical profession and institutions and activities linked with it; to the folk sector belong indigenous healing systems of various kinds (shamanistic, homeopathic, trance media, massage, bone-setting, etc.). The popular sector, by contrast, is defined as "a matrix containing several levels: individual, family, social network, and community beliefs and activities. It is the lay, non-professional, non-specialist, popular culture area in which illness is first defined and health care activities initiated. This sector is excluded from most studies dealing with indigenous healing traditions, yet ironically it is for almost all societies *the* most active and widely used indigenous healing tradition. Self-treatment by the individual and family is the first therapeutic intervention resorted to by most people across a wide range of cultures. This is only one of the essential activities taking place in the popular sector (and especially within the family). The relative inattention given to this sector is responsible in part for the fact that so much past work in medical anthropology and cross-cultural medicine and psychiatry has been irrelevant to practical issues in health care" (1980, 50–51).

2. Because it is the soul (*atma* or *roh*), and not the life force (*bayu*), which is lost or captured, the popular concept *mekesiyab bayune* which is used for "soul-loss" ("our soul has been frightened/surprised") also turns out to be fundamentally misconceived. An expert (a balian *usada*) explained that it should be *mekesiyab rohne,* as only the soul (*roh*) can be surprised or frightened at all.

3. As previously noted, there is dissension on this point. Some think that in trance and when victimized by black magic the *atma* remains in the body, sub-

dued. As proof of the theory that the *atma* actually leaves during such occurrences, Nade Bidja used the example of fire walkers who feel no pain because the source of feeling-thinking is now beyond the body.

4. Covarrubias notes: "Life vanishes when the soul escapes from the body through the mouth" ([1931] 1973, 360). He also refers to the practice of placing a bamboo tube in the mouth of the dying person to make sure the soul will be let out (365). Whatever exits, the *atma* or *bayu*, salient is the experience of vulnerability. A Brahmin woman, in her early thirties, told me how she hoped she would not be chosen (by the gods) to be priestess, for it was very dangerous: every time she would be entranced (*kerangsukan*) she would also be much exposed to black magic (presumably because her resistance would be gone). Another view on exposure due to loss of one's *atma* was offered by a family who related the case of what happened at the tooth-filing ceremony of their youths: When the youth's own *atma* had been expelled, as it must be, by the priest, to make room for the entry of an ancestor's—in that fraction of a second—an intruding evil spirit entered. I'll not go into detail about all the tumults that followed. The point here is the protective function worked by the *atma/bayu*.

5. Cf. Covarrubias: "The Balinese attach great significance to any sort of physical sickness and, having no great hardships to discuss, to complain of illness, no matter how slight, is a favourite subject of conversation. Colds, cough, stomach-ache and other minor ailments make them miserable, although they can cure them effectively" ([1931] 1973, 352).

6. Kleinman has shown that somatization is not a peculiar and aberrant mode of experiencing and expressing suffering. Rather, it is among non-Western peoples *the* most common pattern of response, and even in the West it is highly usual: "Research reports . . . shows that cases of somatization account for between one-third and three-fourths of patient visits to primary care physicians in the United States and United Kingdom . . . (but more so in lower socioeconomic strata). Counter to the established views of Western mental health professionals, from the cross-cultural perspective it is not somatization in China (and the West) but psychologization in the West that is unusual and requires explanation" (1986, 55–56).

7. *Ngambul* expresses a condition of hurt feelings and takes the form of withdrawal/passive resistance. A person who is *ngambul* will not speak and will sometimes physically absent herself, as when a child or a wife leaves home because of *ngambul*. It is a characteristic Balinese reaction which is very common among intimates (family and friends) and is emphatically distinguished from a hostile nonspeaking relationship, termed *puik*. A *ngambul* person only ceases to be so when the offender offers a gesture of reconciliation, acknowledging regret.

8. Exposure to wind causes the very common illness *masuk angin* ("the wind has entered"), a form of common cold/fever combined with headache. Balinese believe that the wind will go into the body and has to be extracted. This is done by dipping a coin in coconut oil, then rubbing neck and shoulders briskly with the coin so that the excess of heat rises to the surface of the body. Another com-

mon method consists of seizing a small portion of the hair, twisting it around the finger, and pulling with all one's might. This is repeated until the patient's whole head has been treated. Drinking coffee with ginger is an additional remedy.

On exposure to sun, the face must not be washed until the heat is gone. Otherwise the heat will "stay inside" and "come out" through ugly brown spots. Exposure to rain is likewise detrimental; getting either head or feet wet gives a feeling of extreme dizziness/imbalance combined with headache.

9. For a critique of the notion of health care *system* as applied to non-Western cultures, see Comaroff 1983.

10. As previously noted, this does not mean that the *bayu* actually fight, but they empower/give strength to the souls/consciousnesses (*roh/atma*) which engage in battle.

11. A strong *bayu* is thought to counteract illness, make the person less susceptible, and speed recovery. An illness will not be "heavy" (*berat*) if one has a strong *bayu*. A friend told how she recovered from an operation on the uterus because her *bayu* was strong. Another told me how her hair had turned white when she was in her teens because she was so unhappy at home, but after her marriage it became, and until now (she is in her forties) it is, quite black. This was confirmed by a medical doctor. The phenomenon/affliction is said to be well known in Bali and is referred to as *lanji*.

12. Examples of hot food are meat, milk, eggs, cheese, coffee, coconut oil, beans, red pepper, durian, grapes, and sugar. Cold foods are sweet potato, sugar apple, and most vegetables. Rice and bananas are neutral.

An excess of hot foods is most detrimental. It leads to high blood pressure, and "the person wants always to be angry"; (s)he will be confused and have headache. A nursing mother in particular must be careful not to eat eggs or meat.

13. A name may be either too "heavy" or too "light" for a person, and how well it fits can also change through life. Name changes are common both to change undesirable character and to cure illness, e.g., a chronic form of malfunctioning called *sakit saketan:* that the person is always sick, is thin, does not like to eat, is tired, is depressed, sleeps poorly. I know of several cases where a change of name is said to have worked an instant cure. The new name is selected by a healer, but it is believed that the first name remains inscribed with the god and continues to be used by the god. Covarrubias also notes name change as a remedy for illness ([1931] 1973, 131).

14. For an important study of the management of anger and other disruptive emotions among Toraja that bears some striking resemblances to that in Bali, see Hollan 1987.

15. C. Geertz also notes the notion of "not caring" from his fieldwork in Java: "a detached and static state of 'not caring'" (1957, 40). My own understanding of "not caring" as invoked by Balinese is very different and evokes none of the overtones of detachment and stasis. Rather, it connotes an active effort and triumph, supreme *involvement* in the attempt to rise above unhappiness and sorrow. The ego is most emphatically involved, and the condition is fluid.

Chapter Ten

1. The translations published here represent only a small selection of a much larger corpus.

Chapter Eleven

1. *Sumpah* means both oath and curse. As an oath or promise expressed at an altar or tomb, it is believed that supernatural punishment will follow if the oath is broken. As a curse, *sumpah* refers to punishment inflicted on a disrespectful subordinate by someone in authority, e.g., a teacher. The most dangerous is the curse cast by one's own mother. A friend told how he had seen with his own eyes the mother of a friend of his cast a curse on her son. She was furious with her son because he neglected her but pampered his wife, and one day at my friend's house she uttered the curse "May my son die in an accident!" A month later he did—in a traffic accident.

The prototype mother curse story concerns the tale of the boy Malin Kundang in Sangkuriang, West Sumatra. He was a poor boy who went out into the world and became rich, but when he returned home with his ship laden with wealth he would not recognize his own mother. She cursed him, and immediately the boat capsized and was turned to stone. It is still to be seen in the form of a mountain shaped like an overturned boat.

On curse, see also Connor 1982b, 784, and Zurbuchen 1989, 245–47, 264.

2. I did not see these poems; the mother told me about them.

Chapter Twelve

1. The following is a gross generalization of practitioner types which over-looks significant differences in practice, both within each category and across them. Nichter and Nordström, in an excellent article published only after this went to press, warn that "while it may be that traditional practitioners share more health concerns in common with the public than do most allopaths, a superficial depiction of practitioner types on the basis of medical tradition is simplistic and misleading" (1989, 369).

2. M. Hobart (1986c, 6): "Healers work in conjunction with the patient or their family. Should they not, they invite suspicion of being the agent of some other, most likely malevolent, agent."

3. For a discussion of neurasthenia, see Kleinman 1987.

4. Indeed, a Muslim doctor explained to me that the very concept of *sumpah*—oath—was also meaningless in terms of Muslim ideology, because of its built-in assumption of supernatural retribution. However, due to the accultura-tion of society, Muslims use it as much as Hindus, as if the logic of *karma pala* applied also to them.

5. The ritual is called *pengulapane*.

6. Also, there is no concept of self-limiting disease. Every illness must be "taken out" by some kind of remedy, or the person's condition will deteriorate.

7. M. Hobart (1986c, 21) observes that *sakti* is often glossed as "mystical power," but as it is established by results, it indicates above all effectiveness. See also 1986c, 26, and M. Hobart 1985c, 10, 13.

8. H. Geertz interprets *sakti* as "a diffuse divine or cosmic energy, which is formless, spaceless, personalityless, timeless, and intangible, but which can fragment or refract and take lesser manifest forms and move about in limited spaces. When manifested *sakti* is very tangible. Human beings know *sakti* by its effects in the immediate world of experience (*sakala*). . . . *Sakti* can be harnessed both for morally good and morally evil purposes, for healing and for causing suffering. . . . [It] is, most often, spoken of as a weapon in an interminable war among those who have it. Whoever has access to *sakti* has an instrument of enormous potential power over others. . . . As far as I know, the term *sakti* is used to refer to cosmic energy when it is used under the control of human beings, but as cosmic energy it is also an attribute of, or perhaps even the substance of divinity. In fact, according to mythic stories, those humans who can be said to be *sakti* share divine or demonic qualities" (1989, 28).

9. For a cogent critique of the pitfalls of this approach, see Keesing 1987a, 1989b.

10. A good heart is a calm heart, and calm is essential to counteract a magic assault. Hence a man told me: "Sometimes at night I get very cold, then warm and nervous, and suddenly I am accosted by an attack as from a flash of lightning. I instantly try to keep calm! If I'm not, if I remain worried, nervous, or cold, I am bound to lose."

11. On the vital importance of faith and hope as resources also for Western medicine, see Jerome D. Frank 1975a, 1975b, H. Benson 1975, R. R. Ryneason 1978, and Arthur Kleinman 1988a, 1988b.

12. I emphatically disagree with Bateson when he notes: "In regard to the offerings which are taken to every temple feast, there is no purpose in this enormous expenditure of artistic work and real wealth. The god will not bring any benefit because you made a beautiful structure of flowers and fruit for the calendric feast in his temple, nor will he avenge your abstention. Instead of deferred purpose there is an immediate and immanent satisfaction in performing beautifully, with everybody else, that which is correct to perform in every particular context" ([1949] 1972a, 117–18). This does not square at all with my evidence, which supports H. Geertz's interpretation: "A ritual is, above all—at least in Bali—a series of tasks which are task-oriented, pragmatic interventions which aim to change the state of affairs in this world, which aim to bring about material well-being and to prevent suffering, however diffusely understood. The possibility that it can accomplish this is based on a set of assumptions which are entirely different from many Western views" (1989, 37).

Chapter Thirteen

1. Because Jero Mangku is possessed only by gods (*dewa*) and not by unpurified ancestors (*leluhur*), he uses only the term *kerauhan* to refer to his own

trance: other words, such as *kerangsukan, kesurupan,* and *kemasukan,* indicate possession also by ancestors.

2. On different kinds of holy water (*tirtah*), see Covarrubias [1931] 1973, 299.

3. The souls of the dead in general are much feared. Consider this response of a woman when her husband threatened her to fear him: "I don't fear you so long as you're alive, but when you will be dead!!!"

4. On *kanda mpat,* see Connor 1986, Hooykaas 1974, Mershon 1970, and Ramseyer 1977, 110.

Chapter Fourteen

1. But another spontaneously exclaimed when she suddenly caught sight of a certain man: "He is very handsome and has high position, but to have two wives—I cannot respect such a man!"

She spoke from a position of having been let down when her own husband took as his second wife her own best friend, and unlike Suriati who spoke from a position of poverty and low rank, this woman is herself wealthy and of aristocratic progeniture. She did not feel that wealth could in the least excuse taking two wives. In her judgment "balance" evidently does not enter at all. At stake is decency, morality, and trust or loyalty.

GLOSSARY

Terms followed with a **B** are Balinese; those followed by an **I** are Indonesian.

abeh B: enlarged stomach which is soft to the touch, from natural cause
abet B: character, action
acuh-tak-acuh I: to do as one pleases, not to care about
aligh-aligh B: demonic figures (statues) lining the entrance of the Hindu family houseyard
ambil pusing I: to get headache, to care about
anggun I: exquisite, dainty, trim, smart
angin hitam I: "black wind," paralysis of half the body due to sorcery
angin merah I: "red wind," swollen face due to sorcery
angkak B: arrogant, conceited: see *sombong*
angker B: a part of nature (wood, tree, stream) suffused with mystical force (*sakti*)
arwah B & I: see *roh*
atma B: soul, the representation of God in the person

badan I: body
baik I: good; sound; decent
balian B: traditional healer, magician
balian kampung B: midwife
balian manak B: midwife
balian tulang B: bonesetter
banci I: homosexual, transvestite
bangga I: obstinate, proud, willful
banjar B & I: village quarter, the smallest administrative unit
bangrok B: the husk of the coconut, used to refer to pregnancy with the husk of the coconut due to sorcery; death magic
bayu B: vital spirit, energy, life force
bebainan B: sorcery-induced illness akin to a kind of hysterical fits
beligh B: grown up, adult
beling batu B: pregnant with stones
beling bulan B: pregnant with the moon

beling sambuk B: pregnant with the husk of the coconut

belorong I: white magical mice that steal and render their owners immensely rich

benci I: angry (unexpressed)

bengkok B: crooked and bent body caused by black magic

bengong I: dazed, dumbfounded

berani I: brave, courageous, audacious

berat I: heavy

bercanda I: to joke

besarkan jiwa I: to strengthen one's spirit or soul

bhatara B: god, goddess; deity of the Balinese pantheon; also used as part of a deity's title, e.g., Bhatara Wishnu

bikas B: action, behavior

bimbang I: anxious, disturbed

bikolpoteh B: see *belorong*

bingung I: confused, headache

boreh B: powder

bodoh I: stupid

buana agung B: the big world or macrocosm

buana alit B: the small world or microcosm

buta kala B: demons

cacad B: handicapped, abnormal

capek I: tired, fatigued, exhausted

cemburu B & I: jealous, angry, envious

cedang B: bright, clear

cerah I: bright, clear

cerik B: little, small

cetik B: poison; see *rajja*

ciri-ciri I: signs, indication, feature

cobaan I: to test, trial

cocok B & I: suitable, fitting

daun kelor B & I: the leaf of the kelor tree

demen ngomong B: gossipy, liking to talk

dendam I: grudge, hate, grievance

dengki B & I: hatred

de runguange B: not to care about

desti B: supernatural spirit, used to work black magic

dewa B & I: god, goddess; purified ancestor/ancestress

diam I: quiet, still

dosa I & B: sin, crime
duke B: sad
dukun I: traditional healer (uually used of a Muslim)

ejek I: to mock, scoff
engal-galak B: quickly given to anger, rash, uncontrolled

galak B & I: furious
gede B: big, strong
gedeg B: angry (expressed); a function of the moment, easily erased
gedenang keneh B: to strengthen one's heart or spirit; see *besarkan jiwa*
gembira B & I: happy
gila I: mad, crazy, insane
girang B: cheerful, happy
goncang B & I: shaken, confused
gotong-royong I: cooperation
guna-guna B & I: black magic, also love magic

harga diri I: self-worth, self-value
hati I: heart, feeling; also used about character and vital spirit; liver
hati kecil I: heart of hearts
hati mulia I: of excellent heart, superior
hayacan I: illusion

ibe B: body
ilmu I: science, knowledge, wisdom; also mystical or magical knowledge
ilmu hitam I: knowledge of black magic
inda B: compassion, sympathy, empathy
iri B & I: envious, jealous

jahat I: evil, bad
jail B: to poke
jamu I: traditional herb medicine
jamu awet muda I: herb medicine to make always young
jele B/jelek I: bad; ugly; evil
jenget B: whirling, dizzy
jerangkong B & I: ghost of dead person
jinn I: supernatural spirit; see *orang alus*
jiwa I: vital spirit, soul

jiwa besar I: strong vital spirit
jiwa cerik B: weak vital spirit
jiwa gede B: strong, large vital spirit

kaku I: rigid, stiff, strict
kakawin B: holy scriptures
kamar suci I: holy chamber, temple
kampong I: settlement, village, quarter, marketplace
kanda mpat B: the "four siblings" of the afterbirth, who can give a person mystical protection through life
karma pala B: fate, determined by your acts in previous incarnations
kasi senang I: to give pleasure, joy, rest, comfort
kata hati I: to speak one's heart, open up secret; heart sound
kayun B: conscience
kebiasaan I: habit, usage, tradition
kebus B: hot; see *panas*
kecewa I: disappointed
kedek B: to laugh
kedudukan I: situation, position, status, rank
kelangen B: sympathy, empathy, compassion
kemasukan I: entranced, possessed by unpurified ancestor or supernatural spirit
kene tamplikan B: (magic by) wrong address
keneh B: feeling, thought, intuition, will, desire; heart
kenehange B: care, concern
kerangsukan B: in trance, possessed by god or purified ancestor
keras I: strong, stiff, hard
kerauhan B: see *kemasukan*
kesadaran I: consciousness
kesaktian B & I: spiritual or mystical power
kesambet B: illness from fright or shock or soulloss
keseimbangan I: balance
kurang ajar I: lacking in knowledge, uncouth, unmannered
kosong I: empty
kuat B & I: strong
kuntilanak B & I: magical bird that sucks vaginal blood of virgin and newly married women

lamaran I: engagement gift
lamas I: weak, tired

langsing B: stomach being level with the waist, sign of beauty in females

lelah I: weak, tired; see *capek*

layu B & I: withered, cloudy, languished

leak B: witch, sorcerer

leluhur B: (unpurified) ancestors

lemah B: daytime

lemah I: weak, limp

lemah-lembut I: soft, trim, calm

lempuyengan B: "motion sickness" characteristic of soulloss; severe trembling, confusion; headache

lengeh B: confused, dizzy, inattentive, drunk

loloh B: traditional herb medicine

lonjang B: moon-shaped face with temple area convex, sign of beauty

lontar B: manuscripts on palm leaves, inscribed in old Balinese or old Javanese

lumpuh B & I: lame, crippled, paralyzed

maideh B: marriage by negotiated contract

malu I: shy, ashamed, embarrassed

mandiri I: selfish

manusia jahat I: truly bad human being

marah I: angry (expressed)

mati I: dead

mati setengah I: "half is dead"; see *angin hitam*

medalem B: compassionate

megah I: fame, pride, glory

mekeneh B: to feel, think, feel-think

mekesiyab bayune B: frightened, suddenly surprised; ill from fright or soulloss

melah B: good, used in relation to all aspects of person and behavior

melahang ngabe keneh B: making one's heart better

melasti B: purificatory ritual by the seaside for sacred objects

memedi B: supernatural spirit

mengejek I: to mock, scoff, ridicule

menghayati I: appreciate

menghibur hati I: to make the heart happy from sadness

menghina I: to mock, ridicule, disdain, offend

menjatuhkan seseorang I: to put someone down

mepeed B: procession of agnates at cremation

merangkat B: marriage by elopement or capture

meseh lawang B: ceremony to erase physical faults or bad characteristics of ancestor reincarnated in a person

moksa B: liberation from the cycle of reincarnation; Nirvana

mue B: face

mue layu B: withered, cloudy face

mue cedang B: clear, bright (happy) face

mue tebal B: thick-faced, lacking in shame

mueg B: not clear

muka I: face

muka cerah I: clear, bright (happy) face

munafiq I: hypocrite, hypocritical

muram I: cloudy, gloomy, sorrowful

nakal I: obstinate, impudent

nasib I: fate, destiny

ngabe B: to guide, bring

ngaben B: main part of cremation ritual

ngambul B: withdrawn; angry

ngamok I: amok

ngedenang bayu B: strengthen vital spirit

ngelah keneh B: resonance

ngesapine B: to forget

ngengkebang keneh B: to hide one's heart

ngidalem B: shame, embarrassment

ngilangang B: to disappear, go away, vanish

ngumpet B: to gossip

nurani B & I: conscience

nyacadim B: to scoff, mock; see *menghina, mengejek*

nyajang jelme B: to put someone down

nyakitang keneh B: disappointed

nyebeng B: grave, stern, a closed face

Nyepi B: Balinese New Year, observed in silence

omong B: stream of talk

orang alus I: supernatural spirit

orang Bali I: Hindu

orang Islam I: Muslim

orang Buddha I: Buddhist

orang Java I: Javanese

panas I: hot, feverish

pantas B: balance, compatibility

pasangan B: death magic; poison; see *sihir, cetik* and *rajja*

patah hati I: brokenhearted

pedalem B & I: to have pity with, compassion

pedanda B: high priest with Brahmana title who is literate in the *lontar* manuscripts

pelajaran berat I: "heavy" or dangerous knowledge

pemaksaan I: force, constraint

pemangku B: family or village priest

pemunah B: to lose the effect of black magic

penolak I: to refuse black magic

penampilan I: performance, attitude

pendiam I: quiet, still

penggambira I: to make glad, happy, to make to laugh

pengiwa B: science of the left hand; black magic

pengorbanan I: sacrifice

penungang karang B: the keeper of the earth, supernatural spirit in the ground

penyakit I: illness

penyakit menular I: contagious illness

perasaan I: feeling, emotional, feeling-thought

perkebel B: village headman

percaya I: to believe, to have evidence of something

perduli I: to mind, care about

pikiran I: thinking, thought, feeling-thought

pingul B: protruding buttocks, sign of beauty in females

pitara B: purified ancestors

polos B & I: smooth, plain, of one color

pura-pura B & I: to dissimulate for good purpose

pusing I: headache, confused

rajja B: short-distance magic, often in form of poison; see *pasangan*

rajun B: see *rajja*

rambut I: hair

rambutan B & I: special fruit delicacy

ramah I: friendly

rameh B: friendly

ratipan I: postmortuary memorial feast among Muslims

rimo B: always content, accommodating

roh I: soul, representation of God in the person
roh jahat I: evil spirit used as agent in sorcery

sabar I: patient, calm
sadar I: conscious
sakit gedeg B: anger-sickness
sakit hati I: anger-sickness; lit. heart-sickness likely to incite recourse to black magic; also predisposes for TBC
sakit keneh B: sickness from envy or jealousy; same as *sakit hati*
sakit rindu I: sickness from longing or loss
sakit saketan I: "always sick": chronic illness characterized by not wanting to eat, fatigue, depression, sleeping problems
sakit salah nama I: chronically sick from having the wrong name
sakti B & I: endowed with mystical power
salah alamat I: wrong address; usually about black magic
salah kaprah I: misconception
salah mati I: death from wrong cause, i.e., by black magic, witchcraft, or supernatural spirit
sambetan B: medicine for illness from fright or soulloss
sanggah B: household temple
satukan jiwa I: to unify, concentrate one's spirit or vital life force
sawan nganten B: "ensuing from wedding": sickness from magic by wrong address
sedeh B: sad
sedih I: sad
segar I: health
sehat I: healthy
seimbang I: balanced
semangat I: spirit, soul, vital life force
sembuh I: fresh, clear, healthy, well
semu I: fiction
semu B: appearance, expression
sempengot B: illness caused by black magic whereby face becomes swollen and disfigured
semug B: enlarged, protruding stomach
senang I: affection, care
seram I: hideous, horrible, frightening
sifat I: character
sigug I: sarcastic
sihir I: death magic, works over long distance

sinar mue B: the light of the face, the expression of the heart via the face

sindir B & I: hint, allusion

sing ngerunguange B: not to care

sinis I: cynical

slametan I: Muslim thanksgiving feast

somboh B & I: healthy, fresh, strong

sombong I & B: headstrong, arrogant, conceited

sopan I: polite, correct, modest

sopan-santun I & B: the moral code, rules in good order; meticulous, trim

susah I: problem, care, difficulty

suka-sukanya B: do as one pleases, not to care about

sumpah I: oath, vengeance

susuk B & I: small golden leaf or pin inserted into the body as charm

tabiat I: nature, character, behavior, attitude

takut B & I: afraid

tampe-tampe B: hint, indication

taqdir I: fate, destiny

tata krama B & I: the moral code, rules in good order

tau mali I: to know, or have shame

tebal muka I: see *mue tebal*

tekejut B: frightened, suddenly surprised

tekanan batin I: inner pressure

tenaga I: vital spirit, life force, energy

tenang I: calm

tenger B: see *angker*

tenung B & I: prediction, horoscope

terkejut I: see *tekejut*

tersinggung B & I: offended, angry

terserah dia I: it's up to him or her

tertawa I: to laugh

tiang keneh B: to speak one's heart, open up the secret

tingkah I: behavior, attitude

tukang I: craftsperson

tukang pijet I: masseur, masseuse

tukang sambet B: healer specializing in treating fright illness

tukang urut B: masseur, masseuse

turutan B: illness from fright or soulloss

usada B: traditional *lontar* manuscripts on healing
usaha I: effort

was-was B & I: worried, anxious

yeh mue B: the expression of the face; luster

REFERENCES

Abu-Lughod, Lila, 1986. *Veiled sentiments: Honor and poetry in a Bedouin society.* Berkeley: University of California Press.

Alisjahbana, S. Takdir. [1966] 1986. *Values as integrating forces in personality, society, and culture.* Kuala Lumpur: University of Malaya Press.

Ammar, Hamed. 1954. *Growing up in an Egyptian village: Silwa, province of Aswan.* London: Routledge and Kegan Paul.

Appadurai, Arjun. 1985. *The private and the interior in Hindu social life.* Philadelphia: University of Pennsylvania (manuscript).

―――. 1986a. Theory in anthropology: Center and periphery. *Comparative Studies in Society and History* 28 (2): 356–74.

―――. 1986b. Is homo hierarchicus? *American Ethnologist* 13 (4): 745–61.

―――. 1988. Putting hierarchy in its place. *Cultural Anthropology* 3 (1): 36–49.

Austin, Diane J. 1979. Symbols and culture: Some philosophical assumptions in the work of Clifford Geertz. *Social Analysis* 3 : 45–49.

Averill, James R. 1968. Grief: Its nature and significance. *Psychological Bulletin* 70 (6): 721–48.

Bailey, Fred. 1979. *The tactical uses of passion: An essay on power, reason, and reality.* Ithaca: Cornell University Press.

Barth, Fredrik. 1966. *Models of social organization.* London: Royal Anthropological Institute Occasional Paper no. 23.

―――. 1988. *Cosmologies in the making: A generative approach to cultural variation in inner New Guinea.* Cambridge: Cambridge University Press.

―――. 1991. *Balinese worlds.* Forthcoming.

Bateson, Gregory. [1949] 1972a. Bali: The value system of a steady state. In *Steps to an ecology of mind,* 107–27. New York: Ballantine Books.

―――. [1967] 1972b. Style, grace and information in primitive art. In *Steps to an ecology of mind,* 128–52. New York: Ballantine Books.

Bateson, G., and M. Mead. 1942. *Balinese character: A photographic analysis.* New York: New York Academy of Sciences.

Belo, Jane. [1935] 1970. The Balinese temper. In *Traditional Balinese culture,* 85–110. New York: Columbia University Press.

Benson, H. 1975. The placebo effect: A neglected asset in the care of patients. *Journal of the American Medical Association* 232 (23 June): 1225–27.

Bloch, S., P. Orthous, and G. Santibanez-H. 1987. Effector patterns of basic emotions: Psycho-physiological method for training actors. *Journal of Social Biological Structure* 10:1–19.

Boehnlein, James K. 1987. Clinical relevance of grief and mourning among Cambodian refugees. *Social Science and Medicine* 25 (7): 765–72.

Boon, James A. 1977. *The anthropological romance of Bali, 1597–1972: Dynamic perspectives in marriage and caste, politics and religion.* New York: Cambridge University Press.

Bouchet, Dominque. 1986. *Fremtiden er ikke hva den har været* (The future is not what it has been). Århus: Forlaget Afveje.

Bourdieu, Pierre. 1977. *Outline of a theory of practice.* Cambridge: Cambridge University Press.

Brown, G., and T. Harris. 1978. *The social origins of depression.* New York: Free Press.

Brumberg, Joan Jacobs. 1988. *Fasting girls: The emergence of anorexia nervosa as a modern disease.* Cambridge: Harvard University Press.

Bruner, E. M., and S. Plattner, eds. 1984. *Text, Play, and Story.* Washington, D.C.: American Ethnological Society.

Cannon, Walter B. 1942. Voodoo Death. *American Anthropologist* 44:169–81.

Clifford, James. 1986. Introduction: Partial truths. In *Writing culture: The poetics and politics of ethnography,* ed. J. Clifford and G. E. Marcus, 1–26. Berkeley: University of California Press.

———. 1988. *The predicament of culture.* Cambridge: Harvard University Press.

Colson, Elizabeth. 1974. *Tradition and contract: The problem of order.* Chicago: Aldine Publishing Company.

Comaroff, Jean. 1976. A bitter pill to swallow: placebo therapy in general practice. *Sociological Review* 24 (1): 79–96.

———. 1983. The defectiveness of symbols or the symbols of defectiveness? On the cultural analysis of medical systems. *Culture, Medicine, and Psychiatry* 7:79–96.

Connor, Linda. 1982a. The unbounded self: Balinese therapy in theory and practice. In *Cultural conceptions of mental health and therapy,* ed. A. J. Marsella and G. M. White, 251–67. Dordrecht: Reidel.

———. 1982b. Ships of fools and vessels of the divine: Mental hospitals and madness, a case study. *Social Science and Medicine* 16:783–94.

———. 1984. Comment on Shankman, "The Thick and the Thin." *Current Anthropology* 25 (3): 271.

———. 1986. Balinese healing. In *Jero Tapakan: Balinese healer,* ed. L. Connor, P. Asch, and T. Asch, 21–36. Cambridge: Cambridge University Press.

Cousins, Norman. 1976. Anatomy of an illness as perceived by the patient: Reflections on healing and regeneration. *New England Journal of Medicine* 295 (96): 1458–63.

———. 1979. *Anatomy of an illness as perceived by the patient: Reflections on healing and regeneration.* New York: Norton.

Covarrubias, M. [1931] 1973. *Island of Bali.* New York: Knopf.

References

Crapanzano, Vincent. 1986. Hermes' dilemma: The masking of subversion in ethnographic description. In *Writing culture: The poetics and politics of ethnography,* ed. J. Clifford and G. E. Marcus, 51–76. Berkeley: University of California Press.

———. 1989. Preliminary notes on the glossing of emotions. *Kroeber Anthropology Society Papers* nos. 69–70: 78–85.

D'Andrade, Roy. 1984. Cultural meaning systems. In *Cultural theory: Essays on mind, self, and emotion,* ed. R. A. Shweder and R. A. LeVine, 88–119. Cambridge: Cambridge University Press.

Danforth, Loring and Alexander Tsiaras. 1982. *The death rituals of rural Greece.* Princeton: Princeton University Press.

Davies, Robertson. 1987. *A mixture of frailties.* Ontario: Penguin Books.

Duff-Cooper, Andrew. 1984. *An essay in Balinese aesthetics.* Hull Center for South-East Asian Studies Occasional Paper no. 7.

———. 1985. Ethnographic notes on two operations of the body among a community of Balinese on Lombok. *Anthropological Society of Oxford Journal* 16 (2): 121–42.

Festinger, Leon. 1956. *When prophecy fails.* Minneapolis: University of Minnesota Press.

Frank, Jerome. 1975a. The faith that heals. *Johns Hopkins Medical Journal* 137: 127–31.

———. 1975b. Psychotherapy of bodily disease: An overview. *Psychotherapy & Psychosomatics* 26: 192–202.

Fry, William F. 1968. *Sweet madness: A study of humour.* Palo Alto: Pacific Books.

———. 1977. The respiratory components of mirthful laughter. *Journal of Biological Psychology* 19 (2): 39–50.

Geertz, Clifford. 1959. Ritual and social change: A Javanese example. *American Anthropologist* 61: 991–1012.

———. [1966] 1973a. Person, time, and conduct in Bali. In *The interpretation of cultures,* 360–411. New York: Basic Books.

———. [1966] 1973b. Religion as a cultural system. In *The interpretation of cultures,* 87–126. New York: Basic Books.

———. 1973c. Thick description: Toward an interpretive theory of culture. In *The interpretation of cultures,* 3–30. New York: Basic Books.

———. [1972] 1973d. Deep play: notes on the Balinese cockfight. In *The interpretation of cultures,* 412–53. New York: Basic Books.

———. 1980. *Negara: The theater state in nineteenth-century Bali.* Princeton: Princeton University Press.

———. [1974] 1984. "From the native's point of view": On the nature of anthropological understanding. In *Culture theory,* ed. R. A. Shweder and R. A. LeVine, 123–36. Cambridge: Cambridge University Press.

Geertz, Hildred. 1959. The vocabulary of emotion: A study of Javanese socialization processes. *Psychiatry* 22: 225–37.

———. 1968. Latah in Java: A theoretical paradox. *Indonesia* 3: 93–104.

————. 1989. A theatre of cruelty: The context of a Topeng performance. Princeton University, manuscript.

Geertz, H., and C. Geertz. 1975. *Kinship in Bali*. Chicago: University of Chicago Press.

Goffman, Erving. 1959. *The presentation of self in everyday life*. New York: Doubleday Anchor Books.

Goris, R. 1960. Holidays and Holy Days. In *Bali: Studies in life, thought, and ritual*, vol. 5, 1–76. The Hague: W. van Hoeve.

Greenwald, Harold. 1975. Humor in psychotherapy. *Journal of Contemporary Psychotherapy* 7 (2): 113–16.

Grotjahn, Martin. 1970. From humour to happiness. In *A celebration of laughter*, ed. W. M. Mendel. Los Angeles: Mara Books.

Hahn, R., and A. Kleinman. 1983. Belief as pathogen, belief as medicine. *Medical Anthropology Quarterly* 1443: 16–19.

Hallowell, A. Irving. 1955. *Culture and experience*. Philadelphia: University of Pennsylvania Press.

Harkness, P. C., and P. L. Kilbride. 1983. Introduction: The socialization of affect. *Ethos* 4 (4): 215–220.

Henry, Jules. 1973. *Pathways to madness*. New York: Vintage Books.

Hobart, Angela. 1987. *Dancing shadows of Bali: Theatre and myth*. London: Kegan Paul International.

Hobart, Mark. 1978a. Padi, puns, and the attribution of responsibility. In *Natural symbols in South East Asia*, ed. G. B. Milner, 55–87. London: School of Oriental and African Studies, University of London.

————. 1978b. The path of the soul: The legitimacy of nature in Balinese conceptions of space. In *Natural symbols in South East Asia*, ed. G. B. Milner, 5–28. London: School of Oriental and African Studies, University of London.

————. 1983. Through Western eyes, or how my Balinese neighbor became a duck. *Indonesian Circle* 30: 33–47.

————. 1985a. Anthropos through the looking-glass, or how to teach the Balinese to bark. In *Reason and morality*, ed. Joanna Overing, 104–34. London: Tavistock.

————. 1985b. Texte est un con. In *Context and levels: Anthropological essays on hierarchy*, ed. R. N. Barnes, D. de Coppet, and R. J. Parkin, 33–53. Oxford: Jaso Occasional Papers no. 4.

————. 1985c. Violence and silence: Towards a politics of action. London: Department of Anthropology, School of Oriental and African Studies (ms.). Paper presented to the conference "Violence as a Social Institution," St. Andrews, January 4–6, 1985.

————. 1986a. Introduction: Context, meaning and power. In *Context, meaning and power in Southeast Asia*, ed. M. Hobart and R. H. Taylor, 7–19. Ithaca: Cornell Southeast Asia Program.

————. 1986b. Thinker, thespian, soldier, slave? Assumptions about human nature in the study of Balinese society. In *Context, meaning, and power in*

Southeast Asia, ed. M. Hobart and R. H. Taylor, 131–56. Ithaca: Cornell Southeast Asia Program.

———. 1986c. The patience of plants: A note on agency in Bali. London: School of Oriental and African Studies, University of London (ms.).

———. 1986d. Summer's days and salad days: The coming of age of anthropology. London: School of Oriental and African Studies, University of London (ms.).

Hochschild, Arlie. 1979. Emotion work, feeling rules, and social structure. *American Journal of Sociology* 85:551–75.

———. 1983. *The managed heart: Commercialization of human feeling.* Berkeley: University of California Press.

Hollan, Douglas. 1988. Staying "cool" in Toraja: Informal strategies for the management of anger and hostility in a nonviolent society. *Ethos* 16:52–72.

Hooykaas, C. 1973. *Religion in Bali.* Leiden: Brill.

———. 1974. *Cosmogony and creation in Balinese tradition.* The Hague: Nijhoff.

———. 1978. *The Balinese poem Basur: An introduction to magic.* The Hague: Nijhoff.

Howe, L. E. A. 1984. Gods, people, spirits and witches: The Balinese system of person definition. In *Bijdragen vor den Taal-, Land- en Volkenkunde* 140:193–222.

James, William. [1890] 1950. *The Principles of Psychology,* vol. 2. New York: Dover Publications.

Keeler, Ward. 1985. Shame and stage fright in Java. *Ethos* 11 (3): 152–65.

Keesing, Roger. 1987a. Anthropology as interpretive quest. *Current Anthropology* 28 (2): 161–69.

———. 1987b. Models "folk" and "cultural": Paradigms regained? In *Cultural models in language and thought,* ed. D. Holland and N. Quinn, 363–93. Cambridge: Cambridge University Press.

———. 1989a. Exotic Readings of Cultural Texts. *Current Anthropology* 30 (4): 459–69.

———. 1989b. Theories of culture revisited. Paper presented to the American Anthropological Association Meetings, Nov. 18–22, 1989.

Kleinman, Arthur. 1980. *Patient and healers in the context of culture.* Berkeley: University of California Press.

———. 1986. *Social origins of distress and disease: depression, neurasthenia, and pain in modern China.* New Haven: Yale University Press.

———. 1988a. *Rethinking psychiatry: From cultural category to personal experience.* New York: Free Press.

———. 1988b. *The illness narratives: Suffering, healing, and the human condition.* New York: Basic Books.

Kleinman, A., and B. Good. 1985. Introduction: Culture and depression. In *Culture and depression,* ed. A. Kleinman and B. Good, 1–33. Berkeley: University of California Press.

Kleinman, Arthur, and Joan Kleinman. 1989. Suffering and its professional transformation: Toward an ethnography of experience. Paper presented to the First Conference of the Society for Psychological Anthropology, San Diego, Oct. 6–8, 1989.

Kroeber, A. L. 1949. *The nature of culture.* Chicago: University of Chicago Press.

Laban, Rudolf. 1974. *The language of movement.* Boston: Plays, Inc.

Laird, J. D. 1984. The real role of facial response in the experience of emotion: A reply to Tourangeau and Ellsworth, and others. *Journal of Personality and Social Psychology* 49:909–17.

Lakoff, G., and L. Kövecses. 1987. The cognitive model of anger inherent in American English. In *Cultural models in language and thought,* ed. D. Holland and N. Quinn, 195–221. Cambridge: Cambridge University Press.

Lakoff, George, and Mark Johnson. 1980. *Metaphors We Live By.* Chicago: University of Chicago Press.

Lange, C. G. [1885] 1922. *The emotions.* Baltimore: Williams & Wilkins.

Leavitt, John. 1985. Strategies for the interpretation of affect. Paper presented to the American Anthropological Association, Washington, D.C. (ms.).

Lutz, C. 1985. Depression and the translation of emotional worlds. In *Culture and depression,* ed. A. Kleinman and B. Good, 63–100. Berkeley: University of California Press.

———. 1988. *Unnatural emotions: Everyday sentiments on a Micronesian atoll and their challenge to Western theory.* Chicago: The University of Chicago Press.

Lutz, Catherine, and Geoffrey White. 1986. The anthropology of emotions. *Annual Reviews in Anthropology* 15:405–36.

Lynch, James J. 1977. *The broken heart: The medical consequences of loneliness.* New York: Basic Books.

Marris, Peter. 1974. *Loss and change.* New York: Pantheon Books.

Marsella, A., and G. White, eds. 1982. *Cultural conceptions of mental health and illness.* Dordrecht: D. Reidel.

Maslow, Abraham. 1966. *The psychology of science: a reconnaisance.* New York: Harper and Row.

McCauley, Ann. 1984. Healing as a sign of power and status in Bali. *Social Science and Medicine* 18 (2): 167–72.

McHugh, Ernestine L. 1989. Concepts of the person among the Gurungs of Nepal. *American Ethnologist* 16 (1): 75–87.

Mead, M. 1942. Introduction. In *Balinese Character,* G. Bateson and M. Mead, 1–54. New York: Academy of Sciences.

Mershon, Katharane Edson. 1970. Five great elementals: Pancha maha buta. In *Traditional Balinese culture,* ed. Jane Belo, 57–66. New York: Columbia University Press.

Moody, Raymond A. 1978. *Laugh after laugh: The healing power of humor.* Jacksonville: Headwater.

References

Moore, C. L. and K. Yamamoto. 1988. *Beyond words: Movement observations and analysis.* New York: Gordon and Branch.

Muninjaya, A. A. Gede. 1982. Balinese traditional healers in a changing world. In *Indonesian medical traditions.* Melbourne: Monash University, Annual Indonesian Lecture Series.

Myers, Fred. 1986. *Pintupi country, Pintupi self: Sentiment, place, and politics among western desert aborigines.* Washington: Smithsonian Institution.

Nader, Laura. 1988. Post-interpretive anthropology. *Anthropological Quarterly* 61 (4): 149–59.

Napier, A. David. 1986. *Masks, transformation, and paradox.* Berkeley: University of California Press.

Nations, Marilyn, and L. A. Rebhun. 1988. Angels with wet wings won't fly: Maternal sentiment in Brazil and the image of neglect. *Culture, Medicine, and Psychiatry* 12(2): 141–200.

Newman, Katherine. 1989. *Falling from grace: The experience of downward mobility in the American middle class.* New York: Free Press.

Nichols, Michael, and Melvin Zax. 1977. *Catharsis in psychotherapy.* New York: Gardener Press.

Nichter, Mark, and Carolyn Nordstrom. 1990. A question of medicine answering: Health commodification and the social relations of healing in Sri Lanka. *Culture, Medicine, and Psychiatry* 13(4): 367–90.

Noronha, Raymond. 1979. Paradise reviewed: Tourism in Bali. In *Tourism— Passport to development?* ed. Emanuel de Kadt. New York: The World Bank and Unesco, Oxford University Press.

Obeyesekere, Gananath. 1985. Depression, Buddhism, and the work of culture in Sri Lanka. In *Culture and depression,* ed. A. Kleinman and B. Good, 134–52. Berkeley: University of California Press.

Osterweis, Marian, Fredric Solomon, and Morris Green. 1984. *Bereavement: Reactions, consequences, and care.* Washington, D.C.: National Academy Press.

Paul, Robert A. 1989. What does anybody want? Desire, purpose and the acting subject in the study of culture. Paper presented to the Society for Cultural Anthropology Meetings, Washington, D.C., May 1989, under the theme "Challenges to the Concept of Culture." Atlanta: Emory University (unpublished ms.).

Peacock, James. 1984. Religion and life history: An exploration in cultural psychology. In *Text, play, and story: The construction and reconstruction of self and society,* ed. E. M. Bruner and S. Plattner. Washington, D.C.: American Ethnological Society.

Pitt-Rivers, Julian A. 1965. Honour and social status. In *Honour and shame in the Mediterranean,* ed. J. G. Peristiany. London: Weidenfeld and Nicholson.

Poole, Fitz John Porter. 1987. The voice of "thinking/feeling" and the power of speech: Ethnopsychological discourse among Bimin-Kuskusmin. Paper presented to the American Anthropological Association meetings. La Jolla: University of California, San Diego (unpublished ms.).

Quinn, Naomi. 1987. Convergent evidence for a cultural model of American marriage. In *Cultural models in language and thought*, ed. D. Holland and N. Quinn, 173–92. Cambridge: Cambridge University Press.

Quinn, N., and D. Holland. 1987. Culture and cognition. In *Cultural models in language and thought*, 3–40. Cambridge: Cambridge University Press.

Ramseyer, Urs. 1977. *The art and culture of Bali*. Oxford: Oxford University Press.

Rorty, Richard. 1989. *Contingency, irony, and solidarity*. Cambridge: Cambridge University Press.

Rosaldo, Michelle Z. 1980. *Knowledge and passion: Ilongot notions of self and social life*. Cambridge: Cambridge University Press.

———. 1983. The shame of headhunters and the autonomy of self. *Ethos* 11 (3): 135–51.

———. 1984. Toward an anthropology of self and feeling. In *Culture theory: Essays on mind, self, and emotion*, ed. R. A. Shweder and R. A. LeVine, 137–57. Cambridge: Cambridge University Press.

Rosaldo, Renato. 1984. Grief and a headhunter's rage: On the cultural force of emotions. In *Text, play, and story: The construction and reconstruction of self and society*, ed. E. M. Bruner and S. Plattner, 178–95. Washington, D.C.: American Ethnological Society.

———. 1989. *Culture and truth: The remaking of social analysis*. Boston: Beacon Press.

Roseberry, W. 1982. Balinese cockfights and the seduction of anthropology. *Social Research* 49:1013–28.

Rosenblatt, Paul. 1983. *Bitter, bitter tears: Nineteenth-century diarists and twentieth-century grief theories*. Minneapolis: University of Minnesota Press.

Rosenblatt, P. C., R. P. Walsh, and D. A. Jackson, eds. 1976. *Grief and mourning in cross-cultural perspective*. New Haven: HRAF Press.

Ryneason, R. R. 1978. Touching people. *Journal of Clinical Psychiatry* 39 (6): 42.

Sacks, Oliver. 1987. *The man who mistook his wife for a hat and other clinical tales*. New York: Harper and Row.

Said, Edward W. 1981. *Covering Islam: How the media and the experts determine how we see the rest of the world*. London: Routledge and Kegan Paul.

Scheff, T. J. 1979. *Catharsis in healing, ritual, and drama*. Berkeley: University of California Press.

Scheper-Hughes, N., and M. Lock. 1987. The mindful body: A prolegomenon to future work in medical anthropology. *Medical Anthropological Quarterly* 1(1):6–41.

Schieffelin, Edward L. 1976. *The sorrow of the lonely and the burning of the dancers*. New York: St. Martin's Press.

———. 1985. Anger, grief, and shame: Toward a Kaluli ethnopsychology. In *Person, self, and experience: Exploring pacific psychologies*, ed. G. White and F. Kirkpatrick, 168–82. Berkeley: University of California Press.

Scholte, Bob. 1984. Comment on "The thick and the thin: On the interpretive theoretical program of Clifford Geertz," by P. Shankman. *Current Anthropology* 25:271.

Shankman, Paul. 1984. The thick and the thin: On the interpretive theoretical program of Clifford Geertz. *Current Anthropology* 25 (3): 261–70.

Shweder, Richard A. 1985. Menstrual pollution, soul loss, and the comparative study of emotions. In *Culture and depression*, ed. A. Kleinman and B. Good, 182–215. Berkeley: University of California Press.

Shweder, Robert, and Robert A. LeVine, eds. 1984. *Culture theory: Essays on mind, self, and emotion*. Cambridge: Cambridge University Press.

Siegel, Lee. 1987. *Laughing matters: Comic tradition in India*. Chicago: University of Chicago Press.

Simons, Ronald C. 1985. The resolution of the *latah* paradox. In *The Culture-Bound Syndromes*, ed. R. C. Simons and C. C. Hughes, 43–62. Dordrecht: D. Reidel.

Simons, R. C., and C. C. Hughes, eds. 1985. *The culture-bound syndromes: Folk illnesses of psychiatric and anthropological interest*. Dordrecht: D. Reidel.

Singer, Isaac B. [1970] 1975. *Passions*. New York: Fawcett Crest.

Solomon, Robert C. 1978. Emotions and anthropology: The logic of emotional world views. *Inquiry* 21:181–99.

———. 1980. Emotions and choice. In *Explaining emotions*, ed. Amelie O. Rorty, 251–82. Berkeley: University of California Press.

———. [1976] 1983. *The passions: The myth and nature of human emotion*. Notre Dame: University of Notre Dame Press.

———. 1984. *Getting angry: the Jamesian theory of emotion in anthropology*. In *Culture theory: Essays on mind, self, and emotion*, ed. R. A. Shweder and R. A. LeVine, 238–57. Cambridge: Cambridge University Press.

Strathern, Marilyn. 1987. Comment on Keesing's "Anthropology as interpretive quest." *Current Anthropology* 28 (2): 173–74.

Stroebe, Wolfgang, and Margareth S. Stroebe. 1987. *Bereavement and health: The psychological and physical consequences of partner loss*. Cambridge: Cambridge University Press.

Suryani, L. K. 1984. Culture and mental disorder: The case of bebainan in Bali. *Culture, Medicine, and Psychiatry* 1:95–113.

Swellengrebel, J. L. 1960. *Patterns of the Cosmic Order*. Volume 5 of *Bali: Studies in Life, Thought, and Ritual*, 1–76. The Hague: W. van Hoeve.

Weber, Carlo. 1970. A God who laughs. In *A celebration of laughter*, ed. W. M. Mendel. Los Angeles: Mara Books.

Weck, W. [1937] 1976. *Heilkunde und volkstum auf Bali*. Jakarta: Bap Bali and Intermasa.

Wellenkamp, Jane. 1988. Notions of grief and catharsis among the Toraja. *American Ethnologies* 15:486–500.

Wierzbicka, Anna. 1989. Soul and mind: Linguistic evidence for ethnopsychology and cultural history. *American Anthropologist* 91 (1): 41–58.

Wikan, Unni. 1977. Man becomes woman: Transsexualism in Oman as a key to gender roles. *Man* (N.S.) 12:304–19.

——. [1976] 1980. *Life among the poor in Cairo.* London: Tavistock.

——. 1982. *Behind the veil in Arabia: Women in Oman.* Baltimore: Johns Hopkins University Press.

——. 1983. *Tomorrow, God willing: Lives in the back streets of Cairo.* Oslo: The University Press (in Norwegian).

——. 1984. Shame and honour: A contestable pair. *Man* (N.S.) 19:635–52.

——. 1987. Public grace and private fears: Gaiety, offense, and sorcery in North Bali. *Ethos* 15:337–65.

——. 1988. Bereavement and loss in two Muslim communities: Egypt and Bali compared. *Social Science and Medicine* 5:451–60.

——. 1989a. Illness from fright or soulloss: A North Balinese culture-bound syndrome? *Culture, Medicine, and Psychiatry* 13:25–50.

——. 1989b. Managing the heart to brighten face and soul: Emotions in Balinese morality and health care. *American Ethnologist* 17:294–310.

——. 1990. Challenges to the Concept of Culture: Towards an experience-near anthropology. *Cultural Anthropology* (in press).

Wojowasito, S., and T. Wasito W. 1980. *Kamus lengkap.* Bandung: Penerbit Hasta.

Worsley, P. J. 1972. *Babad Buleleng: A Balinese dynastic genealogy.* The Hague: Nijhoff.

Zajonc, R. B. 1985. Emotion and facial efference: A theory reclaimed. *Science* 228:15–21.

Zurbuchen, Mary Sabina. 1987. *The language of Balinese shadow theatre.* Princeton: Princeton University Press.

——. 1989. Internal translation in Balinese poetry. In *Writing on the tongue,* ed. A. L. Becker, 215–79. Michigan: University of Michigan Papers on South and Southeast Asia no. 33.

Index

Index

Index

Index